KITCHENS
& BATHS

A Builders' Guide to Design and Construction

A Journal of Light Construction Book

On the Cover: Contractor Herb Clement, of Burlington, Vt., installs custom maple cabinets
on a kitchen remodel.
Photo by Carolyn Bates. Cover illustrations by Tim Healy.

Editor: Steven Bliss
Production Editor: Josie Masterson-Glen
Article Editors: Sal Alfano, Clayton DeKorne, Don Jackson, Paul Spring, Wendy Talarico

Production Manager: Theresa Emerson
Graphic Designer: Sylvie Vidrine
Illustrators: Nate Cleveland, Tim Healy, Joseph Petrarca, Pamelia Smith

Special thanks to the National Kitchen & Bath Association for technical support and the
use of NKBA materials and photography.

International Standard Book Number: 0-9632268-2-7
Library of Congress Catalog Card Number: 94-072403
Printed in the United States of America

A *Journal of Light Construction* Book

The Journal of Light Construction is a tradename of Builderburg Group, Inc.

Builderburg Group Inc.
RR 2, Box 146
Richmond, VT 05477

Introduction

Most successful kitchen and bath jobs are designed to use every inch available to its best advantage. This was true in the 1950s, when designers first developed the concept of the kitchen work triangle, and it's more true today when homeowners have come to expect even greater utility and convenience out of these rooms.

Kitchens are more complex today because they have become the center of family life in many homes — combining cooking, entertainment, recycling, and often a home office space as well. In addition, the types of major appliances have changed and their numbers have multiplied. Bathrooms, too, are changing, as both codes and homeowners demand greater safety, durability, and comfort. And with our aging population, accessibility in both kitchens and baths has moved more into the mainstream of design.

At the same time, there has been an explosion of new materials and technologies — from solid surfacing and thinset tile systems to low-flow toilets and scaldproof showers. Each offers benefits, but demands new skills and knowledge on the part of the contractor and designer.

To help you keep pace with these changes in design and construction, we've selected and updated the best K&B articles from *The Journal of Light Construction*, representing the expertise of over 40 leading kitchen and bath professionals. In addition, we've included the new design guidelines from the National Kitchen and Bath Association, and the accessibility guidelines of the federal Americans With Disabilities Act, both of which reflect the latest research on safety and ergonomics in kitchen and bath design.

We've focused on practical solutions so that you can put this body of knowledge to work on your job sites. The work you do in these rooms will be used and appreciated day after day by your customers and their families — which is good for them and good for your business. So make every inch count.

Steven Bliss
Editor

Table of Contents

Chapter 1

KITCHEN DESIGN BASICS

SAMUEL KULLA, CKD, DESIGNER, COURTESY OF NKBA

Successful Kitchen Layout

by Jerry Germer

A workable design fits standard kitchen functions to unique client needs

Kitchens have changed dramatically since Grandma ran the place single-handedly, whomping bread dough and transforming apples into applesauce. Today, with smaller families and more women in the work force, kitchens must suit a variety of family types and lifestyles. The conventional nuclear family makes up only about one half of American households. Single people, childless couples, one-parent families, and elderly people make up the rest. All make different demands on the kitchen and require different conveniences.

A working couple without children, for example, may want a place to quickly microwave take-out food during the week, but an elaborate workspace where two cooks can prepare gourmet meals on weekends. You won't come up with a responsive design for such a kitchen unless you thoroughly understand the user's needs and lifestyle.

Of course, the kitchen's basic functions still revolve around the management of food and utensils. Food comes in and is stored, processed, and served; waste goes out. A good design is one that makes the management of these functions a smooth, efficient process. Knowing the basic elements of the kitchen and how they relate will help you plan any kitchen, simple or elaborate.

Essential Ingredients

Despite the proliferation of appliances, the most important elements of most kitchens remain the sink, the cooking surface, and the refrigerator.

The sink. Because of its use in both food preparation and cleanup, the sink is the most important item in the kitchen, and a good place to start the planning process. The workhorse of the past is the 32-inch-wide two-bowl sink. Still popular, it is but one of many choices today. An additional single-bowl sink helps if more than one cook is involved or if the kitchen is large. A three-bowl sink provides

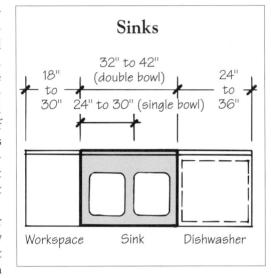

one basin that can be dedicated to washing raw foods.

Sinks have expanded beyond the rectangle to include ovals, circles, and other shapes. American Standard's double-circle *Connoisseur* and Kohler's *Porto fino*, for example, straddle corners elegantly.

One useful option is an integral drainboard, which can be a real plus for people who use the sink for messy chores such as repotting plants.

Regardless of sink choice, remember that the sink is a center of activity and requires generous adjacent counter space. Allow at least 18 inches on one or, preferably, both sides. Increase the adjacent clearance space to 24 inches if a dishwasher is to be installed below. Overhead clearance space can be shared with the clearance required for an adjacent item, such as a cooktop, unless the adjacent space will be permanently occupied, such as by a dish-draining rack.

Ranges, ovens, and microwaves. After the sink, the cooking surface is the next most important item. The all-purpose range with a built-in oven has long filled this role. Now, however, with people baking less often and microwave ovens handling most other oven chores, the oven portion of a range gets less use.

Microwaves

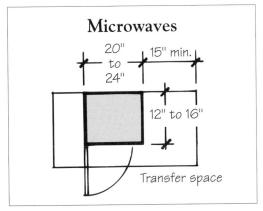

If your clients opt for a range/oven anyway, they can choose between a standard free-standing range, a slide-in unit (sides unfinished), or a drop-in unit (installed into a notch cut out of the counter).

If they don't need an oven, consider a cooktop installed in the counter with a separate microwave. If, on the other hand, your client specifically wants one or more ovens, a separate wall-mounted oven assembly will usually be more useful than a range, because neither oven nor cooktop block access to each other. Locate the oven assembly in a corner or at the end of a counter to avoid interrupting counter space. A heat-resistant working surface, such as tile, should be installed next to the cooking surface and oven to place items before and after cooking.

All cooking surfaces need devices to remove cooking moisture and gases. Ducted range hoods mounted above the cooking surface remain the most common and effective solution. Allow for a 4-inch-diameter duct from the fan through an outside wall.

An accessory until recently, microwave ovens are increasingly seen as necessities.

Although they can adequately roast a whole chicken, they shine at rewarming leftovers or take-out foods — an asset in modern lifestyles.

Originally, microwaves lived on top of the counter. That's not necessarily the best place, because you lose the workspace in front of the unit, which must be kept clear for the door to open. If you are designing the kitchen from scratch, consider installing the microwave near the cooking surface or hanging it from a wall cabinet. Better still are the combination microwaves with built-in exhaust fans beneath; these mount above the cooking surface.

Refrigerators. The refrigerator must be convenient to the sink area, but not so close as to hog needed counter space. Like wall ovens, refrigerators interrupt counter space, making a corner or end-of-counter location a sound choice, except in kitchens where two cooks need constant access.

Refrigerator-freezers come in capacities of up to 27 cubic feet. Models with the freezer above or below vary from 28 inches to 36 inches wide (30 inches and 32 inches are most common) and 65 inches to 68 inches high. Side-by-side units are 32 inches to 36 inches wide, 67 inches to 84 inches high. Remember that built-in ice makers and cold water dispensers require plumbing.

Countertop space for loading and unloading should be provided next to the opening side. The doors of most models open to a full 90 degrees inside the width of the unit, but some models require an additional 5 inches clearance on the hinge side. If that's the case, make sure to allow this extra space if you intend to install the unit in a corner or next to a wall.

Dishwashers. Like microwaves, dishwash-

Refrigerators

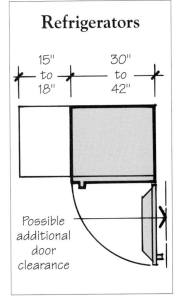

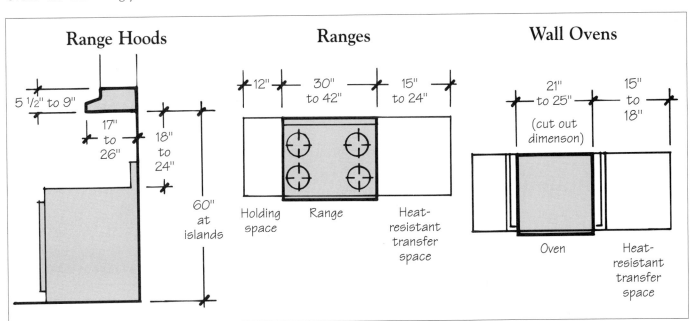

ers are becoming standard equipment. Front-loading units installed under the counter to the right of the sink (for right-handed people) are the most common, followed by top-loading units that slide in and out from under an open counter space. When you lay out the kitchen, sketch the unit showing the door in the open position to avoid awkward conflicts.

Garbage disposals. If your clients' home is served by a septic system, you should advise them that a disposal will mean pumping the tank 30% more often. Another caveat: Drain lines higher than 17 inches from the floor make disposals work harder to pump waste uphill and may eventually cause malfunction. Standard models are rated from 1/2 to 3/4 horsepower and require 120v power.

Noise plagues all disposals, but the better ones are quieter. The thin walls of stainless steel sinks particularly amplify disposal noise. An optional coating on the underside of some sinks (such as Kohler's Hushcoat) can deaden some of the sound.

Trash compactors. By reducing the bulk of non-food kitchen waste — packaging and glass — compactors prove useful in locations where trash disposal is costly or difficult. Standard 12- to 18-inch-wide units 34 1/2 inches high can slide under a counter. Pulled out, the top surface serves as a chopping block.

Residential units come with 1/2- to 3/4-hp motors that require 120v power. The pricier compactors have odor and sound control devices. Although the compactor's location will probably be decided by where under-counter space is available, the best place is probably between the sink and refrigerator or close to any recycling bins. As with dishwashers, sketch in the position of the open door to ensure access and minimize traffic conflicts.

Small appliances. Small appliances such as toasters, mixers, blenders, and processors should ideally be stored near the work area where they are most often used. Processors and blenders, for example, logically fit next to the sink, where vegetables are washed. Mixers are best put where baking will occur.

But because mobile appliances are mobile, their position is likely to change. Locate abundant power outlets around the work counter to allow for flexibility. The electrical code requires a minimum of one receptacle for each separate counter area. Your client will be happier if you provide at least double that.

Kitchen Clearances

Designing a successful kitchen is a challenge. You not only have to organize a slew of parts into a workable whole, but you must also make the space a pleasure to be in. One key to success is making sure your layout handles traffic well. Avoid plans where people have to pass through the main kitchen work area to get from one part of the house to another.

For a two-cook operation, create separate work areas by locating shared appliances (range, refrigerator, and sink) convenient to both cooks. A second, smaller sink can help eliminate conflict. Studies show that two cooks working together tend to prepare individual dishes, rather than do stages of the same item. That is, it's "I'll make the salad, you do the lasagna," rather than "I'll chop the vegetables, you cook."

To maintain enough clearance between cabinets for people to work and pass each other, draw all doors and drawers in the open position. The HUD Minimum Property Standards (1980) stipulates a minimum clearance between cabinets of 40 inches for one person and 48 inches for two. A more generous allowance is 60 inches. Anything over 60 inches just means extra walking between one counter and the next and reduces efficiency.

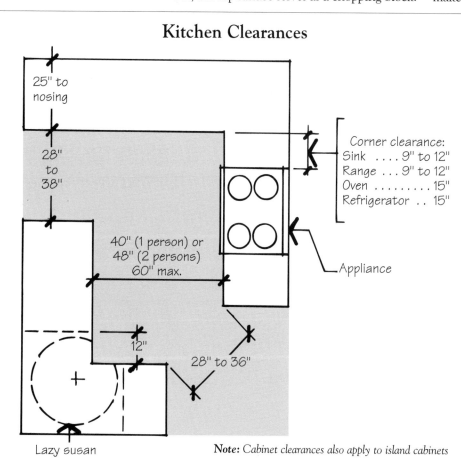

Kitchen Clearances

25" to nosing

28" to 38"

40" (1 person) or 48" (2 persons) 60" max.

12"

28" to 36"

Corner clearance:
Sink . . . . 9" to 12"
Range . . . 9" to 12"
Oven . . . . 15"
Refrigerator . . 15"

Appliance

Lazy susan

Note: *Cabinet clearances also apply to island cabinets*

Four Basic Kitchen Layouts

L-Shape (Optional Island)

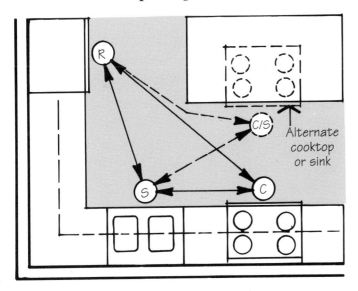

Alternate cooktop or sink

Parallel Wall (Galley)

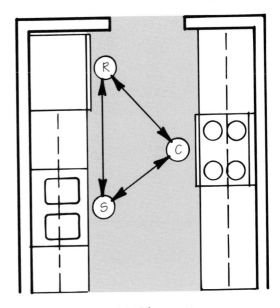

One-Wall In-Line

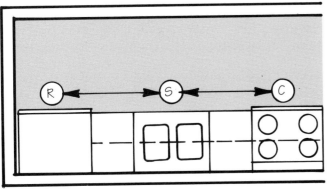

C – Cooking surface
S – Sink
R – Refrigerator

U-Shape

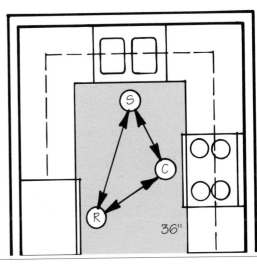

36"

Basic Layouts

"Go with the flow" is a useful concept to remember when laying out a kitchen. The usual flow sequence goes something like this:

Raw materials → Storage (cabinets, refrigerator) → Preparation (sink, countertops) → Cook (range, oven, microwave) → Serve (table, breakfast bar) → Cleanup (sink, dishwasher) → Store (cabinets, refrigerator) or Dispose (wastebasket, garbage disposal).

In a well-organized layout, food flows through this sequence with ease; the paths between the successive stages are short and direct. If two people work together, they shouldn't have to trip over each other.

In the 1950s, researchers at the University of Illinois Small Homes Council identified three critical points in the kitchen — the sink, refrigerator, and cooking surface — and contrived a set of rules to make the "work triangle" efficient. Most of those rules still stand:

- No leg of the triangle should exceed 9 feet
- The total distance between all three points should fall between 12 and 26 feet
- Traffic patterns and cabinets should not obstruct any leg of the triangle

Though the work triangle concept predated the days of two-cook kitchens and the proliferation of specialized appliances, it can still help you organize the space efficiently.

One-wall in-line arrangements are the most cost- and space-efficient. Better suited to apartments than homes, they are definitely one-person kitchens. If enclosed by a back wall, as shown on the previous page, don't waste the wall. Fitted with a pegboard, it can store numerous utensils to compensate for the lack of cabinet storage.

Parallel wall (galley) plans, also compact, add a second work center on an opposite wall. Besides adding more workspace, this plan allows two people to work simultaneously if the space is wide enough. The open end presents no problem if it leads to a pantry or laundry room, but it invites conflicting traffic if it's an entrance door.

L-shaped kitchens offer the most flexibility. They have plenty of easily accessible work surfaces and can be combined with an adjacent island, dining table, or dining area (off either end of the L) for auxiliary preparation space.

U-shaped plans make good use of limited space and have the added benefit of blocking through traffic. The tradeoff is some loss in flexibility. You can't, for example, stick a dining table in the middle without blocking the work triangle.

Variations. The above proven layouts make good starting points. But because they reflect an "average" user's requirements, you may need to vary them to reflect your client's specific needs and desires. Creative use of angles, curves, peninsulas, and islands can make a basic plan extraordinary. Backing counters or islands with eating or desk spaces can help integrate the kitchen into other everyday activities.

For instance, an island or peninsula with three or four sides that are easily accessible can extend the workspace (a real boon for two-cook kitchens), provide an informal eating area, and add storage. Locate them with care; they should neither obstruct the paths to other key points nor be so far removed that they go unused.

Locate any cabinets above the island or peninsula so that their bottoms are at least 61 inches from the floor, to allow people to see under them. (Find out the eye level of your occupants!) A ventilating hood above an island or peninsula should have a high capacity — of, say, 600 cfm — because there is no wall behind it to help funnel the smoke upward.

Storage

There must be a Murphy's Law for kitchen storage that states: The amount of storage needed in any kitchen exceeds that available by one half.

Suggested Storage Capacity

	Kitchen 150 sq.ft. or less	Kitchen larger than 150 sq.ft.
Base cabinet frontage	156 in.	192 in.
Wall cabinet frontage	144 in.	186 in.
Drawers (individual total frontage)	120 in.	165 in.

Storage needs vary with family size and shopping and cooking patterns. People who shop once a week need more space than those who shop more frequently. The table above gives the National Kitchen and Bath Association's suggestions for kitchen storage capacity.

However, the type and location of storage spaces are as important as the amount. Small kitchens suffer not because they contain less storage, but because things crammed into every available piece of real estate are harder to find. If well-organized, such kitchens can be a pleasure to use. Modern prefab cabinets equipped with adjustable shelves, pull-out racks, and various inserts can help meet these and most other storage requirements.

Kitchen expert Ellen Cheever suggests the following guidelines:

• Store items close to where they are used. For example, store dishes either near food preparation areas (their first place of use) or the sink (the last place of use).

• When necessary, duplicate storage space for smaller, less expensive items so that a set may be kept near each likely spot of use. If the owner bakes a lot and measures both at the sink and at a baking area across the kitchen, provide storage for measuring tools and mixing bowls at both locations. This guideline is particularly important for two-cook kitchens.

• Stored items should be easy to locate. Shallow shelves and variable-depth drawers can help here. Consider glass doors or no doors on cupboards.

• The most frequently used items should be the easiest to retrieve. The most accessible location is the front of a cabinet shelf between hip and eye level.

• Stored items should be easy to grasp. Locating heavy pans at eye level is a bad idea, as is nesting one item inside another. To avoid nesting, provide several shallow drawers or shelves, rather than a few deep ones. Store heavy items in base cabinets.

Your clients' preferences also clue you in as to how to handle garbage. They may opt for the simple route where food waste is sent down the disposal and everything else gets chucked into an under-sink waste receptacle. But with recycling on the rise, they may want to set aside wet waste for composting and sort dry garbage into separate containers. At the extreme, you may need separate storage for wet waste, paper, different colors of glass, plastics, and everything else. If so, allow an extra 3 feet or so of base cabinet frontage near the sink for waste bins, unless there is an adjacent utility room or garage that can serve these needs.

Time to Sit and Eat

Because dining can consume a lot of space, make sure you understand your clients' patterns. A dining surface built into a peninsula or island is suitable for quick snacks and meals on the run. The height depends on how the surface is used. Table height (29 or 30 inches) accommodates standard chairs and creates a distinction between an abutting 36-inch-high preparation counter, making it less likely that the eating space will get overrun by pots, pans, and other cooking items pushed aside.

Raising the dining side to a 36-inch counter height eliminates this distinction, but gains you the flexibility of a larger, unbroken countertop. Stools rather than chairs can provide seating at this height. If you boost the surface up higher still, to bar height (42 inches), it will be higher than the adjacent counter (pro-

viding the same distinction between eating and cooking space) and just right for either stand-up access or high stools.

A sit-down table makes for more sociable and relaxed dining, either in addition to or in place of a dining counter (see illustrations, following page). Round tables require more space than rectangular ones for the same amount of seating, but they are more flexible and easier to move around.

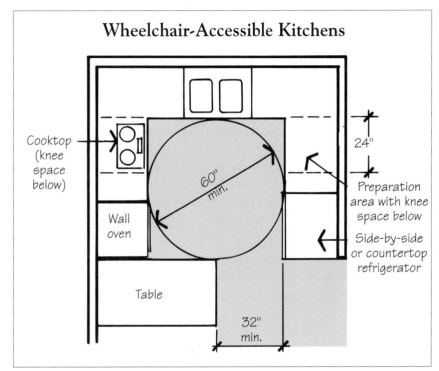

Wheelchair-Accessible Kitchens

Cooktop (knee space below)

Wall oven

Table

60" min.

32" min.

24"

Preparation area with knee space below

Side-by-side or countertop refrigerator

The Accessible Kitchen

Minor adjustments to a standard kitchen can eliminate many accessibility barriers. Better lighting and larger print can aid people with poor eyesight. For the hard of hearing, aural signals, such as buzzers on appliance timers, can be replaced with light signals.

Accommodating the needs of wheelchair-bound people, unfortunately, changes the kitchen in ways that makes it less useful to ambulatory users. This can be a major problem if an ambulatory person shares in the cooking, and it can compromise the resale value of the house. On the other hand, the market for wheelchair-accessible kitchens will grow as elderly people make up an increasing share of the population.

Wheelchair accessibility requires changes in both horizontal and vertical dimensions. Start with an open space on the floor 60 inches minimum in diameter to allow a wheelchair to turn around. No point of passage should be narrower than 32 inches.

Counters should be 30 to 32 inches high instead of the usual 36 inches. Because

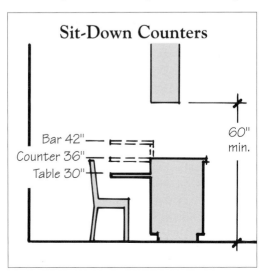

Sit-Down Counters

Bar 42"
Counter 36"
Table 30"

60" min.

Dining Tables

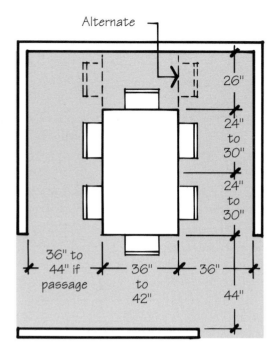

Rectangular Tables		
Capacity	Width	Length
6	36" to 42"	60"
8	36" to 42"	78"
10	36" to 42"	96"
12	36" to 42"	120"

Round Tables	
Capacity	Diameter
4 to 5	42"
5 to 6	48"
6 to 7	60"
7 to 8	72"
8 to 10	84"
10 to 12	96"

wheelchair users can't reach work surfaces without wheeling under them, you'll need to provide open spaces at least 24 inches wide and 24 inches deep under three work centers: the cooking surface, sink, and preparation area. Having that space below the main work counters will help, too. The most flexible design is a counter that's continuously open below, except for the refrigerator and possibly a bank of drawers.

Insulate hot water piping below the sink to prevent burning the user's legs. This leaves only 6 to 8 inches to accommodate sinks and cooktops — not impossible, but make sure the depth of the sink you specify stays within that dimension. The cooking surface can be one or two two-burner cooktops with their burners and controls near the front.

Storage is tricky. Because people in wheelchairs can't easily reach shelves higher than 48 inches or lower than 10 inches, make the best use of this space for storage. Shallow shelves on the backside of cabinet doors are easy to get at when open. Shallow adjustable shelving and pegboards between the counter and wall cabinet will provide additional utility (people in wheelchairs can't easily reach the back 8 inches of a 24-inch-wide counter, anyway).

Ovens, even wall-mounted ones, are awkward for wheelchair users. Microwave ovens are safer and more convenient. Side-by-side refrigerator-freezers offer better access than units with the freezer above. Small refrigerators mounted on top of a counter with knee space below are even better if the person's needs are modest. ■

Jerry Germer is an architect and writer in Marlborough, N.H.

NKBA's 31 Rules of Kitchen Design

In 1992, The National Kitchen & Bath Association (NKBA) introduced new design guidelines based on extensive research conducted by the association along with the University of Minnesota. The guidelines were established to help building and design professionals plan spaces that function well. The kitchen guidelines, in simplified form, appear below. For more information contact NKBA, 687 Willow Grove St., Hackettstown, NJ 07840; 908/852-0033.

1 *Walkways* Make openings at least 32 in. wide at all entrances to the kitchen. Make walkways at least 36 in. wide, and allow at least 36 in. of clearance for cabinet access (distance from cabinet front to a wall or obstacle).

2 *Doors* Entry, cabinet, and appliance doors should not interfere with each other.

3 *Work Aisles* In a one-cook kitchen, make work aisles at least 42 in. wide (from counter edge to counter edge), and passageways at least 36 in. wide. For two cooks working in the same aisle, make it at least 48 in. wide.

Rules 1 & 3: Walkways & Work Aisles

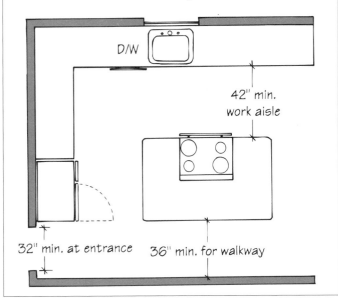

D/W

42" min. work aisle

32" min. at entrance   36" min. for walkway

4 *Wall Cabinet Frontage* Kitchens under 150 sq. ft. should have at least 144 in. of wall cabinet frontage. For kitchens over 150 sq. ft., the minimum is 186 in. (Don't count hard-to-reach cabinets over hood, oven, or refrigerator.)

5 *Dish Storage* Provide at least 60 in. of wall cabinet frontage

within 72 in. of the primary sink centerline. *Alternative:* Substitute a tall cabinet of equivalent size, or provide base cabinets on the back side of a sink peninsula.

Rule 5: Dish Storage

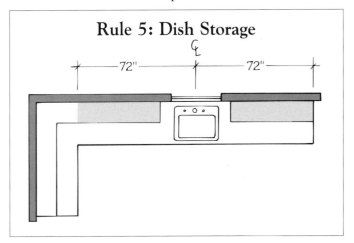

72"   72"

6 *Base Cabinet Frontage* Kitchens under 150 sq. ft. should have at least 156 in. of base cabinet frontage (cabinets must be at least 21 in. deep). For kitchens over 150 sq. ft., the minimum is 192 in. (A lazy susan counts as 30 in.)

7 *Drawer Frontage* Kitchens under 150 sq. ft. should have at least 120 in. of drawer frontage or roll-out shelf frontage. For kitchens over 150 sq. ft., the minimum is 165 in. (Example: A 21 in. base with three drawers or three roll-out shelves counts as 63 in.)

8 *Storage* Include at least five storage items in the kitchen to improve its accessibility and usefulness. (Examples: specialized drawers, built-in bins or racks, swing-out pantries.)

9 *Corner Storage* In a kitchen with corner cabinets, make at least one corner unit functional. (Examples: lazy susan, angled cabinet front, access from rear of cabinet.)

10 *Height of Wall Cabinets* Leave 15 in. to 18 in. of clearance between the countertop and the bottom of wall cabinets.

11 *Countertop Frontage* Kitchens under 150 sq. ft. should have at least 132 in. of usable countertop frontage. For kitchens over 150 sq. ft., the minimum is 198 in. Do not count corner space, or countertops that are less than 16 in. deep.

12 *Work Centers* Never separate two primary work centers (such as the main sink and cooktop) with a refrigerator or full-height, full-depth cabinet, such as an oven or pantry cabinet.

Rule 11: Countertop Frontage

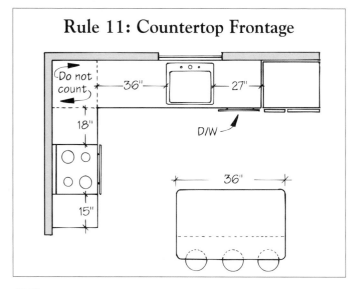

13 *Sink Counter* Provide at least 24 in. of countertop on one side of the sink and 18 in. on the other. For a second sink, minimums are 18 in. and 3 in. If these sections turn a corner, measure along the front edge of the countertop.

Note: Where a section of counter serves two centers, such as sink and stove, take the longest of the two minimum counter lengths and add 12 in. to find the new minimum.

14 *Sink Near Corner* Provide at least 3 in. of countertop from the sink to an inside corner (this requires 21 in. of counter on return). Leave at least 18 in. to a dead-end or hard-to-reach corner.

Rules 13 & 14: Sink Counter

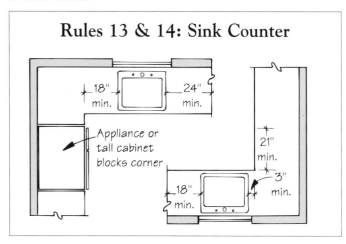

15 *Waste Receptacles* Include at least two waste receptacles: one for garbage and one for recyclables.

16 *Dishwasher Clearance* Allow for 21 in. of standing room extending from each edge of the dishwasher. Also, keep the dishwasher within 36 in. of the sink.

17 *Preparation Center* Provide at least 36 in. of straight, continuous countertop for the preparation center — immediately adjacent to a sink. Add a separate center for a second cook.

18 *Refrigerator Counter* Provide at least 15 in. of countertop on the latch side of the refrigerator or 15 in. on each side of a side-by-side unit. *Alternative:* Provide at least 15 in. of landing space no more than 48 in. across from the refrigerator.

Rule 18: Refrigerator Counter

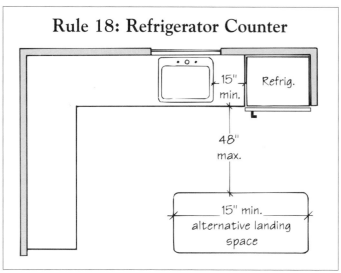

19 *Cooktop Counter* Leave at least 9 in. of counter space on one side of the cooking surface and 15 in. on the other. *Exception:* If the cooktop goes against an end wall, leave at least 3 in. of clearance and protect the wall from heat.

Rule 19: Cooktop Counter

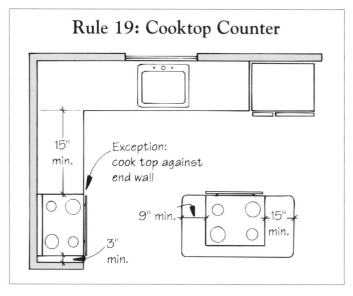

20 *Cooktop Near Window* Do not place the cooking surface below an operable window unless the window is 3 in. or more behind the appliance and more than 24 in. above it.

21 *Oven Counter* Provide at least 15 in. of landing space next to or above the oven if the appliance door opens into a traffic lane. *Alternative:* The landing space can be across from the oven (no more than 48 in. away) if the appliance does not open into a traffic lane.

22 *Microwave Counter* Provide at least 15 in. of landing space below, or adjacent to, the microwave oven.

Rules 22 & 23: Microwave Counter

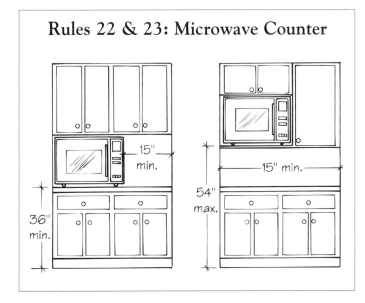

In two-cook kitchens, each cook should have a separate triangle. The two triangles can share a leg but should not overlap. Usually, at least the refrigerator is shared by both cooks.

Rule 26: Two-Cook Work Triangle

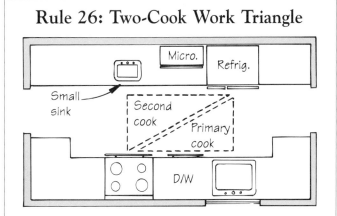

23 *Microwave Clearance* Place the microwave oven so the bottom of the unit is between counter height and user eye-level (36 in. to 54 in. off the floor).

24 *Cooktop Ventilation* All major appliances used for surface cooking must have a ventilation system with a minimum fan rating of 150 cfm.

25 *Cooktop Clearances* Above the cooking surface, leave at least 24 in. to a protected surface (such as a range hood), or 30 in. to an unprotected surface. *Exception:* A microwave/hood combination may be lower than 24 in.

27 *Traffic Jams* No major traffic lanes should cut across the work triangle connecting the primary centers (sink, refrigerator, food preparation, and cooktop/range).

28 *Eating Counter* If the kitchen has an eating counter, allow counter space at least 24 in. wide by 12 in. deep for each seated diner. Provide at least 12 in. of kneespace under an eating counter 42 in. high, 15 in. under a counter 36 in. high, and 18 in. under a counter 30 in. high.

Rule 26: Work Triangle

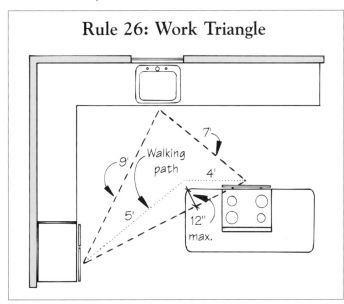

Rules 28 & 29: Kitchen Seating

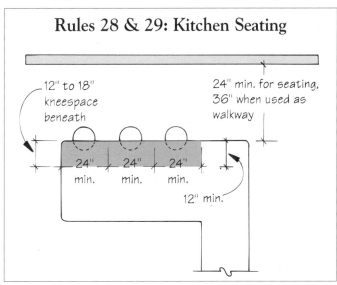

26 *Work Triangle* Make the primary work triangle 26 ft. or less. This is the distance between the refrigerator, primary cooking center, and the primary sink, measured from the center front of each appliance. No leg of the triangle should be less than 4 ft. or more than 9 ft. long. If an island or peninsula obstructs the triangle, measure the shortest *walking* distance (not actually a triangle), as shown. No leg should intersect an obstacle by more than 12 inches.

29 *Kitchen Seating* Provide at least 24 in. of free space behind a counter or table for seating. Increase the clearance to 36 in. if people will need to pass behind diners.

30 *Kitchen Windows* The combined area of windows and skylights should equal at least 10% of the area of the kitchen (or of the living space that includes the kitchen).

31 *Safety* Specify ground-fault circuit interrupters (GFCIs) on all receptacles within 6 ft. of a kitchen water source. Also, include smoke alarms in the kitchen and a fire extinguisher across from the cooktop. ■

Kitchen Design Portfolio

Award-Winning Kitchens: The rules of good kitchen design can take you part way to a design solution. The rest takes creative talent and an understanding of the customers' individual needs. A variety of winning examples from the National Kitchen & Bath Association's annual design competition follow (photos courtesy of NKBA).

Designer: Dagmar Thiel, CKD, Kitchen & Bath Design, Orinda, Calif.

Designer: David Lemkin, CKD, Kitchen Specialists of California, Encino, Calif.

Designer: Patti Lawson, CKD, of Dayton Showcase Co., Cincinatti, Ohio.

Designer: Robert Santoro, Cold Spring Designs, Ridgefield, Conn.

Designer: Candace Ihlenfeldt, The Showplace, Inc., Redmond, Wash.

Designer: Allen Godziebiewski, Cabinets By Robert, Traverse City, Mich.

Beyond the Work Triangle

by Paul Turpin

Even if you haven't tried your hand at kitchen design, you probably know the term "work triangle." Even your clients use the phrase. It's a term that came out of 1930's industrial-style time-and-motion studies, and defines the movement of the cook from refrigerator to sink to range. The basic concept is simple: If the appliances and fixtures are too far apart, you waste time and energy walking around all the time. If they're too close to each other, the work spaces are cramped.

However, like all good ideas, it's easy to turn this one into an absolute rule, rather than a flexible guideline. This can put you in a position of automatically rejecting floorplans that are the best compromise of *all* the variables that need accommodating in today's multi-use kitchens.

New Variables

Kitchen designers need to consider two important changes — new appliance technology and modern lifestyles.

Altered appliances. The kitchen work triangle was conceived when the refrigerator, sink, and range were the three primary kitchen fixtures. But that's changed. The range of yesterday is often several components today: cooktop in one place, a built-in oven elsewhere, and a microwave oven in yet a third place. Larger kitchens often have two sinks, sometimes two refrigerators.

With appliances, frequency of use is a critical measure. An appliance that is used only a few times a year doesn't need to be as handy as one used each day of the work week. For instance, if the cook is a serious microwave user, a conventional oven will probably be used only occasionally for holiday gatherings. In this case, consider including a small microwave near the refrigerator to handle defrosting and leftover food reheating, along with another larger microwave.

Central station. In addition to appliances multiplying, kitchens are used for a great deal more than just cooking these days. Dual-income households leave no one home during the day. As a result, the kitchen gets used for fewer hours, but more intensively. It's now a center for family activity that can include kids doing homework, TV/video viewing, laundry,

end of the day "debriefing," and more than one person sharing cooking and cleanup responsibilities. Entertaining standards have changed too, so that food that used to be prepared in the kitchen and brought out to the guests, may now be prepared with the help of guests and consumed in the kitchen.

These changes add a social element to the kitchen, so the design goal is more than making the work spaces in a kitchen efficient. You also have to integrate these work spaces with other central functions.

To boil it down, start with two principles in mind: (1) the cook needs room to work conveniently. This includes work space plus storage convenience (the *new* "work triangle"); and (2) other members of the household need to have access to the kitchen, and room for interaction without getting in the cook's way.

Plotting patterns. I usually start by assessing the household traffic flow in and around the kitchen, and then test that against the cook's needs. As an example, I try to have the cooking area as far out of the traffic flow as possible, so that household members can use the refrigerator and sink without crossing the cook's path. At the same time, I don't want to cut the cook off from the rest of the activities in the room.

Poor household traffic problems can make kitchen redesign seem more difficult than it really is. Often the clients think there simply isn't enough room for everything they want, when in fact, some rearranging will do the trick. The following case study, in which I rearranged space within the existing footprint, illustrates this point.

Case Study

The clients and the floor plan may look familiar to you: The house was a 1950s ranch with a dining/family room addition that was put up next to the kitchen in 1962. By 1980, the owners had lived in the house with a family of five for 19 years, and were ready for a change. The children were grown, and "mom and dad" wanted a kitchen that was comfortable yet suitable for entertaining.

Before. After meeting with the clients, getting their critique of the kitchen, and making my own study, we drew up this list:

- The kitchen seemed impossibly small and crowded.
- The refrigerator blocked the door to the living room whenever it was open.
- The microwave sat on the counter, eating up space that was already in short supply.
- The main passageway ran right through the middle of the work triangle.
- The kitchen's west partition blocked the line of sight between the cook and the table, and much of the view to the back patio.
- The washer and dryer sat in a corner.
- The 10x20-foot dining/family room felt long and narrow; the southern end was not much more than a passageway.

After. The key structural change was removing the partition between the kitchen and dining room. When we also moved the washer/dryer next to the water heater, these changes created a new "blank slate" on which to lay out the kitchen work area.

The centerpiece — literally — is an oval island cabinet that accomplishes several goals:

- Its Jenn-aire downdraft cooktop adds four more burners (which can also be interchanged with plug-in grill or griddle modules) to the kitchen, and provides a showcase for more flamboyant cookery.
- The island also creates a second approach to the refrigerator, helping to keep the work triangle clear.
- The rounded corners provide good circulation around the island.
- Its shape mirrors that of the dining room table.

The microwave is built in next to the refrigerator, keeping the counter free. A small sink for washing vegetables keeps the cooking area compact, while a large sink with its adjacent dishwasher creates a separate clean-up area. At the southern end of the dining room, interior screens (made of oak paneling that match the kitchen cabinets) hide the utility area and reinforce the sense of having a single large room.

The effect for the clients is a completely transformed room. What was cramped is now spacious. The back patio, once hard to get to, has become a useful part of the living area of the house. And best of all, what used to feel crowded with five people, has had over twenty people circulating through it at one time, with lots of room for the hosts to cook while still conversing with their guests. ■

Paul Turpin is a Los Angeles-based remodeling contractor who specializes in kitchen & bath design and remodeling.

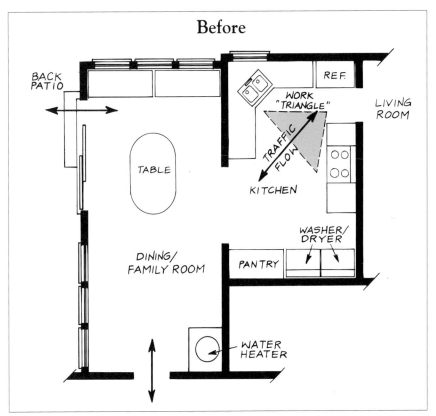

Before: *This floorplan of a 1950s ranch kitchen and 1960s dining/family room addition shows how the work triangle occupies one end of the kitchen, leaving it isolated from the family room and in conflict with traffic to the living room.*

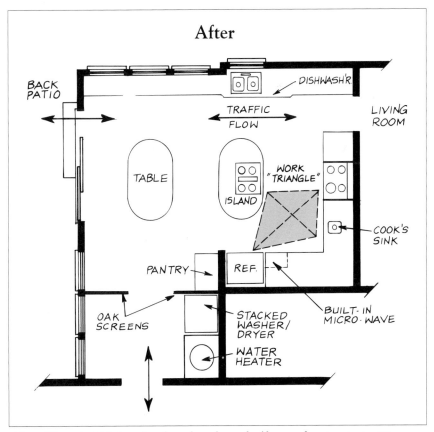

After: *The revised kitchen plan shows how the washer/dryer and an interior partition were removed, and an oval island with cooktop and small sink were added. This shifted the work triangle away from the traffic pattern to the living room, and created better access and line of sight between the kitchen and family room.*

Kitchen Islands

by Paul Turpin

Clearance Around Islands

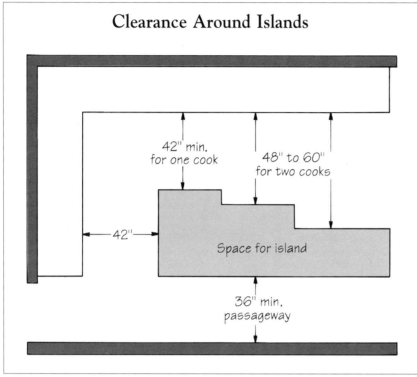

42" min.
for one cook

48" to 60"
for two cooks

42"

Space for island

36" min.
passageway

Figure 1. *The National Kitchen and Bath Association recommends allowing at least 42 inches of clear space between the island and adjacent countertops. If a work aisle is to be used simultaneously by two cooks, allow between 48 and 60 inches of clear space. Passageways should be a minimum of 36 inches wide.*

Figure 2. *A countertop wider than 42 inches should have curved or angled corners to make it easier to reach the entire work surface from all sides. Island storage space (inset) adds convenience.*

Islands serve two main purposes in the kitchen: They give the cook added workspace and they give the kitchen a focal point. Depending on the layout, an island might also provide extra eating space or additional storage. If it is located at the edge of an adjoining room, an island may serve as a border between rooms or as a screen to hide everyday kitchen mess.

An island must be properly proportioned. I've seen large ones crammed into tight kitchens and undersized islands cast adrift in enormous spaces. Passageways and work areas need to be wide enough to allow the cook room to move, but compact enough to prevent the work triangle from becoming too big (see Figure 1). The best way to define the size and shape of an island is to lay out the necessary clearances first. Whatever space remains in the center is what you have to work with. If there's no room for an island, you may be able to remove the wall between the kitchen and dining or family room and put the island in its place.

Island Options

Rerouting traffic is one of the benefits of adding an island: It gives you two possible paths through the kitchen. This is a bonus in an often-crowded family kitchen, although young children like to run racetrack patterns around an island. Warn moms and dads of this possibility and, if it's a problem, recommend a peninsula layout instead.

If the island is particularly large, you can do a variety of things with the ends and backs of the cabinets. For example, on a long island you can provide a mix of seating, storage areas, and decorative trimwork. One option is to put a customized bank of drawers below or next to some open shelves.

Putting standard base cabinets back to back may sound like a good idea, but on top it creates a counter that's 50 inches across. That's usually too wide, although it might be acceptable on a curved or hexagonal island (Figure 2). A

Islands With a Purpose

by Lynn Comeskey

Islands are a hot item in kitchen design, and clients often ask for them. But including one because it's chic is not a good enough reason. It must have a purpose and be an integral part of how the kitchen works.

Islands can serve many purposes. They can be used for food preparation, baking, washing and cleanup, cooking, eating, or as a staging area for the dining room. An island also can be used to define an area visually or divert traffic outside the core kitchen area.

A "complete" food preparation island has a small second sink and disposal unit so produce can be washed and parings ground up right there at the island. But this takes a lot of room. More than half the islands we do are just work surfaces — no sinks or cooktops. For this purpose, you can get by with an island that's 30 inches wide and 24 inches deep. Proximity to refrigerator, storage, and the cooktop is essential. I feel that a 30-inch width is the minimum worth building. Regarding island size, I subscribe to "the bigger, the better" theory. A single-use island 48 to 60 inches long and 30 to 36 inches deep is perfect if you have the room.

If you're lucky enough to have 3 feet or more of depth available for an island, you can use standard-depth base cabinets on the principal side and modified wall cabinets on the other side for books or other shallow storage. Or, if you are designing a kitchen where two people will be cooking, you can use 18-inch-deep base cabinets back to back.

There really isn't much difference between food preparation and baking except that the latter is more specialized and requires a proper working surface — marble. For kneading, most bakers also prefer a work surface slightly lower than 36 inches.

If the island is going to be used for dishwashing and cleanup, you'll need to incorporate a sink, a dishwasher, possibly a trash compactor, and open counter on both ends of the sink.

All this requires a lot of space — often more than you have to work with — and an island plumbing vent (check this out with your plumber). Also be aware that without a backsplash, spills from an island sink often end up on the floor

Setting a cooktop in an island is common. For this you need a minimum of 10 to 12 inches of counter space at one end of the cooktop (preferably at both ends). The biggest problem with an island cooktop is venting. Placing a bulky hood over it takes away a lot of the freedom and openness associated with an island.

Islands can range from a small and simple work station with a bar sink (top) to a large, multi-function space forming the core of the kitchen (right).

The logical solution is to use a downdraft cooktop, but I'm not all that fond of them. To be effective, they require very powerful fans. And if the duct is designed to run down the back of a 24-inch-deep base cabinet, this precludes including a toe kick on that side. ■

Lynn Comeskey, of Palo Alto, Calif., is a remodeling contractor who specializes in kitchens and baths.

Figure 3. *Eating counters work well at standard bar height (42 inches) or dining table height (28 inches). For knee space leave 12 to 18 inches.*

DIANA VALENTINE, CKD, DESIGNER; COURTESY OF NKBA

Eating Counters

Minimum knee space

12"

42"

30"-32" typ.

Minimum knee space

29"

18"

17"-19" typ.

2x8 blocks and, using plenty of screws, affix them to the subfloor. I then set the cabinets over the blocks and screw into them. Some remodelers fasten cabinetry to the stub walls set up for plumbing and electrical chases. These are not stiff enough for the job, however, unless there is a continuous post going up to the ceiling framing.

If the cabinets themselves are flimsy, or if the island is tall and narrow, you have to improve the rigidity of the cabinets. Otherwise, with adequate pressure (such as someone falling against the island), they will collapse like dominoes. I reinforce cabinets with a sheet of $^1/_4$- to $^3/_8$-inch plywood across the back, fastening to each cabinet partition as I go. Then I cover the plywood with whatever finish material the customer selects.

Islands at Center Stage

Nothing will bug your customers more than not being able to see what they're doing. So forget fancy lights and go with floodlights, good general lighting, and, if you want pinpoint bursts of brightness, some spotlighting (see "A Practical Guide to Kitchen Lighting," page 182). Floods are good for task lighting, while spots have a narrow beam spread and should be used strictly for aesthetics.

Remember that overhead floods and spots will emphasize the counter and leave the sides of the island in a pool of shadow. This may be the desired effect: It can make the counter look like it's floating. If you have an island that looks good all around, however, you'll probably want additional lighting to illuminate the sides. Using dimmer switches for island lighting is appropriate for kitchens where one part is primarily functional while the rest serves as a dining or family area.

Pot and pan racks are a nice decoration in a country-style kitchen. Don't come down too low, though. You don't want to cut off the line of sight. Stove hoods pose a similar problem: If they're low enough to function properly, they block lines of sight. But if they're high enough to be aesthetically pleasing, they don't draw well. That's why I like downdraft ventilators here.

As for the cabinetry, custom cabinets allow greater flexibility, as well as dramatic and unusual shapes. If your customers want something different but don't have a lot to spend, try mixing stock and custom cabinets to create an unusual look at a lower cost. ∎

better choice is to limit the counter width to 42 inches, the same as many dining tables. That way the entire work surface can be reached from one side.

If the backside of the island serves as a seating area, the counter must overhang at least 12 to 18 inches to provide knee space. When planning the counter height, consider the following: Standard dining table height is 29 inches, standard bar height (that barstools fit) is 42 inches. Standard kitchen counter height is halfway between these at 36 inches. That makes dining room chairs too short and barstools too tall.

One solution is to find barstools that can be shortened by 6 inches without looking weird. Another is to make the eating portion of the island a separate counter that's raised to 42 inches or lowered to 29 inches (Figure 3). Varying the counter height also creates a division between the work and eating portions of the island.

Anchoring the Island

Most kitchen cabinetry is fastened to the wall, but island cabinets must be secured to the floor. I screw a series of 2x4 blocks to a floor joist, if I can get at one. Otherwise I use 2x6 or

Paul Turpin is a Los Angeles-based remodeling contractor who specializes in kitchen and bath design and remodeling.

Kitchen Peninsulas

by Patrick J. Galvin

From a design viewpoint, kitchen peninsulas are similar to islands. The difference is that rather than float free, they extend out into the room from one of the walls. Peninsulas serve to form an L shape or provide one of the legs of a U-shaped kitchen.

Like islands, peninsulas should be thought of in functional terms. Their purpose is to help create a suitable work triangle. (A triangle of between 12 and 23 feet is most efficient.) The fact that peninsulas might also provide aesthetic value and additional uses — as a brunch counter or workspace — is a bonus.

Cabinet Considerations

Unlike other cabinets, which are installed against a wall, peninsula cabinets are exposed to view. As a result, they must be finished on two sides, and the end cabinet on three. Many cabinets can be ordered with access from both sides, making them more useful. In the case where a dining area is placed on the other side of the peninsula, two-way access cabinets can provide handy storage space for table linens and dishes. This adds considerably to the cost of the cabinets, however, since it doubles the number of cabinet doors. Depending on type, one door can account for half the cost of a cabinet.

It is also quite common to install wall cabinets above a peninsula. If this is in the plan, it is important to order peninsula wall cabinets specially reinforced for this kind of installation. Regular wall cabinets are made to be screwed to a wall, and should not be suspended from the ceiling.

Sizing It Right

The wall from which a peninsula protrudes must be at least 8 feet long. If the peninsula includes an eating area on the back side, that wall has to be at least 11 feet long. This includes 4 feet for the depth of two base cabinets, 4 feet of working space between the two cabinet runs, one foot for a narrow eating counter and 2 feet of clearance for seating (3 feet if people need to pass behind the diners).

Appliances

The next question is what to put in the peninsula. It is usually a poor place for the refrigerator because that puts a massive design element out in the middle of the room and exposes its unattractive backside to the living area.

It is a popular place to put a sink and dishwasher, although this can add to plumbing cost, especially for builders who use plumbing tree layouts that serve two floors through one wall.

That leaves the range, or cooktop, which is the most common choice. As with islands, the main problem here is ventilation. If you have wall cabinets suspended over the peninsula, a standard range hood will work, although ducting to the outdoors can be a challenge and may require a long duct run.

Other options include an island hood, which tends to be large and block the line of sight, or a downdraft hood. Because these require fairly large fans of 300 cfm or more, they can be noisy unless the blower is located remotely, such as in the attic or basement. Also, in this era of ultra-tight houses, the homeowner may need to open a window slightly to provide makeup air for the larger blower. ■

Patrick J. Galvin is the author of Kitchen Planning Guide for Builders, Designers and Architects, *and the former editor and publisher of* Kitchen & Bath Business.

Peninsula To Form U-Shaped Kitchen

24" min.
36" if walkway

12" min.

48" min.

Undercounter dishwasher

Refrigerator

Downdraft vent or range hood

36" min.

Peninsulas help form an efficient work triangle — and, with enough space, can provide an eating counter as well.

Designing the Two-Cook Kitchen

by Joan Eisenberg

With two-cook kitchens I always start the planning process by surveying the needs of both people. Some of the questions I ask are:

- What are the physical attributes of the two people? A very tall cook working with a short cook will need different counter heights than two cooks of about the same height. A right-handed person will have different needs than a left-handed person.
- Who shops and puts away groceries, and when? Does one family member stop on the way home from work, bringing packages into the kitchen as another member is preparing dinner? If so, I consider having a separate unloading counter near the pantry space so as not to disturb the cook.
- Which cook does what? This is a crucial question — its answer tells me whether the kitchen needs extra appliances or whether shared equipment will work.

Two-Cook Categories

The National Kitchen and Bath Association identifies several categories of multiple cooks:

Team cooking. With team cooking, two or more people share equally in the preparation and cleanup of meals. In this situation, it's best to design the room with as little shared space as possible. If the budget can afford it, the only shared equipment should be the refrigerator, and it should be placed so that one cook does not have to cross the path of the other to reach this very important leg of the work triangle.

Assistant chef. In this scenario, the assistant is generally given preparation tasks such as washing and chopping vegetables. This situation calls for a second preparation center with a small sink that will keep the assistant close at hand but out of the primary cook's way.

Specialty cooks. This type of two-cook

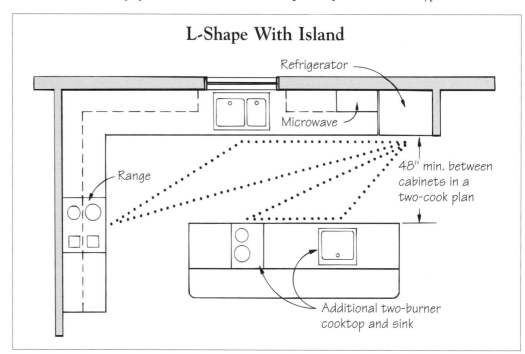

L-Shape With Island

Refrigerator

Microwave

Range

48" min. between cabinets in a two-cook plan

Additional two-burner cooktop and sink

The island counter with a sink and small cooktop makes a workspace for an assistant cook, who shares the refrigerator with the main cook.

kitchen involves a primary cook for most preparation and cleanup and another cook (or cooks) who has a special interest in one type of cooking — someone who loves to make bread, for instance. A separate baking center, designed with this activity and person in mind, will create an ideal kitchen for this household.

Avoiding Traffic Jams

Once I determine the family's general category, I examine the traffic flow. In a one-person kitchen, I try to create traffic paths that keep noncooking family members out of the work triangle. In a two-cook kitchen, I use either a greatly expanded triangle, or more often, two triangles that may share one or two common points. This allows the two cooks to work without interruption and without getting in each other's way.

Another way to avoid traffic jams is to widen walkways. The standard 42-inch space between cabinets or appliances is not adequate in a two-cook kitchen. Allow 48 to 54 inches between cabinets for edging by, and 60 to 64 inches if it serves as walking space. To determine which end of these ranges to use, I go back to the survey of the physical attributes and look at the size and weight of the individuals in question.

Double Triangles

To establish two work triangles, you must have adequate counter space. This prevents the traffic jams that occur when one of the two cooks spills over into the other's work space.

At a minimum, allow 36 inches of clear counter for each cook. It is best when this counter space is in two separate areas rather than in one 72-inch stretch.

Depending on the configuration of the room, any of the three major appliances — sink, cooktop, or refrigerator — can act as a divider. The interview helps determine which appliances can comfortably be shared and which need to be duplicated. Usually, the sink is the first fixture requested to be duplicated, with cooking equipment second, and the refrigerator a distant third.

If space or budget does not allow for duplication, concentrate on placing the fixtures where they are convenient to both cooks. Also, strive for easily accessible storage of spices and cooking utensils.

Islands useful. Consider using a large island to provide an accessible shared work

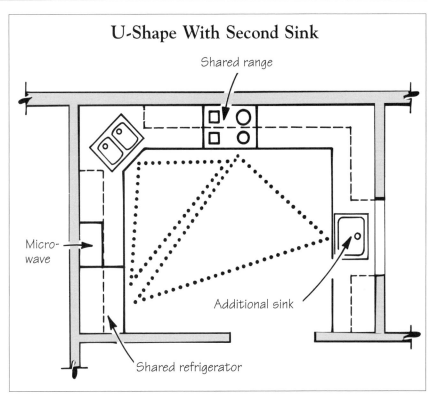

U-Shape With Second Sink

A U-shaped kitchen can be ideal for two cooks. A second sink creates two work triangles, with the range and refrigerator shared.

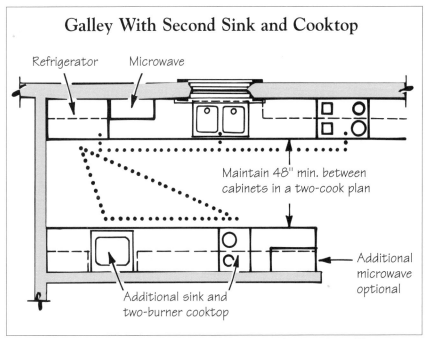

Galley With Second Sink and Cooktop

A galley can work for two cooks — this plan uses a second sink and an additional two-burner cooktop.

space. It can have a sink or cooktop that is accessed from both legs of an L-shaped kitchen. An island can also offer a secondary work counter for an assistant cook. ■

Joan Eisenberg, CKD, is the principal of JME Consulting, an independent kitchen and bath design firm in Baltimore, Md.

Chapter 2
KITCHEN CABINETS

ALLEN GODZIEBIEWSKI, DESIGNER; COURTESY OF NKBA

Shopping for Kitchen Cabinets

by Rick Fournier

For beauty and performance that last, you have to look beneath the surface at materials and joinery

People shopping for kitchen cabinets are usually looking for something better than what they already have. Unfortunately, their wants often exceed their budget. And it only gets worse when they enter a showroom like mine, where they can see five or six full-size displays incorporating most of the styles and accessories available. I handle several different cabinet brands; within each one there are several levels of quality and price. The first thing I try to do is narrow the choices and match the customer's budget to a cabinet that will also fit their need.

Good, Better, Best

The best tool I have for this is a drawing that shows a typical L-shaped kitchen floor plan and perspective (see"Matching Cabinets to the Budget," facing page). The accompanying chart compares oak raised-panel cabinets for all of the manufacturers I carry, and shows separate costs for the cabinets, the accessories, and the moldings. This system works for people who have no idea what a kitchen costs, as well as for those who come in with a general plan and rough dimension.

In either case, I can count the number of cabinets (tall cabinets count as two pieces because of their size) and apply the per-unit coast at each level of quality. It gives customers a good idea of the total cost (within 10%) and

helps to shape their expectations. Once customer see which grade of cabinet they can afford, they can better focus on door styles and accessories.

The cost chart also provides a timetable for order and delivery. There's no way I can satisfy people who need their cabinets in two weeks. Depending on the cabinet, production tim e is three to eight weeks, plus a week for delivery.

Box Construction

The quality and price of a cabinet depends on the materials and methods used to put it together. Cabinet boxes come in two designs — framed and frameless (Figure 1, page 32). Framed cabinets have a wood facing surrounding the door and drawer openings, and inset, full overlay, or partial overlay doors that let the frame show through, giving them a traditional look. Frameless cabinets (sometimes called Euro cabinets) have no facings and always use full overlay doors and drawers. Frameless cabinets often have laminate door and drawer fronts, which add to their flush, streamlined appearance. But most manufacturers have started to offer wood door and drawer fronts on a frameless cabinet. This leaves a small strip of the cabinet box exposed, which is usually faced with vinyl that matches the cabinet interior (wood-grained or white). Higher-grade cabinets use solid wood banding or wood veneer.

Matching Cabinets to the Budget

Using this perspective drawing and floor plan for a standard L-shaped kitchen helps clients compare costs among various brands and models of cabinets. The chart gives prices for the kitchen shown both with and without accessories.

MOLDING:
V60 – Valance 60" Straight
3 Crown Molding
2 Matching Toe Kick
1 Touch-up Kit
27 Pieces of Hardware

ACCESSORIES:
1 Spice Rack
2 Wall Lazy Susans
1 Appliance Garage
1 Cutlery Divider
2 Tray Dividers
1 Tilt Down
1 Towel Bar
2 Roll Outs

Cabinet Price Comparison

	Cabinets Only		Cabinets With Accessories		
Manufacturer	Total	Unit Cost	Accessories/ Moldings	Total	Unit Cost
Jim Bishop II	$2,785	$199	$450/190	$3,425	$245
Jim Bishop	3,115	223	455/210	3,780	270
Imperial	3,570	255	605/275	4,450	318
Plato	5,015	358	945/205	6,165	440
Millbrook	3,195	228	750/530	4,475	320
Millbrook 500	3,705	265	800/565	5,070	362
Millbrook 1000	4,640	331	900/565	6,105	436
Millbrook 2000	6,015	430	955/660	7,630	545

Note: Most manufacturers require three to eight weeks to produce cabinets, plus one week for delivery.

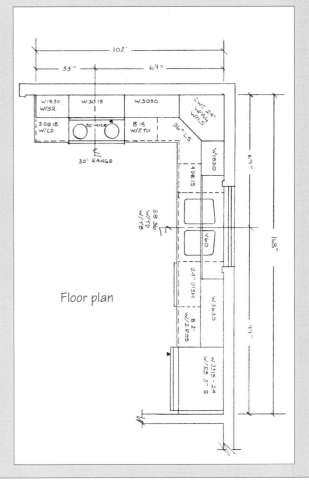

Floor plan

Figure 1. *In a framed cabinet box* (top), *the door and drawer openings are bordered by a solid wood "face frame." A frameless box* (bottom) *is almost completely hidden by the door and drawer fronts.*

Plywood vs. MDF. One of the factors that determines cabinet quality and price is the material used to build the box. Cabinet boxes are sometimes made of cabinet-grade plywood (which has a wood veneer), but usually they are constructed of 1/2-inch-thick particleboard with sides and edges veneered in vinyl. The quality of the particleboard varies from one manufacturer to another, with better-quality cabinet lines using MDF (medium-density fibercore).

It's difficult to determine the difference visually — a low-grade product can look as good as a high-grade product, but the cost can vary greatly. Plywood resists moisture well, and it's easier to patch a scratch in a wood veneer than in a vinyl veneer. Plywood is also stronger than MDF, which in turn is more durable than low-grade particleboard.

It's not necessary, however, to pay a premium for plywood to get a good cabinet. Cabinets take the most abuse during shipping and installation. Once they're in place, the 36- or 38-pound density MDF used for most cabinets is strong enough. (Some manufacturers, like Millbrook, use even more dense, 42- to 48-pound MDF.) MDF is also more stable than plywood. While it's true that scratches that penetrate through to the MDF base material are harder to repair, the 4-mil vinyl veneer resists scratches well. (This is less true of lower grade cabinets that use 2-mil vinyl.) And the veneer is smoother on MDF than on plywood.

When I'm trying to cut costs to fit a budget, I recommend MDF cabinets, except in a couple of problem areas. To reduce the chances of moisture damage, I go with plywood cabinets for the sink base and both sides of the dishwasher. If scratches are a concern, I order plywood for the finished end panels.

Other considerations. Some high-end custom lines put a solid top on their base cabinets. Even though this gives you more places to fasten the countertop, to me it's not a necessary part of the construction. Most companies use corner blocks, which together with hanging rails, are strong enough to keep the cabinet square.

Curved fronts are common on frameless cabinets with plastic laminate, although you can get certain radiuses done in wood (Figure 2). To keep the cost down, I try to work with standard sizes on curved units before requesting a quote on a special cabinet.

The least expensive way to finish the back side of a peninsula or island cabinet is with a flush veneered panel, which all manufacturers supply. A step up is wainscoting, which is basically a series of cabinet doors glued together

Figure 2. Curved fronts *are more widely available with laminate-faced cabinets, but a limited number of radiused wood fronts are available. Stock sizes are much cheaper than custom curved units.*

Figure 3. With inset doors, *a gap is visible between the doors and drawers and the cabinet frame. This leaves little room for error, and expansion and contraction may cause the fronts to rub against the frame.*

without the frame. Wainscotting requires more labor to install than a plain panel, especially if you have to miter the corners or if the cabinets are set at an odd angle to each other.

Doors

Appearance is a priority for most people, so the door style is what they look at first. Wood doors are always more expensive than laminate doors, but most people have a definite preference for one or the other, so price is not necessarily the determining factor. What the average customer doesn't know is that even though a cabinet door appears to be solid wood, many are actually less expensive particleboard with a wood veneer. It's difficult to tell the difference with a flat panel door, but the milling of raised panel doors differs depending on whether it's solid wood or veneer. If the panel has a flat slant toward the frame, it's probably solid wood; if it's a raised cove, it's probably veneer. Particleboard is more stable than solid wood, but it's harder to mask scratches in the veneer.

With laminate doors, the main differences in quality are in the finish surface and the edge treatment. High-pressure decorative laminate (HPDL) is much more durable than melamine (see "Cabinet Finish Glossary," page 35). The thinner melamine, however, is adequate for the back side of a door, and is widely used for cabinet boxes. For edge banding, HPDL leaves a black line at the seam, so most doors have

PVC or wood edge banding, or plastic T-molding. Impregnated paper is used only on low-end cabinets.

Inset doors. Builders who have no experience with inset doors may get callbacks from fussy customers. Unlike an overlay door, which covers the cabinet frame, an inset door is mounted flush with the frame, so the gap between the door and the frame is exposed (Figure 3). It looks great when the cabinets are new, but even a slight misalignment — from expansion and contraction or a slipping hinge — can cause the edges to rub or make the door look tilted. The best cabinet lines bevel the edge of the doors and drawers so they will shut without rubbing even if they've moved a little. To avoid callbacks, I explain all of this to customers and I tell them that I will make one adjustment after installation. After that if it moves, it moves.

White painted wood. Another popular style that may cause complaints is white painted wood — usually a birch or maple framed cabinet finished with some type of catalyzed enamel paint. There are two problems with this type of finish. First, despite the paint's durability, scratches and nicks are harder to touch up than those on stained or even regular painted surfaces. It's like a chip in the paint on your car. Do you sand the whole panel or just the spot? The other problem is that when the wood expands and contracts, even a slight separation

Figure 4. *Over time, white painted hardwood cabinets* tend *to show small cracks at the joints (right). An alternative is to use a foil-wrapped MDF front (far right).*

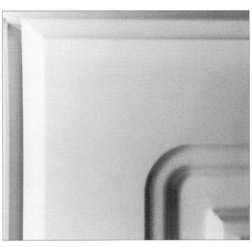

Figure 5. *Knife hinges are partially concealed and are adjustable in two dimensions. The one shown is self-closing.*

Figure 6. *Fully concealed cup hinges* (top) *are adjustable in three dimensions, making it easier to keep doors aligned. Many cup hinges allow you to easily remove the door by unclipping the hinge body from the base* (above), *after removing the hinge cover plate.*

at the joints is very visible (Figure 4). Sometimes the floating center panel also shows a line of natural wood color where the panel has moved away from the white frame.

One solution is to use an MDF door with a foil wrap. The finish is harder than paint so it's less likely to scratch and chip. Because it's a one-piece door, it's also more durable and stable, and it usually costs 20% to 40% less than real wood.

Drawers

Drawer glides have improved a lot in the last ten years. Every manufacturer I know of uses glides rated for at least 75 pounds that wrap around the bottom edge of the drawer. This simplifies drawer construction because the glides support and strengthen the drawer.

Some high-end cabinets still build drawers with dovetailed corners, but it's really not necessary for strength. Most drawers are solid wood, stapled and glued together, with a separate drawer front attached to the box with screws from the back. To reduce cost, some drawer boxes use softer poplar instead of maple or birch, and some have an integral drawer front, which is a less durable construction. Lower-grade cabinets use MDF or particleboard wrapped with wood-grained vinyl, but it's not something you'd notice unless you're told or you take the drawer out and look at the back edges.

On good-quality cabinets, drawer bottoms are hot-melt-glued into dadoes in the drawer sides. Lower-grade cabinets use particleboard with an impregnated paper print, and on very cheap cabinets, the underside is left unfinished. (Plastic drawers with single center-mounted glides are virtually nonexistent today.) Higher-grade cabinet drawers use melamine or plywood, which wears much better. You can upgrade cabinet drawers at a cost of $10 to $20 per drawer.

A lot of people don't realize that you can also special-order upgraded drawer glides. For example, if you want full-extension glides for a heavy-duty pots-and-pans drawer, you can change the cabinet spec for that one drawer. It's an inexpensive way to improve a cabinet without busting the budget.

Hardware

Most customers don't notice cabinet hinges, but for the installer, hinge quality and adjustability is an important consideration.

Barrel and knife hinges. Most lower-grade cabinets use a barrel hinge or knife hinge in one or two finishes (Figure 5). These hinges are adjustable in two directions (up and down, and in and out), and are self-closing, eliminating the need for magnetic or mechanical catches.

Cup hinges. Fully concealed hinges, or cup hinges, give you more control because they're adjustable in three directions, making them ideal for frameless cabinets, where alignment of full overlay doors is critical. Also, with some cup hinges you can unclip the hinge body from the base plate to remove the doors (Figure 6). This makes the cabinets lighter during installation and keeps the doors out of the way when plumbers and electricians are working inside the cabinet.

Most cup hinges allow the door to swing open 95 or 105 degrees. If your customer prefers doors that open more than this, you can either move to a higher-grade cabinet or upgrade the hinges (hinge swing angles vary between 95 and 175 degrees). For one cabinet, swapping hinges will cost about $25. But for a whole kitchen, it could cost as much as $600, which is probably as expensive as stepping up to the next higher cabinet grade.

Pulls. Cabinet knobs and pulls are always shipped loose and have to be installed on site. With most lower-grade cabinets you have to order and pay for the hardware separately, and your choices are limited to about ten styles, often fewer. Many low-end cabinets are not predrilled for pulls, and those that are don't give you a choice of location.

Higher-grade cabinets give you 20 to 25 different hardware styles to choose from, most of which are included in the price of the cabinet. The cabinets are always predrilled, and you can specify the location (if you don't, you get the standard location). Some of the hardware is solid brass, and if your customers choose that particular style, they're getting a good deal. However, if there's absolutely nothing they like from the manufacturer's selection, you cannot get a credit for omitting the hardware. Buying hardware separately could cost $300 to $500.

Accessories

At all levels of quality, a standard base cabinet is equipped with a drawer and one or two adjustable shelves. But every manufacturer also offers accessories that make the storage space easier to use. The cost varies quite a bit from brand to brand, but on aver-

Figure 7. Many corner cabinets *now contain a Super Susan, which rides on ball bearings on the cabinet bottom or on an intermediate shelf, eliminating the need for a center post.*

Cabinet Finish Glossary

Even though the finish surfaces of factory-built cabinets often look the same, they vary in durability and cost. Here's a brief description of the materials used by most kitchen manufacturers to finish the interiors, exteriors, doors, and drawers of their cabinets:

High-pressure decorative laminate (HPDL) is a multi-layered material familiar to most builders by trade names like Formica, Wilsonart, and Nevamar (it's often called plastic laminate). A single paper sheet printed with a pattern or solid color is sandwiched between a base material composed of several layers of resin-saturated kraft paper, and a top layer of melamine. The entire assembly is squeezed together under high pressure. Kitchen cabinets use .03-inch-thick vertical grade HPDL; the thicker (.05 inch) horizontal grade is used primarily for countertops.

Melamine is a generic name for a clear polymer. Unlike HPDL, melamine is not produced in separate sheets. Instead, manufacturers buy ready-made boards on which melamine

has been applied as a wear surface over printed paper glued to particleboard. The paper can be a solid color or a wood-grain print. Melamine boards are used for cabinet box panels, although some low-grade cabinets may also have melamine door and drawer fronts.

Vinyl is a flexible sheet of plastic that, like melamine, is supplied to manufacturers as ready-made boards. Vinyl is thicker and more resilient than melamine, but less wear-resistant. It is used chiefly for cabinet and drawer box panels.

Impregnated-paper is a phenol- or melamine-based overlay. It is used as a veneer on plywood panels (melamine cannot be applied to plywood) for cabinet interiors.

Rigid thermal foil (sometimes called RTF) is a European process that has become popular recently in this country. The process uses heat and pressure to wrap a solid plastic sheet around a medium density fibercore (MDF) door that has been shaped, for example, as a raised panel. Foil has good durability,

but the quality of the finish depends on the fabrication process and the quality of the MDF used. Poor quality MDF sometimes allows surface defects to telegraph through. Rigid thermal foil should not be confused with hot-stamped foil, which is not nearly as durable and is used as a finish on low-end furniture.

Polyester paint produces a lustrous, clear or colored finish to cabinet door and drawer fronts. It is a very expensive finish, however, because like lacquer, it requires many coats, and each coat must be wet-sanded by hand. But polyester paint doesn't craze or crack as much as lacquer.

Catalyzed enamel paint is one of a new generation of two-part paints used as a lower-cost substitute for polyester paint. Some manufacturers use vinyl enamel (Plato), while others use lacquer enamel (Millbrook) or some other formula. But in each case, the result is a lacquer-like finish with good resistance to yellowing, chipping, and cracking.

— R.F.

Fancy Fasteners

Better-looking than drywall screws: *Fasten cabinets using a plastic collar and cap (at left, in photo), a sleeve and through-bolt (center), or a plated screw with finish washer (right).*

Most contractors still hang cabinets with drywall screws because it's convenient — there's always a handful of drywall screws lying around the site. But when I open the door on a white or wood-grained cabinet interior, the last thing I want to see is the black head of a drywall screw. With a little foresight, you can order special fasteners that do a much cleaner job of fastening cabinets to the wall and to each other.

One type isn't really a fastener at all, just a white plastic collar that you drive a screw through, and a removable cap that snaps over the collar (photo, right). The collar helps prevent over-driving the screw, and the cap provides a finished appearance that blends well with both white and wood-grained veneers.

Another type of two-piece fastener consists of a metal or plastic sleeve and bolt. After clamping two cabinet boxes together and predrilling a slightly oversized hole through both sidewalls, the sleeve friction-fits into one side to receive the through-bolt from the other side. This works for framed cabinets, too, but requires longer sleeves and bolts. You can use this through-bolt system to gang base or wall cabinets together before installing them or to pull them snug once they're in place.

Both types of fasteners must be ordered separately. The cost for an average kitchen — about $25 — is easily justified by the improved appearance. But if you'd rather use materials you can get at the local hardware store, try using #6 or #8 Phillips head screws (chrome for white cabinets, brass for wood grain) with matching finish washers. You'll need several different lengths, one to fasten cabinets to each other and one to attach them to the wall. The washers not only give a clean appearance, but also keep you from over-driving the screws.

— R.F.

Figure 8. Another option for corner cabinet storage combines roll-out trays with pie-cut shelves on the door.

Figure 9. Adjustable pull-out trays can be mounted on full-extension glides and come in widths up to 36 inches.

fixed shelf, eliminating the need for a center post (Figure 7). This allows the trays to ride on ball bearings, so they will hold more weight and take more abuse. And a Super Susan is bigger than an ordinary lazy susan — 32 inches in diameter instead of 28 inches.

There are lots of other options for corners, too, like swing-out half-moon shelves, trays that slide out of the corner, and racks for the door (Figure 8). Fixed wraparound shelving is a recent — and inexpensive — improvement on the old blind corner. The L-shaped adjustable shelves let you pack a lot of stuff in the corner, but make it easy to get to it.

Pull-out tray. Most pull-out trays are adjustable so you can change the height to fit whatever you're storing (Figure 9). They are mounted on full-extension glides and come in widths up to 36 inches. Adding two pull-out trays to a typical 24-inch base cabinet will cost $100 to $150.

Many suppliers will install cabinet accessories at no extra charge, but unless you specifically tell them to do it, they'll ship them loose. It's silly not to take advantage of free mounting, especially since some accessories, like a tilt-down sink front, are tricky to install. A few items, however, like the inner components of big pantry cabinets, are always shipped loose because of their weight. ∎

age you can easily add $200 to $500 per kitchen in accessories.

Corners. Higher-grade cabinets offer a Super Susan for both diagonal and pie-cut corners. The door opens separately from the lazy susan (pie-cut corners have a bifold door), which rolls on the floor of the cabinet or on a

Rick Fournier owns Interior Creations in Barre, Vt.

Cabinet Installation Basics

by Bob Cox

A step-by-step guide to fast and accurate kitchen installation

CAROLYN BATES

Installing kitchen cabinets is a precise task. If you proceed logically and measure accurately, you'll get good results.

The following steps are a time-tested and proven method for properly installing cabinets at controlled costs.

Step 1: Check Specs

Start out by fully familiarizing yourself with the details of the kitchen installation. Unfortunately, errors in paperwork or cases where the specs and the drawings differ occur too frequently. There is no better time than now to correct or adjust for discrepancies.

Step 2: Check Materials

A missing or damaged cabinet or part could delay installation. Depending on your past experiences with the supplier, you may want to unpack or unwrap each cabinet. If you do so, repack and/or rewrap the cabinets to protect them during the preliminary work. Unprotected cabinets are easily damaged.

Step 3: Check Dimensions

One of the most costly errors in kitchen planning and design is incorrect or missed measurements. It doesn't take long to verify floor plan dimensions, but it could make the difference between a profit or loss on the entire job.

Make sure you have adequate clearances — that you are not trying to fit 144 inches of cabinets into a 144-inch space. Where a row of cabinets fits between two walls, make sure you leave 1 to 3 inches for fillers at one or both ends.

Also, check now to see if walls are so far out of square or plumb that you'll need to spec a smaller cabinet or make other adjustments.

Step 4: Find the High Point

Start the layout by locating the high point on the floor. Regardless of whether you install wall cabinets or base cabinets first, the following procedures will ensure that all the cabinets on all walls will be level.

If the kitchen to be installed is:
- On one wall only, mark and locate the high point of the floor along this wall.
- An "L" installation, determine the highest point along both walls.
- A "U" installation, determine the high point of the floor along all three walls.

If the kitchen contains a peninsula, you must also check this floor area. Whatever the layout, you must find the one high point in the floor for the entire installation.

Many installers use a 6- to 8-foot straight piece of lumber (2x4 or 1x3) and a 4-foot level to check out and locate the high point. A builders' level also works well.

Step 5: Draw Horizontal Lines

Next, locate and draw horizontal lines on all walls where base cabinets are to be installed

Locate Cabinet Tops/Bottoms

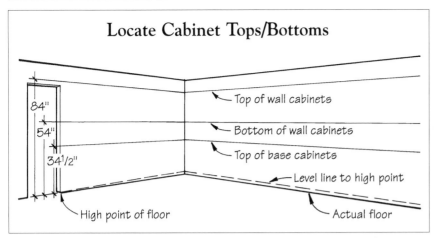

Figure 1. *Starting at the high point on the floor, draw level lines to locate cabinet tops and bottoms.*

Locate Cabinet Centerlines

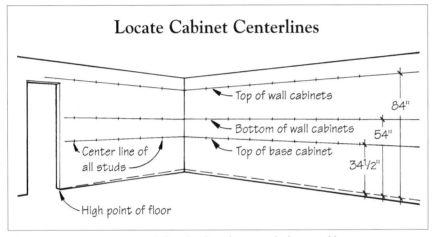

Figure 2. *Mark the centerline of all studs where they cross the horizontal lines.*

Cabinet Scribe

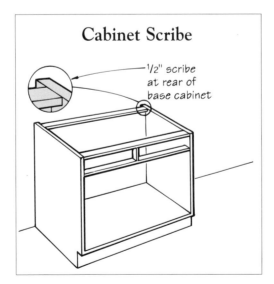

Figure 3. *Where necessary, scribe the back edges of exposed cabinet sides to the wall.*

again from the high point) using the 4-foot level. Draw this line on all walls where you will hang wall cabinets. Finally, draw horizontal lines to mark the bottoms of the wall cabinets (at 54 inches for standard 30-inch-high wall cabinets).

Step 6: Locate Stud Centers

Locate and mark the centerline of each stud where it crosses the horizontal lines drawn at $34^1/2$, 54, and 84 inches high.

Draw short vertical lines to mark the studs (Figure 2). For each wall with cabinets, start by finding one stud, then measure off it to locate the others. Double check stud location. Then repeat for each wall on which cabinets are to be installed.

Step 7: The Final Check

Check 90-degree corners and vertical walls where cabinets are to be installed. Use a framing square to check corners and a straightedge and level to check walls. It is rare that any room has corners that are exactly 90 degrees or walls that are all exactly plumb.

Slightly out-of-square corners and out-of-plumb walls are easily corrected when installing cabinetry. On most cabinets, the sides project beyond the back by up to $1/2$ inch. These extensions allow you to scribe the back of the cabinet to fit to irregular surfaces (Figure 3).

Use shims in back of the cabinets to pad out a depressed section of wall. If you discover variances that are beyond the reach of normal corrective steps, however, you must evaluate the problems and decide on corrective measures before starting the installation. If this occurs, ask these questions:

• Will additional or wider fillers compensate for the variance?
• Are new wall or base cabinets needed?
• Can the countertop (if prefabricated) be used as furnished?

Then make your decisions.

Step 8: Layout on Walls

Measure and mark on the walls the width of each wall and base cabinet to be installed, as well as each open space — for appliances, windows, kneeholes, and such (Figure 4).

After completing the layout, double check the floor plan and measurements. When you're sure everything will fit, proceed with the installation.

Step 9: Install Base Cabinets

In L-shaped layouts, it's common to start the installation from the corner. In U-shaped lay-

(Figure 1). To do this, measure from the high point of the floor up to $34^1/2$ inches and draw a short line. If the finished floor has not been installed, remember to take its thickness into account.

Using a 4-foot level (or builders' level), draw this horizontal line at $34^1/2$ inches on all the walls that will receive base cabinets.

Next, draw a line 84 inches high (measured

outs, many installers start from the corners and fit the cabinets in between, though this varies depending upon the location of appliances and fillers. Where a line of cabinets is closed in by walls at each end, start from one end but allow for fillers at one or both ends. If the wall of cabinets is open at both ends, you can start in the middle of the wall and work your way out in both directions.

In fact, if you've done your layout accurately, left space for fillers, and marked all the cabinets on the wall, as described, you should be able to start the installation anywhere without running into problems.

Install first base cabinet. If you're starting with a standard cabinet (not a corner cabinet) proceed as follows: Remove the doors and drawers form the cabinet. Then locate its position marked on the wall.

Set the top of the base cabinet to the 34½-inch line and plumb the front of cabinet. Use shims on the bottom of the toe kick and back of the cabinet, as needed.

Drill pilot holes through the inside of the cabinet back. Place the holes slightly down from the top and slightly up from the bottom at each stud marked on the wall. The holes should be sized to accept an 8- or 10-gauge wood screw.

After running the screws through the back into wall studs, recheck all levels and adjust as necessary. Loosen the screws and adjust shims as needed to level and plumb the cabinet, then retighten the screws.

Install lazy susan and adjacent cabinet. In a U- or L-shaped kitchen, you typically start in a corner with a lazy-susan cabinet. Most lazy-susan cabinets take up 36 inches of wall space, but are built in a 27-inch box. This means you'll need to attach two furring strips to the wall to support the counter in the corner. Align the top of the furring strips with the top-of-base-cabinet line (Figure 5).

Next, install the adjacent base cabinet on either the right- or left-hand side. The side of this cabinet must be placed precisely 36 inches out from the corner as marked on the wall.

Shim and scribe, if necessary, and secure the adjacent cabinet as described above for the first base cabinet. Next, place the corner cabinet in position. Shim it level to the 34½-inch line and flush with the front of the adjacent base cabinet. Then clamp together the corner cabinet and adjacent cabinet, as shown. Drill four holes through the sides of both cabinets (in the four corners) and secure them together with connector screws.

Mark For Cabinets/Appliances

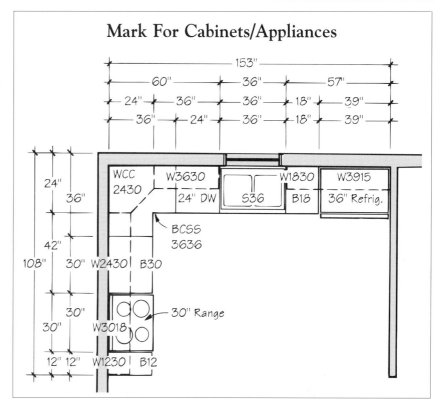

Figure 4. *Measure and mark spaces on the walls for all cabinets and appliances.*

Start With Corner Base

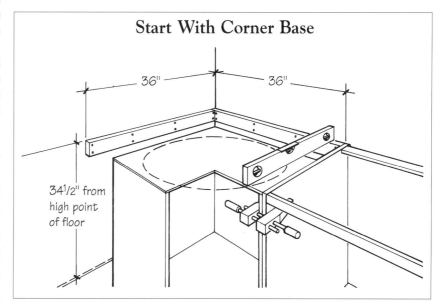

Figure 5. *With L- and U-shaped kitchens, start with a corner base cabinet and one of the adjacent cabinets.*

Other base cabinets. Remove the doors and drawers from the next cabinet to be installed. Set it along side of the cabinet installed previously and shim it level and flush with the front of the cabinet. Clamp the sides of the two cabinets together (Figure 6).

To join the two cabinets, drill four holes through the adjacent sides. Make two holes near the top (front and rear) and bottom (front and rear). With 32-mm (European-style) cabinets, these holes may already be partially drilled and will line up automatically. Install the four connectors and tighten. After connecting the side panels, drill holes

Figure 6. *Line up adjoining cabinets, clamp the sides, and fasten with threaded connectors in the four corners.*

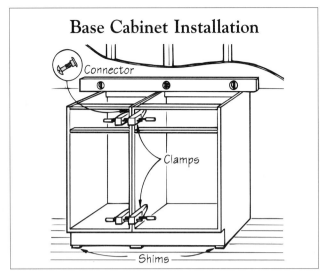

Base Cabinet Installation

Connector

Clamps

Shims

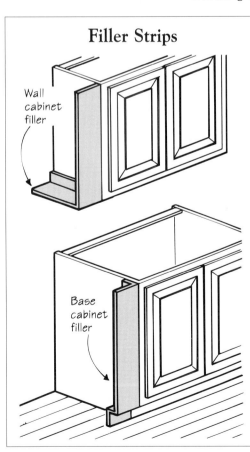

Filler Strips

Wall cabinet filler

Base cabinet filler

Figure 7. *Attach fillers with wood screws from inside the cabinet. Allow room for fillers during layout — otherwise the cabinets may not fit.*

through the back of the cabinet, near the top, at each stud. Recheck all the cabinets for level, then fasten to the studs.

Install doors and drawers on the first cabinet. Reinstall the doors and drawers on the cabinets as soon as possible. This will reduce the likelihood of their being damaged while laying around the job site.

Repeat this procedure until all the base cabinets have been installed.

Installing base fillers. Cabinet fillers come in varying widths for base and wall cabinets (Figure 7). Both types shown attach to the side of the case near the front.

In a run of cabinets fitting between two walls, you usually want the fillers to be symmetrical on each end. If the gap is small, however, one thin filler will do. This should be planned in your layout.

In all cases, install the cabinet before the filler. After the cabinet is secure, scribe the filler to the wall and cut it to fit with a sharp fine-tooth saw. File or sand as needed for a tight fit.

The easiest way to attach a filler is to drill through the cabinet side or face frame from inside the cabinet and use two wood screws.

Step 10: Install Wall Cabinets

Most contractors install the base cabinets first. Some, however, prefer to hang the wall cabinets first so they don't have to lean and reach over the base cabinets as they work. In either case, they use the same procedure to install wall cabinets and fillers as described above for base cabinets.

Install first wall cabinet. Remove the doors. Lay out and predrill holes in the back of the cabinet so the wood screws will hit wall studs. The holes should be slightly down from the top and up from the bottom of the cabinet.

Align the cabinet to the proper level line and drive the screw to within about 1/4 inch of its final tightness. Level the top, sides, and bottom of the cabinet. Use shims where necessary. Drive the screws home and recheck all levels.

Second and additional wall cabinets. Remove doors. Set the second cabinet next to the first. Clamp the two at top and bottom while aligning the fronts flush and level to the first cabinet.

Drill four holes for connectors and install them. Drill holes through the back of the cabinets and install wood screws into the wall studs. Shim for level and plumb as necessary. Install wall fillers in the same manner as base cabinet fillers.

When all the cabinets have been installed and trimmed out:
• Clean out the insides of cabinets and drawers.
• Adjust all doors, drawers, and catches.
• Make minor touch-ups where practical, such as brad holes in molding.

Occasionally, the connectors will not pull adjacent cabinets tightly together — particularly in tall cabinets — leaving a gap in the joint at the front. You can usually correct this by driving a few short flat-head wood screws through the side of one cabinet into the adjacent cabinet.

Step 11: Adjust Hinges

Many cabinets now come with 35-mm cupstyle hinges, which allow cabinet doors to be adjusted in three directions. This adjustment is especially important in frameless cabinets, which are less forgiving and have smaller tolerances than the more common face-frame cabinets.

Your main goal is to keep all the cabinet doors flush and to keep the reveals even between doors. In remodels with surfaces out of level and plumb, you may need to "split the difference" in some cases to make the cabinet run blend in visually. ■

Bob Cox is a 36-year veteran of custom kitchen and bath remodeling. He now consults in the Baltimore, Md., area.

A Kitchen Installer's Tips

by Lou duPont

Guidelines to help your kitchen cabinets go up quickly and without blunders

What follows is a description of some of the methods and techniques I use when installing kitchens. Whatever size or type of kitchen I'm installing, following these guidelines has helped me work efficiently and avoid mistakes, and has kept my kitchen installing experiences mostly happy ones.

Delivery and Inspection

I keep two things in mind before the cabinets arrive at the job site: they are not that easy to move and are very easy to damage. I make sure they arrive when I'm good and ready for them. The less I have to move them, the better.

Cheap or fancy, factory-made or custom, I thoroughly inspect the cabinets for damage or flaws in workmanship. Problems found before installation begins are much easier to deal with than those discovered later. For example, during a recent installation of factory-made cabinets I found a badly warped door and staples coming through an exposed side. I called the kitchen designer/distributor and she warned me that "installation constitutes acceptance." Time constraints being what they were (it would take three weeks to get a new cabinet from the factory), I repaired the blown-out side, while the manufacturer replaced the door.

Reality check. I measure each cabinet to make sure it conforms to the plan. As I do this, I arrange the upper and lower cabinets according to the plan to help visualize how they will best go together, and in what order.

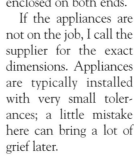

Whether the plan I'm working from is a rough shop drawing or a seemingly infallible blueprint, I give it an extensive reality check. Nine times out of ten, the kitchen designer or cabinetmaker has measured the space accurately, but it pays to be certain.

At this point I tally up the cabinet runs and appliance dimensions plus any filler strips that are provided. These tallies should be slightly greater than the space where the cabinets will go: The difference will be trimmed from the filler strips for a snug fit. This is especially critical when the cabinets are enclosed on both ends.

If the appliances are not on the job, I call the supplier for the exact dimensions. Appliances are typically installed with very small tolerances; a little mistake here can bring a lot of grief later.

Layout

At this point I get the lay of the land. If there's an inside or outside corner, I check to see how square the walls are to each other. I determine how plumb the walls are and whether the floor is level. If the floor is out of level, I find the highest point in the area where the base cabinets will go. This is an important step because it establishes the minimum counter height. I set the counter height 36 inches above the high point, and shim the cabinets in other areas as necessary. This way I avoid having to do a hatchet job on the bottom of a cabinet to account for the high spot.

Soffits. If the kitchen has a soffit, I pay close attention to the vertical layout, especially

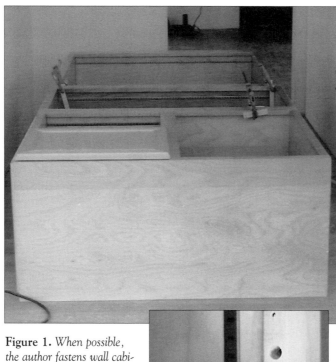

Figure 1. *When possible, the author fastens wall cabinets together while they're still on the floor (above). The face frames are held tightly together by screws concealed behind the door hinge base plates (right).*

Figure 2. *Starting in the corner, the author fastens a temporary ledger to the wall to support the first cabinet, a blind corner cabinet.*

when there's an appliance garage (a cabinet that rests on the counter). These cabinets fill up the space between the counter and the soffit, leaving no room for error. In that case I measure down from the soffit the height of the appliance garage plus the crown mold and the countertop thickness, and strike a level line on the wall through this point.

This line shows me how much I'll need to shim the base cabinets. Just above this line is a good place to find and mark the studs you will be fastening to. Any nail holes you make will be covered by the counter. If the height of the wall cabinets is not determined by a soffit, I strike a second level line 18 inches above counter height for the bottom of the wall cabinets.

Marking the layout on the wall. I mark on the wall where each cabinet or appliance will be placed. I start with the cabinets or appliances whose locations are absolutely fixed — such as a sink base centered under a window, or a range that's centered on a wall. With the layout marked on the wall, the nerve-racking part of the job is over and installation can begin.

Uppers First

I always hang the upper cabinets first. If you have ever hung them after the base cabinets are in place, your back can tell you why this is a mistake.

Often, if I am putting up several wall cabinets in a row, I screw them together before hanging them (see Figure 1). With the doors off and the cabinets on their backs, it's easy to clamp them with the frames flush and then screw them together. If possible I hide the screws in the frames behind the hinge baseplates. I use a minimum of four fasteners — either screws or cabinet bolts — between cabinets.

Support ledger. For hanging wall cabinets, I use a temporary ledger board fastened with drywall screws 1/4 to 1/2 inch below where the cabinets will eventually go (Figure 2). By taking the weight of the cabinet, the ledger makes it easier to get the cabinet exactly where I want it. I use shims on the ledger to push the cabinet up that last 1/4 inch into place. Once the cabinet is hung I remove the ledger and patch the screw holes with spackling.

Spacer blocks. When working to a level soffit, I attach a strip of wood to the top of each cabinet before hanging it. This strip serves two functions: It gives me a nailer for the crown moldings to be installed later, and acts as a spacer to keep the cabinets an even distance down from the soffit.

Starting point. If the kitchen has an inside

corner, this is a good place to start. Sometimes the corner configuration has two cabinets, with one runing by — a so-called "blind" cabinet. Sometimes it's a single cabinet, such as a lazy susan unit. Either way, starting in the corner allows you to make sure the two walls of cabinets come together plumb and level, and tight to the back wall.

If the corner has two cabinets, the blind one goes up first (Figure 3). I make sure that the front face is absolutely plumb so that the abutting cabinet will be level. I may have to shim behind the cabinet at the top or bottom to achieve this. If the blind cabinet has an exposed side, I scribe it to the wall.

Filler strips. After hanging the blind cabinet, I determine what width to rip the filler strip that goes between it and the abutting cabinet. For example, in a recent installation the wall cabinets had to be spaced evenly on each side of a window (Figure 4). This space was dictated by the location of the refrigerator. Once I had established that, I marked out where the cabinets stopped on each side of the window and measured back the width of the cabinet. This gave me the filler width.

Typical filler strips for factory-made cabinets are from 1½ to 4 inches wide, depending on

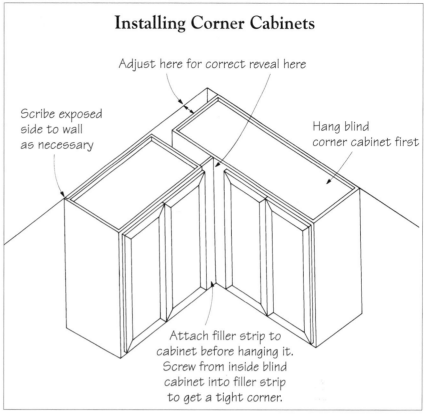

Installing Corner Cabinets

Adjust here for correct reveal here

Scribe exposed side to wall as necessary

Hang blind corner cabinet first

Attach filler strip to cabinet before hanging it. Screw from inside blind cabinet into filler strip to get a tight corner.

Figure 3. *When installing cabinets, start from a corner and work out in each direction. The procedure illustrated here is the same for wall and base cabinets.*

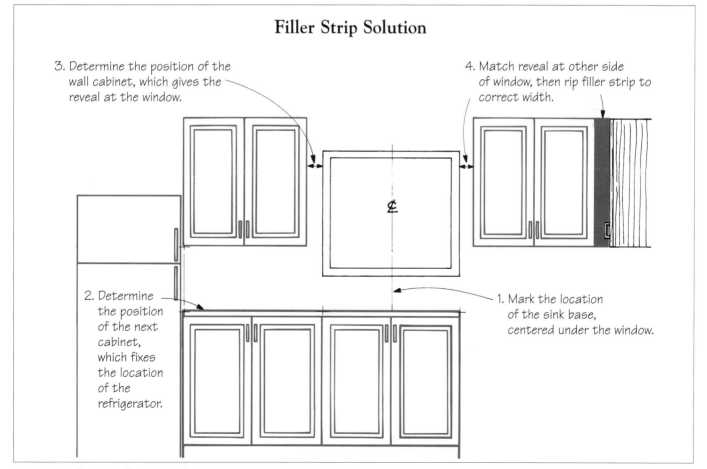

Filler Strip Solution

3. Determine the position of the wall cabinet, which gives the reveal at the window.

4. Match reveal at other side of window, then rip filler strip to correct width.

2. Determine the position of the next cabinet, which fixes the location of the refrigerator.

1. Mark the location of the sink base, centered under the window.

Figure 4. *Filler strips allow you to fine-tune the spacing on factory-made cabinets. In the example above, the strip is ripped to give an equal reveal on both sides of the window.*

Figure 5. *After checking measurements, the author rips a filler strip for the corner cabinet (above, left), then glues and screws it to the cabinet (above). With the cabinet held temporarily in place the author checks the fit against the blind cabinet (left).*

simplify the leveling process.

Installation of base cabinets proceeds much like that of the wall cabinets. I start in the corners, locate the cabinets that have fixed locations, and adjust the spacing with filler strips.

Islands. When installing an island cabinet I mount 2x blocks securely to the floor. Ideally, I place the blocks so the cabinet will just barely slip over them. If the screws won't show I screw through the sides and the kick space into the blocks. Since nail holes are easier to fill than screw holes, I toenail any exposed sides with 8- or 10-penny finish nails.

Counters. Our kitchens often have specialty countertops, such as Corian, tile, granite, or marble. Except with simple, straight-run situations, we usually sub out the Corian to a local cabinetmaker who knows solid surfacing. For tile tops, we lay down one layer of 3/4-inch BC plywood. Our tilesetter tops this with a layer of cement backerboard for a solid substrate. Slab counters we set in thinset on particleboard or MDF.

We usually install our own plastic laminate tops. When cutting laminate counters to length at the site, I use a circular saw with a carbide finish blade and cut along a straightedge. I always make a test cut to see how the blade performs. I use masking tape on the laminate surface to minimize chipout. The tape also allows me to make a visible pencil line for scribes.

When scribing countertops or splashes to a wall, I use a Bosch jigsaw on the metal-cutting setting with a metal/plastic-cutting blade. I fine-tune the cut with a belt sander. To attach a separate backsplash to the wall, I use an adhesive caulk called Phenoseal (Gloucester Co., P.O. Box 428, Franklin, MA 02038; 800/343-4963, 508/528-2200). I clamp blocks to the front edge of the counter and cut prop sticks to wedge the backsplash against the wall while the adhesive dries.

After the countertop is in place I set the remaining cabinets. On cabinets that go from counter to soffit I leave off the nailer for the crown mold that I use elsewhere. This gives a little more room to slide the cabinets into place. To avoid scratching the counter, I use kraft paper or cardboard. ∎

Lou duPont is a project manager for Birdseye Building Co., in Richmond, Vt.

where they go. They are designed to be trimmed to take up the slack between a cabinet and a wall, or between runs of cabinets at corners. At corners, wider filler strips allow doors and drawers to operate unobstructed.

I rip the corner filler strip and glue and screw it to the cabinet (Figure 5). To get a proper fit, I hoist the cabinet onto the ledger, scribe it to the other cabinet, then plane it to fit. This is where a sharp block plane is essential.

When installing the second corner cabinet I clamp it to the blind cabinet. I screw from the inside of the blind cabinet into the filler strip. A right angle drill is very helpful for this.

Base cabinets. In a typical installation, I hang all of the upper cabinets that I can, leaving aside any cabinets that sit on the counter. Then I move on to the base cabinets.

My level layout line tells me how far I need to shim the base cabinets up from the floor. If most of the bases need to come up 3/8 or 1/2 inch, I cut a bunch of plywood shims and fine-tune with shim shingles. In some cases the cabinets come with adjustable legs, which

New oak doors, drawers, and trim spruced up these tired old cabinets. Quarter-inch oak plywood, laminated to face frames and end panels, completed the facelift.

Cabinet Refacing: The Big Cover-Up

by Jim Cavanagh

Put new doors and new veneer on old cabinets for an economical kitchen facelift

Your clients want a new kitchen, but have a limited budget. You have three choices: You can tell them it can't be done; you can sell them the cheapest cabinets and accessories you can find; or you can suggest refacing the existing cabinets.

When you reface cabinets, you cover all the flat surfaces, including the face frame, with thin veneer, plastic laminate, or veneer plywood. Then you install new doors, hardware, and drawers (or drawer fronts). You may also make some minor modifications to the cabinets.

Refacing cabinets can be a good deal for both the customer and the contractor. When done, the refaced cabinets can brighten up a drab kitchen and usually cost less than cabinet replacement.

Reface or Replace?

First, determine exactly what the customer expects to get out of the job. An inexpensive basic job can quickly grow past the point of cost effectiveness if you try to make a totally "new" kitchen. To decide, you need to consider two questions:
• Does the existing layout work?
• Are the cabinets sound?

If the present layout works, has decent storage, and the customer likes it, then the refacing job will go smoothly. But if you have to move a sink, stove, or refrigerator, or significantly modify the cabinets to accommodate modern size appliances or new drawers or roll outs, this may tip the balance in favor of the new cabinets (see Figure 1).

Major structural changes to cabinets, or cabinets that were poorly made to begin with, are not worth refacing.

Refacing isn't always cheaper. In fact, one reason refacing appeals to buyers is that it can provide much nicer doors, drawers, and hardware than they would find on low-end cabinets. Moderate or high-priced cabinets will make the refacing option look better. This comparison is important to the decision and depends heavily on the responsibility and integrity of the contractor, and on the tastes and standards of the buyer. I frequently do $30,000 kitchen remodels, but this investment is beyond the reach of most refacing customers.

We often do cost estimates for both refacing and new cabinets. This satisfies the customer. If refacing looks like the way to go, work with the client to select the laminate or wood species and stain. Also work together to choose the hardware and style of the new doors and drawers.

Many Possibilities

You can reface a kitchen in a number of ways. The cabinet frames

Figure 1. *Minor on-site cabinetwork, such as this microwave surround, can dress up a refacing job. But with too much custom work, refacing is no longer a bargain.*

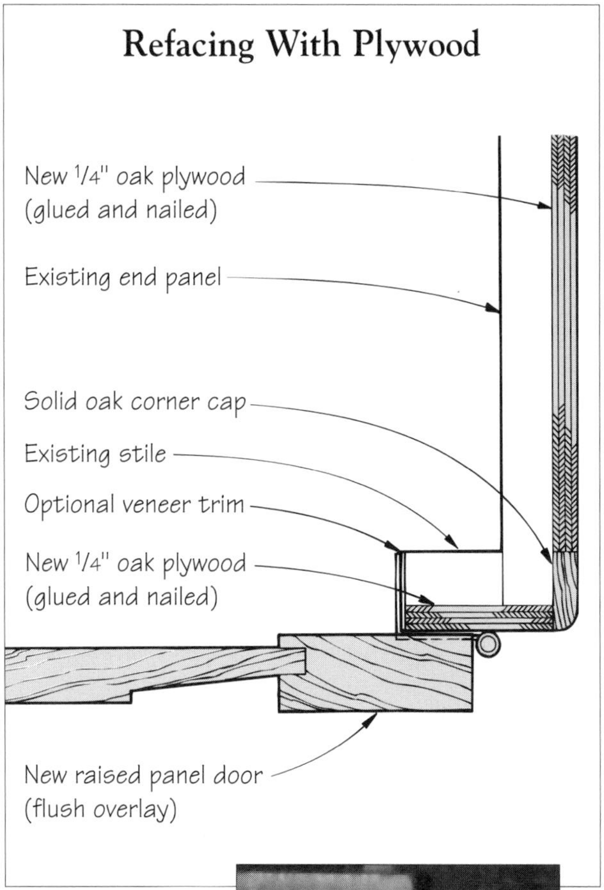

Refacing With Plywood

New 1/4" oak plywood (glued and nailed)

Existing end panel

Solid oak corner cap

Existing stile

Optional veneer trim

New 1/4" oak plywood (glued and nailed)

New raised panel door (flush overlay)

Figure 2. *The author typically covers face frames and exposed end panels with 1/4-inch hardwood plywood, glued and nailed in place. The thick surfacing material can conceal uneven frames. New overlay doors with self-closing hinges (photo, inset) are easy to mount on refaced frames and can hide out-of-level cabinets.*

can be covered with a thin veneer, plastic laminate, or 1/4-inch plywood. Laminates give a modern, European look if solid colors are used, but a somewhat tacky, fixed-up look if a wood-grained design is applied. The new doors can also be wood, in any style, or high- or low-pressure laminate.

Veneers. Thin veneers (1/16-inch or less) work well if the cabinets are perfectly smooth. They come in different wood species with or without a glue backing. I buy mine from a mail-order hardwood supplier or local hardwood dealer, depending on what species of wood the customer wants.

Thin veneers are easy to work with and apply. I cut large pieces of veneer on a table saw, with a piece of cardboard under the veneer to stabilize it while the saw is running. I cut the piece 1/8 inch oversize and trim it with a router and wood scraper when it's in place. For edge material, I use veneer that comes precut in 1 3/4-inch by 12-foot rolls. Some edge veneer has a hot-melt adhesive backing, allowing you to efficiently iron on the veneer.

With thin veneer, I use contact cement because it provides a barely visible glue line and perfect mating with the substrate. You can also use a veneer with peel-away backing, but the bond is not as reliable. You can trim the veneer with a utility knife and/or sandpaper. The edges are thin enough that they are virtually invisible at the corners.

To get a good job, however, you must make sure that all seams and joints are even on the

surface. Any unevenness will show through the thin material. You need to sand or fill high and low spots before you spread on the contact cement. Also, make sure you put these veneers on very clean surfaces. You may have to wash, sand, or strip the finish before you can trust the adhesive for long-term bonding.

Paneling. My favorite technique, because it's quick and covers almost all problems, is to use 1/4-inch hardwood-faced plywood laminated to the frames and end-panels. I use panel adhesive, shoot 1/2-inch brads or staples into the paneling, and fill the holes with color putty. I prefer overlay doors and surface-mounted self-closing hinges to finish the job (Figure 2).

I order my doors from a local cabinet company or from one of the larger suppliers like Quality, Towncraft, Porta Door, or Conestoga. And I have the company that makes the doors pre-stain the veneer or hardwood plywood to match the door stain. I have the doors made 3/4 to 1 inch larger than the openings both ways. This allows me room to jockey the doors until they are plumb and level and cover the opening. I clamp a level to the bottom rail to set the doors on, and the entire run looks perfectly level, regardless of whether the cabinets are level or not.

Laminate. If you want to use plastic laminate to reface cabinets, you may have a more difficult job finding a local source for doors and drawers. One company that specializes in supplying contractors with doors, drawers, and refacing materials is Facelifters (800 Snediker Ave., Brooklyn, NY 11207; 718/257-9700). But the job may still be difficult because the hinges that give the Euro-look cabinets their touch of class aren't designed to fit on cabinets with face frames or cabinets that have face frames made thicker by the extra layer of laminate. You must be careful to use the correct hinge. Look into Blum, Grass, and Hafele, which offer a variety of hinge choices for face-frame cabinets and provide good technical information on hinge installation.

A Typical Plywood Job

When you start a refacing job, remove all doors, drawers, and trim, including any non-cabinet trim that may interfere with the work. Clients can leave their food in the cabinets (few want to) because most of the dust is created in the on-site shop in the garage or porch. If the countertops and any tiles are to be replaced, remove them. You want bare boxes to work with, and a clean room.

When the room is ready, set up shop. A table saw with a paneling blade, power miter box, compressor and shooter, hand and power planes, and belt sander are the tools you need. You'll also need a good panel adhesive (such as Sonneborn 200 or Dap 4000), thinner, color putty, and spray lacquer. For lacquer, I like to use Deft; it dries quickly and comes in convenient 13-ounce canisters.

Next, take care of any mechanical changes. These could be additional outlets, undercabinet lighting, phone lines, intercoms, plumbing, or ductwork changes. Also, if there are any layout changes, like cutting in a dishwasher, compactor, hood valance, or any cabinet changes, get them done now so that the refacing can proceed without interruption. I'll do simple cabinets, bookshelves, nooks, or small drawers on the job. Small jobs like this are nuisance work for local cabinet shops, so it's cheaper and faster to do them yourself.

Job flow. I generally rip pieces for the stiles and rails first, and plane down the widths to fit the face-frame dimensions. Then I rip the larger pieces for the cabinet end panels and cross-cut them to length on a table saw.

I install the stiles first, setting the bottoms flush with the cabinet bottoms. Cut the rail pieces a little long so you can bow them a bit. They will spread out against the stile pieces, creating a prefect fit. Apply a bead of panel adhesive and attach the strips with small staples (or brads). This bonds the material securely to the old cabinets. The prep work, especially with 1/4-inch material, is negligible.

Make the new end stiles flush with the existing corner. Then cut a piece of solid material, usually 1 inch by 1/4- or 5/16-inch thick, and apply it to the end of the cabinet, flush with the new front. This covers the edge of the paneling and means you don't have to miter the corner. Then rip the end panel to fit between this solid piece and the wall.

On most jobs, I leave the inside edges of rails and stiles as is — with the edge of the 1/4-inch plywood exposed. On the few jobs where the customers wanted it, I've mitered and returned the plywood on the inside edges. Another option would be to use the thin veneer edging discussed above.

When you have a valance above the sink or window, you may want to change this procedure slightly. In this case, skin the end of the cabinet first, making it flush with the face frame. Then install the stile veneer, and cover the joint with a wood strip (Figure 3).

When all of the skins are applied, put up any additional trim, such as the cornice, gallery, plate rail, or base shoe. Fill the holes with color putty, and touch up seams. Wipe the color-putty residue off with a rag, and then shoot the entire job with a coat of spray lacquer.

It's easier to keep the tops of doors level if you use the trim as a reference. As with most remodeling, dimensional compromise is the rule: Trust your eye, not a tape or level.

When hanging the doors, the important points to remember are to cover the entire opening, keep the doors symmetrical with each other, and fiddle with them until they open and close properly. You may have to shim or bend a hinge here and there. A helpful trick is to double up on the felt pads, using two if one doesn't quite touch the frame.

You have to use face-mounted hinges with 1/4-inch panel veneer because you increase the stile and rail thickness to 1 inch (most wrap-type hinges are made for 3/4-inch stock). Also, be sure to use 5/8-inch screws that will go all the way through the paneling and secure the hinge to the solid frame stock.

Figure 3. *The new valance (at top, right) is locked in place with a narrow hardwood strip. The strip also trims out the cabinet corner and conceals the edge of the 1/4-inch veneer on the stile.*

Final Touch

The final touch is to sand and finish the paneling edges that are visible in the door openings. Also, sand the bottom edges. Set the countertops, tile, sink, and appliances. On about half the jobs I do, the countertops are in good shape. On the others, I install new ones. From start to finish, the job takes two to three days on site. Compared to a full-blown, long-lasting kitchen remodel, these jobs fly by.

Refacing can be good business. The clients are less distressed and the work usually progresses without any big unknowns. But it's only a face lift, and it doesn't completely erase all the wrinkles. If this compromise is acceptable to the clients, and if you've used good planning and installation techniques, the results can be pleasing and profitable and can save your clients a good deal of money. ■

Jim Cavanagh remodels kitchens in Kansas City, Mo.

A Lazy Susan
In Every Corner

by Don Jackson

The author prefers half-round lazy susans for base cabinets because they blend well with the frameless style cabinets he builds. For upper corners, he likes the full-round type shown.

I never built a kitchen where convenient access to storage and space-efficiency were not important to the client. Over the years, kitchen hardware makers have answered these needs with catalogues full of pull-out, fold-down, pop-up, and swivel devices designed to make kitchen storage more accessible and to make use of every inch of space. Years ago, though, when I was starting out as a custom cabinetmaker, space-efficiency basically meant a good design and a lazy susan in every corner — at least insofar as the budget would allow.

There were originally two types of lazy susans — the full-round version, usually found in upper corner cabinets, and the pie-cut version, for L-shaped base cabinets. I never really liked pie-cut lazy susans — the L-shaped cabinets and doors were more trouble to build, the on-site installation was always a nuisance, and even when fine-tuned, the action seemed stiff and cumbersome. Plus, the doors on pie-cut units — whether the bi-fold type or the attached ones that turn around inside the cabinet — always looked different from the rest of the doors in the kitchen. So when manufacturers developed a third variation on the lazy susan — the half-round version — I began to steer customers away from pie-cut units. Once I explained how the half-round lazy susans worked, I never met any resistance. I've also never had any complaints or callbacks on installed units. On the contrary, most people are delighted with the smooth action of the half-round units.

Half-Round Lazy Susans

For the cabinetmaker, the advantages of using half-round units are clear: You build an ordinary, rectangular blind corner cabinet with an ordinary, well-proportioned door (photo, left). Installation of the half-round units is simple: The support bracket attaches against the back of the cabinet blind side and the shelves slide down over the post and lock into place with set screws.

There's no wrestling with L-shaped or bi-fold doors. In my estimates, the overall cost of a blind corner with a half-round unit, including cabinet fabrication time, is less than the cost of a pie-cut lazy susan in an L-shaped cabinet.

Half-round lazy susans come in several sizes — from about a 14-inch to a 20-inch radius — to allow you to adjust the size of the blind cabinet as needed. The units are available with either coated wire or solid plastic shelves. If the customer wants extra convenience, there is a separate sliding bracket — about a $20 upgrade per shelf — that brings the half-round shelves 12 inches or so out of the cabinet for easier access to items in the back.

Figure 1 shows a basic blind corner cabinet. I usually build European-style, or frameless, cabinets, using 3/4-inch birch or maple plywood for the carcasses, and covering exposed edges with hardwood to match the doors and drawer fronts. The half-round units install just as easily in face-framed cabinets.

The semicircular shelves pivot independently. Typically, the bottom shelf attaches to the cabinet door and pivots out as the door is opened. Since European hinges project out from the inside face of the door, they get in the way of the bottom shelf, so I use butt or piano hinges at these locations. At least one manufacturer, Rev-A-Shelf, has recognized the problem and makes a 1 1/4-inch offset bracket for use with Euro hinges.

Upper Corners

For upper corners, the basic full-round, two-shelf lazy susan makes the best use of cabinet space. Figure 2 shows a simple upper corner cabinet that works with standard 12-inch-deep frameless cabinets. I typically use a 45-degree angled bracket for mounting the Euro hinges; another option is to use 45-degree hinges made specifically for angled-front cabinets.

Blind Corner Base Cabinet

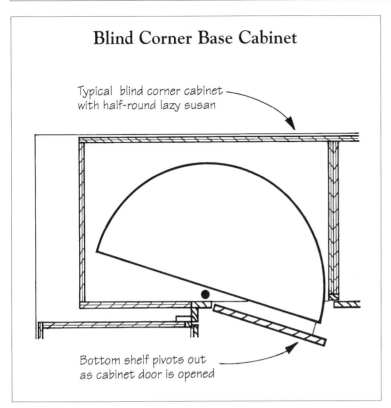

Typical blind corner cabinet with half-round lazy susan

Bottom shelf pivots out as cabinet door is opened

Angled-Front Upper Corner Cabinet

Angled-front upper corner cabinet with lazy susan

Use sides of cabinet for vertical storage or small shelf

Figure 1. A blind corner base cabinet *for a half-round lazy susan is simple to build, especially in a frameless style. The author uses butt hinges for the doors, since Euro hinges tend to get in the way of the lower pivoting shelf.*

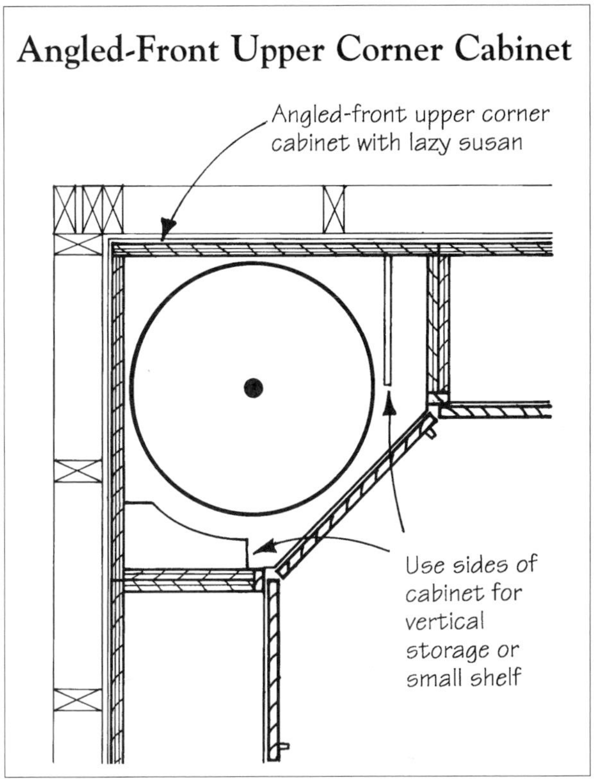

Figure 2. This angled-front upper corner cabinet *fits an 18-inch-diameter, full-round lazy susan. Because the cabinet is frameless, beveled cuts are kept to a minimum in the cabinet's construction.*

The corner cabinet shown will fit an 18-inch-diameter lazy susan. The extra space at the sides of the cabinet can also be used without interfering with the lazy susan. In some cases I've built in vertical tray storage here or put small shelves halfway up.

Although they are never my first choice for corner base cabinets, full-round lazy susans work well in angled base cabinets.

They are useful in ordinary rectangular base cabinets, as well. Make sure when ordering that you check the height of the post — an extension is usually needed for upper cabinets. ■

Don Jackson, a former cabinetmaker, is the managing editor at The Journal of Light Construction.

Sources of Supply

The following companies manufacture the types of lazy susans discussed in this article:

Amerock Corp.
4000 Auburn St.
Rockford, IL 61125
815/963-9631

Feeny Manufacturing Co.
P.O. Box 191
Muncie, IN 47308
800/554-1410

Hafele America Co.
3901 Cheyenne Dr.
Archdale, NC 27263
910/889-2322

Mepla Inc.
909 W. Market Center Dr.
High Point, NC 27261
910/883-7121

Rev-A-Shelf Inc.
2409 Plantside Dr.
Jeffersontown, KY 40299
800/626-1126

Small Kitchen Recycling Center

by Paul Turpin

The problem of what gets thrown away and how has changed a lot over the last decade. Recycling is on its way to becoming a regular part of life. Fitting this into a small kitchen, however, is a tough proposition. The containers have to be smaller, and typically recyclables are mixed together in one bin. But it's still possible to efficiently fit trash, recycling, compost, and disposal, into a 33-inch sink base cabinet.

Disregarding the disposal for a minute, there are four basic components to consider: waste container, recycling bin, compost bucket, and the sink itself. I mount the waste and recycling containers on the two cabinet doors (see photo below).

My favorite waste container is Hafele's Built-In Waste Bin (Hafele America Co., 3901 Cheyenne Dr., Archdale, NC 27263; 910/889-2322). At $30 to $50, it features a self-closing lid on a removable plastic bucket that attaches to the door. It's available with a 4-gallon or 5¼-gallon bucket.

I mount a recycling hamper on the other door. I use a 5-gallon Rack-Sack (Extrufix, Inc., 4542 L.B. McLeod Rd., Suite E, Orlando, FL 32811; 800/327-9780). This wire frame unit uses a standard supermarket plastic shopping bag, and comes equipped with a lid. It costs about $17. It comes in 1-, 3-, and 5-gallon sizes, making it an option for waste containers in other cabinets.

For compost, I suggest my clients buy a sturdy plastic container with an airtight lid and keep it under the sink where it can be emptied frequently.

The final issue is finding space under the kitchen sink. The two containers that attach to the doors take up a lot of space inside the sink base, so not all sinks will work. The one I use most often is Kohler's Executive Chef. Its main virtue is that its drains are located at the rear. This pushes the sink's waste pipes, including the disposal, to the back of the sink base, creating extra room at the front for the waste and recycling containers.

The space below the sink is tight, and you must figure the

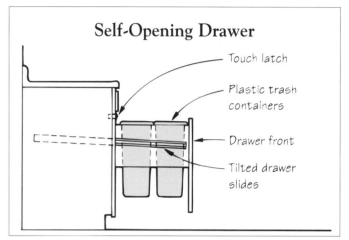

Self-opening drawer: This oversized drawer holds two containers for trash or recyclables. A touch latch and downward-sloping drawer slides allow operation with no hands.

dimensions of all the components carefully if everything's going to fit. The bins often have a clearance of less than ¼ inch.

But still there's a bit of space that can be used for storage — the area behind the false drawer fronts. To take advantage of this space, I use "false front trays" (Amerock Corp., P.O. Box 7018, Rockford, IL 61125-7018; 815/963-9631).

When You've Got More Space

An alternative for larger kitchens with more available cabinet space is a pull-out trash drawer. Amerock, Hafele, and Feeney Manufacturing Co. (P.O. Box 191, Muncie, IN 47308; 800/554-1410) all make variations on a slide-out trash container that fit standard base cabinets. But you or your cabinet sub can make a unit that matches the rest of the kitchen and doesn't require any hands to operate.

Here's how: Make a drawer deep and wide enough to hold the plastic trash container of choice. Attach a cabinet door (as if it were a drawer front) to your large drawer body. Then, mount a set of heavy-duty full-extension drawer slides so they tilt down slightly toward the front (see illustration above).

Now attach a positive-hook touch latch and presto. A little pressure from your knee will release the touch latch, and the weight of the drawer combined with the downhill tilt of the slides will roll the unit on its own.

There are a couple of things to watch out for. First, don't tilt the slides too much or the drawer will come shooting out like a roller coaster. Also, since the drawer moves down slightly as well as out, you have to provide enough clearance so the bottom of the drawer clears the bottom of the cabinet. ■

Paul Turpin is a Los Angeles-based remodeling contractor who specializes in kitchen and bath design and remodeling.

One-stop recycling center: *This 33-inch sink base includes two door-mounted containers for trash and recyclables, a separate compost bucket, and false-front trays for dishwashing utensils.*

Customizing Stock Cabinets

by Joan Eisenberg

Manufacturers of stock cabinets have come a long way in the past few years. While stock cabinets are still limited in size, they are available in a new range of shapes and styles. A creative remodeler can successfully complete even the most sophisticated projects using stock parts. The key to keeping costs down while creating a custom look is to familiarize yourself with the many accessories and options cabinet manufacturers offer.

Most European and American companies manufacture their cabinets using a modular system. One advantage of the European system is that it offers many more standard sizes (in metric). European makers also tend to place more emphasis on design and offer numerous customizing features and accessories.

Fortunately, many American companies now offer just as many accessories as the Europeans. For example, Merillat Industries (2075 W. Beecher Rd., Adrian, MI 49221; 517/263-8282) and American Woodmark (3102 Shawnee Dr., Winchester, VA 22601; 800/388-2483) each offer a wide variety of options, including window moldings, chair rail, and countertop bullnose trim, all stained, painted, or laminated to match cabinetry. Other options include integral cutting boards and knife trays, and cutlery partitions. Most manufacturers also offer hardware options that make cabinets and drawers easier to use, such as roll-out trays, pull-out wire racks, recycling centers, and lazy susans.

Here are some other design techniques to help create a custom look:
- Use a valance along the bottom of wall cabinetry to provide a place for undercabinet lighting, such as fluorescent strips or halogen spots.
- Run a line of customized shelving midway between the countertop and the wall cabinets.
- Substitute a bread drawer for two small drawers. These are deeper, usually 9 to 12 inches, and feature plastic or wooden lids and metal liners.
- Instead of a false drawer in front of the

Improved storage: Storage accessories can make kitchen space more functional and accessible. Shown (clockwise from top, left) are roll-out shelves, covered bread drawer, tilt-out sponge storage, and cutlery drawer.

Recycling and waste: With the growing emphasis on recycling, Merrilat's roll-out containers (left) or American Woodmark's three-bin lazy susan (right) can simplify sorting and storing of trash.

Cabinet upgrades: *Finishing touches available on many stock cabinets include (clockwise from top, left) glass lights, curved end panels, and decorative hardwood moldings. Some manufacturers offer matching wood-paneled range hoods (bottom, left).*

kitchen sink, use a tilt-down drawer front with attached storage bins for bottle scrubbers, sponges, soaps, and rubber gloves.

• Add a glass-front door or two to break up a solid bank of wall cabinets. Some companies offer these in stained or beveled glass as well.

• For a furniture finish, use a decorative end panel that matches the doors, instead of a flat panel at the end of a run.

You can also create variety and interest with stock cabinets by arranging them creatively. For instance, I sometimes create a bookcase or plant shelves in a run of wall cabinets by inserting a cabinet 6 to 12 inches shorter than the others and leaving the front of the cabinet open. Or I might make a baking center by using a matching bathroom vanity (with matching doors) in a base run. Vanities are generally 28 to 30 inches tall, just the right height for kneading and rolling bread dough. If I want a shallower base cabinet, then I'll use a wall cabinet and add a base with a kick space to match the other base cabinets. ∎

Joan Eisenberg, CKD, CBD, is a home economist and president of JME Consulting, a kitchen and bath design firm in Baltimore, Md.

Chapter 3

Countertops

JASON LANDAU, DESIGNER, COURTESY OF NKBA

Solid Surfacing Options

by Ryno Wretling

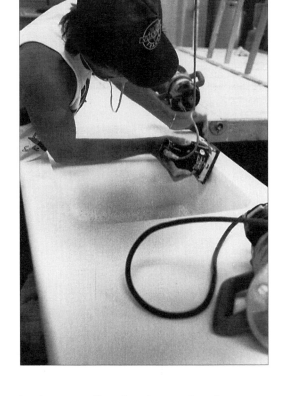

All surfaces of this counter and its double sink are sanded thoroughly before the top leaves the fabricator's shop. Solid surfacing's homogeneous nature means that nicks and scratches — whether from fabrication, installation, or wear — can be quickly sanded out.

As these products grow in popularity, so does the sophistication required to fabricate and install them

It wasn't very long ago that solid surfacing was represented by a single brand that came in two shades of white, and was glued up with silicone. Now it's an industry with several major manufacturers, over 50 colors, and fabrication techniques that include near-invisible seaming, inlaying, and thermoforming.

This rapid evolution has made fabrication and installation of solid surfacing a lot more complex. Although manufacturers still advertise that the materials can be shaped with ordinary woodworking tools, in most cases you're best off leaving the work to a company like ours that specializes in solid-surface fabrication.

Working With a Fabricator

Although we bid most jobs from blueprints, we don't fabricate anything without measuring it ourselves unless it's a "will call" item like a small vanity top. In residential work, we prefer to help the homeowner with design decisions even when it's the contractor's job because we know the material, its tolerances, and how it can be used creatively.

We typically need four to six weeks of lead time, and a 50% deposit. This puts the contractor on the scheduling board. When his cabinets are permanently installed, we take our field measurements and we are back to install within four to five days.

We do something a little unusual when it comes to measuring — we use full-size, corrugated cardboard or 1/4-inch door skin templates. The salespeople scribe them to the walls with a knife, and bring them back to the shop. The lightweight cardboard is particularly handy, because by scoring the top layer of paper, you can fold an entire U-shaped kitchen into the cab of a truck.

Using templates helps reduce error and allows us to mark exactly where cabinet supports fall (so we can plan where to put field seams for the support they need) and mark centers on sinks and cooktops. It also allows us to do as much of the fitting as possible in the shop. Fabricating solid surfacing is a very dusty business, and the less of this we bring into the homeowners' lives, the happier they and their contractor are.

We charge a flat fee for putting down underlayment, but in many ways it's a nuisance charge — we're happy to have the contractor do it. Corian requires only a perimeter underlayment. (In fact, you'll void the warranty by putting down continuous plywood over the cabinets because it doesn't allow heat to dissipate rapidly around stoves or when the homeowner puts a hot pan down on the counter).

The height of the underlayment should be discussed early on. We typically use 3/4-

inch plywood to bring the countertop up to 36 inches, and to provide drawer clearance under the built-up edge. European cabinets allow as little as $1/8$-inch clearance even with 1-inch plywood. In our area, many homes have bow windows whose sills are near countertop height; they can be included in the surfacing if everything planes out correctly.

Design Options

The creative possibilities with solid surfacing are limited only by the client's budget and imagination. However, the items I've listed here are fairly typical of our standard residential work.

Edge details. To price our edge work, we've divided it into four categories according to the thickness (1 inch, $1^1/2$ inches, 2 inches, or more), and the difficulty of routing and sanding the profiles. Like most shops, we offer radiuses of $3/16$, $1/4$, $3/8$, and $1/2$ inch, along with coves, beads, bevels, ogees, and combinations of these. Some of our more creative standard options are shown in Figure 1.

Inlays and inserts are popular in edges, but I'm very particular about how we detail these. We use thin acrylic or laminate color strips or brass recessed slightly in a dovetail dado to keep them in place and protect them. We also use oak and other woods in solid surface edges, but as $1/4$-inch-thick inlays (in the $1/2$-inch material) rather than full-width laminations. In fact, the only thing we will laminate to a piece of Corian is another piece of Corian.

Backsplashes. The standard solid surfacing backsplash is $1/2$-inch material, 3 to 4 inches high, siliconed to the deck and wall. But a coved backsplash looks nicer and provides a stop for water and a much easier intersection to wipe with a dishcloth.

There are several different ways of detailing a coved backsplash. A common method involves rabbeting the back edge of the deck to accept the coved splash (see Figure 2). This creates a tight joint, but because you're dealing with a straight channel, it doesn't allow you to scribe the splash to the wall. This leaves gaps at the top of the splash to fill with silicone. I hate to see silicone showing anywhere on my jobs, so I use a profile that sits flat on the deck but conforms to the wall. A slight disadvantage of this cove is that you are cutting the glue joint at a very steep angle, which shows a slight line in the granites. I use a $1/2$-inch cove and sand it with a Makita narrow-belt sander whose

front pulley fits snugly in the cove. A $3/8$-inch cove is more common.

Another cove that I began fabricating out of Corian about five years ago is what I call a $1/2$-inch or tile cove. It rises above the deck just $1/2$ inch, providing a ledge for tile in the kitchen or mirror in the bathroom.

I use $1/2$-inch material for all backsplashes because there is typically a lot of wall movement and a lot of cutouts for outlets (each of these has four inside corners that create stress points). In fact, on full-height backsplashes, I don't go over 12 inches in height without creating a break. This shouldn't be a hard seam (glued with proprietary adhesive), but a butt joint with dabs of silicone to the wall. I usually disguise this joint as a feature stripe by beveling the edges of the material or introducing a contrasting color.

Sinks. One of the advantages Corian has had for many years is their shaped products: bar sinks, lavs, and kitchen sinks that can be undermounted, top-mounted, or inlaid (seamed) into a counter or vanity top. Other manufacturers have now come out with bowls in their own materials.

Figure 1. *Counter edge details are built up from $1/2$-inch-thick material. The ones above are all 1 to $1^1/2$ inches thick and require at least two router passes. Wood or acrylic inlays add several dollars per foot to the cost.*

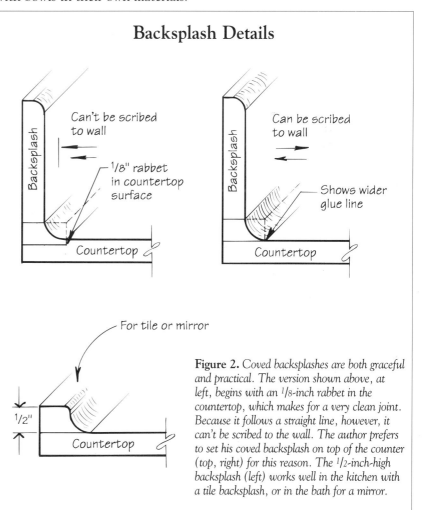

Backsplash Details

Figure 2. *Coved backsplashes are both graceful and practical. The version shown above, at left, begins with an $1/8$-inch rabbet in the countertop, which makes for a very clean joint. Because it follows a straight line, however, it can't be scribed to the wall. The author prefers to set his coved backsplash on top of the counter (top, right) for this reason. The $1/2$-inch-high backsplash (left) works well in the kitchen with a tile backsplash, or in the bath for a mirror.*

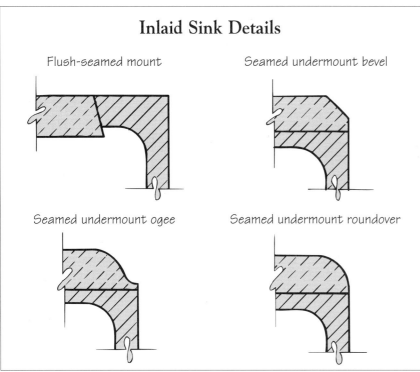

Inlaid Sink Details

Flush-seamed mount

Seamed undermount bevel

Seamed undermount ogee

Seamed undermount roundover

Figure 3. *Two different ways of inlaying solid surfacing sinks are the flush-seamed mount, (top, left) which requires an absolutely perfect cutout, and the seamed undermount. The seamed undermount can be detailed three ways, as shown: with a bevel, ogee, or roundover. If seamed by an experienced fabricator, the transition from bowl to countertop is invisible when the same color is used.*

The two most dramatic treatments are the flush-seamed mount (this style requires an absolutely perfect cutout), and the seamed undermount (see Figure 3). Most manufacturers also have an integral top and bowl (ITB). Dupont also makes a kitchen model with an integrated drainboard. But given a good fabricator, independent bowls allow you much more flexibility because you can put them almost anywhere in any combination.

Although it takes most homeowners and contractors by surprise, using a solid surface sink with its ten-year warranty comes within $100 or so of undermounting a cast-iron one.

If the customer does opt for an undermounted, cast-iron sink, it has to be chosen with this application in mind. Many sinks have a slight rise at the outside edge of the lip, which creates a gap between the sink and the underside of the solid surfacing where it lips the bowl. With this kind of sink, the fabricator has to hold the material back to the rise.

Breakfast bars and overhangs. Different solid surfaces vary in their cantilever ability. Half-inch Corian is good for 6 inches unsupported; 3/4-inch material is specced at 12 inches, but I keep it to 9 inches. When I need to bring the material out farther, I use 3/4- or 1-inch-square aluminum stock, rather than corbels, to support the counter.

Tubs and showers. Showers are a perfect application for solid surfacing, and I think we will see a real switch to this material in the near future. Although Dupont shows a two-piece back wall, I hard-seam my material 60 inches or even wider to eliminate the batten and silicone look. The panels, however, are kept independent of each other behind corner pieces. We build soap dishes and shampoo storage out of Corian as well. While solid surfacing runs a good 15% more than tile on kitchen counters, in the shower it's competitive.

Thermoforming. This technique is fairly new still, and it is not encouraged by all of the solid surfacing manufacturers. A temperature of about 325°F gives Corian the flexibility to be postformed to a fairly tight radius. We've used this technique so far in creating rounded skirts for bathroom basins, teller windows, and round table edges. This is an area that I think will take off in the next few years as more fabricators learn where the limits are with the material.

Fabricating Standards

All of the major solid surfacing manufacturers hold training classes for fabricators, but even a two- or three-day seminar doesn't allow enough time to pass along all you need to know. Even something as rudimentary as seaming the material can be made much less risky by learning advanced techniques and tricks of the trade that have developed over time.

Of all the problem installations I've seen in the field (both my own and ones I troubleshoot for Dupont), 90% were caused by fabricator or installer error. The worst of these involved warping at the seams and stress fracturing. The causes were a lack of proper support, stress points at interior corners that weren't relieved with radiusing and finishing, and the failure to isolate the heat from cooktops. Only 1% of the problems were caused by the material, and the remaining 9% were from homeowner abuse: roasting pans straight from the oven, heavy objects dropped from upper shelves, etc.

Dupont and some of the other manufacturers of solid surfacing have been very generous in taking care of problems in the field in order to maintain the reputation of their products. But as the network of experienced fabricators builds, the manufacturers are warning that they will be less tolerant of errors in fabricating and installing that are covered in their technical bulletins. Soon, I think you will see much tougher standards in enforcing the warranty clauses.

Installation

Installation is in some ways more critical than shop fabrication. We install all our own work for that reason (see box, at right). The most disastrous installation mistakes usually involve cooktop cutouts. Other common mistakes include not paying enough attention to interior corners; gluing down backsplash with seam adhesive or Superglue; and not allowing enough expansion space between walls.

A standard rule of thumb for us on most kitchens is that cutouts, field seaming, and setting the countertop and splash pieces (the latter two rely on dabs of silicone) is a day's work. If the backsplash is coved, we're looking at two days.

We do all of our cutouts on-site in custom work. We insist that sinks and cooktops — not paper templates or a list of dimensions — be on site for us. If the job calls for an undermount cast-iron sink, we ask that the contractor have it installed since it must be supported by blocks attached to the sink cabinet. It has to be absolutely even with the top of the underlayment in this case. Because there is less weight involved, we undermount lav bowls in the shop using brass brackets supplied by Dupont.

All cutouts are made with a router for the smoothest possible cut. Because cooktop cutouts have to deal with heat as well as normal stress, every edge has to be as smooth as possible to keep from establishing fracture points. Even the slightest surface crack or tool mark will hold heat and could cause the surface to fail. So we use a 3/16-inch roundover bit on the perimeter of the cutout on the top (and the bottom if we have access), and polish the inside of the opening as smoothly as the front edge of the countertop.

Inside corners are always radiused. We use a 1-inch-diameter bit and actually go out beyond the cutline by 1/2 inch on the sides (this is covered by the cooktop trim) for as much relief as possible. Then we use 4-mil aluminum conductive tape to line the perimeter of the opening as shown in the literature.

We keep the stove and sink cutouts, but bring the customer two small, finished cutting boards from the same dye lot. This way we have something nice to give them when we're finished with the job. And because they'll use the cutting boards, there is more likely to be a matching piece of stock available on the site if for some reason we have to seam in a patch at a future date. ∎

Ryno Wretling is the owner of BYGG, Inc., a Greenbrae, California-based fabricator. Wretling, a native of Sweden, has contributed many details and procedures to Dupont's fabrication manuals.

Fabrication in the Field

A

B

PHOTOS BY PAUL SPRING

C

D

E

After making the sink cutout on site, the fabricators set a countertop section into place (A). Two-part proprietary seam adhesive is squeezed into the joint in one pass (B) to avoid bubbles that leave voids. A quick but effective clamping system (C) holds the seam together using offcuts spot glued into place with hot-melt glue. Once the adhesive cures, the inside corner is radiused with a router (D), and the seam is ground lightly (E) before finish sanding.

Fabricating Solid Surfacing Countertops

by Chuck Green

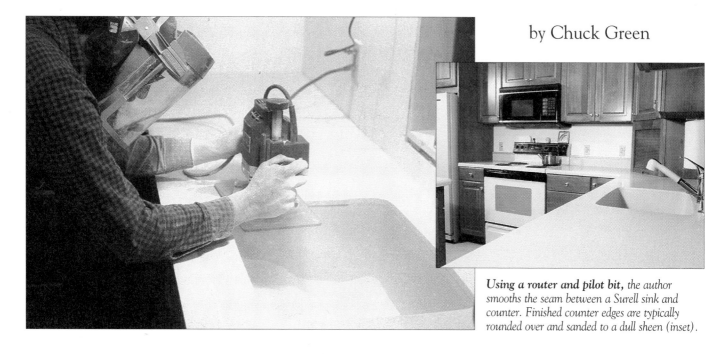

Using a router and pilot bit, the author smooths the seam between a Surell sink and counter. Finished counter edges are typically rounded over and sanded to a dull sheen (inset).

Careful preparation, precision cuts, and a cool head under pressure are the keys to success with solid surface materials

In my remodeling business, customers often ask me for "Corian" countertops. Corian, a DuPont product, was the first brand of solid surfacing introduced, and for a long time it was the only brand. But DuPont's original patent on Corian has expired, and six different companies now make solid surfacing materials (see manufacturers list, page 63). Builders and remodelers can now offer people more choices.

Fabricating with solid surfacing isn't too hard to learn, though the techniques vary a little from brand to brand. To use any of them, you need to get some training from the manufacturer. I've taken the introductory training seminars offered for both Corian and Surell, Formica's brand of solid surfacing, and I've worked with both products. In this article, I'll go over the steps in an on-site fabrication job I recently completed using Surell. The job was a custom kitchen. Usually I make up countertops in the shop, but this time I did all the fabrication on site because of the cold weather. (My shop isn't heated at night and wasn't warming up to the required 70°F temperature fast enough.) The tight kitchen space complicated matters, but it also proved just how versatile and easy to use solid surfacing is.

Ordering the Material

Always stick with one company's material and seaming compound when you use solid surfacing. Different brands aren't compatible, and the colors won't match. In fact, any sheets that you plan to seam together should come from the same production lot, because color varies a little from one run to the next. With Surell, the sheets are stamped on the back with "skid numbers." Your distributor can get you sheets with the same skid number to ensure a consistent color throughout.

Sizes. Sheets come in 30- and 36-inch widths, in several lengths from 4 to 12 feet, and in 1/4-, 1/2-, and 3/4-inch thicknesses. My distributor has been willing to sell me half sheets as well. You can also get narrow strips for backsplashes, but these will come from a different skid number. I offer my customers that choice, because you save a little money that way, and the slight color variation between the backsplash and the counter usually isn't noticeable.

Cost. Sheets are expensive (around $25 per sq. ft. for 1/2-inch stock), so plan your cutting list before you buy. When you're deciding what size sheets to order, keep in mind that joints have to be placed away from inside corners or heat sources such as cooktops. Otherwise, stresses can build up and crack the material. Also remember to order extra material for backsplashes and built-up edges.

Not all colors and sizes are instantly available, so give your distributor some advance notice. Both the Corian and Surell distributors in my area have jumped through hoops at times to get the material I've asked for, even if it meant trucking sheets in from out of state. With their help, I can usually reduce waste to a minimum.

For this job, I ended up buying two thicknesses of material, $1/2$ and $3/4$ inch. I used the $3/4$-inch stock for the island countertop because it could handle the 12-inch cantilevers without any support. The main part of the cabinets formed an L-shape with a 1-inch overhang, and for this I used $1/2$-inch-thick stock, the most common size. The $3/4$-inch-thick stock is more expensive, but it's easier to build up the visible edges to $1^1/2$-inch thickness, which most customers want. With $1/2$-inch stock, bonding one layer below will produce a 1-inch-thick edge, but you'll have to add a second strip for the thicker look.

Getting to Work

When I make countertops in the shop, I make cardboard templates at the site, then use them as guides in the shop. On this job, we just measured and rough-cut the pieces, then did our seaming and finish-cutting in place. This worked okay, although dust was a special challenge (see box, above).

Modifying the cabinets. Solid surfacing must be well supported, so we had to slightly modify the stock cabinets we used. On the island, this meant recessing the metal corner brackets so they would sit flush with the surface — a time-consuming task (Figure 1). On the cabinets along the walls, we installed a

Dust Control

Surell dust is considered a "nuisance" dust — it isn't toxic, but there's a lot of it and it gets everywhere. I've seen big fabrication shops where the dust could be found in offices way down the hall from the shop itself. On our job, we sealed off the kitchen with plastic sheets and used a zippered Dust Door (Brophy Design Inc., 524 Green St., Boylston, MA 01505; 508/393-7166) in the door opening. We set up an exhaust fan to the outdoors and turned it on when we were cutting or routing. Then it was just a matter of frequent vacuuming.

A tight-fitting dust mask is important for solid surfacing work. My job foreman, Dave Deganhart, uses 3M masks with foam gaskets, but I have a full beard and can't get a good seal with any simple mask. I use the Airlite Air Visor (Airstream Dust Helmets, P.O. Box 975, Elbow Lake, MN 56531; 800/328-1792), a battery-powered unit that has a full-face mask and blows filtered air down across my face (photo on facing page). It costs about $230, but my lungs are worth more than that to me.

— C.G.

continuous 1-inch-thick cleat along the back, and crosswise supports every 18 inches, to match the thickness of the tripled-up material on the front edge.

Cutting. You can work solid surfacing with the same tools you use for woodworking: table saw, miter saw, router, power planer, and circular saw (Figure 2). All blades must be carbide-tipped. You need to be extra careful not to scratch the surface. I put nonscratching covers on some of my tools (clear packing tape works well), and I leave the solid surfacing's protective plastic in place, just pulling it aside to mark my cuts, then replacing it for the actual cutting. I spray DriCote lubricant (Bostik, 211 Boston St., Middleton, MA 01949; 800/726-7845) on the table saw before each cut.

After rough-cutting each piece, you have to smooth the saw cut with a planer or router. Even with the 80-tooth carbide blades I use, no

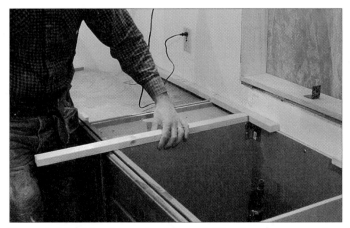

Figure 1. Modifying the stock cabinets. *Solid surface counters must be well supported from underneath. To match the one-inch buildup on the front edge of the counter, the author added a continuous one-inch-thick wood strip to the top of the cabinets along the wall and crosswise at every cabinet side (left). To provide a perfectly smooth bearing, he also had to recess the cabinets' metal corner brackets (right), which protruded above the top surface of the cabinets.*

Figure 2. Solid surfacing can be cut with standard woodworking tools equipped with carbide-tipped blades. Here, the author rips a piece of Surell on a portable table saw.

saw cut is smooth enough for a seam. Edge irregularities can cause stresses to build up and crack the material over time. My practice is to smooth each edge right after it's cut, then label the pieces and their edges so I will remember how each piece fits into the puzzle. Pieces that will be routed in place later can be left rough.

On our kitchen project, we first rough-cut the two big pieces that would make up the L, leaving 1/2 inch of extra material to allow for scribing and fitting. Only the exposed end of the L needed to butt perfectly to the wall. Gaps at the back of the counter would be hidden when the backsplash was installed.

The seam where the two legs of the L met, however, had to be cut and fit with precision. To ensure a perfect match, we positioned the two pieces 3/8 inch apart and ran a 1/2-inch spiral router bit down the center, using a guide for the router (Figure 3). This was a little more complicated on site, with the wall in the way, than it is in the shop. We had to rig up quite a complicated array of clamps to keep everything steady.

We set the jig up so that the router would have to remove only 1/16 inch from each side of the joint. The router bit could more easily remove this small amount, and it was easy to hold the router to the guide. After unclamping, a test-fit showed that the seam cut was perfect.

Installing the Sink

To make things easier for ourselves, we decided to install the sink before seaming the two counter pieces together (see box, facing page). Seaming the sink requires flipping the countertop over several times, which is hard to do with a big, unwieldy L in a confined kitchen space.

You install sinks by joining them to the countertop with seaming compound. You can take your time with layout and preliminary cuts, but when the time comes to actually seam the sink in, you have to act fast before the compound sets up. Once it's mixed, seaming compound gives you only about eight minutes to work.

The sink was attached to the underside of the countertop sheet. After carefully laying out the sink location on both the top and bottom of the sheet (double-checking your layout is well worth it with this stuff), I roughed up both the sink lip and the area it would be joined to. Then I cut a 4-inch hole in the sheet to accept a bar clamp. The clamp would extend through the sink's drain hole to hold the two components together while the seam cured.

I like to glue maple blocks around the sink's layout perimeter to act as guides. I tack them in place with hot-melt glue. The blocks make setting the sink in place quick and simple. The less fussing the better during those precious eight minutes. Afterwards, the blocks come loose with a hammer tap. Hardwood works best for this — softwood blocks tend to splinter instead of breaking loose cleanly.

The last step before seaming is cleaning. To get a good bond, the joint has to be perfectly clean. You use denatured alcohol for this, swabbing both sides of the joint thoroughly with paper towels.

Seaming compound. Mixing and applying the seaming compound is a little tricky. Luckily, the stuff comes with directions. Surell's two-part seaming compound comes in a special cartridge with an adaptor that fits electric drills. You chuck the mixing wand into your drill, then break the seal between the two

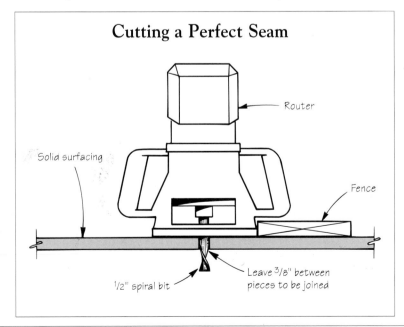

Cutting a Perfect Seam

Router

Solid surfacing

Fence

1/2" spiral bit

Leave 3/8" between pieces to be joined

Figure 3. To cut matching edges for a seam, the author first clamps the two pieces of solid surfacing 3/8 inch apart. Using a straightedge as a guide, he then runs a router down the center with a 1/2-inch spiral bit.

Installing a Solid Surface Sink

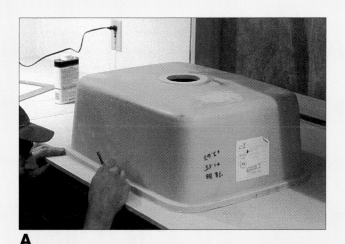

A

B

The author outlines the sink location on the underside of the countertop (A), then attaches wood guide blocks along the line with hot-melt glue to help position the sink during the seaming process. After cleaning the surfaces to be seamed, he applies seaming compound to the lip of the sink (B) and clamps the sink into place (C).

As soon as the compound has set up, the top is flipped into place and the sink hole is cut out with a router and pilot bit (D). Wood strips hot-glued to the corners prevent the top from falling through while the cut is made. The finish pass with the router rounds over the sink edge and smooths the joint (E).

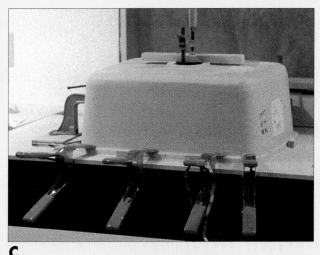

C

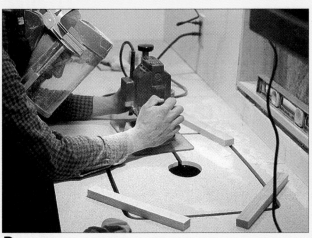

D

E

Figure 4. *The countertop joint is clamped together using strips of hardwood attached to the two counter pieces with hot-melt glue. A clamp screwed to a plywood block, also fastened with hot-melt glue, holds the two surfaces flush.*

Figure 5. *Counter edges are built up with two 1/2-inch strips of Surell, seamed together with compound and thoroughly clamped to minimize joint lines (above). Trimming with a router and straightedge yields a smooth, one-piece finish (right).*

parts by pushing down the plunger. Then you mix for the specified time, and quickly put the cartridge into your caulking gun. Oh, and don't forget the adaptor for the caulking gun.

It's worth reviewing this procedure in advance each time until you get the hang of it. One misplaced item or forgotten step, and you've got big problems. There's no time to think when you're seaming.

Cutting out the sink. I finished the sink cutout with two passes of a router, using bits I buy from Fred Velepec Co. (71-72 70th St., Glendale, NY 11385; 800/365-6636). The first pass was with a bit that left a 1/8-inch lip. The second was with a finishing roundover bit that makes a smooth curve and blends the countertop perfectly into the sink. A little hand sanding and we had an integrated unit with no visible seam.

Assembling the Countertop

Seaming the countertop was another case of mixing the compound, then rushing to fit and clamp the joint. Again, we made a point of preparing in advance so we could act fast when the time came.

To hold the countertop joint together, we attached a maple strip to each piece with hot-melt glue, then applied clamp pressure. Another set of clamps held the surfaces flush. Hot-melt glue came in handy again for attaching a surface-mounted clamp in the center of the joint to keep that area flush (Figure 4).

If there's a lot of extra seaming compound squeezed out of the joint, don't wipe it off: You might leave voids in the glue joint that would cause cracking later. Instead, let the squeeze-out cure and remove it later with a router. This time, we had just a minor squeeze-out that we could easily sand off.

Perimeter edging. We built up the front edge of the countertop to 1 1/2 inches by seaming together three layers of 1/2-inch stock (Figure 5). We started from the inside corner and worked out, taking care to stagger the joints (aligned joints would create a weak spot in the finished piece). With clamps spaced every 3 inches along the edge of the counter, the thing looked like a clamp porcupine before we were done.

Once the edge was tripled up, it could be cut and rounded off with a bullnose router bit. For inside and outside corners, we first made templates for the router to follow, then clamped them in place. After routing the corners, we clamped a straightedge in place and routed off the straight front and sides.

Installing the Countertop

For final installation, we propped the finished countertop up on 2x6 supports, being very careful in lifting not to stress the sink area, the joints, and our backs. We then applied dabs of silicone caulk every 6 inches to the upper surfaces of the cabinets, the cleats, and our reinforcing members. Silicone is the recommended fastener with solid surfacing because it flexes to allow for thermal expansion in the countertop. Finally, we carefully lowered the top into its proper location, and checked for any areas where silicone might have squeezed out onto the cabinet top rails.

We also used silicone to bond the backsplash to the countertop. The edges of the pieces had to be planed smooth as always. Then we applied a continuous bead of color-matched caulk to the bottom edge of the backsplash and dabs of silicone to the back side. Clamps and sticks wedged against the ceiling kept pressure on the joint as the silicone cured. We used wet rags to clean up any silicone that oozed from the joint during the first few minutes.

Plumbing installation is pretty straightforward with solid surfacing. Cutouts for the plumbing are done with a router — leaving rough jigsaw cuts could cause the material to crack. Dishwasher installation can be tricky: Some dishwashers need to be secured at the top by screws into the counter, to keep the unit from tipping out when the door is open and the racks are extended. Since you can't screw directly into solid surfacing, we solve the problem by drilling an oversize hole in the underside of the countertop and setting the screws in a gob of silicone caulk in the hole. The threads don't bite into the solid material at all, so the screws don't have much withdrawal strength, but they resist the sideways pull of the dishwasher.

The island. After the complicated L-counter and sink, the island was a piece of cake. With no joints, no inside corners, no sink and only a double thickness at the edge, this stage of the project went quickly and smoothly.

Finishing. The last step is sanding the surface. You can polish these materials to a high gloss, but it isn't recommended because it's hard to maintain and all minor irregularities show up, as with a high gloss paint on a wall. We sanded these counters to a dull sheen. Starting with 150-grit paper in an orbital sander, we progressed to 240-grit with a little water. We then hand-sanded with wet 300-grit and wet 60-micron paper.

Formica says wet sanding works best with these fine papers, but you have to watch out for the shock hazard. Air sanding equipment is the safest; at a minimum, use double-insulated tools, and be sure every work outlet is equipped with a GFCI. ∎

Chuck Green is a NARI certified remodeler and owner of Four Corners Construction in Ashland, Mass.

Solid Surfacing Manufacturers

You have three choices if you want solid surface countertops: Order custom tops from a k&b shop or fabricator, who might also install them; fabricate them yourself; or buy premade tops with bowls from a lumber yard or plumbing supply store. This last route limits your selection to a smaller range of colors and styles.

Each manufacturer has an 800 number. If you call the manufacturer, they'll tell you where to find the local distributor for their brand. The distributor in turn can introduce you to fabricators in your area, or help you get certified as a fabricator yourself.

— C.G.

Avonite
Avonite Inc.
1945 S. Highway 304
Belen, NM 87002
800/428-6648
Three different product lines with different compositions. The Class III high-end line is translucent and takes a high shine but requires maintenance.

Corian
DuPont Company
Box 80702, Room 1218
Chestnut Run Plaza
Wilmington, DE 19880
800/426-7426
Five lines and three price ranges of acrylic-based material in a range of colors.

Fountainhead
Nevamar Division
International Paper
8339 Telegraph Rd.
Odenton, MD 21113
800/638-4380
A polyester-based thermoset product, available in three lines: 4 solid colors, 13 matrix styles (granites), and 6 Classix, which are like the matrix but with large particles.

Gibraltar
Ralph Wilson Plastics
1110 Industrial Blvd.
Temple, TX 76504
800/787-3223
Acrylic and polyester, available in 16 solid colors and 16 granites. Gibraltar claims greater heat resistance than other solid surface materials.

Surell
Formica Corporation
1504 Sadlier Circle
Indianapolis, IN 46239
800/367-6422
Polyester-based, available in three product lines: 9 solid colors, 14 granites, and three Revolution Collection styles (the most expensive).

Swanstone
Swan Inc.
One City Center, Suite 2300
St. Louis, MO 63101
800/325-7008
A reinforced modified acrylic, available in 5 solid colors and 13 granites. Swanstone comes in 0.41-inch thickness, and claims to have greater strength than other brands. Only Swanstone has stock sinks available in the granites.

Laminate Countertops On Site

by Michael J. Barnes

With a few basic tools and techniques, you can produce professional-quality plastic laminate counters at the job site

Contractors who rely on specialty shops to supply all of their countertops may regard laminate work as too difficult, too time-consuming, or too expensive to be done on site. But the skills required to work with plastic laminates are no more sophisticated than those you employ on any finish project: an ability to measure and cut accurately, and a willingness to fuss over 32nds of an inch.

Tools

The only new tools you might have to purchase are a very inexpensive router, a laminate flush trim bit, and a few hand tools.

Light-duty router. For laminate work, you must be able to handle the router easily with one hand. If the only router you own is a 3-hp plunge model weighing 12 pounds, I suggest you buy the lightest-weight, lightest-duty router you can find. This may be the only opportunity you'll ever have to buy a truly cheap piece of equipment and feel good about it — light weight and small size are the only attributes that matter.

I recommend an all-plastic router with no fancy geared adjustment, no light, no slick adjustable handles, and practically no horsepower. We're talking $29.95 here. The tool freaks among you are probably asking, "Why not just buy a laminate trim-

mer and get it over with?" The main reason is that they cost about four times as much as an inexpensive router. Unless you're going into production on countertops, you're only going to be routing laminate for about five minutes per month. At that rate, the additional cost of the trimmer may not make sense.

Trim bit. The flush trim bit you'll need is available in a variety of diameters and lengths. I recommend a 1/2-inch-diameter bit that's 1/2 inch long. Exposing more than 1/2 inch of cutting edge below the router base is very risky when trimming laminate, so bits longer than 1/2 inch are just not that useful.

Hand tools. Occasionally you will encounter an awkward inside corner where a router just won't fit. A hacksaw blade will cut the laminate without chipping — it's not much fun, but it works. For routed edges that didn't turn out perfectly flush, use a machinist's all-purpose file.

All of the big cabinet shops apply the contact cement with a spray gun, but I've never tried it, and it's not at the top of my "must do" list. For small jobs, I use a cheap 2-inch or 3-inch brush. On jobs larger than a few square feet, a short-nap 9-inch roller spreads the cement easily and uniformly. For edges, a 1 1/2-inch brush works well. You can leave the brush in the can with the cement, rather than allowing it to harden

Postformed Laminates

by Paul Turpin

Postformed countertops have some friendly features, including a raised lip at the front edge, which keeps spills off the floor, and a coved transition to an integral 4-inch backsplash. Since they are prefabricated, these countertops are easy to install. And you can buy lengths of the material cut to size. (You can cut it with a carbide-tipped blade, but the countertop is bulky and hard to get a saw through. Also, the plastic laminate has a tendency to chip when you're cutting it.)

Despite its friendly features, postformed laminate is my least favorite countertop material. The first problem is finding a technique for joining the precut mitered corners on an L-shaped counter. Drawbolts are typically used to pull the two sides of the joint together, but the two surfaces don't always line up. I've seen joints where one side of the miter is slightly concave and the other is slightly convex. The easiest technique I've found for keeping the surfaces flush is to use a plate joiner. I set the biscuits 6 inches on-center.

But no matter how tight the joint is, you'll still have a crack (see photo above, right). It's essential to keep water from seeping in since it will swell the particleboard and cause the laminate to crack. You can run some caulk in this joint or glue a strip of metal over it. But the best solution I've found is to fill the crack with SeamFil (Kampel Enterprises, 8930 Carlisle Rd., Wellesville, PA 17365; 717/432-9688). This is a one-part, solvent-based plastic that is applied as a liquid but cures to a hard finish. It's available in standard and custom laminate colors. Be forewarned that your countertops must be secure. If there's any movement, the filler will crack and pop out of the seam.

Self-rimming sinks are almost always used with laminate countertops, but these can be a nuisance for the

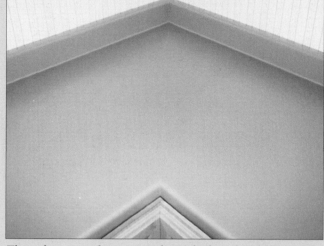

The author uses a plate joiner and special solvent-based fillers to help keep miter joints watertight in postformed counters.

homeowner. The rim is like a roadblock when you're trying to sweep scraps or water into the sink with a sponge. While it takes time and effort to make a template and rout the more accurate hole required for a flush-set sink, the results are worth it (photo below). I use a metal trim ring to cover any stray cuts (available from Vance Industries, 7401 West Wilson Ave., Chicago, IL 60656; 708/867-6000).

When the counter ends abut a wall or cabinet, I make an endsplash by gluing a scrap section of laminate to the vertical surface and butting the countertop to it. This serves as a bumper for wet, soiled sponges, protecting adjacent walls and cabinets. I use an adhesive caulk to attach the endsplash, which allows me to float the endsplash out a little if things aren't even and square. The piece of laminate should match the height of the backsplash and run to the outermost edge of the nosing. ■

Paul Turpin is a Los Angeles-based contractor who specializes in kitchen and bath design and remodeling.

VANCE INDUSTRIES

A flush-set sink, like this one, makes it easy for the homeowner to sweep water and kitchen scraps into the basin. But the installation takes more time and precision than with self-rimming models.

Substrate Details

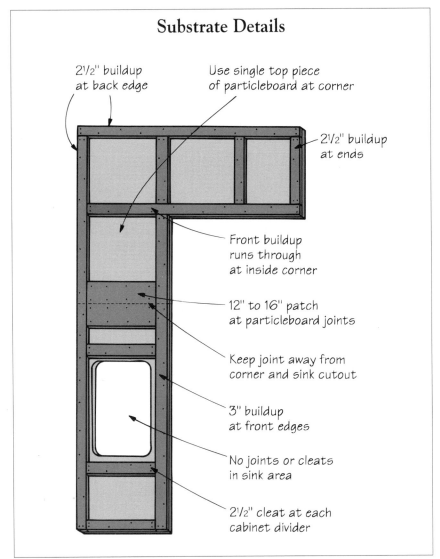

2½" buildup at back edge

Use single top piece of particleboard at corner

2½" buildup at ends

Front buildup runs through at inside corner

12" to 16" patch at particleboard joints

Keep joint away from corner and sink cutout

3" buildup at front edges

No joints or cleats in sink area

2½" cleat at each cabinet divider

Figure 1. *When making a laminate countertop substrate, avoid joints in the particleboard at corners and sink cut-outs. Where joints do occur, support them with a large patch on the substrate bottom. Build up the countertop thickness to a standard 1½ inches with bands at the edges, and use cleats to support the top at each cabinet divider location.*

between jobs, but only if it has a wooden handle (the cement will attack a plastic handle).

To ensure complete adhesion between the laminate and the particleboard substrate, wonderful hardwood and rubber rollers are available in the catalogs. But I find that tapping a palm-sized block of wood with a hammer works just fine.

That's about it for tools, except for hearing protection and a good full-face shield. This kind of work requires you to get very intimate with the router, and at close range it can be a thoroughly nasty device. Those "granny glasses" you've been calling eye protection are just not going to be adequate.

Materials

I build all of my substrates with very fine-grained ¾-inch particleboard. Every manufacturer has a different name for this stuff, but virtually all of them offer it in an over-sized sheet (49x97 inches) specifically for

making countertops. The smoother the sheet, the easier it is to rout the edges of the laminate facings and endcaps. A smooth surface also makes for a more uniform bond to the laminate. Don't use coarse "underlayment" grades of particleboard, and avoid plywood, which is neither dimensionally stable enough nor smooth enough for use in countertops. Multi-purpose screws or drywall screws, along with plenty of wood glue, work well for fastening the various layers of substrate together.

Laminate is produced in sheets up to 5x12 feet, and in every texture and color imaginable. The major brands are uniformly excellent; some lesser-known brands suffer from uneven quality. Most good yards stock the most popular colors of one or two brands, and will order whatever you need. For a countertop, make sure you're working with standard grade laminate. Vertical grade, which is made specifically for door and drawer fronts, is too thin and brittle (although it might do for the backsplash).

If you live in a state or locality with strict air-quality regulations and fire codes, you might not be able to buy really great contact cement. The old solvent-based type does an excellent job of what the folks in the hills call "adhesing," but it has a few undeniable drawbacks, not the least of which is its amazing flammability. In fact, contact cement is what they use in the movies when a character staggers from a burning building with his clothes afire. On top of its flammability, the fumes from contact cement are both explosive and toxic. Nice stuff.

Luckily, there are some "user-friendly" alternatives. One of these is a solvent-based cement similar to the original formula, but lacking the explosively flammable drying agents. The tradeoff is that it takes somewhat longer to dry. The other alternative is a latex acrylic cement that requires both higher ambient temperatures and long drying times. These cements still produce fumes that the manufacturers warn against breathing, so make a serious effort to ventilate your workspace.

Substrate Construction

I prefer to build countertops after the base cabinets are in, but before the wall units are hung. That way I can get precise measurements of the installed bases and still be able to tip in large, tight-fitting countertops without interference from wall-mounted units above.

Your workspace should be at least partially heated and free of other tradespeople. If you are providing heat with an open-flame heater, reread the previous section and make a sane decision about which kind of adhesive to use.

The substrate consists of two layers: a top layer made up of the largest pieces possible, and a bottom layer of edge buildup bands, joint stiffeners, and cleats to support the top at every vertical divider of the cabinets below (see Figure 1). This produces a top that is a standard $1^1/2$ inches thick, and is easily strong enough to span dishwasher and trash compactor openings in the base cabinets.

Whether you use a table saw or a portable circular saw to cut parts for substrates, the saw must be capable of turning out a true 90-degree edge. Because the flush trim bit in the router can work perfectly only on a true 90-degree edge, even minor inaccuracies in your saw cut can cause disasters in the routing. Angles less than 90 degrees cause the bit to leave the top piece of laminate hanging over the face piece, a problem that can be corrected only by intensive hand work with a file. Angles greater than 90 degrees cause the bit to cut into the face piece — definitely a mood-altering experience.

There are only a few rules for substrate design. First, this is not a good place to use up a lot of scrap underlayment. Try to use the fewest number of pieces possible to make the top layer — a single piece is ideal. On an L shape, make sure that the entire corner is cut from one sheet. Joints at or near the corner make the top too weak to move safely. If joints in the substrate are necessary, locate them away from sink openings, and in places where joints in the laminate will miss them by a foot or two.

Secondly, every vertical divider in the base cabinets should have a corresponding cleat in the countertop. Also, make sure that buildup bands at the front edge and ends are absolutely flush with the edge of the top — otherwise, routing the laminate will be a nightmare.

Finally, avoid using screws near the sink cutout. Since all edging and cleats should be glued, you can remove any screws you use as clamps in this area after the glue has dried.

Rough-Cutting Laminate Sheets

The first time you try doing your own laminate work, rough-cut all the pieces with a full $1/2$-inch overhang on each edge. After you gain more confidence, you can reduce the overhang to $1/4$ inch or even $1/4$ inch. It's a lot easier to trim a $1/8$-inch overhang than a $1/2$-inch overhang, but it makes sense to give yourself a little room for error in positioning the sheet for gluing.

Using a table saw. If you have a table saw on site, you can cut even the largest sheets cleanly after making a few minor modifications to the saw. Clamp a straight strip of scrap particleboard or other material to the fence to close the gap between the bottom of the fence and the saw bed. Otherwise, the sheet will try to slip under the fence, spoiling both the cut and your day.

Plastic laminate can chip if you're not careful when you cut it. Use a veneer or plywood blade, or any blade with at least 5 tips-per-inch. This should keep the worst chips down to about $1/16$ inch to $3/32$ inch — easily within the margin you will be trimming off with the router. If you need a completely chip-free cut, raise the blade higher than normal to provide a more vertical angle of attack for the saw teeth.

Handling large, floppy, brittle sheets of laminate can be challenging. I like to loosely roll the sheet, and slowly unroll it as I feed it into the saw (Figure 2). If space is

Figure 2. *When ripping a full sheet of laminate on a table saw, unroll the sheet as you feed it into the blade and have a helper roll it up again on the outfeed side. A scrap of wood clamped to the saw fence eliminates any gap between the fence and the saw table.*

tight, your helper can reroll the sheet on the outfeed end of the saw.

Using a circular saw. It's possible to rip laminate with a portable circular saw. The main difficulty is keeping the sheet flat and stable while you hack away at it. If you're blessed with ample working space, the substrate, blocked up on sawhorses, makes a fair workbench.

Joints

Making clean joints in the surface laminate requires cutting both sheets at the same time with the router. A simple jig made of scrap particleboard makes this process nearly foolproof (Figure 3).

Marking. First draw a line on the substrate, indicating exactly where the joint will occur. Continue the line down the face and back edge — you'll need it later to accurately position the sheets for gluing. Next, place one of the surface laminate sheets to be joined on the substrate and align it precisely where it will ultimately be glued. Be sure to get all the overhangs in the right places. Now transfer the joint line from the substrate to the surface laminate. Finally, draw a second line parallel to and $1/4$ inch away from the first to mark where you'll rough crosscut the laminate. Confusion about which line is which can lead to disaster, so a penciled notation on the sheet is a good idea. Then repeat the marking process with the other sheet to be joined, and rough crosscut both sheets using a tablesaw or circular saw.

Cutting. Arrange both sheets on your jig, with the joint lines dead parallel to the jig and to each other, making sure they're exactly $1/2$ inch apart — the width of the router bit. Clamp everything firmly, being careful to allow room for the router to pass between the clamps. Run the router down the center of the jig, cutting both sheets simultaneously.

To be certain you've got everything right before applying adhesive, dry fit the sheets on the substrate. A few light pencil lines across the joint will help you to correctly reposition the sheets in relation to each other during gluing. When you're ready to stick down the laminate, the original joint line on the substrate will show through the cement. Make sure to make contact at the joint first.

Applying Laminate

For the cleanest appearance, I prefer to install the laminate end caps first, followed by the face pieces, and then the tops. Apply two coats of contact cement to the particleboard substrate and one coat to the laminate, allowing the cement to dry between coats. Don't get too sloppy with the cement or you may gum up the router bearing later.

Everyone develops their own way of determining when the adhesive is dry enough for assembly. I figure that when the little hairs on the back of my hand stick to the glue — but my skin doesn't — the glue is dry. This seems like a good time to point out that this stuff is called "contact cement" for a reason. Once two coated surfaces touch, a nearly miraculous bond takes place, making it just about impossible to reposition the pieces. If you find you have to reposition a piece, you can continually score the glue joint with a razor blade, rolling the laminate away from the particleboard as you go, until the sheet comes free. Then you have to start over again and reapply cement. It's much easier to be careful while positioning pieces for gluing the first time.

Step by step. For end caps and facing strips, use a hardwood roller or wood block and hammer to work out any air bubbles and ensure complete adhesion. Regardless of which tool you use for this, try not to break off the overhanging edges of the laminate. When this happens, all you can do is start over with a fresh strip of laminate.

Now rout off all the overhanging edges (Figure 4). This requires some one-handed

Figure 3. *When making a laminate butt joint, cut both pieces at once using a simple particleboard jig. The base of the router rides against the top left piece of particleboard, which acts as a straightedge.*

work with the router on the short ends of the pieces, and makes you really appreciate that new lightweight router. If the top has an L shape, you'll have to use a hacksaw blade to trim the laminate for about 3 inches at the inside corner overhangs. I like to use a file on all of the edges of the facing, just to be sure that the laminate edge is truly flush on every side.

Apply the top pieces of laminate last. You can do this alone, but it's easier with a helper. The trickiest part is keeping the laminate from touching the substrate until the laminate is positioned just where you want it. I lay $^1\!/_2$-inch dowels or $^1\!/_2$ x $^3\!/_4$-inch stickers about 12 inches on-center between the laminate and the top (Figure 5). I've heard that strips taken from old Venetian blinds also work well. Whatever you use, make sure that the stickers are free of dust and that the cement is dry.

With the laminate positioned on the stickers, start at one end — or at a joint if there is one — and remove the stickers one at a time, firmly pressing the two surfaces together as you go. Use a sweeping motion with your hand to keep air bubbles from forming. Seat the entire surface with a roller or wood block, paying special attention to the front edge. Before routing the top piece, adjust the router to expose the absolute minimum of cutting edge on the bit. This makes it much less likely that you'll nick the face piece. On an inside corner, you will again need to use a hacksaw blade and file to trim the edge.

Final Details

Contact cement solvent will remove excess glue from the laminate surfaces, but read the label carefully and protect yourself against hostile chemicals and fumes. Inspect the finished top, looking for edges that could benefit from a little filing. No matter what, I like to use very fine sandpaper (shoe-shine style) to break the sharpness of the routed edges a little.

Some people are particularly sensitive to gases emitted by particleboard. Consider sealing the bottom of the countertop with polyurethane if you anticipate that kind of problem. At a minimum, it's good practice to seal the bottom of the countertop above the dishwasher opening, since warm, wet air can play havoc with particleboard over time.

All of this probably sounds like quite a project, but a little experience speeds things up markedly and allows you to be competitive with rates charged by specialty

Figure 4. *Apply and trim laminate edges first, beginning with the ends of the countertop.*

Figure 5. *Place stickers 12 inches on-center to keep the surface laminate from adhering to the substrate as it is being positioned.*

laminate shops for custom work. If you're the kind of finish carpenter who looks forward to a challenge and never tires of hearing "wows" from your clients, you'll really enjoy site-laminating plastics. ■

Michael Barnes is shop supervisor at the University of Maryland School of Architecture and a carpenter of 23 years.

Custom Work With Plastic Laminates

by Joshua Markel

Creative details can give you an edge with this versatile material

When I first became a cabinetmaker 17 years ago, I would become queasy when someone asked for plastic laminate. At that time, "plastics" symbolized phoniness to many of us.

In time, however, I came to realize that plastic laminate, when it wasn't trying to imitate something else, could be a valid and useful material for many applications. In kitchens, its water resistance and durability made it a logical choice. And it even began to dawn on me that the dense and uniform colors of its surface presented some definite design advantages for a room like a kitchen.

Around the same time, I also began to realize that it was senseless for me to try to compete with the many mass-produced plastic-laminate cabinets and tables already on the market. I needed to use plastic laminates in ways that were not generally available. Any custom builder who works with plastic laminates should have unique design ideas to offer to clients.

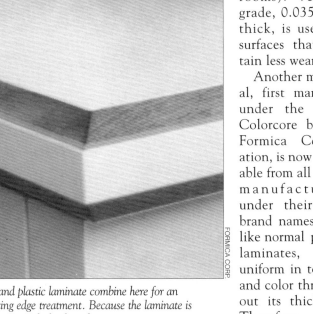

Wood and plastic laminate combine here for an interesting edge treatment. Because the laminate is Colorcore, no dark edges show.

FORMICA CORP.

What Are Laminates?

Plastic laminate is composed of several layers of special paper, bonded under heat and high pressure. The top coat is a protective overlay of melamine, a hard themosetting resin. The other layers are saturated with either melamine/formaldehyde or phenolic resin, creating a dense and durable surfacing material, suitable for wet areas.

The material is available in two thicknesses. Horizontal grade is 0.050 inch thick, and generally used for countertops and heavy-duty cabinetry (as in commercial installations or medical examining rooms). Vertical grade, 0.035 inch thick, is used for surfaces that sustain less wear.

Another material, first marketed under the name Colorcore by the Formica Corporation, is now available from all major manufacturers under their own brand names. Unlike normal plastic laminates, it is uniform in texture and color throughout its thickness. Therefore, there are no dark lines at the seams, and deep scratches don't show as much because the color remains uniform.

In exchange for these benefits, you must pay at least twice the material cost. Also, Colorcore-type laminates are brittle. They should not be used if a tight bend is necessary, and large sheets must be handled very carefully to prevent shattering. They should never be rolled up for shipment.

Substrates

Plastic laminates must be adhered to more substantial material, called the substrate, in order to gain structural integrity. Flakeboard is useful as a substrate because it is both inexpensive and dimensionally stable. If you use solid wood, it will change in size with the seasons, causing delamination. If you use one of the lower grades of plywood, the surface is not smooth enough to provide good adhesion when coated with contact cement.

Some applications may call for different substrates, however. If you are combining tile and laminate on a countertop, for example, you might want to use a plywood made with waterproof glue. In cabinet applications, laminate is sometimes used in conjunction with melamine-coated particleboard (MCP). This is simply flakeboard with a surface coating of melamine on one or both of its faces. MCP can form the inner surfaces of the cabinets, with plastic laminate used to cover the doors, edges, and exposed exterior surfaces.

What MCP lacks is resistance to gouges and deep scratches. Also, when you cut it, the surface coating will chip at the edge if it's not handled properly. It's usually best to cut it with the coating up and the table-saw blade raised all the way. If that doesn't work, cut it coated-side down with a sharp blade and score-cut it first to no more than 1/16 inch before final cutting.

If the MCP coating is on both sides, the surface should be scuffed up before applying plastic laminate.

Contact Cement

Plastic laminate is adhered to the substrate using contact cement. The contact cement may be sprayed, brushed, or rolled on. For most fabricators who aren't making a specialty of laminate work, short nap rollers are the best choice. The cement itself comes in three forms: neoprene base with either flammable or non-flammable solvent, and water-soluble latex base.

Like so many other choices in life, the option which is the easiest initially may be the most dangerous in the long term. The flammable material is the cheapest and fastest to use and provides a good strong bond. The non-flammable neoprene-based material has similar characteristics, and both should be used only with proper ventilation and an organic vapor mask. A dust mask is useless here, and the fumes are quite toxic.

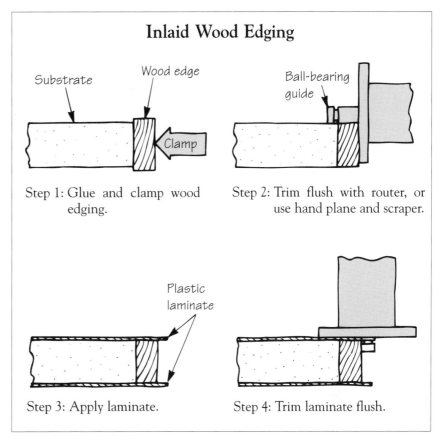

Inlaid Wood Edging

Step 1: Glue and clamp wood edging.

Step 2: Trim flush with router, or use hand plane and scraper.

Step 3: Apply laminate.

Step 4: Trim laminate flush.

Figure 1. *The easiest way to add wood edging is to sandwich it between two pieces of laminate. The above sequence works well with open shelving.*

I tried the latex material a few years ago, and it had a long drying time and unreliable bond. It's possible that the material has been improved since then or that my technique was not adequate, so you many want to test it. Latex is non-toxic and non-flammable, so a less controlled working environment is possible (as in your client's home if you are remodeling).

Pre-cut the laminate slightly oversized, both for the edges and the faces of the panel to which it is to be adhered. Once the contact cement is no longer tacky on both the laminate and the face of the panel, lay down the laminate piece with dowels or kraft paper to separate it from the surface of the panel. Make sure the laminate overlaps the substrate around the entire perimeter. Then remove the intervening medium and press the laminate onto the substrate. Take a hard rubber J-roller or the edge of a piece of wood and slide it over the entire surface while bearing down.

Panels are generally laminated on the edges first and then trimmed flush. Trimming is done either with a router with a flush trimming bit, or with a specialized router called a laminate trimmer. The latter is smaller and lighter, and has an adjustable bearing attachment on the bottom and a one- or two-flute cutter.

The face of the panel is then laminated, and flush-trimmed to cover the edges. This makes the edges less vulnerable to being chipped or sheared off.

If you make a mistake in laminating, it's not the end of the world. Slip a sharp knife under an edge at a corner and slowly begin to work lacquer thinner (in the case of solvent-based contact cement) under the laminate while prying it up. Once the piece is removed, make sure the surface of the substrate is smooth before attempting to laminate a new piece; scrape if necessary.

Wood Edging

If you want to offer something more interesting to a client who has more than a bare-bones budget, consider using solid wood edging along with conventional plastic laminate construction.

The simplest form this technique can take is in open shelving, with a piece of wood glued to the edge of the substrate and laminate on the top and bottom (see Figure 1).

Cut flakeboard pieces $5/16$ inch narrower than the final necessary dimension for the sides and shelves. Then glue a wood strip, $5/16$ inch thick, to the front edges. Select wood that will contrast nicely in color with the plastic laminate. Machine the wood edging $1/16$ inch wider than the flakeboard. Make sure that the edging overlaps the flakeboard on both sides for its entire length.

At this point, most people would jig up a router with a partial sub-base and flush off the edging to the flakeboard. I personally prefer to do it with a hand plane and scraper. This is not simply for reasons of nostalgia. In my experience, a router increases the chances for error. If the work surface is not flat, the router will not cut flush down the full length of the board. Neither will the plane, but you will have a better idea of what's going on before it's too late. The router is also more likely to chip the wood. If you've taken care and truly left only a $1/32$-inch overlap, you can do the job quite quickly with a well-tuned plane and scraper.

Forming the Edges

Next, laminate the faces of the board, and use a router to flush off all of the edges. For the front, choose an edge-forming bit that will give the solid wood strip an attractive appearance, such as the cove cut shown in Figure 2. You must not choose a bit that cuts deeper than the thickness of solid wood that you applied. Since there are many bits that remove $1/4$ inch, I specify $5/16$-inch wood above. But that number could be modified to suit the application.

Molding bits that cut the laminate at a slant should be avoided. These forms (such as a round-over) would reveal a very wide area of the paper-like material that underlies the coating of the laminate.

If you wish to use a round-over, you could laminate the faces of the boards first, and then add the wood edging (Figure 3). This requires that you flush the wood strip to the surface of the laminate. Otherwise the router will not have a flat surface to ride on. With this procedure, the consequences for mistakes are much higher, as the ruined surface will be the final laminate rather than the substrate. Once the wooden edging is applied, round over very carefully

Coved Wood Edging

Figure 2. *A decorative bead can be routed into the edge of the wood and laminate (at left), but don't use a profile that exposes too much of the laminate edge (at right).*

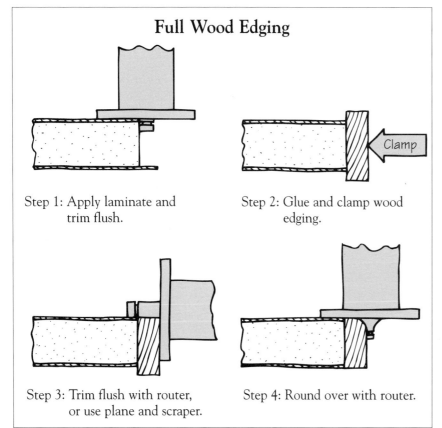

Figure 3. *Applying the edging after the surfaces are laminated can be risky because a mistake could damage the laminate. The advantage is that the wood edging can be rounded without cutting the laminate.*

so as to avoid damaging the surface of the plastic laminate.

Countertops

In making countertops with wooden edging, you have the same choices concerning the order of operations. If you laminate the surface first and then apply the wood edge, you face the same risk of ruining the counter surface when flushing off the wood. Perhaps you have a method of gluing the edge dead-on without having to flush it off. If so, please let me know. People have a habit of running their hands over countertops, and even the most oblivious consumers are unfortunately blessed with the ability to feel a discrepancy of a few thousandths of an inch on a surface.

As previously mentioned, the downside of sandwiching the edging is that the edge profile must cut through the laminate at nearly 90 degrees or too much of the back will be revealed. It is also good practice to ensure that whatever finish is applied to the wood is well absorbed by the exposed edge of the laminate as well. Counters get a lot of moisture on and over them; if any of this moisture is absorbed by the edges of the laminate, it could cause swelling.

Cabinets

The technique described above for shelving can also be used quite handsomely on cabinet doors and drawer fronts. When applying wood on all four edges, you have to keep in mind what the panel will look like after you machine the edge profile. It will look best, and chances of splitting will be diminished, if you miter the wood edging strips at all four corners.

If you must cheat, think about the location of the edge in relation to the viewer's eye. For instance, on a base cabinet door, you might miter the top two corners and butt the bottom two, which are below the viewer's line of sight. Just remember to clamp a block of wood to the bottom edge of the panel at the corner when routing through the butt joint and across the grain of the bottom strip. Otherwise there will be chip-out problems.

If you are making a cabinet with face-frame construction, a nice touch is to make the face frame of substrate pieces with a thin wood strip glued to the inside edge (Figure 4). Flush off the wood strips as described above. Make the face frame about 1/16 inch oversize and attach it to the cabinet carcase and flush it off all around.

Here I would recommend using MCP for a substrate and only applying plastic laminate to the outer face. Apply a large laminate

Exposed Hardwood Edging

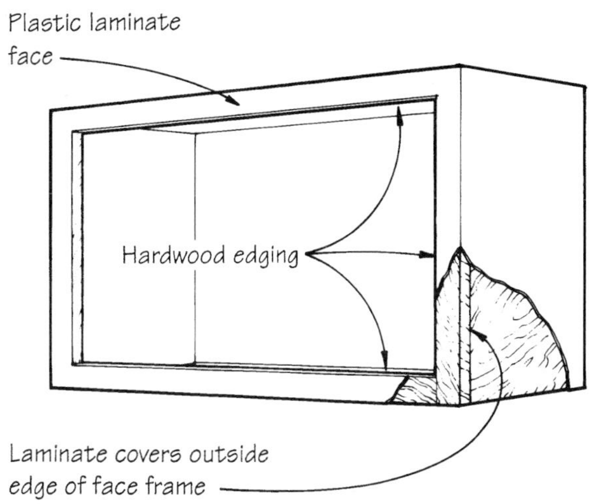

Plastic laminate face

Hardwood edging

Laminate covers outside edge of face frame

Figure 4. *With face-frame construction, a sandwiched strip of solid wood adds an elegant touch. Use melamine-coated particleboard (MCP) as the substrate, and laminate the exposed surface last to cover the rough edge of the face frame.*

sheet over the entire face frame. Cut out the opening with a router and flush-trim the edges. This wastes material somewhat, but gives a seamless result not usually available in mass-produced cabinetry. Here a molded edge is not called for, only wooden edges sandwiched between laminate.

If the face frame is attached to a carcase which will have an exposed side, laminate that side after applying and laminating the face frame so that the raw outside edge of the face frame is covered. This also might be an occasion for using Colorcore economically. On the carcase side, use Colorcore that's the same color as the face frame. Since the exposed edge will be Colorcore, the effect will be the same as if the entire unit were laminated with Colorcore.

I don't recommend making the face frame of solid wood and then laminating, as the expansion and contraction of the wood may eventually cause delamination.

Other Possibilities

It is not hard to extend the techniques described above into the realm of backsplashes or kitchen tables, or to the use of a decorative and functional wood drawer front, or cabinet door pull. Wood edging has become quite popular, even on mass-produced plastic laminate cabinetry. It adds warmth to the laminate, which can be quite sterile if unrelieved. But a single wood edge, molded and stuck on the top or bottom of a kitchen cabinet as a pull is about the limit of production cabinetry. The builder doing custom work can easily top that. ■

Joshua Markel is a developer and cabinetmaker based in Philadelphia.

On Site With Nuvel

by Chuck Green

A **Nuvel counter** has nearly invisible seams, according to the author, but is easier to work and less costly than solid surfacing.

I n early 1993, the Formica Corporation introduced a new surfacing material called Nuvel. When a customer recently asked me about the product, I hadn't yet heard of it, so I called Formica and my local distributor to get the lowdown. Soon after Nuvel became available, my company, Four Corners Construction, fabricated our first Nuvel job for this same customer, a large U-shaped countertop with hardwood edging (see photo above).

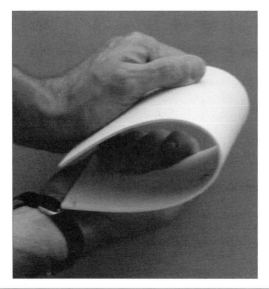

Figure 1. Much less brittle than plastic laminate, Nuvel will bend to tight radiuses without cracking.

Characteristics

Nuvel is a "high-density, mineral-filled thermoplastic polymer" manufactured by General Electric for Formica. It comes in thin sheets — 0.090-inch-thick (about $^3/_{32}$-inch) — and in five sizes: 30 inches by 8, 10, and 12 feet; 4x8 feet; and 5x12 feet.

A Nuvel countertop is fabricated partly in the manner of solid surface materials, and partly like plastic laminates. It is applied to a substrate using both ordinary contact adhesive and a special seaming compound. Nuvel can be formed to tight bends, up to a $^3/_{16}$-inch radius (Figure 1). It can be postformed, vacuum-formed and thermoformed, as well. Nuvel has a Class 3 fire rating and works in other applications, such as tub and shower surrounds.

Seaming compound. The seaming compound comes in odd-looking double-cylinder cartridges. The large cylinder holds the seaming compound base, while the smaller one holds the activator. The large, European-made applicator gun, which sells for about $130 (we rented), applies the two viscous liquids in the proper proportions. It looks like a weapon the Terminator would carry, but is easy to use (Figure 2). One beauty of the system is that the seaming compound cartridge can be used for up to three sets of seams, made minutes or days apart. The gun ejects only what is needed at the time, plus what remains in the mixing tube. The plastic mixing tube is discarded and a new tube attached for the next seaming run. Each cartridge comes with three mixing tubes.

Advantages

Nuvel has a lot going for it. Like the laminates, it's thin and lightweight. But because it's much stronger and far less brittle, handling it before and during fabrication is less of a concern. Colors are homogeneous all the way through, and damage to its surface, such as cuts or burns, can be repaired by sanding and buffing, as with solid surface materials. Done properly, seams between sheets of Nuvel are not easy to detect, as with solid surface materials.

You can work Nuvel with the same tools you use for laminate jobs, though Nuvel cuts more easily. Even so, Nuvel has greater impact resistance than laminates, according to the manufacturer. Formica also claims that Nuvel has greater heat-resistance than laminates, so a pot can be put on it directly from the stovetop.

One advantage over solid surface materials is that the dust produced in fabricating Nuvel is tolerable even when working inside an enclosed living space. My experience with Surell and Corian is that with seam and edging work, the routing and sanding produce great quantities of extremely fine dust that goes everywhere quickly. Routing the edges and seams of Nuvel inside an almost-finished kitchen produced mainly shavings, which looked like thin rice grains. There was no billowing dust, and cleanup was easy.

Finally, Nuvel is priced competitively. It costs about $7 per square foot — about one third to one half the cost of $1/2$-inch Surell, Formica's solid surfacing material. There are some additional costs with Nuvel: the substrate, contact adhesive, seaming compound, and rental of a Nuvel seaming compound application gun ($10 per day). As for labor, on our job, Nuvel worked somewhat slower than laminates but faster than solid surfacing.

Disadvantages. On the down side, Nuvel is limited in color choice. For now, white, two off-whites, almond, and Folkstone (light gray) are available, though Formica reports that they expect to add patterns and more solid colors. Also, though Nuvel can be well integrated with Surell sinks to give a smooth countertop-to-bowl transition, you can't get the perfectly matched color that you can with solid surface sinks and counters.

Figure 2. *This futuristic application* for seaming compound automatically mixes the compound and catalyst in the correct proportions. The nozzle, which contains unused mixed portions, is disposable.

Working the Material

We started our kitchen countertop the same as for laminate, making a $3/4$-inch high-density particleboard substrate, built up at the edges to a $1^1/2$-inch thickness. Next we laid out and dry-fit the Nuvel sheets. Rather than trusting the factory edges to be perfectly straight, we used a router to cut the joints (joints must be cut accurately, even though seaming compound will be used).

At this point, surface preparation takes a unique turn, with the application of the seaming compound at all Nuvel-to-Nuvel joints (Figure 3). The only areas to receive seaming compound in our job were the butt joints, which we masked with $1^1/2$-inch masking tape on both the underside of the Nuvel and the top of the substrate. After masking these areas, we spread ordinary contact adhesive on both surfaces, let it dry, then removed the masking tape, leaving the masked areas adhesive-free. Because we used a maple edge treatment, we didn't need seaming compound along the counter perimeter.

The awkward stage of the work came as we set the sheets permanently. When Nuvel sheets are laid down, there must be enough seaming compound to allow for a small amount of squeeze-out at the joint. The next sheet is carefully slid tightly into this squeeze-out. Most of the area is bonded using contact adhesive, so the pieces are not adjustable once in place.

This step is mildly awkward with laminate work, too, but with Nuvel the seaming compound imposes two limiting time factors. Once mixed, the seaming compound sets up in eight to ten minutes — so you must apply

Figure 3. Nuvel attaches to the substrate with ordinary contact cement except at seams, which receive a proprietary seaming compound. The author first masks the seamed ends with 1 1/2-inch masking tape, spreads the contact cement on both surfaces, then removes the tape and spreads the seaming compound on the adhesive-free ends.

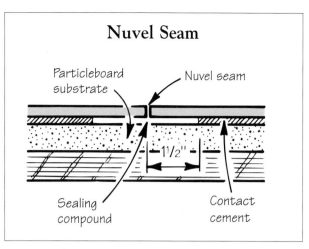

Nuvel Seam

Particleboard substrate

Nuvel seam

1 1/2"

Sealing compound

Contact cement

the stuff, spread it, and accurately place the Nuvel within this time. Secondly, joints (and edges, if you're using a Nuvel edge treatment) must be clamped with clamps and cauls (boards used to spread the clamping pressure) within the compound's working time. (Clamps remain in place for an hour.)

Laying the first sheet. We started with a 10-foot-long sheet. I discarded the first several inches of compound to be sure of a perfect mix. Since we couldn't physically lay more than the first sheet — including spreading the seaming compound and putting on clamps — within the ten-minute limit, we applied seaming compound to only one side of the first joint.

With the gun I squeezed a thin line of the gooey compound along the middle of the previously masked area at the butt end of the sheet. We placed the sheet carefully, using several stickers between the Nuvel and the particleboard as we positioned it. We pulled the sticks out one by one, as with laminate work, except that we had to carefully lift each one over the seaming compound — and we had a real time restriction for doing it all. We rolled the Nuvel out with a hand roller, working from the middle to remove any air bubbles, then clamped the seamed end with cauls.

Clamping produced a fine line of squeeze-out. While the compound was still workable, we scraped out all the excess from where the next sheet would go, so we'd get a tight fit when it went in. It was moderately hectic, but it went smoothly as could be. Compound got on everyone's skin, but soap and water easily removed the stuff before it set. Excess compound in other places came off later with a router.

With the second sheet, I spread the line of compound closer to the joint so the compound would be sure to squeeze into the joint. We worked the second sheet from the joint back, making sure the seam with the first sheet was tight. We got a slight buildup from the squeeze-out at the seams — perhaps 1/16 inch high — as we wanted.

We laid the next two joints in one operation, since the pieces were more manageable and we had some confidence at that point. It went very well. It then took about 20 minutes to strip off the protective film that comes on the product.

Trim work. Router work was next, to trim off overhanging Nuvel along the perimeters and to trim down the thin lines of hardened compound that had squeezed through at the seams. We set up a router with a carbide hinge-mortising bit, and lay two equal-sized wood slats on each side of the joint, held back about an inch, for the router to run on top of. With the bit set to cut 1/64 inch higher than the main surface, we ran the router down on the two strips, leaving less material to sand off.

In places where the router didn't fit, Nuvel trimmed easily with a chisel or utility knife. It's really easier to trim than any countertop material I know — because it isn't brittle and has no "grain" to pull the cutting edge off course.

The shavings were surprisingly manageable. They fell down without blowing around, and we just swept up. We used a 3-inch Porter Cable belt sander with a good dust bag, using medium grit paper to take the seams down flat. We then edged the front perimeter with maple, keeping it slightly higher than the Nuvel surface, since it proved to sand down more easily than the Nuvel. We belt-sanded the Nuvel-to-maple joint flat, which took a half hour for 26 linear feet. Then followed an hour of random orbital sander work, using an AEG TXE 150, which has an excellent dust collector. We worked up from medium to very fine grit pads, going over the entire counter to leave a consistent sheen.

We cut the two sink openings with a Bosch jigsaw and a fine cutting blade. We didn't feel any need to use a router for this since the Nuvel, with its strength and non-brittle nature, seemed unlikely to chip during cutout operations.

I should note again that Surell's kitchen and lavatory sinks are not perfectly color matched to Nuvel. Surell's arctic white sink is only fairly close to Nuvel's white. A contrasting color might be a better choice, but the two are not so very different in hue that everyone will be bothered by it. For this job, though, we went with stainless steel. ■

Chuck Green is a NARI certified remodeler and owner of Four Corners Construction, in Ashland, Mass.

Thinset Tile Countertops

by Brad Compton

PHOTOS BY JIM HART

When I install tile countertops, I want a finished product that will draw attention for the right reasons. Poor tile placement, unlevel surfaces, and cracked grout lines can make a tile job a real eyesore and open the way to water damage. From the sizing and placement of the plywood base right on through to the removal of the excess grout, many decisions are made that will make or break a tile job's appearance and durability.

Scoping Out the Job

When I arrive on a job, the first thing I do — sometimes before I unpack my truck — is grab my 2-foot level and check the cabinet installation from front to back and end to end. I often find cabinets out of level. While I can compensate for some leveling problems in a mortar-bed job, with thinset on backerboard there's not much I can do. I have to either install the backsplash out of level to match the countertop, or level the backsplash and make up the difference in the backsplash grout joint. The lesson to learn from all this is to start with level cabinets.

The next task is to answer some critical design and layout questions. Don't wait to address these issues or you're bound to wind up with a shoddy job.

What size and type of tile am I using? The homeowner typically chooses the tile on a custom job, but I can advise them on how their decision will affect the tile layout. For instance, clients will sometimes ask me to use a floor or shower tile for a countertop. Some of these tiles — though very attractive — don't have countertop trim pieces available. My job is to find trim pieces sold by another manufacturer that match in color, thickness, and size, or to modify the tile pieces available (see "Trim Tiles," page 79).

Is the client looking for a full tile layout? In most cases the plywood base is cut flush with the cabinet frame, keeping the trim tile tight to the cabinet. But on rare occasions I'm asked to do a "full-tile" layout with no cut tiles. In this case, I may need to extend the countertop beyond either the front or side edge of the cabinet by more than a few inches, and the cantilevered plywood will need some reinforcement. Usually this is done by adding a second layer of 3/4-inch plywood as a base or installing some type of metal or wood brackets or moldings.

What style backsplash and trim are called for? In kitchens we usually tile the backsplash all the way from the counter to the bottom of the wall cabinets. On a bathroom cabinet, the backsplash is usually one full tile. We trim the exposed sides of the 1/2-inch backerboard in either quarter-round, or "radius bullnose," or apply "surface bullnose" directly to the finished wall.

Whether the perimeter of the countertop is to be trimmed in V-cap, speedcap, or wood, you need to know the dimensions of the trim.

Any through-the-backsplash switches or outlets required? Since I'm the only one who knows how all the layers (plywood base, substrate, thinset mortar, tile top, and backsplash) stack up dimensionally, I sometimes have to play electrician in order to get a

A long-lasting and attractive job starts with precise layout and a sturdy substrate

Tile Countertop Detail

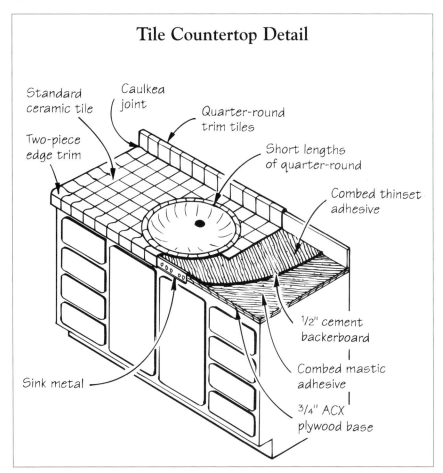

Standard ceramic tile

Caulked joint

Quarter-round trim tiles

Two-piece edge trim

Short lengths of quarter-round

Combed thinset adhesive

Sink metal

1/2" cement backerboard

Combed mastic adhesive

3/4" ACX plywood base

Figure 1. *The author uses short lengths of quarter-round trim tile to finish around an inset oval sink. Sink metal reinforces the counter edge and provides a backing for the thinset adhesive.*

switch or outlet through a backsplash. This work sometimes requires cutting out drywall to access the wires, so it is best to move any electrical boxes before installing the tile.

Besides adjusting the boxes for elevation, they should be adjusted for depth in the wall. On remodels, I find myself with three options: screwing on extension plates that pull the outlets and switches out about 1/2 inch, installing new boxes the correct distance out from the wall, or buying longer screws and cutting the tile carefully so the tabs on the outlet or switch rest on the tile. The third option is most common in my area, but check with your local electrical inspector. Also, most codes require electrical outlets every 2 feet along the countertop, and any countertop outlet within 6 feet of a kitchen sink must be wired with a GFCI outlet.

What type of sink is used and what is its dimension? There are two basic types of sink installations: self rimming and inset. The self-rimming type is easiest to install since the rim of the sink rests directly on the field tile. But clients typically prefer the inset type — whether "undermount" or "flush mount" — because cleanup on the countertop can be done with a sweep of a sponge into the sink. Also, the inset type is just

a little more sanitary, because it doesn't have a sharp corner where food and dirt can collect. The inset sink sits on the plywood base, and the substrate butts up to its outer edge or overhangs inside the bowl slightly.

Knowing the dimensions of the kitchen sink is critical to making an attractive layout. Because most kitchen sinks are rectangular and sit centered on the sink cabinet, they are a fixed part of the tile layout. Especially with an inset sink, you don't want to place a narrow band of tile along any of its sides.

Bath sinks, on the other hand, are usually oval, making tile layout much simpler, but the trim can be a little fussy around an inset sink. Typically the tile is set back about 1/2 inch from the sink, with the field tile cut in an arc and trimmed with 1- to 1 1/2-inch segments of quarter-round tile (see Figure 1). Keep the grout lines small or the edge will look like it has more grout than tile, which can be very unattractive.

The Plywood Base

After these layout questions are answered, it is finally time to get to work. I use mostly 4-inch ACX for my tile base. I use an exterior grade plywood for water resistance, and the good face grade gives me a smooth surface. This grade also has a tight core, which assures me I won't hit a void when screwing sink metal onto the plywood edge.

After cutting the plywood to size, I lay the sheet with the factory edge toward the cabinet face so that I have a nice, straight edge for the trim tiles. To secure the tile base, I screw through the plywood to the cabinet frame every 6 inches with 1 1/2-inch drywall screws.

Next, I trace the template that comes with the sink, and with a jigsaw cut a hole that is typically 1/2 inch smaller than the outer rim of the sink. I check the dimension of my hole a few times to make sure it is accurate, because this lip becomes the reference for knowing where to cut my tile around the sink hole.

Tile Substrate

Once the plywood base is on, we install the tile substrate. Because most countertops get wet, it is not advisable to use plywood as a tile substrate. Cementitious boards such as 1/2-inch Wonderboard or Durock work well, although recently I've been using Dens-Shield (Georgia-Pacific, 133 Peachtree St. N.E., Atlanta, GA 30303; 404/652-4000). This is a gypsum-based product with a watertight plastic facing on the front and fiberglass mat on the back. It is quite a bit lighter and easier to cut than the cementitious boards, although it's about twice as expensive.

Both types of substrate are fairly simple to install using a thinset latex-modified mortar to bond to the plywood. First, comb the thinset onto the plywood, then cut the substrate for the sink. For a self-rimming sink, carefully cut the hole to the same size as the plywood opening. For an inset model, I usually cut the substrate back 1/2 inch from the plywood so that the sink lip rests on the plywood. Screw the substrate into the plywood with 1 5/8-inch drywall screws about every 6 inches on-center. Drive all screws flush with the surface. Take extra caution, however, not to countersink screws through the Dens-Shield, because breaking the facing can ruin the product's ability to resist water.

Seams for both Dens-Shield and cementitious products are handled in a similar fashion. Spread 2-inch-wide fiberglass tape evenly over the seam and embed it in tile adhesive. Be sure to tape between the deck and the backsplash if tile is to be adhered to the drywall. This reinforces a joint that typically sees a lot of stress from the movement of dissimilar materials. Taping the joint won't stop this movement, but it will strengthen the joint.

Sink Metal

Though primarily used with mortar bed jobs, I often use sink metal with backerboard. Sink metal is galvanized metal that has closely spaced holes for mortar or thinset to key into. It also has periodic slots for an adjustable screw connection to the plywood base. Sink metal reinforces the edge of the counter and provides an accurate edge to connect trim tile to if you need to hang a "skirt" under a surface bullnose (see "Steps to a Thinset Countertop," next page). Sink metal is not necessary if you are using V-cap.

Tile Layout

With the substrate screwed down, I am ready to begin the tile layout. Having made the major layout decisions before the plywood base was set, the goal now is to transfer marks to the substrate as guides for the tile.

The best way to lay out any tile job is to create what is affectionately called an "idiot stick." This is a stick that has the tile width plus grout joint width marked for

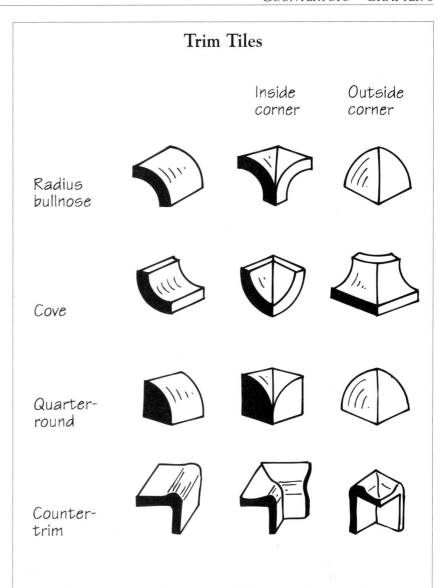

Trim Tiles

Inside corner   Outside corner

Radius bullnose

Cove

Quarter-round

Counter-trim

Note: These common trim tiles are not available in every style or type of tile. Check with your tile supplier for the appropriate trim before buying the field tile.

several tiles in a row. For a large countertop, I start by placing the trim tile on the counter edge and make a mark at its back edge on the counter surface. I make similar marks at all corners and snap chalk lines around the perimeter of the counter, defining the "field." This is where the idiot stick enters the picture.

On an L-shaped counter, I start the layout from the inside corners. In other words, I place a full tile at the corner and tile away from it in both directions. By placing the idiot stick in a couple of different directions from the corner, I can see how the rest of the field will lay out. The backsplash then simply corresponds to the field tile layout.

For bathroom vanities and straight kitchen countertops, the easiest layout approach is to start with a full tile at an end that is not against a wall. Then if the "idiot

Steps to a Thinset Countertop

(A) In preparation for laying the tile on this vanity top, the author fastens the tile backer (Dens-Shield) over the 3/4-inch plywood base, then attaches sink metal to the counter edge.

(B) To ensure an accurate layout, he draws a line parallel to the sink-metal edge, using a sample tile for exact measurement.

(C) Before setting the tiles, he tapes the substrate joints with 2-inch fiberglass mesh and coats the tape with adhesive to strengthen the joint.

(D) The edge tiles are set first, beginning at the outside corner and working towards each end.

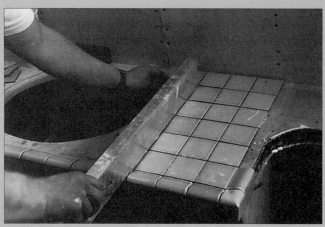

(E) With the edge tiles in place, the author spreads the thinset with a 1/8-inch square-notched trowel.

(F) He lays the field tiles in place, checking for exact alignment with a straightedge.

stick" shows that I end up with a small strip at a sink or at the very end, I split the difference at the two end tiles. For example, if I'm using a 6-inch tile and the stick tells me I'm going to be left with a 1-inch strip along the wall, I'll put a $3^1/2$-inch cut tile at each end. This eliminates the narrow strip and creates a symmetrical look (Figure 2).

Applying the Thinset

With the layout finished we are ready to start tiling. Tile can be secured to the substrate with either a mastic or with thinset cement-based adhesive. I prefer the thinset for a number of reasons. First, I can buy it pigmented to closely match the color of my grout. That way, if any grout lines wear through to expose the thinset, it won't look awful. Mastic is more expensive and is difficult to remove from a tile face after it dries.

To get a proper mix, follow the directions on the package. With most, you add two parts thinset to one part water or add water until the consistency is like mashed potatoes. Don't mix with a drill and paddle-bit, unless you keep the speed below 300 rpm. Any more velocity and you can whip air into the thinset, which will weaken the bond to the tile. Also, never add water to a thinset mixture after it has started to stiffen. Instead, simply mix it up again and it should loosen up to its original state. If your thinset sits for much over an hour, however, it might not loosen up and you'll need to mix a new batch.

I also use an additive in my thinset to increase bond strength and give flexibility to the hardened thinset. This helps the counter resist impact and stand up to freezing and thawing. The product I use is Acrylic Mortar Admixture, from Custom Building Products (13001 Seal Beach Blvd., Suite 200, Seal Beach, CA 90740; 310/598-8808).

All adhesives are applied with $1/8$-inch notched trowels. My trowels, which I acquired in Germany, have square teeth. I haven't seen them locally, but similar trowels are made by A. Richard Ltd. (Impex Can-America, c/o J.V. Carr, Elm St., Champlain, NY 12919; 800/724-5928). V-notched trowels are more commonly available, and will do the job adequately.

Laying Trim Tile

I begin by setting the trim tile on the counter edge. The trim tile is sometimes thicker than the field tile. By setting the trim tile first, I can raise the field tile to the right height by applying more thinset if necessary.

The quickest trim type to install is a single piece V-cap. To lay V-cap, I "butter" the back of each cap and set it on the chalk line. To keep a neat line, I use an aluminum straightedge and frequently sight down the edge of the counter. At inside and outside corners on an L-shaped counter, I miter the trim, or use special corner pieces if available.

Another option is to use two tile pieces to create a "skirt," as shown in Figure 1. This takes more time to install straight, but sink metal will help to ensure a neat job.

Laying Field Tile

Holding a $1/8$-inch notched trowel at a 45-degree angle, comb the thinset material onto the field. It is important to apply the thinset consistently or the tile will be uneven. Do not comb more thinset than can be tiled in 20 minutes when working at ordinary indoor temperatures. In very hot weather, you may have only 10 minutes, while cooler weather may buy you 30 minutes or more. If thinset starts to cure before the tile is in place, the bond is significantly weakened.

If my grout line is greater than $1/16$ inch, I place spacers between the trim tiles and the field tiles and carefully set the first row in place. If my grout line is $1/16$ inch or less, I eyeball for consistent grout width. Some tile has built-in spacers for narrow grout lines.

I then take a mallet and firmly tap the tiles so that they get maximum coverage of

Figure 2. Poor tile layout. *Instead of leaving a narrow strip of tile along the backsplash, the tilesetter should have used one less full tile and set two "half" tiles at front and back.*

Figure 3. Critical joint. *The joint between the countertop and backsplash is very susceptible to cracking because the cabinet base and the wall expand and contract at different rates with moisture and temperature changes. Instead of grout, the author recommends using a flexible colored caulk to match the other grout lines.*

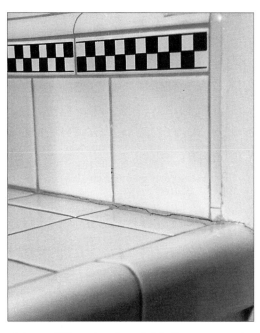

thinset. If I notice that field tiles are not sitting evenly with the trim tiles, I'll pull them up and add or remove thinset as needed.

I repeat this procedure, placing spacers between all the tiles, and use a straightedge to keep them straight in both directions. I keep a water bucket and paint brush handy to clear away any thinset that works its way up into the grout joints. I also use a sponge to wipe any thinset off the top of the tile before it cures.

Setting the Backsplash

With the field and trim installed, I mark out the top of the first backsplash tile (tile plus one grout joint) with a level line and carefully comb the drywall with thinset up to, but not covering, the line. Then I use wedges or spacers on their sides to keep the tile on the level line.

If I am tiling a bathroom vanity, I usually install just a single row of surface bullnose. If tiling a kitchen with a backsplash that extends up to the wall cabinets, several rows of tile are needed. In that case, I trim out the outside edges of the backsplash with surface bullnose cut to match the width of the V-cap on the countertop, typically 1$\frac{7}{8}$ inches.

Grouting

After the tile has had all night to set, we are ready to grout. For joints $\frac{1}{8}$ inch or smaller, unsanded grout is the appropriate material. For joints larger than this, sanded grout is recommended. I generally use the same additive that I use in the thinset mix to improve the performance of grout.

To mix, I pour the grout into a dry bucket and premix it dry to get all the pigments out of the bottom of the bag. I then put back in the bag what I don't need, add water and additive, and mix until it reaches a firm consistency.

I install the grout with a grout float, combing it diagonally over the tile. It is best not to install too much grout at a time because it will dry quickly; once dry, it is very difficult to remove. I also keep the grout out of joints to be caulked, typically the joint between the backsplash and field tile, and the joint between trim tile and an inset sink.

Once the initial grout is worked into all the joints, I remove most of the excess by running the grout float parallel with the joint. Finish cleanup is done with a grout sponge slightly dampened with water. By passing my sponge along the joints, I can shape the grout so that it is slightly concave and doesn't cover too much of the tile edges. With each pass, I rinse and ring out the sponge in a bucket of water, keeping the sponge as clean and dry as possible. If the sponge is too wet, the water can remove pigments and cause inconsistent shading after the grout has cured.

The grout on a kitchen counter should be sealed with one of the many water-based sealants available. Sealing keeps grease and other liquids from penetrating the grout and causing permanent stains. Manufacturers recommend that grout cure at least three weeks before sealing, so this requires a visit back to the site.

Caulked Joints

The next day, after the grout has cured, we caulk the joints that are the most susceptible to cracking. These include the joint between the countertop and backsplash, around the sink, and any joint between tile and another material, such as a cabinet or stove top. Many tile setters avoid this step, mainly because finding a matching caulk color is difficult and caulking requires one more trip to the job. If these joints are grouted, however, they will probably crack and allow water to penetrate within a matter of weeks (Figure 3). Some grout makers, like Custom Building Products, make caulk colors that coordinate with their grout colors, but any silicone or mildew-resistant caulk that matches in color will be fine. The wider the joint, the more critical it is to accurately match the color of the grout. ■

Brad Compton leads tile jobs for tile contractor Rainer Hoelsher of Ceramic Dimension in Cupertino, Calif.

Backsplash Details

by Nancy Thomas

Adding a small amount of detail to the backsplash can really make the kitchen sparkle. But we must always be aware of the kitchen's utilitarian nature. Water, grease, and heat are the primary sources of aggravation to keep in mind when choosing materials and details.

First and foremost, the counter must be fully sealed to the backsplash to prevent liquids from seeping down the back — leading to rotting plywood or swelling particleboard.

Second, whatever material is used, it must be easy to clean. In some cases, especially with commercial ranges, fire retardation and clearances are a third concern.

The 4-Inch Splash

Take the standard 4-inch laminate backsplash. This ordinarily comes as a one-piece coved riser referred to as a postformed splash. A variation of this is an attached square-jointed backsplash.

The advantage of the formed top with no joint is its ability to prevent seepage. But there are tradeoffs. These tops are pre-made, come only in specific sizes, and are often made of thinner laminate stock. The square-edged counter is generally made of thicker laminate, and the factory-made seams are usually fewer and better than with postformed counters.

The square-jointed backsplash may be mounted and sealed by the fabricator, or can be installed in the field. It is very important, however, that the backsplash be attached to the counter itself rather than the wall. Otherwise, wall movement or the settling of the house is likely to break the seal between counter and splash.

Get Creative

Once we've determined how to make the backsplash functional, the question becomes how to make it more interesting. There are numerous possibilities:

- Top a 3- to 4-inch backsplash with ceramic tile to add color and texture. Or cap it with wood.
- Match the color of the backsplash to a complimentary accent. For example, it could match the counter edge, tile floor, or sink.

- Bevel the edge of the counter and the splash, then insert a color-core pinstripe, or a small detail of wood. Be sure to fully finish the wood.
- Soften the room by using bullnose edges on counters and backsplashes, in laminate, wood, or synthetics.
- If the backsplash is solid surfacing, your fabricator may be able to rout in a decorative pattern, and inlay an alternate color using resins or other materials. Or these materials can be shaped to provide interesting details, such as ogee edges, bullnoses, coved joints, and other profiles.
- The backsplash need not be one height. You can step it up and down from 1 to 16 inches or so. The steps can be symmetrical or irregular.
- Consider pulling the cabinets forward and building a small ledge (4 to 6 inches deep) on top of the backsplash. This can be a good solution in houses that need heat distribution from behind the cabinets. This type of ledge can also be built without pulling the base cabinets forward if you can sacrifice counter space. What are these ledges good for? Besides the design effect, they make good storage space for spices and decorative items. They also provide areas for vertical knife slots and for inserting stainless restaurant-style utensil holders.

Tile and Other Materials

Other materials to be considered for backsplashes include: wood, furniture-type moldings,

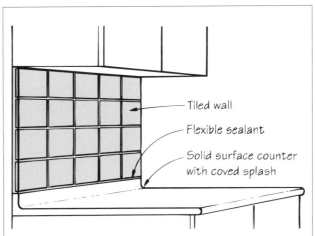

Tiled wall

Flexible sealant

Solid surface counter with coved splash

Tile over solid surface: For an attractive and watertight detail, create a cove in the molded-plastic or solid surface counter, then add a ceramic tile splash.

Mixing materials:
(clockwise from top left) wood molding, ledge with utensil holder, wood and tile combo, and tile with spice shelf.

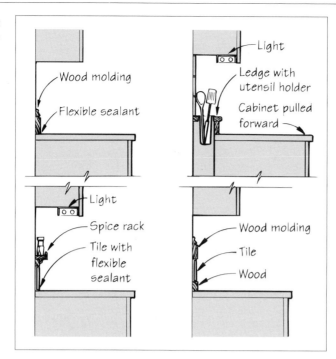

Tile step-up:
When the counter area is wider than the wall cabinet, you can step tile up the wall — as shown in these two details.

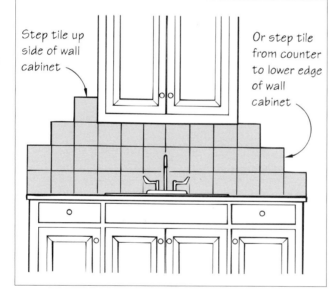

Multi-use space:
This detail shows an appliance garage, an overhang that looks fine with no backsplash (at the right end), and a backsplash that mixes plastic laminate and wood moldings.

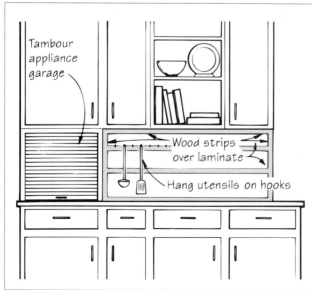

mirror, granite, and marble (now available as wall tiles).

Tile, of course, is commonly used. It is durable and adds texture. Tiles range from simple 4x4-inch solid-color tiles, to hand-painted custom tiles. Whatever you use, pay attention to ease of cleaning. Durability is also a concern, particularly on horizontal surfaces, which are prone to chipping. Keep grout lines tight to minimize the exposed surface of this problem area. Also use a silicone compound to seal the grout or use grouts with additives to make them impervious to water. Avoid light-colored grouts since these are more likely to discolor. Greys, tans, and other colors are more suitable for this use.

Using a different color of tile on the lower portion of the backsplash creates a border effect. You can create an interesting backsplash by sandwiching tile between sections of wood, solid surfacing laminates, other tiles, or stonelike materials. However, where tile meets the countertop or joins a dissimilar material, such as wood, a grout joint is likely to crack. Use a flexible sealant such as silicone instead.

Use the Space

Backsplashes needn't be simply covered walls. They can also serve as utilitarian space, such as for shelving. You don't want to reduce the counter depth in all areas of the kitchen, but an extra deep backsplash may work well in some areas. Another example is appliance garages, which have become very popular recently. These are compartments built into a corner of the backsplash — sometimes with a tambour door. Also on the market now are metal and wood wall racks — for hanging utensils, cups, pots and pans, bins of dried goods, and so on. If the backsplash walls are on the interior, and not filled with pipes or ducts, small shelf areas can be recessed between the studs.

In all applications, consider varying materials, colors, and utilitarian uses of the backsplash spaces. Remember to seal all joints well, and detail the locations of electrical outlets and switches so they don't interfere with the function of the backsplash. Make these small details special and useful. Your clients will rave about it. Surprisingly, it is often these details, rather than the cabinetry or layout, that make more of an impact on the client. ∎

Nancy Thomas is a kitchen and bath designer and a former instructor for the National Kitchen and Bath Association.

Chapter 4
BATHROOM DESIGN BASICS

RICHARD M. RAWSON, CKD, CBD, DESIGNER. COURTESY OF NKBA. PHOTO BY SEAN CRANOR

Successful Bath Layout

by Jerry Germer

Good bathroom design starts with laying out the fixtures for comfort and function

All bath planning starts with the fixtures — their features, sizes, and clearance requirements. The following sketches show several proven fixture layouts. The dimensions represent the minimum clearance for code or physical accessibility. Where two dimensions are given, the larger one yields a more comfortable space. You may want to provide even more clearance to suit your client's requirements.

Toilets and Bidets

The size and shape of toilets hasn't changed much, but minimum clearances are crucial. The only real improvement to the basic toilet in the last 50 years is the new generation of water-saving toilets, which reduce the amount of flush water from seven gallons to as little as one.

Bidets, long in use in Europe for personal hygiene of the pelvic area, are gradually catching on in the U.S. Since hookups and clearances are similar to those of toilets, these fixtures are often placed side by side.

Lavs

Lavatories are currently available in four main types: pedestal, wall-hung, countertop, and integral (illustration on facing page). Pedestal lavs, popular in the early decades of this century, are making a comeback, but their higher cost and space requirements limit them mostly to upscale baths. Wall-hung units come with or without a backsplash. Supply and waste piping are exposed.

Some countertop units are joined to the counter surface by a metal flashing strip (mounting frame); others have an edge that overlaps the counter surface (self-rimming). Lavs that fit under the counter surface (undercounter) work only if the countertop is designed to allow water to run off the edge, as with cultured stone, synthetic solids (e.g., Corian, Nevamar), stone, or tile.

Integral lavs unite countertops and lavs in a single unit. Some resemble wall-hung lavs, but sit atop a cabinet base. Composite plastic models contain one or more lavs molded into countertop lengths of up to 10 feet. (You'll have to order anything over 4 feet custom made.)

If you provide side-by-side lavs, remember that the goal is for two people to be able to use them at the same time. Aim for the more comfortable, on-center dimension of 36 inches.

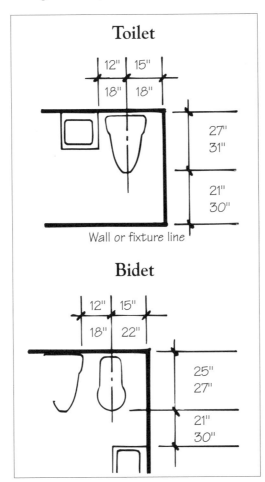

Toilet

12" 15"
18" 18"
27"
31"
21"
30"
Wall or fixture line

Bidet

12" 15"
18" 22"
25"
27"
21"
30"

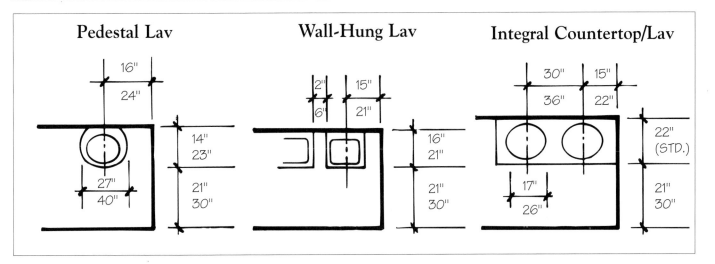

Pedestal Lav — **Wall-Hung Lav** — **Integral Countertop/Lav**

Tubs

Sometime early in this century, the 30x60-inch rectangular tub edged out the classic clawfoot tub, and still reigns as the most common fixture for bathing. Available in various materials and colors, it comes as tub-only or as a complete enclosure, with one- to three-piece wall surrounds, and sometimes ceiling panels. While the standard 60-inch length suits most people, a 66-inch unit offers much more comfort to tall people. A 54-inch tub is too cramped for almost any adult. Square tubs fit neatly into corners and can be moved out into the room.

During the last decade, Americans began to think of bathtubs as more than just places to get clean. The change in attitude requires rethinking the layout. Instead of merely stashing the tub in the end of the bathroom, designers and builders now have to think of ways to enhance the whole bathing experience. Tubs can be pulled out into the room, recessed into the floor, elevated on platforms, and surrounded with plants. If space permits, separate the bath from the toilet with a divider.

Whirlpool baths are now preferred by a growing number of consumers. Sixty percent of remodeling jobs included whirlpool tubs, according to a 1986 survey by *Kitchen and Bath Design News*. Whirlpools start as small as 32x60 inches and grow from there.

Basic Tub/Whirlpool

Corner Tub

Showers

Showers combine easily with tubs when space is scarce, but separate showers are more in demand. Homeowners prefer showers when adding a fourth fixture to a three-fixture bath, and as the bathing fixture in second (three-quarter) baths. Another plus, showers are more accessible to older persons and the physically handicapped because the curb is lower.

Showers can be completely site-built, site-built on prefab bases, or ordered

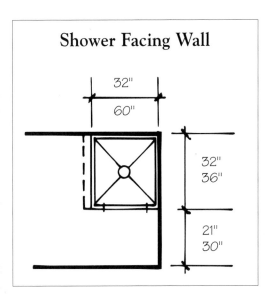

Shower Facing Wall

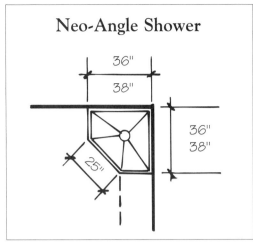

Neo-Angle Shower

as one-piece molded units. They can open beside a wall, or diagonally into the room, as above (neo-angle).

Bath Layouts: General

When planning bath layouts, remember that the fixtures are only the tip of the iceberg. The unseen parts — water, waste, and vent piping systems — have to work without conflicting with each other or with the building structure. While you can force the piping to fit almost any fixture placement, a little thought given to logical arrangements will save costs and headaches during installation.

Try to align baths above each other, floor to floor, so that all fixtures can easily tie into a single waste/vent stack running up from the basement or crawlspace and out through the roof. Single-wall plumbing arrangements are somewhat more economical than those that require piping in two or three walls.

It's not always easy, but there are definite advantages to keeping waste/vent pipes out of exterior walls. For one thing, you won't have to worry about getting enough insula-

tion between the pipe and outer wall sheathing (even in a 2x6 wall, you can only get 1 1/2 inches of insulation behind a 4-inch pipe). And you won't be stuck with a fat, ugly vent pipe poking through the roof just above the eaves line or gable wall.

Unless the room is planned for wheelchair access (as discussed later on), I have found no advantage to a door wider than 28 inches. A larger door can be downright awkward in a small room.

Windows are always desirable in baths for light, view, and ventilation. Small windows placed high on the wall offer the most privacy. If you want a window above a toilet, you will have to offset the stack. Some designers avoid placing windows above tubs because of the likelihood of people slipping when reaching to open or close them.

Half-Baths

Every home needs at least one full bath, but when you add a second or third bathroom, half-baths can save space and money. Because people use lavs and toilets much more often than tubs and showers, half-baths are particularly well-suited to the public part of the house (kitchen/living/dining).

The simplest half-bath aligns the two fixtures on the same wall. Of the three possible door locations, the spot near the lav is least awkward, and eliminates the direct view of the toilet when the door is left open.

If the space is long and narrow, such as under a stairway, you can fit in a half-bath by installing the fixtures on opposite walls. But beware of positioning the toilet where it can't be vented. In most cases you can probably offset the piping to an adjacent sidewall.

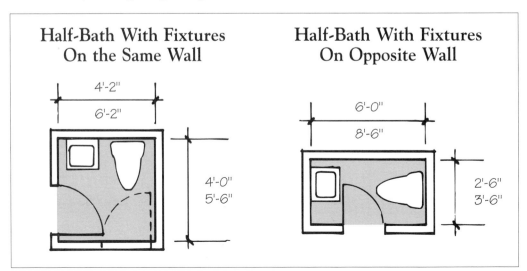

Half-Bath With Fixtures On the Same Wall

Half-Bath With Fixtures On Opposite Wall

Site-Built Medicine Cabinets

Case Study #1
Basic Hardwood Box

by Lynn Comeskey

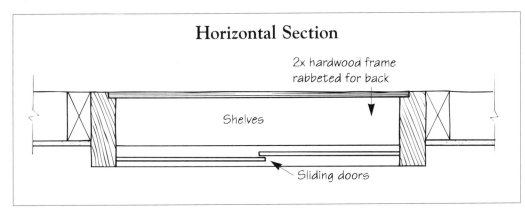

Horizontal Section

2x hardwood frame rabbeted for back

Shelves

Sliding doors

This simple custom medicine cabinet uses a 2x hardwood frame that protrudes beyond the stud cavity. The doors typically are mirrors mounted on standard track; shelves are tempered glass or wood.

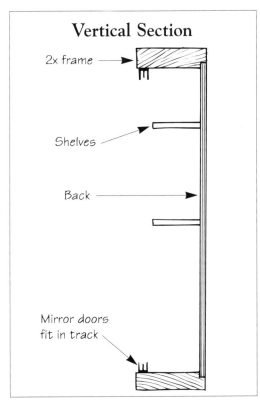

Vertical Section

2x frame

Shelves

Back

Mirror doors fit in track

This design is best used where the clients need a lot of storage. Basically, it is a box made of 2x6 oak, maple, or birch assembled on edge. The wood can be stained, finished clear, or covered with plastic laminate. The 2x should be ripped to approximately 5 inches so that about 1 inch protrudes past the face of the drywall when the frame is recessed in the wall (see illustration). We install the unit before the drywall, and flat tape right up to the edge of the frame.

We drill holes on the inside for adjustable shelf supports; the shelves can be made of wood or tempered glass. The height and width of the unit is flexible. If the unit gets too wide for the shelves to be self supporting, then we install a vertical divider. For doors, we typically use mirrors mounted on KV wheels and track. If the mirrors get too large, though, you'll have to use extra wheels to take the weight.

In using this design, it will probably be necessary to install a header, since Murphy's Law says there won't be adequate space between the studs where you want it. You'll also want to inform the homeowner that plumbing vents have a way of appearing in these spaces, and that moving them will cost extra.

Lynn Comeskey is a remodeling contractor who specializes in kitchens and baths. His firm, Mac & Lou Construction, is based in Mountain View, California.

Although it's not always necessary to make up your own medicine cabinet, it's still a useful option if you want something a little out of the ordinary. Our custom designs are based on the notion that medicine cabinets should err on the side of being understated — there are too many other bath fittings that should be the center of attention.

Case Study #2
Small Bath Storage

by Greg Gossens

The cabinet's large mirror surface area makes the room look and feel larger. Adjustable glass shelving provides lots of storage space for small items.

One of the most essential storage components in a bathroom is the medicine cabinet. Manufactured units can be expensive and don't always match the room's size or fixture arrangement. Often, the owner's taste and storage needs are such that only a custom cabinet will do.

We have used designs similar to this one on several projects. It's made of inexpensive materials that can be assembled on site, and is versatile enough to be used with many different interior finish schemes.

In this case, the medicine cabinet solved several design problems in a second-floor bathroom renovation. The cabinet was surface mounted because the fixtures are on an exterior wall, but it could also be recessed. It had to be shallow because the room is small and narrow. We made it as wide as we could to satisfy the owner's need for plenty of storage space for small items. And the tall, mirrored doors are close enough to the

Cabinet Details

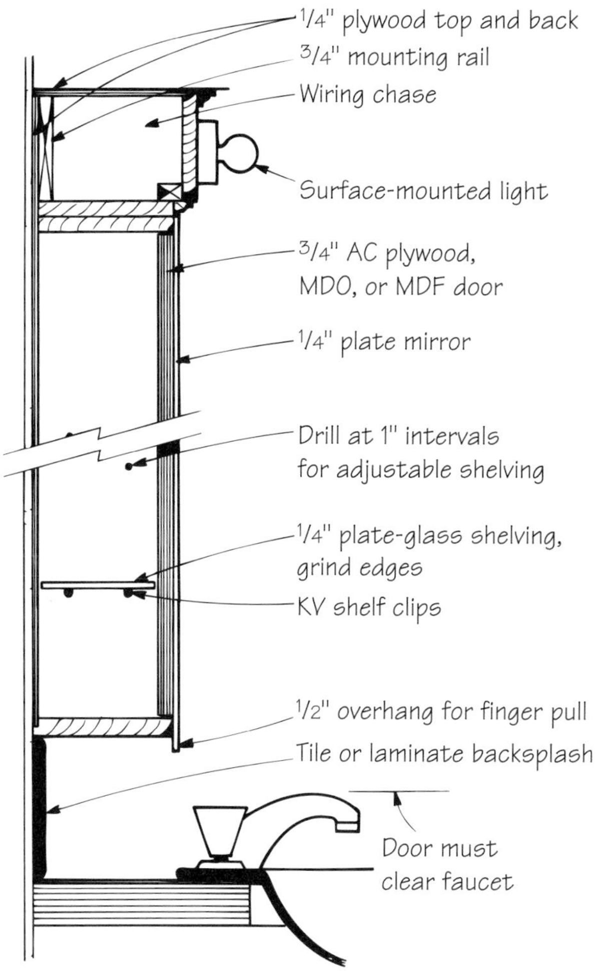

1/4" plywood top and back

3/4" mounting rail

Wiring chase

Surface-mounted light

3/4" AC plywood, MDO, or MDF door

1/4" plate mirror

Drill at 1" intervals for adjustable shelving

1/4" plate-glass shelving, grind edges

KV shelf clips

1/2" overhang for finger pull

Tile or laminate backsplash

Door must clear faucet

Attach the plate mirror to the doors with a mirror adhesive such as Mirro-Mastic. For an uninterrupted mirror front, use narrow strips of plate mirror to trim the front edges of the carcass. Allow the mirror to overhang the bottom of the cabinet by about 1/2 inch for a finger pull.

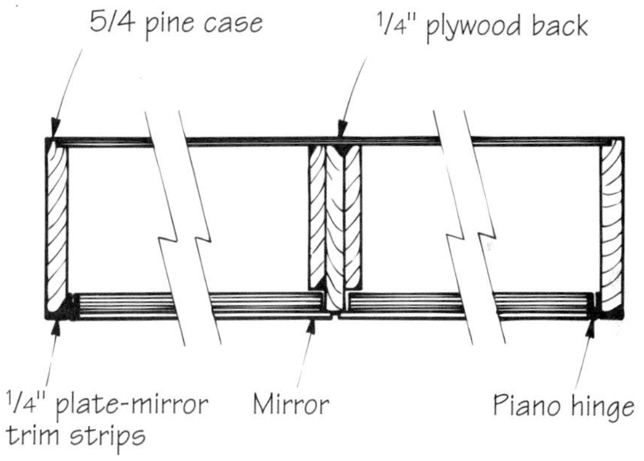

Section Elevation

5/4 pine case

1/4" plywood back

1/4" plate-mirror trim strips

Mirror

Piano hinge

Plan Section

countertop for the owner's children to use.

The cabinet was built and finished entirely on site by one person in about ten hours. The frame is painted pine with a 1/4-inch plywood back. The painted AC plywood doors are fastened to the cabinet body with piano hinges, which provide strength and stability. (Concealed cup hinges haven't worked as well with the heavy doors.) The shelf system uses KV shelf clips (Knape & Vogt, 2700 Oak Industrial Dr. N.E., Grand Rapids, MI 49505; 616/459-3311) adjustable in 1-inch increments, with 1/4-inch plate-glass shelving.

Once the cabinet was mounted to the wall, the plywood doors were hung in place.

Then the mirrors were glued on with Mirro-Mastic adhesive (Summer and Maca, 345 Lodi St., Hackensack, NJ 07601; 800/631-1321). In previous installations, J-channel was used at the perimeter of the mirrors, but here the builder found a supplier who would guarantee the mirrors without it.

The overall effect of this kind of cabinet is to make small bathrooms look and feel larger. Where deeper wall cabinets are possible, we have eliminated base cabinets altogether. This gives the countertop a "free-floating" appearance. ■

Greg Gossens is a principal in Gossens Bachman Architects, Inc., of Montpelier, Vt.

Making Small Baths Feel Bigger

by Paul Turpin

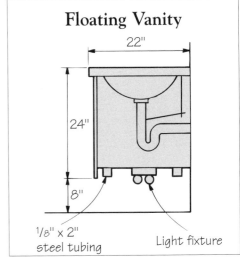

Floating Vanity

22"

24"

8"

1/8" x 2" steel tubing

Light fixture

Floating vanity. The vanity floats about 8 inches above the floor, sacrificing a few inches of storage, but creating the illusion of added floor space. Steel tubes support the cabinet (detail at right) and a fluorescent fixture provides soft accent lighting.

Most of the bathrooms we remodel are small, so unless our customers are willing to move some walls around, we're stuck with the original size and outline.

Since there's little you can do to make the fixtures themselves take up less space, we rely on color, light, layout, and some other design tricks to make the room appear larger.

Creating Floor Space

The more floor space that is visible, the bigger a room appears. Dining rooms are a perfect example: While the table typically occupies a large area at the center of the room, you can see the floor underneath it. As a result, the table doesn't seem massive.

So how do you translate this principle to the bathroom? Clawfoot tubs are a good way to open up some floor space, but they are undesirable or too expensive for many homeowners. Pedestal sinks, which have become as popular in the past ten years as they were in the 1920s, work well since they have a small footprint. But more often, customers need the storage area and counter space that only a vanity cabinet can provide.

One solution I've found is the "floating vanity." Instead of sitting on the floor, this vanity is raised about 8 inches off the floor, and is supported by two steel rails that are bolted to the walls at each side of the unit (see illustration, above). The countertop is still at the same height but you lose the kickspace and about 4 inches of vertical cabinet space. However, this permits the flooring to continue under the vanity and back to the wall.

This size vanity needs to be custom made. When you're discussing the project with the cabinetmaker, it's critical that you determine the vertical height needed for the sink and its waste piping.

A normal vanity is 33 or 34 inches high, but depending on the sink, you may have to go higher. If you're roughing in a new waste line, make sure you consult with your plumber to decide exactly where the sanitary tee should go.

For the steel rails that support the vanity, I use $1/8$x2-inch square stock. I've spanned up to 8 feet with this steel, and then watched the electrician stand on it while installing the overhead light fixture with no noticeable deflection. I found suppliers for the tubing under "Steel Distributors and Warehouses" and "Metals" in the Yellow Pages.

In small baths, the vanity is often only 30 inches wide (the minimum for a plumbing fixture). This small size eliminates the need for the steel rails since the vanity can be screwed directly to the walls. In this case, I usually minimize the height of the cabinet so that it just covers the water and waste piping under the sink.

Enhancing the Illusion

You can do a lot with color, line, and light to make small baths feel larger.

Color. By now, most of us know not to paint a small bathroom brown. Dark colors feel heavier, while light colors seem to recede and make a room feel more spacious. Dark colors are not forbidden in small baths, but keep them low in the room, and use lighter shades as you go higher. In this way, the portion of the room above your waist feels bigger, which seems to give you more elbow room.

For instance, you can use a dark-colored wainscot, either tile or wallpaper, that's between 30 and 42 inches high. The paint or wallpaper above this should be a lighter shade, while the ceiling should be even lighter (usually bright white). In traditional homes, a picture-rail molding set several inches below the ceiling can serve as the transition between the wall and ceiling colors.

Line. Another way to create spaciousness is by using lines to direct the eye. In a square room, for example, lay ceramic or vinyl floor tiles at a 45-degree angle. This way, the joints between the tiles attract the eye across the diagonal of the room. This is especially beneficial in an L-shaped room, since this provides a longer diagonal.

Another trick is to use a chair rail molding at the top of the wallpaper or wooden wainscot to create a horizontal line that the eye will follow around the perimeter of the

Leading the eye. *Horizontal design elements, such as the chair rail (photo above), lead the eye around a room — enlarging its apparent size. Also, reserve dark colors for surfaces low in the room, like the wainscoting shown.*

room. And using wallpaper with vertical stripes above the chair rail draws the eye up, away from the mass of the bath fixtures.

Light. The best design and installation job will still feel like a cave if it's poorly lit. If the bath is windowless, or if the windows look into a solid wall or a shady grove of trees, consider a skylight. For nighttime lighting, I try to provide at least three levels: dim (for a nightlight), normal, and very bright. Even with a single fixture, you can achieve these levels with a high-wattage bulb on a dimmer switch. A three-way bulb will reduce the humming noise at low settings.

A fringe benefit of the floating vanity is that you can use the space below the cabinet as a light valance. This provides indirect lighting without glare that's ideal for a leisurely bath or for those midnight trips to the bathroom. This light can be either a standard fixture box or a plug-in unit with a switched plug in the back wall. Set the fixture as high as you can to let brooms and mops reach under the vanity without hitting the bulbs. ∎

Paul Turpin is a Los Angeles-based remodeling contractor who specializes in kitchen and bath design and remodeling.

Bringing the Bathroom Up to Code

by Iris Harrell

A clear understanding of the rules will help you build safely and keep the inspectors happy

As a contractor in California, I have to conform to some of the strictest codes in the country. I think it's only a matter of time, however, before codes become equally strict in other parts of the country as well.

I'll focus in this article on some of the lesser-known code requirements for bathrooms. The boxes at the end of each section give the relevant code references for the western states. Since regional codes vary somewhat across the country, I've also included references to other regional codes and key points of difference (see "Key to Code References," below). Finally, I've included some items not required by code, but which I feel are essential to minimize callbacks and make the bathroom safe.

Review Plans With an Inspector

During the design phase of a bathroom remodel, I imagine myself building that bathroom with the strictest inspector peering over my shoulder, and I design accord-ingly. It's not as much fun as letting fly with all your wildest ideas, but it's a lot more practical.

All codes have gray areas subject to interpretation by the inspector. To guard against surprises, I check out anything that's unusual or questionable in my design with the toughest inspector in town. For example, I'm especially thorough about checking out any expensive custom parts and European products before I order them.

Answering questions is part of the inspector's job, and I've never found one who wasn't willing to help out. Since most inspectors here are overworked, I try to be brief and to the point. Sometimes I call with my questions, but in many cases I take the plans down in person and ask them to have a look. This not only ensures accurate information, it also helps build a personal relationship with the inspector and gets him involved in the job before he comes to see us for the first inspection.

Working with inspectors this way

Key to Code References

Code Body	Document Name	Abbreviation
International Conference of Building Officials (ICBO) (5360 S. Workman Mill Rd., Whittier, CA 90601)	Uniform Building Code Uniform Plumbing Code	(UBC) (UPC)
Building Officials and Code Administration International (BOCA) (4051 W. Flossmoor Rd., Country Club Hills, IL 60478)	National Building Code National Plumbing Code	(NBC) (NPC)
Southern Building Code Congress International (SBCCI) (900 Montclair Rd., Birmingham, AL 35213)	Standard Building Code Standard Plumbing Code	(SBC) (SPC)
National Fire Protection Association (NFPA) (Batterymarch Park, Quincy, MA 02269)	National Electrical Code	(NEC)

Minimum Shower Size

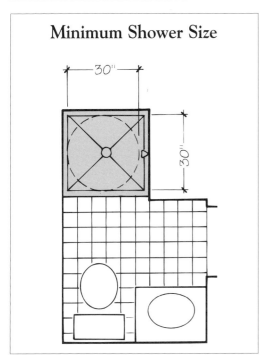

Figure 1. *The Uniform Plumbing Code requires a minimum of 1,024 square inches of shower area, and also that a 30-inch sphere can fit throughout the entire height of the shower.*

Figure 2. *A worker removes ceramic tile from a crumbling green board substrate in a tiled whirlpool bath. The failed substrate will be replaced with cement backerboard.*

involves some extra steps at the front end of the job, but it saves time and money in the long run.

Many of the codes that pertain to bathrooms are logical and easy to find. But some items are little known or may be hidden in other parts of the code and require some detective work.

Shower Size

The UPC (Uniform Plumbing Code) requires that you have a minimum of 1,024 square inches in the entire shower area and that you are able to fit a 30-inch-diameter sphere throughout the full height of the shower (see Figure 1). Both of these rules are true regardless of the shower's shape. This can be difficult to achieve when you are exchanging a tub for a shower since some of the old tubs measure 30 inches or less in width compared to 32 inches for newer models. If this is the case, depending upon how the tub is situated in the room, you'll probably need to fur out the walls at either end of the tub so there's enough room for the new curb.

Code References:

Shower Size
NPC-1216.4, 900-square-inch minimum; UPC-909(d).

Shower Enclosures

Shower doors must open out. They may open in, as well, but if someone falls in the shower, the door must open out so you can get to the person. Many architects and designers don't know this until their plans get red-marked by the building department.

By now, all of the model codes require that shower enclosures be made from safety glass. If that glass is tempered, the word "tempered" must be etched or otherwise permanently marked on each piece of glass. In the past, companies were printing up labels that said "tempered," and dishonest builders and glass contractors were sticking them to glass that really wasn't tempered. However, for laminated glass (a glass/plastic sandwich) a sticker is sufficient.

Shower walls must be impervious to water up to 70 inches above the drain. This usually isn't a problem, but we've gotten stuck in the past with wood windows. If you have one lower than 70 inches, you may have to pull it out. We have tried painting the trim with a marine-type paint, but some inspectors won't approve this.

Code References:

Shower Doors
UBC-5407

Glass Shower Enclosures
SBC-2703.2; NBC-2203.2; UBC-5406 (d).

Waterproof Shower Walls
SBC-2002.3; NPC-1216.4; UBC 510(b).

Water-Resistant Drywall

Code requires water-resistant gypsumboard (often referred to as "green board") in showers and tubs. All of the codes allow contractors to set tile on green board, but I think this will change soon. The material is not stiff enough to serve as a good substrate, and once water gets into it, water-resistant drywall will crumble.

The Gypsum Association says proper maintenance of the tub area (regrouting any spots where the grout is missing, caulking around faucets and the tub lip, and so on) will prevent significant water entry. But I've seen too many tile walls fail that had a green board substrate (Figure 2). Use of a vapor barrier seems to speed up the decay of the green board, since moisture collects between the plastic and the board. High-humidity areas, such as saunas or steam rooms, will also degrade the material.

A better choice for these applications is one of the cementitious backerboards (see "Tile Backerboards: Alternatives to Mud," page 149). A proper vapor barrier is a must with backerboard.

We used to hang leftover sheets of green board on the ceilings, but code now prohibits this. According to the Gypsum Association,

the material sags unless it is attached to framing that's a maximum of 12 inches on-center. Because the material's core and paper facing is treated for water repellency, it's not as strong as standard gypsum board.

Code References:

Water-Resistant Drywall
SBC-1803.4; UBC-4712.

Hand-Held Showerheads

These are popular with our clients, but some of the models don't pass code because they lack an antisiphon valve. Without this valve, dirty water can backflow into the pure water lines if the showerhead is allowed to dangle into a full tub. Manufacturers don't always supply the antisiphon valve as a standard feature because it raises the price of the unit.

If you purchase a unit without an antisiphon valve, install the hand-held showerhead so that, fully extended, it falls at least one inch above the tub's overflow valve. Otherwise the inspector will ask that the plumber install an access panel and put an antisiphon valve in the lines — a small but annoying expense.

Code References:

Hand-Held Showers
SPC-1204.3.4; NPC-1223.1.2; UPC 1003(n).

Toilets and Bidets

If you could draw a line down the center of the toilet bowl, code requires you to have at least 15 inches of space on either side of that line (Figure 3). When there's space, I allow at least 18 inches to either side. This is more comfortable, especially for those who are stocky. You also need 24 inches of space in front of the toilet. I use the same dimensions for a bidet.

As of 1994, all states require 1.6-gallon toilets in new construction and remodeling. In California, you can apply for an exemption if your plumbing system is incompatible with low-flow toilets (usually due to low water pressure).

There is a good deal of controversy about low-flow toilets. Some people argue that, because the waste isn't always fully evacuated on the first flush, some models require two flushes, negating the water savings. I've also heard plumbers complain about the lines getting clogged when there isn't sufficient water

Toilet Clearances

24"

15"

15"

COURTESY OF KOHLER

Figure 3. *California codes require a front clearance of 24 inches and 15 inches to each side (left). Where space is tight, the author uses this 1.6-gallon toilet made by Kohler (right).*

pressure and slope to pull the waste all the way through.

I've had good results with the Kohler Wellworth-Lite and the Kohler Rialto (Kohler Co., 444 Highland Dr., Kohler, WI 53044; 414/457-4441). The Rialto is especially nice because it is not as large as other varieties and fits into small spaces where we're pushing to meet that 24-inch code limit.

Code References:

Toilet Clearances
SPC-903.5, no frontal minimum; NPC-1204.2 requires 18 inches to the front; UBC-511(a) or UPC-907.

Jetted Tubs

These require an access panel so the motor and electrical parts can be serviced. It's important to remember this when you're still in the design stage. Since most of my clients don't want to see this panel, I often put the motor in a remote location, usually inside the vanity or closet.

But the inspectors have something to say about this, too. You cannot install any shelving in front of the access panel. Their concern is that people will pile all kinds of stuff on the shelves and the plumber or the electrician won't be able to find the access. There's also some concern that the items put on the shelves may be combustible.

Here is a good example of a gray area in code enforcement: Some inspectors will permit shelving as long as it's removable. It may be worth having a delicate discussion with the inspector before you rule it out. Your customers will certainly be happier with more shelf space.

Code References:

Whirlpool Access Panels
SPC-923.1; NPC-1221.2; UPC-912.

Bathroom Lighting

While the NEC (National Electrical Code) requires light switches to be at least 5 feet from a hot tub, spa, or jetted tub (Figure 4), different inspectors have made different interpretations. In remodels, some inspectors allow us to put light switches closer than 5 feet, as long as they are connected to a ground-fault circuit interrupter. We've also found discrepancies in the way that 5 feet is measured. The code is trying to prevent people from standing in 3

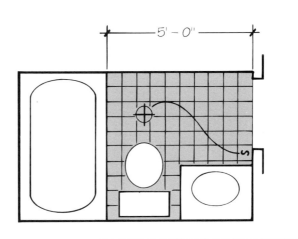

Bathroom Light Switch

5' – 0"

Figure 4. *The National Electrical Code requires light switches to be located at least 5 feet from a spa or jetted tub.*

inches of water and operating the light switch. It's best to find out how the inspector will rule before you start wiring.

Certain parts of the bath may be designated either "damp" or "wet." Again, this is subject to some interpretation, but it affects the type of lighting you can use in that area. For instance, a tub and shower combination is considered a wet location. (An example of a damp location is a tub with no shower.) So recessed lights over a tub/shower combo must include a vapor-proof lens cover. The goal here is to keep water from splashing inside the fixture. Also, homeowners have been known to change the light bulb while standing in the shower.

There is a sticker on the light or packaging that says whether the fixture is approved for a damp or wet location. As a rule, lighting that's approved for wet locations can go in damp locations, but usually not vice versa.

One of the newer energy-oriented amendments to California's Title 24 requires a fluorescent light in each new bathroom. That fluorescent fixture must be the main light, and it must be operated by the first switch inside the door. The idea is to save energy, but many designers are not excited about working this into their plans. Even though there are many different lighting colors and fixtures available, fluorescent lighting has a bad reputation. I've had good luck with full spectrum and daylight fluorescent tubes. Both of these create a bright, natural light. I normally put the fixture over the vanity area.

Code References:

Wet Location Lighting
NEC-410

Watch Your Step: Stairs in the Bathroom

Bathtub Step

40"

10" min.

7 1/4" max.

Ergonomic experts recommend no more than one step leading to a tub platform. This allows the user to sit on the platform at the tub edge and swing in safely. Grab bars are also essential for safety.

Steps leading up to a whirlpool tub, or other level changes in a bathroom, can look very dramatic — but are very unsafe as well. We don't build them often, but when the design calls for stairs, we do all we can to make them as safe as possible.

The model codes say little specifically about bathroom stairs. Some inspectors apply the rules that govern standard stairways, but most consider bathroom stairs decorative, so few rules apply. Regardless of the code, however, railings or grab bars, nonslip flooring, and other safety items make good sense.

One step best. Walking up two or three steps, then stepping down into a deep tub, is awkward and unsafe. In addition, a bather may be lightheaded when standing up to exit the tub. This is from hypotension, an abrupt lowering of blood pressure caused by moving from a prone position to standing, and is exacerbated by soaking in hot water.

One solution for raised tub platforms is to use just one step, at least 10 inches wide and no more then 7 1/4 inches high (see illustration). This approach is approved by the National Kitchen & Bath Association (NKBA), based on the ergonomic research of Alexander Kira. The step should be continuous along the front of the tub platform or run around the entire tub. The platform at the tub lip should be wide enough to sit on. This allows the user to sit down and safely swing into the tub. Ideally, the tread should be level with the bottom of the bathtub.

Railings. According to the UBC (sec. 3306-i), if a set of stairs has four or more risers, you need a handrail. But this is one of those gray areas. Inspectors have different ideas about what constitutes four steps and what constitutes three steps and a landing. Regardless, for safety reasons you should include a railing (or a grab bar) even if you have fewer than three steps.

The vertical distance from the nose of the steps to the center of a handrail must fall between 34 and 38 inches, according to the UBC. The railing should be 1 1/2 inches away from the wall to allow room to grasp it, and should be 1 1/4 to 2 inches in diameter. There are some beautiful handrails available that, unfortunately, don't meet code.

Grab bar. Grab bars are a good idea even without stairs. The most critical area is where users enter and exit the tub (that's where the user may be on one foot). So I usually put a grab bar at the end of the tub where bathers get in and out. A vertical bar centered at about 40 inches above the finished floor or step is recommended. If you want to be extra safe, install both a grab bar and a handrail, or two grab bars, one as a substitute for the handrail.

Most of the grab bars available look like they belong in a hospital. Check with local bath showrooms for the best selection. Some manufacturers have grab bars that match their faucets. I've also used clear plastic ones, although one inspector wouldn't pass it for fear it would shatter like glass.

Risers and treads. While risers can be up to 8 inches and treads as little as 9 inches by California code, in bathrooms I feel it's safer to limit risers to 4 to 7 inches, and make treads at least 11 inches wide. Risers and treads should not vary in size from one another by more than 3/8 inch. If you've ever climbed steps with inconsistent sizes, you know it's an easy way to get hurt.

We often use a different tile color on the risers so that elevation changes are clear. You can even install low-voltage lighting under the nosing to further emphasize the location of the steps.

Flooring. Almost any kind of flooring is slippery when wet and soapy — especially tile. The glossier the tile, the more slippery it will be. Some manufacturers make tile with abrasive grit embedded in the surface. Another option is to use unglazed mosaic tiles (which are hard to keep clean and have no water resistance) or to install nonslip strips, available at hardware stores.

— I. H.

THOMAS TRZCINSKI, CKD, CBD, DESIGNER, COURTESY OF NKBA.

Ventilation

There's just no substitute for fresh air. That may be part of the philosophy behind the fact that the UBC code does not require a fan in bathrooms with operable windows if the open area is equal to at least 10% of the floor area. But since people don't always open that window, especially in the dead of winter, I recommend installing a fan anyway. Doing so is a good way to avoid callbacks for things like mildewed grout and wallpaper.

If you use a fan that doesn't sound like a Volkswagen coming through the bathroom, and put it on a timer, your customers will be more apt to use it (Figure 5). I like NuTone's QT-80 and QT-9093 (NuTone Inc., Madison and Red Bank Roads, Cincinnati, OH 45227; 513/527-5100). The latter is a combination fan, heat source, light, and nightlight. Both of these have low sone ratings: The QT-80 is 1.5 and the QT-9093 is 2.5 sones.

Figure 5. *Clients will be more likely to use the bathroom exhaust fan if you install a quiet one, like this model from NuTone's QT series.*

Code References:

Bathroom Plumbing Vents
SPC-1404.4, must be 10 feet away or 2 feet above the roof; NPC-904.2, same as SPC; UPC 506(b).

Plumbing Vent

The vent pipes must be at least 10 feet from the nearest operable window or skylight. This is, of course, to keep odors and sewer gases, which are potentially dangerous, from being sucked back into the house. But you can't put the vent 10 feet away from an operable skylight when the bath is only 5x8 feet. You can raise the vents 3 feet higher on the roof, but most people don't want to see it, especially at the front of the house. The other, more costly, alternative is to dogleg the vent through the attic and out.

Grab Bars and Antiscald Valves

Grab bars are not mandatory in residential bathrooms, and antiscald valves are only required in some jurisdictions. But, budget permitting, I try to include them anyway. As a designer, it's my responsibility to make the bathroom safe as well as attractive. As a builder, I know there are plenty of lawyers out there trying to make a living off people who are injured due to negligent building practices.

Grab bars. These are not mandatory unless there are steps up to the tub (see "Watch Your Step: Stairs in the Bathroom"). But the National Kitchen and Bath Association, in its recent publication, *27 Rules of Bathroom*

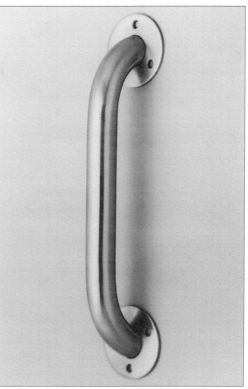

Figure 6. *Though not required by residential code, the National Kitchen and Bath Association recommends installing grab bars in tubs and showers to help prevent falls.*

Design, recommends installing a grab bar in the tub and shower to facilitate entry and exit (Figure 6).

Antiscald valves. The NKBA also suggests that all showerheads be protected with some type of antiscald device, and most of the model plumbing codes have adopted this requirement. I would expand this to include bath faucets, as well, since children can easily reach the levers, turn on the water, and burn themselves. ■

Iris Harrell, CBD, is a general contractor and the owner of Harrell Remodeling Inc., a $1.5 million design/build firm in Menlo Park, Calif.

NKBA's 27 Rules of Bathroom Design

In 1992, The National Kitchen & Bath Association (NKBA) introduced new guidelines for K&B design based on extensive research conducted by the association along with the University of Minnesota. The guidelines were established to help building and design professionals plan spaces that function well. The bathroom guidelines appear below. Some have been elaborated on based on other NKBA literature. For more information, contact NKBA, 587 Willow Grove St., Hackettstown, NJ 07840; 908/852-1695.

1 *Entrances* Make a clear walkway at least 32 in. wide at all entrances to the bathroom.

2 *Doors* No doors (entrance, closet, or cabinet) may interfere with fixtures.

Rule 2: Doors

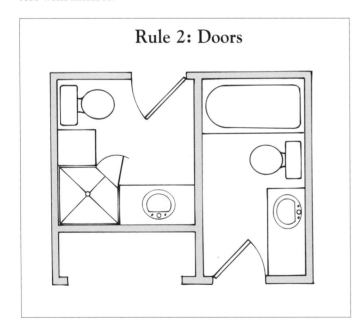

3 *Ventilation* Provide mechanical ventilation in every bathroom to provide a minimum of 8 air changes per hour when operating (more for jetted tubs, spas, etc.). Choose a fan with a noise rating of 3 sones or less at high speed.

4 *Electrical* Specify ground-fault circuit interrupters (GFCIs) on all receptacles. No switches should be within 60 in. of any water source. All light fixtures above tub/shower units should be special-purpose, moisture-proof fixtures.

5 *Cleaning Access* Where floor space exists between two fixtures, provide at least 6 in. of space for cleaning.

Rule 5: Cleaning Access

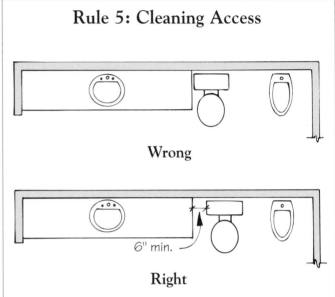

Wrong

Right

6" min.

6 *Walkway at Lavatory* Provide a clear walkway of at least 21 in. (30 in. recommended) in front of a lavatory.

7 *Lavatory Clearance* Provide at least 12 in. (18 in. recommended) from the centerline of the lavatory to any side wall.

Rules 6 & 7: Lavatory Clearances

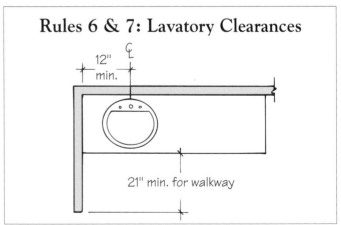

12" min.

21" min. for walkway

8 *Double Lavatory* Provide a minimum of 30 in. (36 in. recommended) between multiple lavatories, measured centerline to centerline.

9 *Toilet Clearance* Provide at least 15 in. clearance (18 in. recommended) from the center of the toilet to any obstruction, fixture, or equipment on either side.

10 *Walkway at Toilet* Provide a clear walkway space of at least 21 in. (30 in. recommended) in front of the toilet.

Rules 9 & 10: Toilet Clearances

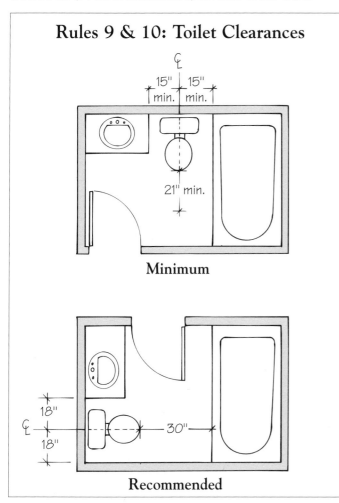

11 *Toilet Paper Holder* Install the toilet paper holder within reach of a seated user. The ideal location is slightly in front of the toilet bowl, and centered 26 in. above the finished floor.

Rule 11: Toilet Paper Holder

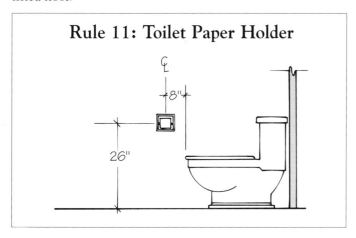

12 *Bidet Clearance* Provide at least 15 in. clearance (18 in. recommended) from the center of the bidet to any obstruction, fixture, or equipment on either side.

13 *Walkway at Bidet* Provide a clear walkway space of at least 21 in. (30 in. recommended) in front of the bidet.

14 *Storage near Bidet* Install soap and towel storage within reach of a person seated on the bidet.

15 *Steps at Tub* No more than one step should lead to a bathtub or a tub platform. The step must be at least 10 in. deep and no more than 7$\frac{1}{4}$ in. high.

Rule 15: Steps at Tub

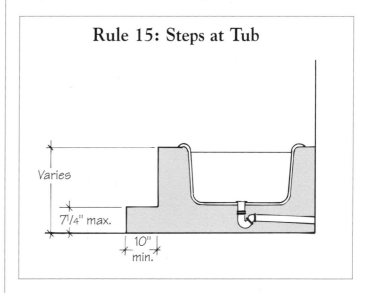

16 *Tub Faucet* The bathtub faucet should be accessible to an adult standing outside the tub.

17 *Jetted Tub Motor* Provide access to jetted tub motors for maintenance and repair.

Rule 18: Bathtub Grab Bar

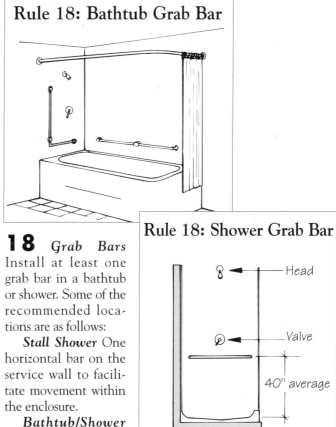

18 *Grab Bars* Install at least one grab bar in a bathtub or shower. Some of the recommended locations are as follows:

Stall Shower One horizontal bar on the service wall to facilitate movement within the enclosure.

Bathtub/Shower One horizontal bar

Rule 18: Shower Grab Bar

centered on the service wall and a vertical bar near the outside edge where bathers enter and exit.

19 *Shower Stalls* Make the interior of a shower stall at least 32x32 in. The preferred size for a typical adult is 36x42 in., which allows space for the user to step out of the stream of water. A fixed showerhead should be roughed in at 72-78 in. high.

20 *Shower Bench* Install a bench or footrest within the shower enclosure. A 6x6x6-in. triangle in the corner can serve as a footrest. A built-in seat, 16-18 in. high by 12-20 in. deep, is ideal.

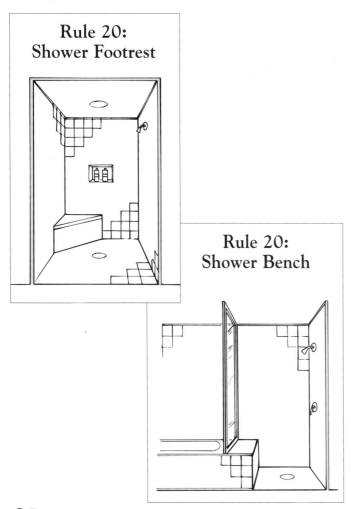

Rule 20: Shower Footrest

Rule 20: Shower Bench

21 *Walkway at Tub/Shower* Provide a clear walkway of at least 21 in. (30 in. recommended) in front of a tub/shower.

22 *Shower Door* Shower doors must swing into the bathroom, not into the enclosure, to avoid trapping an injured or ill bather. The door should have tempered safety glass or plastic glazing, and should not block access to the shower controls.

23 *Scald Protection* Protect all tubs and showers with a pressure-balancing valve, temperature regulator, or other temperature-limiting device.

24 *Nonslip Flooring* Make all flooring from slip-resistant materials.

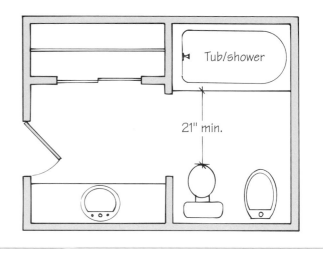

Rule 21: Walkway at Tub/Shower

Tub/shower

21" min.

25 *Storage* Provide adequate storage in the plan, including the following: counter or shelf space around the lavatory; space for grooming equipment; space for shampoo and soap in the tub/shower area; and hanging space for bathroom linens.

26 *Heating* Provide adequate heating in the bathroom. For comfort, this may require temperatures 3° to 5° F warmer than the rest of the house. A quick-response auxiliary heat source may be helpful.

27 *Lighting* Provide adequate general lighting and task lighting (see chart, below). ■

Bathroom Lighting Rules of Thumb	
Application	**Guidelines**
General Lighting	For surface-mounted fixtures, 1 watt of incandescent or $1/3$ to $1/2$ watt of fluorescent light per square foot. For recessed fixtures, $2\frac{1}{2}$ to 4 watts incandescent or $1/2$ watt of fluorescent per square foot.
Small Mirrors	One 75-watt incandescent or 20-watt warm-white fluorescent on each side of mirror, about 30 in. apart.
Large Mirrors (36 in. or wider)	Along the top of mirror, three or four 60-watt incandescents in a fixture at least 22 in. wide; or a 36 in. to 48 in. fluorescent. For a theatrical look, 15- to 25-watt G bulbs along the top and sides.
Shower	60-watt incandescent in wet-location ceiling fixture (check local code).

Bathroom Design Portfolio

Award-Winning Baths: Combining good design principles with a creative sense yields bath spaces that are both enjoyable and functional. A sampling of winning designs from the National Kitchen & Bath Association's annual design competition follow (photos courtesy of NKBA).

Designer: Margie Little, CKD and Dianne Hynes, Independent Kitchen & Bath Designer, Pleasant Hill, Calif.

Designer: Thomas Doty, International K&B Exchange, Sunnyvale, Calif.

Designer: Thomas D. Kling, CKD, York, Pa.

Designer: Molly Korb, CKD, CBD, MK Designs, Newcastle, Calif.

Designer: Diana Valentine, CKD, The Showplace, Inc., Redmond, Wash.

Designer: Kathleen Donohue, CKD, Neil Kelly Designers/Remodelers, Beaverton, Oregon

Chapter 5

BATH FIXTURES

CAROLYN B. THOMAS, DESIGNER, COURTESY OF NKBA. PHOTO BY WALTER SMALLING

COURTESY OF DUSCHQUEEN, INC.

Sleek frameless enclosures, like this one with mitered glass corners (above), require precise fitting by the installer. Kohler's Profile enclosure (right) gets support from round aluminum extrusions finished in high-gloss colors.

Custom Tub and Shower Enclosures

by Lynn Comeskey

Without question, the biggest change in tub and shower enclosures in recent years has been the increased use of clear glass. Almost all of the units we have installed in the last few years have been clear. Although clear glass enclosures are less private and require frequent cleaning, they make the bathroom appear larger and show off attractive tile jobs in the shower.

This trend is most prevalent in high-end work. Also at the high end are smoked and tinted glass, but they represent less than 5% of sales. Most lower priced units — the majority of the market — are still fitted with obscure or etched glass.

Enameled Frames

A trend that emerged in the late 1980s, and is really gaining momentum at the designer level, is enclosures with enameled frames. White is by far the most popular color, with almond second. Other typical colors are black, red, gray, silver, and gold.

Kallista was the first to offer this type of high-quality enclosure nearly a decade ago. Their imported extrusions, fittings, and $3/8$-inch tempered glass (compared to $3/16$ inch in most enclosures) are impressive, with basic units starting at about $1,000. The thicker glass allows you to eliminate corner extrusions by mitering the glass panels. This increases the cost by 5% to 10%, but improves the look of the enclosure dramatically. Even without mitering the glass, high-end units are difficult to install because there is little adjustment in the frame and the glass is very heavy. The first one we tackled took us a couple of days.

Another high-end brand that we install occasionally is made by The Majestic Shower Company. They import their extrusions and fittings from Kallista's original British supplier, also named Majestic. Majestic's extrusions and fittings have a heavily anodized finish that is machine- and hand-polished.

But for most customers, we need to keep the enclosure cost to well below $500. A no-frills tub enclosure — chrome with obscure glass — costs about $135 plus $65 for installation in this area. A shower enclosure costs $200 to $500 installed, depending upon the number of panels. From there, an additional charge is levied for clear glass ($40 to $110, depending on the number of panels), and gold trim ($30 to $70). You also pay a premium for a non-standard height or for a half wall.

What we look for in selecting a glass shower enclosure is a good finish, well-designed gaskets, doors that move and shut securely, and extrusions that cover for some irregularities but don't look heavy and unattractive.

Our clients like frameless doors and open tracks on sliding units, but there are trade-offs (see Figure 1). Frameless doors are easier to clean but aren't as well supported. Open-track units look nicer but closed tracks are stronger. In general, sliding units work fine on tub enclosures, but the ones I've seen and used on shower doors were embarrassingly wobbly and flimsy because of the height involved.

Shower Remodel

When remodeling an existing shower, we're often starting with a space that looks like a cave. These tiled shower stalls typically have a low, 7-foot ceiling, and the entrances are even lower. The door jambs are 24 inches wide, and the doors themselves are made of obscure glass.

When we are asked to repair or remodel such a shower, we typically open it up. We remove the low ceiling; the 24-inch opening is widened by removing the jambs, and we recommend clear glass (Figure 2).

We have been quite successful with this approach. The bathroom visually extends into the shower, which creates a sense of more space in what is typically a small room. Remodeling a shower this way can be economical since it uses less trim tile — the most expensive part of tile work — than an older style enclosure. Also, there is often less field tile to install.

If the shower is a walled-in "neo-angle" unit (a square with one corner cut off), we still remove the walls to open up the room. The results are even better in terms of the room feeling bigger. If the lav butts to the shower wall, we leave a short wall in place between it and the shower, and build a tiled vanity there. The wall can be the same height as the counter. But if you make it 4 inches higher, you can create an end splash (Figure 3). In either case, the shower and counter would have the same tile. We then install a shorter fixed-glass panel on top of the short wall as a part of the enclosure.

Built-In Features

Probably the most popular built-in feature is a soap and shampoo niche. We find out where the homeowner wants to put these niches, but we suggest they use existing stud openings to

Figure 1. *This sliding glass tub enclosure from Century Shower Door features frameless doors and heavy-gauge anodized aluminum tracks, available polished or in a variety of colors.*

COURTESY OF ALUMAX

Figure 2. *When remodeling a shower, the author often removes the low ceiling, widens the narrow jambs, and installs clear glass to create a modern, open look.*

avoid special framing.

When framing, remember that the finished opening will be at least 2 inches smaller in each direction, to account for the thickness of the mortar and tile. Also, we measure the homeowners' soap and shampoo containers to be certain they will fit. There is quite a bit of layout time involved, and with the trim work for the tile setter, the niche can cost as much as $200 to complete.

Benches are also popular. But make sure you have the space to make them big enough to comfortably sit on. Also, it is important that you build the framed bench to be completely watertight.

Multi-Head Showers

On some high-end jobs, we install several showerheads on opposing walls or high and low ones on the same wall. This is a nice feature. As soon as you plan more than one head, however, it is a good idea to consult with your plumber to make sure the pipes are large enough to provide an adequate volume of water.

Also, when the heads are on opposing walls, water will spray in all directions. Make certain the heads are located so the water will stay inside the enclosure when the door is opened.

Installation

Since most of our showers and tubs are custom installations, we sub out the enclosures. It usually takes about ten days to make up the tempered glass and get the installer on the job.

Some contractors like to install ready-made units themselves. Tub enclosures are relatively easy since their sliding doors are adjustable for plumb. Less expensive shower units typically have tolerances of at least one inch for out-of-plumb walls so they don't present an unusual challenge. Higher-end units with no fillers and tight tolerances should be left to a specialty installer. The glass will have to be cut out-of-square if the fit isn't near perfect.

Installations over fiberglass or acrylic shower units are straightforward; tile is a little trickier. Be sure to use a sharp carbide bit and a low-impact hammer drill. But first, check to see if the tile is at all loose where you'll be drilling. If it is, you're taking a chance of chipping or breaking it no matter how careful you are. And if the tile isn't replaceable, it goes without saying that you'll want to send in your best people to do the installing. Also, remember not to drill into the sill or curb; let gravity and silicone do the work. They both work great. (Our contractor uses GE Contractors 1000 Silicone or Sanitary White, which contains a mildew inhibitor.)

Maintenance

Unfortunately, you don't get the sleek look of clear glass with no maintenance. When soap-laden water dries on clear glass, it leaves a film of soap. Regular cleaning with clean water and a squeegee are needed to keep it spotless. There are also some glass cleaners with wax that will help water — and the soap and mineral film it carries — roll off the glass. But the homeowner will still have to scrub the glass and the metal occasionally. Some of the glass and metal cleaners that will cut through the residue are Hi-Sheen, Bath-Brite, and Lime-A-Way. The only caution is not to leave them on the metal over an extended period because they're acidic and can remove the finish. ■

Lynn Comeskey is a remodeling contractor who specializes in kitchens and baths. His firm, Mac & Lou Construction, is based in Mountain View, Calif.

Figure 3.
In remodels where the vanity abuts a shower, the author often leaves a short wall in place and tiles it. This works nicely with a neo-angle unit, as shown.

Neo-Angle Shower Remodel

Sources of Supply

Alumax
1617 N. Washington, P.O. Box 40
Magnolia, AR 71753
800/643-1514
501/234-4260

Basco
7201 Snider Rd.
Mason, OH 45040
800/543-1938

Century Shower Door, Inc.
250 Lackawanna Ave.
West Paterson, NJ 07424
800/524-2578
201/785-4290

Duschqueen, Inc.
40 Lawlins Park
Wyckoff, NJ 07481
800/348-8080
201/848-8081

Hansgrohe, Inc.
2840 Research Park Dr., Suite 100
Soquel, CA 95073
800/334-0455
408/479-0515

Kallista Inc.
2701 Merced St.
San Leandro, CA 94577
415/552-2500 (showroom)
516/895-6400 (manufacturer)

Kohler Co.
444 Highland Dr.
Kohler, WI 53044
414/457-4441

The Majestic Shower Company
1795 Yosemite Ave.
San Francisco, CA 94124
415/822-1511

Installing Jetted Tubs

by Gene Fleisch

Jetted tubs are a popular item in bath-room remodels, and often the most costly. Along with the high price tag comes high client expectations. If the tub installation is not what my customer had in mind, I probably won't get any referrals from the job — despite an otherwise perfect bath remodel.

A jetted tub, often referred to by the brand name "Jacuzzi," is a bathtub that massages the user with water circulated through a pumped system. Unlike spas or hot tubs, jetted tubs are emptied after every use, so they don't need a filtration system. I've installed dozens of jetted tubs in the past 12 years and, over that time, have developed an installation approach that satisfies even the fussiest clients.

In-House Design/Build

We work only from our own designs, and unlike most companies, we use virtually no subcontractors. This gives me full control over the project from the first meeting with the homeowners. Also, I know that my two workers and I will be the only ones who step into the tub during construction. If you have plumbers, electricians, painters, and other subs all stepping into the tub, you'll undoubtedly find damage, even to the most well-protected tub.

Doing in-house design also helps me educate the customer about the realistic cost of a project before the final plans are drawn. A jetted tub with enclosure typically costs over $5,000. In addition, the home often needs a second water heater near the new jetted tub. The cost of the new heater, and creating interior or exterior space for it, is significant, but an outside designer may overlook it.

I can also figure out the best way to position a tub to allow clear access to the motor and pump for maintenance, and not have a hatch in an unsightly place.

Once we have a rough plan and budget, I go with my clients to a reputable bath show-room. I offer advice about materials, accessibility, noise, heaters, and other options, but leave to them the final decision of which tub to buy. I've worked with acrylic tubs from Jacuzzi, Pearl, Kohler, and several other reputable companies and have had no problems with the materials or pumping equipment (see "Sources of Supply" at end of article). Once my clients have selected a tub, I sit down with them to resolve several key issues before drawing the final plans.

Tub accessibility. What good is a large jetted tub if it's difficult to get into or out of? Usually I install the tubs raised a couple of feet off the floor, but I've also installed them level with the floor, creating a sunken look. Most clients are more comfortable with raised tubs. Also, these are safer in homes with small children (see Figure 1, next page). I strongly recommend installing grab bars where possible to help with moving into and out of the tub and to prevent slips.

If the tub is also used as a shower, it's important to discuss enclosure options. On

The author installed contrasting floor and wall tile, grab bars, and a skylight above to make this tub area pleasing and functional.

many units I install a single swinging door, rather than the more common sliders (Figure 2). A swinging door at the shower end of the unit makes it easy to bathe children. And with the door swung open, soaking in the tub is a much less claustrophobic experience. I typically use a door made by Majestic Shower Company (1795 Yosemite Ave., San Francisco, CA 94124; 415/822-1511).

Tub size and color. Clients generally prefer large tubs that comfortably hold two people. It is important to let them know, however, that larger tubs can cramp a bathroom's

COURTESY OF KOHLER

▲

Figure 1. *Most customers choose a raised surround, which is safer than a sunken tub, particularly for children. The glass block window (at right, in photo above) provides privacy and easy maintenance.*

Figure 2. *For tub/shower combinations, the author prefers Majestic's single swinging door to sliders. The swinging door provides better access and feels less claustrophobic to bathers.* ▶

floor plan, not to mention that it can take forever to fill. I almost always recommend a white or beige unit, because the soap and mineral buildup isn't as obvious as with darker colors. Colored models need to be wiped down almost daily.

Noise. All jetted tubs make noise, both during filling and when the pump is running to circulate water. Most tubs I install are acrylic, which tends to magnify the sound. The installer can take steps to minimize this — which I'll discuss below — but the noise is often noticeable in adjoining rooms and in the room below. It's best to let your clients know about this in advance.

Windows and skylights. When designing a bath remodel, I pay careful attention to creating a feeling of openness around the tub. If the tub goes against a wall, a window helps with this. I recommend glass block because it is practical and attractive. Patterned glass block offers privacy and blends in nicely with the geometric pattern of the ceramic tile. Also, it is a lot easier to clean than the sliding metal windows commonly used here, and is less vulnerable to decay than wood windows.

Skylights also help create an open feeling and give bathers something more appealing than a blank ceiling to look up at. An operable skylight also offers quick natural ventilation for steam.

Trims and accents. A jetted tub is one of the few places in a home where someone may remain motionless for close to an hour. In that hour, details around the tub get noticed. So I view every time my client soaks in a tub as an opportunity to show off my design skills and craftsmanship. Whenever possible, I budget for extra attention to trim and finish details.

Framing and Rough-In

Installing a jetted tub is not a lot different than putting in an ordinary tub. But because they are typically deeper and heavier, and have electrical hookups, jetted tubs do have a few special requirements.

Floor concerns. Following demolition, I check out the floor framing where the tub is going to sit. With up to 400 pounds of water (50 gallons) plus two people in a jetted tub, I have to be sure the floor can handle over 800 pounds of weight distributed over a small area. For a typical installation, this works out to a load of about 60 pounds per square foot.

As a quick-and-dirty test, I jump up and down on a floor to see if it has a lot of deflection. If so, I add solid blocking or beef up the joists by sistering on 2xs. Sometimes the floor joists have been notched for the drainage of a pre-existing tub. In that case, I strengthen the cut joists by sistering on solid lumber. If the structure is too flimsy, or is seriously compromised by notching, you should get an engineer's opinion.

The floor should be close to level. If it's not, you'll need to adjust the framing of the surround so that the tub sits level.

Plumbing rough-in. New plumbing should be routed to the approximate drain location of the jetted tub. I prefer cast-iron drainage to ABS because it is quieter. Even

with cast iron, I let the client know that noise occurs when the tub drains. Leave an opening in the subfloor large enough to have good access for installing the drain, but not so large as to reduce the support under the belly of the tub.

As I mentioned before, we often need to add a large water heater near the jetted tub. Since the average tub holds about 45 gallons when filled, I recommend a 50-gallon water heater as a minimum size. I also plumb both the hot and cold water supplies with 3/4-inch copper. Half-inch supplies don't provide the rate of flow needed to fill a tub quickly. I make sure the copper pipe is secured to the

Jetted Tub Surround

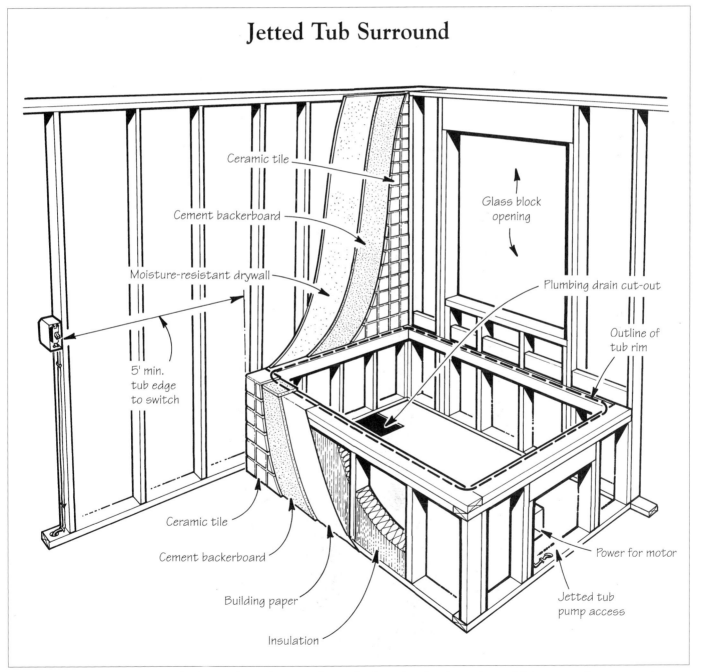

A typical tile tub surround by the author has sturdy 2x4 framing and is insulated to reduce heat loss and noise. Make sure you leave a convenient access panel for maintenance and repair of the pump system. Also, keep electrical switches at least 5 feet from the tub.

Shopping for a Tub

by Tom Harrison

Choosing a jetted tub is far more complicated than choosing a standard bathtub. There are at least two dozen manufacturers offering different sizes and shapes of tubs composed of various materials and with numerous options. A visit to a tub showroom can be a bewildering experience for a contractor, not to mention the client.

To help you and your client make the best selection, consider the following issues:

Acrylic tubs. The contractor wants a tub that can be cleaned up to look like new at the end of the job. The client wants a tub that will be easy to maintain years after the installation. For both of these purposes, I feel that acrylic is the best choice.

An acrylic tub is actually a $1/8$-inch-thick acrylic sheet that is heated and molded to the shape of a tub and laminated to a fiberglass structure. Because the acrylic is $1/8$ inch thick, even deep scratches can be sanded out with 400 or 600 grit sandpaper, and buffed out with baking soda. This can easily be done by the contractor or homeowner, saving the expense of a tub repair specialist.

Gel-coated tubs. It's important not to confuse acrylic tubs with gel-coat tubs. A gel-coat finish is an acrylic resin combination that is sprayed onto the fiberglass structure. The sprayed finish is just 125 mils thick. The thin finish produces a more economical tub but scratches are difficult to remove. Also, the gel-coat finish is far more porous than the acrylic type, making it nearly impossible to keep stain free. For example, a watercolor marker applied to this finish can never be completely removed.

Gel-coat finishes nearly killed the jetted tub industry a decade ago, as homeowners complained that their tubs were deteriorating in appearance soon after they were installed. Even a gel-coat tub straight out of the package will have a "wavy" finish because of the sprayed-on manufacturing process.

With few exceptions, both contractors and clients should steer away from this material. One important exception is with extra-deep tubs (approaching 3 feet), where the acrylic sheet finish will not work. A gel-coat tub may be the only choice. Also be aware of manufacturers' efforts to hide the bad name of "gel-coat" by using more technical language.

Cultured marble tubs. Cultured marble has a history of being temperature sensitive. If you've seen cultured marble sinks with "crazing" and discoloration around the drain, you've seen what can happen to a cultured marble tub. The damage occurs when very hot water hits the bottom of the tub, which is a lot cooler on the outside surface. The temperature differential produces hairline cracks, which fill with dirt or mineral deposits resulting in an ugly finish. One tub manufacturer has combated this problem by insulating the outside of the tub, but I'm not yet convinced that this works.

Other tubs. Cast-iron tubs with a porcelain finish are an option offered in a limited selection by a few manufacturers. These are high-quality products, but for larger tubs the weight is substantial. Also, scratches and chips almost always need to be dealt with by a specialist.

Self-leveling tubs. Don't believe it. When a manufacturer mentions their tub is "self leveling," all it means is that some kind of level base is adhered to the bottom of the tub. The base is usually plywood, with foam filling the gaps. While this is more substantial than the typical plastic pan, the floor must still be level under the tub for this installation to work. Also, in some cases, the base isn't perfectly level in relation to the rim of the tub. I recommend these "self-leveling" tubs be installed like other tubs with about a half a dozen pyramids of wet mortar underneath the tub belly. And don't get in the tub or fill with water until the mortar has dried.

Quiet tubs. If noise is a big concern, a contractor can look for tubs that have flexible hoses leading to and from the pump. This helps dampen vibration between the pump and the tub. Also, I often recommend that bolts be removed that connect the pump to the plastic pan under the tub. This allows the pump to freely vibrate on the surface of the pan instead of shaking the whole pan with it.

A word on jets. Jets, whether installed by the manufacturer or by a tub retailer, should have proper drainage so they don't allow

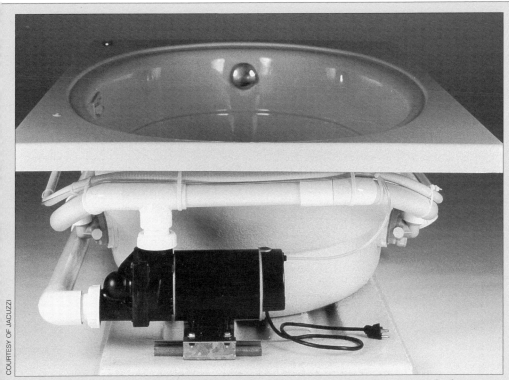

Tub material, jet location, and pump placement are key considerations when selecting a jetted tub.

standing water between uses. In California, tub retailers that do their own custom jetting are required to use IAPMO-labeled jets and be on the approved installer list of Underwriters Laboratory or another testing authority. Building inspectors in our area are trained to check these credentials. Check to see if tub retailers in your area follow similar guidelines.

Choosing jet locations in a tub requires clients to decide whether they want a jetted massage experience or a swirling pool. The former requires jets located near areas on the body that the client wants massaged like the lower or upper back, hips, or legs. If the client just wants a swirling pool of water that lightly massages the surface of the body, then the jets should be high and to the sides. In either case, it's best if the customer can get in a tub and try it out before buying.

Some tubs come with recessed back jets, which I'm fond of. With the jet recessed, the user's back can rest directly against the tub without an annoying protrusion.

Pump location. When ordering the tub, there is one option that the contractor will be very interested in: pump location. Most tubs come with the pump opposite the fill and drain end of the the tub, tucked into the area created by the sloped backrest. Some manufacturers will allow you to request one of the corners for pump location, while other man-

ufacturers just center the pump unit. Plan the pump location for clear access for maintenance and repair.

If the access door needs to be on an exterior wall, preprimed metal-hinged doors, some of which are designed to receive stucco on the surface can be a good solution. These doors come in a variety of sizes and are more durable than a site-built wood door. One supplier I've used is Karp (5454 43rd St., Maspeth, NY 11378; 800/888-4212).

Tub accessories. According to budget and preference, there are many options available to the client. About half of the tubs I sell have heaters to help maintain the temperature of the water during a long bath. Larger tubs need larger heaters. Jets that can be turned indiviually on and off are becoming more popular. Built-in grab bars are important to consider, but clients may not know they need one until they stand up after soaking in hot water for nearly an hour. Cushions and arm rests are also popular items to add to a tub.

Finally, before picking up the tub and taking it to the job site, make sure that it has been water tested. It's better to find a problem in the warehouse than after the tub has been installed. ■

Tom Harrison has sold jetted tubs for 15 years. He owns Tubz in Fremont, Calif.

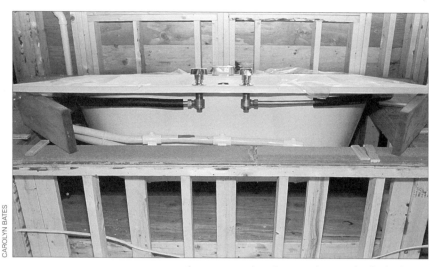

CAROLYN BATES

Figure 3. *After lifting the tub into place to test the fit, the author lifts it out again in order to lay wet mortar under the base.*

framing with plastic clips, which help to reduce noise.

Jetted tubs have three or more options for where the faucet set can mount on the wall or deck. I'm careful to not rush my clients about where to locate the controls, the showerhead, or the tub spout. I encourage them to get in the tub and imagine taking a shower or bath, and always emphasize ease of use over aesthetics. After the tile goes on, changes are expensive.

Tub walls. A jetted tub needs short walls framed under the rim wherever it's not against a wall (see illustration, page 113). I build this support structure out of 2x4s and size it to hold the tub about $1^{1}/2$ inches above the subfloor. This leaves room for a mortar base (explained below). In designs that have an extended deck, I put a plywood top on the platform.

When building the platform, make sure you plan for good access to the pump. I've hidden access doors in vanity cabinets and back walls of closets. Where a hatch needs to be in plain view in a bathroom, I've installed cabinet doors that match the style and finish of the vanity doors.

Where the tub abuts a wall, I prefer to install it directly against the wall framing with the lip resting on a ledger. This allows the tile to come down over the rim of the tub, and eliminates a cavity where soap and water can collect.

After we finish framing the tub support walls, we insulate around the pump and tub with fiberglass batts to cut down the noise. The insulation also helps keep the tub water warm. At the framing stage, you should also install 2x8 or 2x10 blocking wherever you might want to install a grab bar.

Setting the Tub

At least two, and sometimes three, workers are needed to set the tub, which can weigh up to 200 pounds and be very awkward. With the

framing complete, I wrap the adjacent walls and short walls of the tub with building paper, and — if there's a plywood top — cut a hole for the tub to rest in. We then muscle the tub into place and make sure it fits (Figure 3).

Mortar base. Next, I mix about a cubic foot of mortar, keeping it thick, and mound it on a piece of building paper underneath the belly of the tub but away from the drain. We then lift the tub back into position, working it into the mortar until the rim sits flush with the deck.

Although installation instructions are not clear on this point, I feel the mortar is essential for a solid base. Some tubs have fittings on the bottom to receive wood shims, and others have an inverted plastic pan on the bottom that screws to the subfloor for support. I use the mortar with these as well for the added stiffness it provides.

Flashing. At least one major tub manufacturer includes a plastic "J" flashing to be installed around the perimeter of the tub rim for waterproofing. While this seems like a good idea in theory, we haven't found a way to bend the flashing neatly around the tub corners unless the flashing is scored with a knife, which undermines its purpose: to keep water from leaking onto the deck. I discard the flashing and seal the unit as described below. Other builders I've spoken with do likewise.

Plumbing connections. You should never seal the drain flange with standard plumber's putty because it's not compatible with acrylic tubs. Acrylic tub instructions recommend the use of silicone sealants, which can be matched to the color of the tub. A word of warning, however: When threading on a brass drain, make sure you select a sealant that states that it does not react with brass. Some silicones are okay to use; some aren't. I generally use Dap 50-year silicone.

After the tub is in place, the drain overflow assembly can be installed. I prefer the air-activated pop-ups over the manual type. The manual types are clumsy to adjust and noisy, while the air-activated ones are easy to adjust and operate smoothly.

Wiring. A jetted tub may require up to a 30-amp dedicated circuit if it has a heater, as about half of the ones I install do. Besides being GFCI-protected, the motor and pump unit are required in our area to be bound together by a #8 ground wire. Also, when wiring switches around the tub, I make sure to keep them 5 feet away from the rim of the tub, as required by code in my area.

I also install a high-volume bath fan near the jetted tub to help ventilate the room. I've

Waterproofing Details

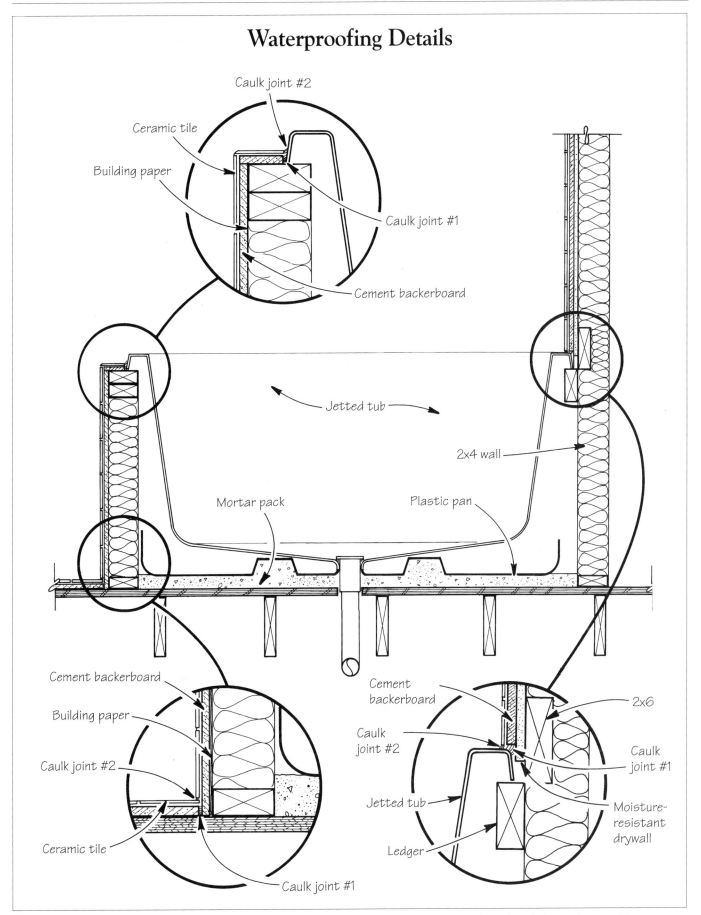

Caulk joint #2

Ceramic tile

Building paper

Caulk joint #1

Cement backerboard

Jetted tub

2x4 wall

Mortar pack

Plastic pan

Cement backerboard

Building paper

Caulk joint #2

Ceramic tile

Caulk joint #1

Cement backerboard

Caulk joint #2

Jetted tub

Ledger

2x6

Caulk joint #1

Moisture-resistant drywall

For a long-lasting watertight seal at the tub lip, the author makes a double caulk joint: backerboard to tub and tile to tub, using 50-year silicone sealant. At the wall, the tub generally goes directly against the framing so there's no space for soap and water to collect. Wet mortar packed under the base of the tub provides rigidity.

had good luck with the Nutone QT Series fan rated at 110 cfm.

Finishing Touches

Now that the tub is plumbed and wired, I check on the operation of the controls, make sure there aren't any leaks, and test the jets. After everything checks out, it's important to protect the tub. I use cardboard, often provided with the tub packaging, and cover it with a thick canvas cloth taped securely to the tub. We use the blue 3M painter's tape because it doesn't leave a hard-to-clean gummy residue when it comes off.

Tile work. I do a lot of thinset granite and tile work and often set accent strips of contrasting color tile around the tub. Another nice touch we add to many jobs is a recessed niche for soap or shampoo. Both items take more tile cutting, but help my jobs stand out among the competition.

Creating a lasting watertight seal around the rim of a jetted tub is a big concern. Because of flexing caused by the constant filling and emptying of the tub, plus the vibration of the pump, it's important that the seal around the tub rim be flexible.

To address this I make a double seal at the rim: using Dap 50-year silicone, I caulk my cement board underlayment directly to the tub around the entire perimeter, and I caulk, rather than grout, the joint between the tile and tub rim (see illustration, previous page). I make a similar seal where the short tub walls meet the floor, because water tends to collect in this joint. I also caulk around all penetrations in the tile wall where water might seep in, including where grab bars screw into blocking.

Trim and wall finishes. I'm a firm believer in oil-base enamels, because they look better and are more durable in the harsh moisture conditions surrounding a jetted tub. All wood trim and drywall surfaces get an oil-base primer and oil-base topcoat. After they are primed, I sand the walls with a #120 sanding screen to improve the bonding between coats and make a smooth topcoat. (The sanding screen doesn't gum up like sandpaper.)

All joints in the room between wood trim and the wall get caulked with a flexible sealant to prevent moisture from seeping in.

Tub finishes. After the tile is complete, the escutcheon plates, handles, and showerhead go on. It's best to keep the tub protection in place for these and other finishing touches, because dropping parts or tools is inevitable. After the protection comes off, the tub will need to be cleaned to get off dirt, adhesives, and grout. Use a non-abrasive cleanser that meets the manufacturer's specifications, such as the household cleaners 409 or Fantastic. When the job is done, and for years after, your customers will appreciate the attention to detail you've given to both aesthetics and function. ■

Gene Fleisch is a remodeling contractor in Atherton, Calif.

Sources of Supply

American Standard
P.O. Box 6820
Piscataway, NJ 08855
800/524-9797, ext 100

Aquatic Industries
P.O. Box 889
Leander, TX 78641
512/259-2255

Caldera
1080 W. Bradley Ave.
El Cajon, CA 92020
619/562-5120

HessCo Industries
160 E. Foundation
La Habra, CA 90631
800/854-3465

Hydro Swirl
2150 Division St.
Bellingham, WA 98226
206/734-0616

Hydro Systems
50 Moreland Rd.
Simi Valley, CA 93065
805/584-9990

Jacuzzi
2121 N. California Blvd.
Walnut Creek, CA 94596
800/678-6889

Jason Intl.
8328 MacArthur Dr.
North Little Rock, AR 72118
800/255-5766

Kohler Company
444 Highland Dr.
Kohler, WI 53044
414/457-4441

Pearl Baths
9224 73rd Ave.
Minneapolis, MN 55428
800/328-2531

Sunset Plastics
6270 Parallel Rd.
Anderson, CA 96007
916/365-5494

Swirl-way Plumbing Group
1505 Industrial Dr.
Henderson, TX 75653
800/999-1459

Plastic Tub/Shower Units

by Paul Spring

All plastic bath fixtures are not alike. In most cases, you get what you pay for.

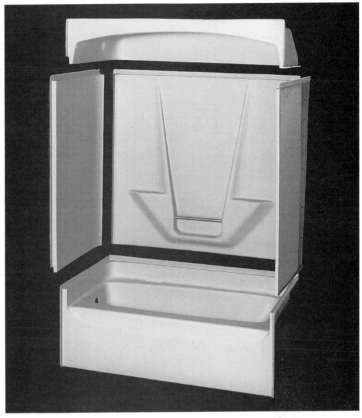

Remodeling combos, like this domed, five-piece unit from Aker Plastics, fit through any doorway, but have to be assembled in place with fasteners and caulk.

Plastic tub/shower units come in a much wider range of quality than most builders realize. And there are a number of new materials to choose from. Here's an overview of what's available, along with some important installation tips.

No Longer One Material

Tub/shower combos (as well as shower modules and bath surrounds) can be made from a half dozen polymer plastics. The two most common are the original *gelcoat* product, and its more expensive challenger, *acrylic*. These two represent the broad middle of the market, with gelcoat at the lower end and acrylic at the upper. Both of these surfaces are used with substrate materials to form a structural laminate. The greatest demands are on the surface layer: It has to be glossy, scratch resistant, repairable, and shouldn't stain or fade. That's a tall order, and each material presents different tradeoffs.

Gelcoat. A pigmented polyester resin, gelcoat is sprayed on a mold in a thin layer, about $1/64$ inch thick when dry. Once it's cured, fiberglass (technically called FRP, or "fiberglass reinforced plastic") is applied to the back in several applications that add up to about $1/8$ inch. This provides strength and most of the bulk. Gelcoated units are often referred to as "fiberglass" even though fiberglass is also used as the backing material for acrylic tubs.

Gelcoat isn't as hard as acrylic, and will scratch and dull over time (most manufacturers suggest a coat of automotive wax to protect it and keep it shiny). It's also not as stain resistant, and is susceptible to caustics such as drain lye. However, gelcoated units cost about half as much as acrylic-faced ones, and can be restored to original appearance by a trained repair worker at the local level.

Acrylic. The lamination of an acrylic tub/shower is similar to that of a gelcoat unit, except that the acrylic begins as a thick sheet ($1/4$ inch for tubs; $3/16$ inch for tub/shower modules) that is heated and vacuum-molded to a form. Then a fiberglass-reinforced laminate is applied to the back for strength.

Although acrylic is known for its durability and high gloss, petrochemical solvents will dull the surface. Repairs have to be made by a factory-trained technician, who may be hard to come by. Further, acrylic tub repairs below the water line may not last the life of the unit.

Both acrylic and gelcoated laminations

use additional materials, called "inclusions," for bulk and rigidity. These can include corrugated paper, foam, balsa or other types of wood and wood composites, and chemical and mineral fillers. Although the industry is full of claims and counterclaims about which material is best, most achieve the goal of a strong, lightweight section that won't delaminate over time.

Other plastics. The other materials used for tub/shower combinations aren't susceptible to delaminating because they're monolithic. These account for both the very lowest end of the market (high-gloss ABS and acrylic-fortified PVC), and the high end (sheet-molded compounds, or SMCs).

SMCs are made from chopped glass fibers, polyester resins, and fillers that are compression-molded into a very strong, rigid product with color throughout. This allows tub supports and even interlocking pins for joining panels to be molded in. One manufacturer, Sterling Plumbing Group, Inc., has had real success with its brand-name SMC product, Vikrell, despite a relatively high price tag.

Shapes, Sizes, and Features

All manufacturers offer numerous colors with both acrylic and gelcoated modules. Color does raise the price of the unit by $20 to $50; white remains the most popular. Most tub/showers also come with a slip-resistant floor, and a choice of the drain on the left, right, or in some cases, center.

Models. The classic tub/shower is a one-piece gelcoated unit (see Figure 1), but all manufacturers offer "remodeling" units that are designed to fit through standard door openings ranging from 2'-4" to 2'-8". These are broken down into two or more pieces (the tub counts as one) that lock, bolt, screw, or caulk together. The tubs themselves typically rely on a simple nailing flange or require a 1x ledger for support. Some, however, use a system of clips that attach to the tub rim and nail to the studs.

Both for ease of installation and watertightness, the fewer pieces the better. It pays to examine both the joining system and how the pieces are configured. For instance, some four-piece systems (a tub and the three walls of the surround) join right at the tub's rim. But many others, such as the one made by Aker Plastics Co. Inc.,

Tub Installation Tips

In general, the installation literature of most manufacturers is pretty good, and the procedures are straightforward. However, here are a few tips garnered from conversations with plumbers, contractors, and manufacturers:

• Inspect any plastic tub or shower module with care before accepting delivery; most damage happens in transit.

• Leave the unit in its packing with the 1x4 in place across the opening as long as possible. Check with the supplier to make sure it can be stored outside; some can't because the inclusions they use will absorb moisture.

• The framed "pocket" that the unit slides into should be about 1/8 inch oversize. Don't ever force a module into place; the stress you put on it can show up in the finish a few years later.

• None of these units acts as a firestop. Check to see if you need drywall behind the surround.

• *Always* drill for plumbing from the finished side, and use masking tape so you don't scratch the finish.

• Use galvanized roofing nails (1 to 2 inches long) for fastening a gelcoat unit to the studs, predrilling if necessary.

• Consider using non-rusting screws (#8s by 1½ inches) for acrylic, which doesn't repair easily if you should happen to miss with a hammer.

• While checking for plumb and level, tack the corners of the tub first, and then nail in from each side at the top of the wall surround to make sure you don't permanently rack the unit.

• It isn't necessary to "bed" any of these units in plaster to meet minimal standards. However, if you shim beneath them, or better yet, "wet set" them in drywall mud, clean mortar, or industrial casting plaster, it will eliminate much of the "give" that some consumers find objectionable in the floor of the unit. It will also cut down sub-

stantially on the chances of having a problem later on.

• If the module includes a whirlpool, "wet setting" is important in reducing vibration and noise.

• However, don't set the tub bottom on sand (you can't contain it), or foam (some will break down after a while).

• Some manufacturers also recommend using panel adhesive and 1xs or plywood to shim the walls of the surround to the existing walls, creating a more solid feel.

• Take the time to use 1/8-inch furring beside the nailing flanges so the drywall stays flat.

• Stay out of the bathing well when installing; damage below the waterline is more than a cosmetic issue.

• Make sure you follow the particular manufacturer's installation instructions; warranties are strictly enforced along these lines.

— P.S.

make the break about 6 to 8 inches above the tub (see lead photo).

Most gelcoated and acrylic units require fasteners and caulking as well as a system of overlaps to make the connections between the panels watertight. Even systems that claim not to need caulking to prevent leaks sometimes suggest using a bead of silicone at corner seams to fill in where soap scum and mildew could accumulate.

SMC units by Swan Corp. and Sterling rely on proprietary systems of factory-installed clips and receiving channels, or molded, interlocking "pins" that allow panels to snap together in a watertight seal without the use of caulk.

Tub/showers that incorporate accessible design for the handicapped and elderly are also produced in both one-piece and remodeling configurations. These are usually equipped with larger diameter (1¼- to 1½-inch) grab bars in code-required locations, and often include removable seats.

Accessories. Most tub/shower designs incorporate at least one soap dish; some sport up to four ledges and niches. These not only provide depth and interest to an otherwise flat wall, they help stiffen the panel to keep it from deflecting (called "oil canning" by manufacturers).

Most units also have a built-in central grab bar that averages 12 to 18 inches long. Major manufacturers design these ³/₄-inch to 1¼-inch stainless-steel or clear acrylic bars to meet voluntary ASTM Consumer Safety Specifications. That means they'll support a 250-pound load. Check for certification to be sure.

Most units can also accommodate larger-diameter, contractor-supplied grab bars bolted to shower walls, although they often have to be backed up with solid material where the bars attach. Some manufacturers instruct you to do this yourself just prior to installation; others will incorporate the backing in the fiberglass if you specify it on your order. But ignoring this need could mean tearing the unit out later in order to retrofit it.

Bells and whirlpools. Many tub/showers can be fitted with a whirlpool, but don't assume this. These units need a removable skirt or access panel for servicing the motor and jets, and enough room to accommodate the plumbing and electricals.

Still another luxury is a steam generator; this requires a domed unit with tightly sealed doors (Figure 2). Acrylic is the best

Figure 1. *This single-piece, gelcoated unit from Lasco is designed for new construction. Measuring 60 inches wide, 72 inches high, and 32 inches front-to-back, it can accommodate a matching dome to create an enclosed module.*

Figure 2. *Aqua Glass's Maxima II is a 72-inch-wide acrylic unit that includes a whirlpool, steam unit, and shower all in one.*

finish for steam since gelcoat can develop pinhole blisters after a few years.

Judging Quality and Price

Although there is a wide range of quality in tub/shower units, pricing is a fairly good indicator in this industry — you typically get what you pay for.

Standards. Most manufacturers subscribe to ANSI Z124.1 for tubs, and ANSI Z124.2 for showers, which dictate minimum finish thickness and durability, as well as structural integrity. Whether a manufacturer goes beyond these standards is often hard to determine. And with both acrylic and gelcoat, the quality of the workmanship is as important as the type and thickness of the material. With either, you should examine the finish for blisters, delamination, dull patches, crazing (especially in corners), and thin sections that allow light to pass through.

When it comes to structural integrity, the good units don't rack quite as easily, and you can tell a lot from lightly bouncing on the bottom of a tub that's fixed in place. All tub bottoms incorporate support (from plywood, composite board, balsa, or softwood slats) with polyester resin and fiberglass, but some are less bouncy than others.

But the best gauge for quality is still the manufacturer's track record. Take the time to ask your supplier which lines have the least problems and the best manufacturer support, including in-place repair if it's ever needed.

Cost. An average one-piece, tub/shower unit runs about $200 to $250 in gelcoat; a similar acrylic unit will cost about twice that.

Larger acrylic units with luxury features from manufacturers like Kohler can cost well over $1,000. And multi-piece remodeling units run about 30% more than comparable one-piece modules.

You can expect to pay a bit less for locally or regionally produced brands because of the lower transportation costs of some national manufacturers.

Warranties. Warranty periods tend to be all over the map, though there's a definite middle ground. A few manufacturers have stayed with only one year, while Sterling warranties Vikrell for 10 years in a residential setting, and Swan offers 20 years on its tub and surround. More typical are companies that warranty their gelcoat products for three years, and their acrylic units for five. ■

Paul Spring was formerly editor of the western edition of The Journal of Light Construction.

Sources of Supply

For more information on units mentioned in this article, contact:

Aker Plastics Co. Inc.
P.O. Box 484
Plymouth, IN 46563
800/348-2211
219/936-3838

Aqua Glass Corp.
P.O. Box 412
Adamsville Industrial Park
Adamsville, TN 38310
901/632-0911

Bathease
2537 Frisco Dr.
Clearwater, FL 34621
813/791-6656

Kohler Co.
444 Highland Dr.
Kohler, WI 53044
414/457-4441

Lasco Products
3255 E. Miraloma Ave.
Anaheim, CA 92806
800/795-2726
714/993-1220

Sterling Plumbing Group, Inc.
2900 Golf Rd.
Rolling Meadows, IL 60008
708/734-1777

Swan Corporation
One City Centre, Suite 2300
St. Louis, MO 63101
800/325-7008
314/231-8148

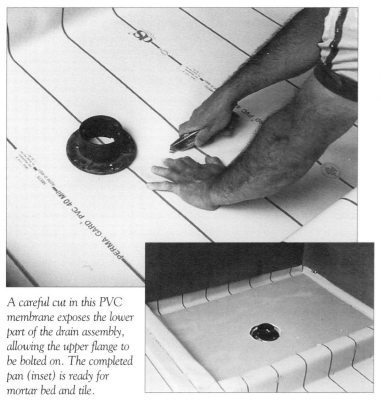

A careful cut in this PVC membrane exposes the lower part of the drain assembly, allowing the upper flange to be bolted on. The completed pan (inset) is ready for mortar bed and tile.

Leakproof Shower Pans

by Scott Duncan

With a plastic liner and attention to detail, there's no excuse for a leaky shower floor

Considering the damage they do over time if they fail, it's amazing how little architects, general contractors, and homeowners know about shower pans. Anyone who has worked in remodeling has seen the damage. The leaks usually start very slowly and continue to get worse, often going undetected for a number of years. In that time, the water can cause thousands of dollars worth of damage. Subflooring, joists, girders, even exterior siding can be completely rotted away.

One of the reasons that pans get so little attention is that lots of people assume a good tile job is completely waterproof. Most aren't. It depends on the width of the grout joints, and the type of tile, grout, grout additives, reinforcing wire, attachment, and tile backing used. That's why any tile subjected to a lot of water, especially in a horizontal application like a shower floor, must have a waterproof liner beneath it.

Years ago, most pans were metal; they had sides and soldered corners, and looked like pans. These days, shower pans are also made of hot-mopped felt, fiberglass, elastomeric coatings, and several kinds of plastic fabrics. I've tried most of them, but I think plastic membranes offer the greatest longevity with very few disadvantages.

Plastic Pans

In the Pacific Northwest where I worked for a number of years, plastic pans are about all you see. Although they haven't been around as long as metal or hot-mopped pans, I've never seen a problem with one that wasn't the result of poor installation. They are generally considered to have a life expectancy in the 50-year range, and I suspect they'll last a lifetime.

There are other reasons to use plastic. Unlike metal or hot-mopped pans, there's just one sub to deal with: the tile setter. This eliminates the scheduling hassles of getting a metal pan made up and installed, or making sure the hot mopper gets to the job when he's supposed to. It also keeps the tile contractors happy because they have complete control over the quality of the work that goes into the pan, and they get to take home the profit from the pan installation.

There are two basic types of plastic shower pan membranes: *CPE*, which stands for chlorinated polyethylene, and *PVC*, or polyvinyl chloride. With either material, you should make sure that your tile setter is using the 40-mil (not the 30- or 20-mil) version, not only because it is more difficult to puncture, but also because codes often call for this thickness.

The brand of CPE membrane I use is

called *Chloraloy* (made by The Noble Co., 614 Monroe St., Box 350, Grand Haven, MI 49417; 616/842-7844). The Noble Company was one of the first to manufacture a plastic pan material, and they did it right. It uses a fusion cement for seams that makes them as strong as the material itself, and preformed inside and outside corners are available to help at intersections. Chloraloy is guaranteed for 50 years, and claims superiority over PVC because it is less susceptible to microorganism growth (although I've never heard of a case of either PVC or CPE deteriorating).

There are a couple of disadvantages to Chloraloy: price and workability. Even though the material is the standard 40 mils thick, it works more like it's 60 mils. When it's less than 60°F, Chloraloy loses some of its flexibility, and a hot air gun is helpful in folding corners.

As for PVC products, there are a number of manufacturers of shower pan membranes. Compotite Corp. (Box 26188, Los Angeles, CA 90026; 800/221-1056) and Pasco Specialty & Manufacturing (11156 Wright Rd., Linwood, CA 90262; 310/537-7782) both make good liners, but my current favorite in the PVC category is made by Dallas Specialty & Manufacturing Company (1161 Ruggles, Grand Prairie, TX 75050; 800/222-5644). Like other plastic liner manufacturers, Dallas Specialty uses a proprietary cement to fuse folds and seams, and they sell preformed corners.

This liner is more pliable than Chloraloy and a good deal cheaper. It runs a little more than 50¢ a square foot; less than one third the price of Chloraloy. You also have a choice of 5- or 6-foot widths. A 5-foot-wide roll works fine for a standard 3x3-foot shower, but on oversized showers, the extra foot often saves me the considerable time required to seam the material.

Another nice bonus with this product is that it has been tested by most of the pertinent building code agencies and has the approvals stamped right on the pan material. This can make a difference to building inspectors who normally want

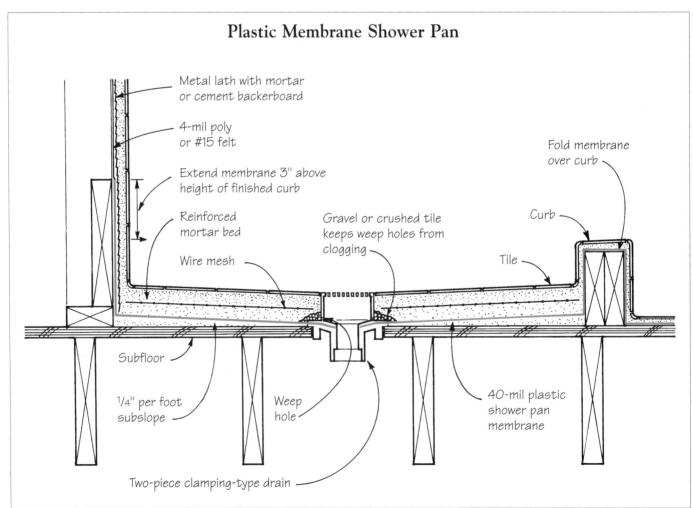

Plastic Membrane Shower Pan

Metal lath with mortar or cement backerboard

4-mil poly or #15 felt

Extend membrane 3" above height of finished curb

Reinforced mortar bed

Wire mesh

Gravel or crushed tile keeps weep holes from clogging

Fold membrane over curb

Curb

Tile

Subfloor

¼" per foot subslope

Weep hole

40-mil plastic shower pan membrane

Two-piece clamping-type drain

Figure 1. *In a typical tiled shower, the pan liner extends above the curb height on walls and is sealed in place by the two-part subdrain assembly. Any moisture that penetrates the tile floor and accumulates will exit through weep holes.*

backup literature if they aren't familiar with the product you're using. Dallas Specialty also makes a nice drain that is adjustable in height and can be fused to the pan material.

Prep Work

The shower pan works in tandem with the drain by carrying to it any water that has leaked through the tile floor. That's why shower pans need to be sloped and need a drain with weep holes. Sounds simple, but at one point a number of years ago tiled showers were almost written out of the codes because their flat floors and sealed drains created what is called a *concealed fouling space*. Translated, that means that the standing water in this space is a fertile environment for decay-producing microorganisms, as well as acids and salts.

The drain needed to avoid this problem is the two-piece clamping-type, sometimes referred to as a subdrain assembly. The plastic liner clamps between the two pieces of the drain, which is held tightly by three bolts (see Figure 1). The weep holes are in the top flange between the bolt heads.

A shower pan must have at least a 1/4-inch-per-foot slope to the weep holes (Figure 2). In my area, the general contractor is responsible for this sloped floor, which is usually built by a carpenter on the job using shims and plywood over the existing subfloor. If I'm doing it myself, I use a dry mix of sand and cement, about 4:1, to get the proper slope. Unfortunately, this usually means an extra trip to the site because the mortar has to set up before I can put the pan on it.

Another requirement for the shower bottom (metal pans are the exception) is continuous blocking between the studs to a height of 4 inches above the rough curb. In my area 2x10s or 2x12s are commonly used, nailed flush between the studs.

This works out well when the wall tile is laid on mortar, as I hope it is. The vapor barrier and reinforcing wire overlap the pan at least 2 inches, and then everything ends up in the same plane. But with cement backerboard or (heaven forbid) drywall, the studs must be notched or the sheet material furred out to keep everything flat.

Installing the Pan

Plastic pan materials come in rolls of 50, 100, and 200 feet, and can be laid out and cut on any flat surface where there are no sharp projections.

Figure 2. *The author used a dry mortar mix to create the slope to the drain in this shower. The two parts of the drain assembly are shown here. The weep holes are visible on the top part of the bolting flange, at left of the drain.*

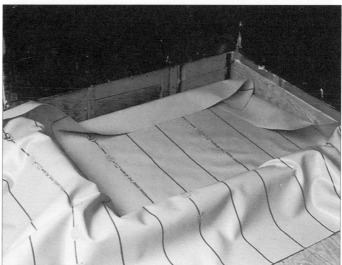

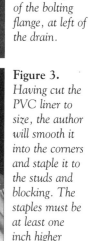

Figure 3. *Having cut the PVC liner to size, the author will smooth it into the corners and staple it to the studs and blocking. The staples must be at least one inch higher than the finish curb.*

The pan should run up the wall at least 3 inches above the height of the finished curb; this typically means allowing 9 to 10 inches of material on each wall. The membrane should also wrap around any jambs and fasten on the outside of them. The same is true of the rough threshold.

If a seam is required, it needs to be done carefully. Following the manufacturer's directions, your tile setter will coat both sides of the seam with bonding cement and create at least a 2-inch overlap. Seams should be pressed together firmly with a seam roller. Drying times vary for different materials, but I err on the cautious side when I can by letting them dry overnight.

Before draping the pan loosely in place (Figure 3), it's important to sweep the shower floor clean and check for anything that could puncture the membrane. With a wood subfloor, I also like to round off the drain cutout with my utility knife to make sure it's smooth, and I always check the two parts of the drain to see if they mate cleanly. I file off any little bumps of metal left

Metal Pans & Other Options

Working the tile trade in both Washington and California, I've seen a multitude of leaky shower pans. Some failed because of poor installation; others failed over time because the material just wasn't up to the job.

Metal Pans

Metal pans — lead, copper, and galvanized steel — have the reputation in some quarters for being the best water protection you can get. They are definitely expensive. In the case of copper or galvanized steel, the pan is fabricated by a sheet-metal shop, and then brazed to the bottom flange of the drain. They're typically installed by plumbers.

Electrolysis is a problem with metal pans. Since they are attached to a drain of a dissimilar metal (brass or cast iron), a dielectric (nonconducting) fitting must be used. If it's not, this joint will deteriorate rapidly. I have replaced shower floors where, once the tile and mortar were removed, you could lift the copper pan straight up and out without even touching the drain. It looked as if someone had cut around the drain with tin snips.

Even the interaction of the mortar bed and the metal pan, when saturated with water, will create problems. Once the metal pan is installed, it must be completely protected from contact. The best way to do this is to hot mop over the metal pan, but that strikes me as an awful lot of work and expense. Still, you frequently see them specced this way.

Another problem with these pans is that they must be fabricated in advance. A change in shower size, or the addition of a shower seat at the last minute means someone is going to have to buy a new shower pan.

With all of these obstacles, why specify a metal pan? I can only guess that there are still some designers who feel that if it costs more money (as long as it's not their own) and takes more time (still not their own), it must be better.

Hot-Mop Pans

These are the most popular in California, although their popularity seems to be waning with the increased awareness of alternatives. In some parts of the country it's difficult, if not impossible, to find someone who can install a hot-mop shower, and there are air-quality issues with heating the tar as well.

A hot-mop shower pan should consist of three layers of felt, each swabbed in place with hot tar. The Ceramic Tile Institute specs call for a woven-glass fiber webbing in the corners for reinforcement, but this isn't common practice.

Good hot moppers can do a 3x3-foot shower in about a half hour. They typically charge $100 to $150. A bad hot mopper will charge the same amount, but will create a buildup of tar in the corners, which makes it a real challenge to get the tile on the walls flat and plumb.

Hot-mop jobs will withstand a lot of abuse prior to installation of the tile. It is fairly common to have the hot mopper come in before the drywall is hung, and I've seen drywall nails and screws mashed into these pans without a hint of a leak. But asphalt does tend to get brittle and deteriorate over time. From my experience, I'd set their life expectancy at 12 to 25 years. (However, I have been told that overheating the tar, which is common, reduces the pan's life.)

Elastomeric Membranes

These are premixed formulas that are either troweled or brushed on. Some require the use of a fiberglass matting embedded in the membrane. I never use these in a stall shower. They are difficult to apply properly and have a high chance of failure. In addition, they're very messy to work with and usually require at least two applica-

tions. Plus, I don't know of an elastomeric membrane that bridges gaps with any success. This is important since, at the very least, you'll have cracks where the floor meets the walls.

The few times I've used elastomeric membranes, they all failed the first water test, and I had to coat the entire pan again. I also had one shower pass the original water test, but develop a leak a year later.

Roman Tub Choices

Since the purpose of these tiled tubs is to hold standing water, choosing a membrane system and installing it carefully is vital.

If the rough tub is formed in concrete, then hot mop is definitely the best method. If the tub is made of wood, then fiberglass is typically required. Anybody experienced in working with fiberglass tape and resin can do a tub liner quite easily because it doesn't have to be beautiful, just watertight.

Although plastic liners are my first choice for shower pans, I shy away from them in Roman tubs. The Noble Company, a leading manufacturer of CPE plastic liners, recommends that their Roman tub membranes be preformed in their factory with the seams *dielectrically heat welded*, not just glued. Something I worry about even more is sealing the protrusions — air jets and overflows — from the sides of the tub. Even if you do get a seal that passes a water test, it's going to have to last for the life of the pan. Pretty risky.

But if you want to be absolutely sure your tub won't leak, use fiberglass and then hot mop over it. This may sound like overkill, but fiberglass liners are susceptible to cracking if there's movement in the framing, so the extra $400 or so is cheap insurance when you consider your liability from a leaking tub. Since many Roman tubs are upstairs in master bathrooms, you can imagine the nightmare a leak could produce.

— *S.D.*

over from the casting process, since they could interfere with a good seal.

The easiest way to attach the liner to the surrounding framing is with a staple gun. Make sure the staples are in the top inch of the material (or at least one inch above the height of the finished curb).

Corners take time. Inside corners require a fold sometimes described as a "pig's ear" (Figure 4). The bonding fluid helps the folds lay flat. Outside corners, like you find on an L-shaped shower, are the most difficult. They have to be done in place and require several patches and lots of solvent.

I install the drain last. I cut a small hole in the pan over the center of the drain so that I can put a bead of butyl caulk between the bottom flange of the drain and the underside of the plastic pan (Figure 5). At least one membrane manufacturer claims this isn't necessary, but I have seen showers leak due to a poor seal here. It's important not to trim out for the bolt holes, but just to pierce the membrane slightly at each location. Once the bolts have been pushed through the material, they can be tightened evenly but firmly with a socket wrench.

Finishing Up

Every pan needs to be tested. No tile setter wants to hear that a pan is leaking, but it's better to hear it now than after the tile is in.

The test should be done over the period of a day with enough water to fill the pan at least an inch above the top of the drain. Make sure a test plug is used in the throat of the drain. I've seen tile setters leave the membrane inside the drain intact and use it instead of a drain plug. This ignores the fact that one common place for a pan to leak is between the bottom flange and the underside of the membrane.

After the pan tests out, there's one small but important last step before floating in the mortar bed: Protect the weep holes from getting plugged with mortar. Almost anything — gravel, broken tile, a handful of spacers — can be used as a barrier around the drain.

Creating the mortar bed is pretty straightforward, but there are two things that the mortar shouldn't be without. The first is a waterproofing additive (I use a product called Anti-Hydro, from Anti-Hydro International, Inc., 265 Badger Ave., Newark, NJ 07108; 800/777-1773). This will reduce the amount of water (up to 85%) absorbed by the mortar bed. This, in

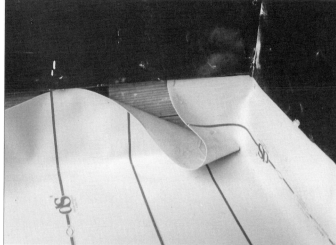

Figure 4. *Inside corners require a fold known as a "pigs ear" (left). Use solvent to keep the fold tight to the wall (below).*

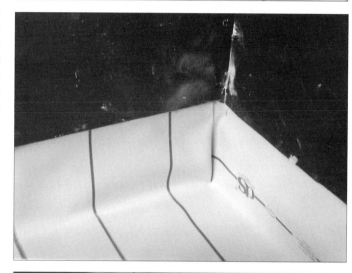

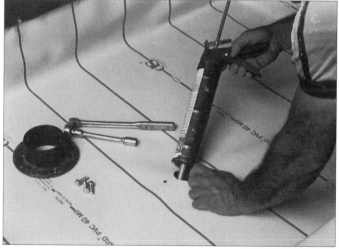

Figure 5. *Using a small access hole cut at the drain throat, the author caulks the base flange of the drain before bolting down the top half. Once the pan is water tested, he will pack gravel around the drain to keep the weep holes from clogging up with mortar when the floor is floated.*

turn, reduces the amount of water the shower pan has to deal with. The other thing to look for is reinforcing wire in the bed. It will go a long way toward preventing cracks, and it's another indication that you're getting a quality job. ■

Scott Duncan of Classic Enterprises, in Saratoga, Calif., has been setting tile for 26 years.

Sauna Design & Construction

by Steve Andrews

Traditional design and grade-A materials will guarantee you a successful product

The word "sauna" refers to a special kind of cleansing, relaxing, dry-heat bath and to the room in which it is taken. Sauna rooms must be built to withstand temperatures in the 170°F to 200°F range, plus exposure to sweat, splashed water, and frequent pulses of humidity.

Proper design and installation of saunas require planning, the right selection of building products, and quality finish work.

The explosive growth of health clubs during the past decade has introduced an increasing number of Americans to sauna bathing. Total U.S. sauna heater sales are roughly 25,000 units per year.

Costs vary and can be a bit steep, often $75 to $100 per square foot of floor area.

The Basic Product Choice

If you haven't built a sauna before, buying a product through a manufacturer may help you sort through some of the design issues. Also, some manufacturers buy lumber directly from mills and have access to higher-grade materials than your average local lumberyard.

A prefab kit (called a "modular system" by some manufacturers) comes with pre-assembled structural walls that include insulation, wiring, and control boxes. The walls can be ordered with either one or both surfaces of finish-grade material, because you may want the sauna to look good from both inside and outside. A prefab's shipping and purchase price may run 30% more than buying your own components, though that should be offset somewhat by quick installation time — a few hours plus wiring hookup.

A second option is to purchase a precut package, which typically provides the finish material with which to line your sauna. You supply the framed enclosure. Someone with experience can usually install the finished unit in about eight hours.

With both the prefab and precut approaches, you have to build your frame to exact dimensions if you want to avoid re-cutting the precut material. If your schedule allows it, finish the framing before you order a custom precut.

A third approach is the custom route. You can either order a custom package or shop the parts yourself through local lumberyards and a sauna heater manufacturer. Buying from a single manufacturer eliminates the need to order materials from various sources, but you will pay additional handling, shipping, and overhead.

Keep It Simple

Keep in mind the objective of designing and building a relaxing environment. The sauna bather is there to escape the day's stress, so there's no need for electrical outlets or phone jacks.

When pressed to identify the most common problem with American saunas, Finnish craftsmen and manufacturers will answer, "The location is wrong." A sauna should be near a shower and should have space for a relaxation chair just outside the door. A lot of bathers take a quick, cool shower between each 10- to 20-minute session in the hot sauna room. After finishing up, the homeowner won't want to walk to a shower at the home's far end, dripping sweat all along.

For whatever reason, Finns seem to feel comfortable in a relatively dark, simple sauna. The stateside buyer may want a more visually inviting room, especially where it is added as part of a larger exercise/hot tub space. Distinctive touches can strike a chord with U.S. buyers: selecting a wood that retains its bright color; picking a door with a large light of etched glass; adding a window or even a wall of glass.

Design Layout

The first design criterion is size. How many people will the sauna hold? Figure at least 2 feet of upper bench space per seated person, and 5 feet per person lying down. A 6x6-foot sauna — the minimum for L-shaped benches — will hold three people comfortably, four if none lie down. Today's homeowners tend to use the sauna in ones or twos rather than as a family. This drives demand toward smaller sauna models, typically 5x7-foot or 6x6-foot units.

Saunas generally have a 7-foot ceiling height to conserve energy and keep the heat down near the benches. Since a bather either lies or sits in a sauna, always maximize bench area. Layout will require two levels of approximately 20-inch-wide benches with the lower level 20 inches off the floor and the higher level up an additional 18 inches (see Figure 1). Finlandia Sauna's Reino Tarkiainen stresses the need for two levels, since a sauna with 195°F air at the ceiling drops off to 155°F for someone

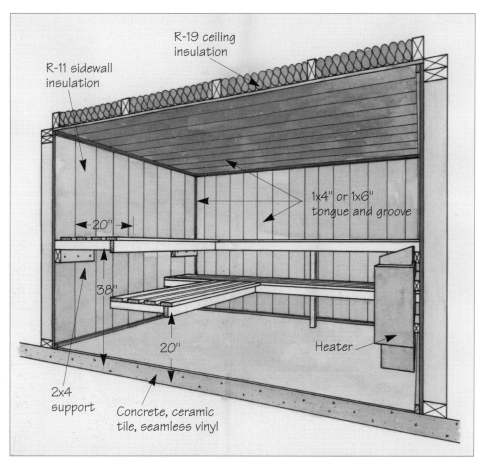

lying on the upper bench.

Floors will be exposed to sweat plus a bit of water splashed on the rocks in the sauna heater. Concrete, masonry, ceramic tile, or seamless vinyl are all appropriate floor surfaces; avoid solid wood floors or carpeting, which would soak up and hold perspiration. Removable duckboards, which can be taken out periodically and washed, are provided for areas in front of the benches. A floor drain will facilitate sauna cleanup, but is not critical.

Typical layout will include a sauna heater, door, and window along one wall. For safety, the wood door should swing out and have wooden handles and ball-catch closure. Most sauna heaters require wooden guard rails around them. Lighting should be subdued.

Sauna Heaters

A good heater must be capable of raising temperatures from 65°F to 180°F within about 30 minutes in a moderately insulated small sauna. Typical residential heaters are wall-mounted and have between 4.5- and 9-kilowatts output; a 6x6-foot sauna will usually require a 6-kilowatt heater that draws 25 amps. Most heaters are wired for 240-volt, single-phase current or three-phase,

Figure 1. Home saunas often measure 5x7 feet or 6x6 feet, which is comfortable for three people. Ceilings are 7 feet high to conserve energy. Typical bench heights are 20 and 38 inches — the higher seat sits in hotter air. Tongue-and-groove wood lining should be blind nailed and seats should be screwed and glued from beneath to avoid exposed metal screw or nail heads.

208-volt current; they should be UL-listed.

Sauna heaters typically come with thermostats, heat indicator lights, and 60-minute timer controls that are built into the unit or mounted on a separate prewired panel outside the sauna. (Since sauna lighting is intentionally dim, exterior controls are easier to read.) If the 60-minute timer is not standard, it is good to buy it as an option; it is a good safety and energy-control feature. Expect the heater and controls to cost $400 to $600.

The heat control should be by natural convection, not radiation. Most sauna heaters provide electric resistance heat to coils running through a double- or triple-shell steel box (Figure 2). The box is filled with 10 to 70 pounds of fracture-resistant igneous rock, often imported from Finland. Usually, air enters at the bottom, flows up through rocks in direct contact with heating coils, and flows out the top. Water periodically ladled on the heated rocks flashes to steam. Most units have a built-in high-limit control that will automatically cut off power to prevent overheating.

There are variations among heater designs. Traditionalists insist on direct contact between rocks and heating elements. Others prefer designs that isolate heating elements from the rocks (and water ladled on them) in a stainless-steel pan atop the heater, claiming this results in less maintenance.

When shopping for heaters, follow these guidelines:

- Check the length of heater warranties. A few manufacturers provide five-year protection.
- Some manufacturers (Tylo) provide triple-wall construction and a heat-resistant finishing layer that eliminates the need for a sauna heater guard rail.
- If space is tight, as it often is, an optional triangular heater design (Amerec) takes up less space.
- A few companies (Finnleo, Finlandia) offer wood stoves, and at least one (Vico) offers sealed-combustion, gas-heated models. Both wood and gas models take up slightly more space than an electric heater with the same output, but the wood and gas models will require flue venting.

Ventilation

While some American installers don't bother with sauna room ventilation, and codes often don't require it, Finns would never build a sauna without it. The American argument seems to be: Why allow the heat built up in a sauna to escape so quickly? But Finns counter that in a confined space where breathing increases, you must introduce fresh air to keep up the oxygen content for a healthy sauna.

In standard Finnish practice, vents are closed during sauna warmup. Once people enter the sauna, a small vent near the sauna heater is opened to allow air from adjacent rooms to enter the sauna; a vent of the same size exhausts stale air from high on the opposite wall (Figure 3). Introducing air from the home rather than from outside will prevent cold-air drafts; venting sauna exhaust air back into the home will at least help offset winter heating needs.

Finlandia specifies 4x10-inch adjustable vents both high and low. Other manufacturers recommend up to 15 square inches for each vent. The Finnish Sauna Society recommends at least six air changes per hour.

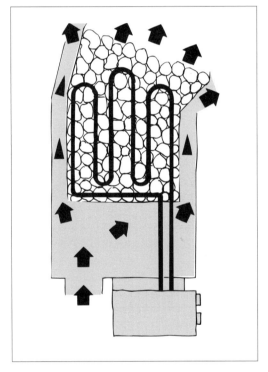

Figure 2. *Most sauna heaters are electric with a double- or triple-wall steel box filled with igneous rocks. The heater coil either runs through the rocks or sits atop them in a stainless-steel pan. Most units are mounted behind a guard rail to prevent accidental burns, and most are wired with a high-limit shutoff.*

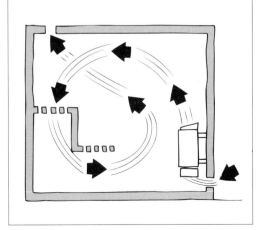

Figure 3. *Finns highly recommend circulating household air through the sauna by natural convection. Place vents high and low, as shown, with the low inlet feeding the bottom of the heater.*

Sauna Wood Performance

Wood	REACTIONS UNDER SAUNA CONDITIONS			Color of Heartwood	Advantages	Disadvantages
	Movement & Expansion	Warping	Resistance to Decay & Fungus			
Western Red Cedar	very small	stable	very high	very colorful cream to dark brown	pleasant cedar odor, no pitch or resin	wood can be stained by metal
Atlantic White Cedar	very small	stable	very high	straw brown	pleasant odor	splits easily
Redwood	very small	stable	very high	light red to deep reddish-brown	straight grained, strong, nice smell	stains easily from perspiration
Eastern White Pine	small	stable	moderate	cream to light reddish-brown		subtle resinous odor
Sugar Pine	small	stable	very low	light creamy-brown		faint resinous odor
Aspen	large	stable	very low	greyish-white to light greyish-brown	straight grained, resists splintering	
Western White Pine	moderate-large	stable	very low	cream to light reddish-brown		can be knotty, slight resin content
Ponderosa Pine	small-moderate	stable	very low	orange to reddish-brown	straight grained	quite resinous with distinct resinous odor
Red Pine	moderate-large	stable	very low	pale red to reddish-brown	straight grained	strong resinous odor, may leach resin
Sitka Spruce	small-moderate	slight	very low	light pinkish-brown	uniform texture, straight grained	
Hemlock	moderate-large	slight	very low	very pale; pale-brown with reddish tinge	even grained, strong	faint sour smell when fresh
Cypress (Bald Cypress)	small	slight	high	light yellowish-brown to dark brownish-red	quite strong	slight musty smell, very dense

Wood and Materials

Wood used in a sauna should be light in color, low in density, and resistant to stains. At high sauna temperatures, hardwoods get too hot to sit on or lean against. The wood also should be kiln-dried (specify below 15% moisture content), clear heart, vertical grain, grade-A material — expensive stuff. Types of wood used in a sauna include redwood, western red cedar, Alaska yellow cedar, Nordic white spruce, hemlock, aspen, birch, and pine (see table above).

On the West Coast, sauna manufacturers and installers tend to favor western red cedar over redwood. Besides costing less, they say, cedar is more aromatic, resists staining, and remains lighter in color. Over time, the heat in a sauna draws tannic acid out of redwood, which darkens it: To some users, dark saunas feel smaller.

Dimension choices vary significantly. Most wall and ceiling material is 1x4 or 1x6 tongue-and-groove. Stay away from fragile 1/2-inch tongue-and-groove. Base, corner, and ceiling molding is typically 1x2.

You'll want to order a wood door that matches your walls. Including a large window in the door (a popular feature with buyers) reduces the possibility of warping.

If you decide to assemble your own package rather than work through a manufacturer, be picky at the lumberyard. Avoid knots and exposed resin, which get very hot in a heated sauna. If you order tongue-and-groove material with more than 12% moisture content, especially 1x6, you may find it susceptible to splitting.

Make sure other materials are designed to survive in a hot and occasionally humid environment. Fasteners and hardware, including vents, should be rustproof. Lights must be vapor-proof by code.

Construction Tips

For framing, use relatively dry 2x4s at 16 inches on-center. Use rot-resistant wood for bottom plates.

Use at least R-11 sidewall and R-19 ceiling insulation; upgrade the insulation where you are against a cold basement wall or an exterior wall, or where electric rates or cooling loads are high. For a vapor barrier, a number of installers favor a sturdy foil radiant barrier, figuring it will slow down heat loss (if adjacent to an airspace) and outlast polyethylene in the warmer-than-normal wall system. Some codes require an interior 5/8-inch layer of standard gypsum board over the framing before nailing up the wallboards.

Generally, the ceiling should go up first. Face-nail the first piece close enough to the edge for trim to cover the nail heads. Then blind-nail through the tongues into ceiling joists, and rip the last board to fit.

Next, install the back wall, then the side wall, moving from the floor up and hiding any blemishes in courses below the benches. Exposed fasteners, on trim or elsewhere, should be countersunk, since nail or screw heads are very hot to the touch in a heated sauna.

To minimize exposed screws, especially on benches, pick thicker (2x) bench-top boards; then glue and screw them through the bottom of the horizontal 2x4 supports.

Unless your sauna heater manufacturer specifies otherwise, install a guard rail around the heater. Finnleo advises holding the rail 4 inches away from the heater; check your sauna heater specs for guard rail requirements.

Don't treat the interior surfaces with any stains, polyurethanes, or preservatives that might emit toxic fumes at high temperatures. U.S. Sauna & Steam recommends "curing" the sauna after construction is completed, by leaving the door slightly open with the sauna heater on high for six hours.

Costs

Quotes from manufacturers for a 6x6-foot precut sauna kit range from $1,500 to $2,000. Opting for the prefab package — normally a do-it-yourselfer option — increases costs by as much as $800. If you ask the dealer or distributor to install your precut kit, add another $400 to $600. The most common quote given for an installed precut kit is around $2,500. Generally, the precuts do not include the cost of framing, insulation, and a finished floor, so you have to factor them into your tab. If you work through a manufacturer, make sure you compare apples to apples in terms of features provided at a given price for the same size models. What is standard with one manufacturer can be optional with another.

A word about operating costs: One Swedish study found that each warmup and use of a four-person sauna consumes about 4 kilowatt hours of electricity (32¢ at the national average of 8¢ per kilowatt hour), while heating water for a bath typically consumes 6.5 kilowatt hours. Used three times a week, an electric sauna heater would cost $4 a month, and a gas unit would cost less. ■

Steve Andrews is a Denver-based residential energy consultant and technical writer.

Sources of Supply

Finlandia Sauna Products
14010-B S.W. 72nd Ave.
Portland, OR 97223
800/354-3342

Finnleo of the West
9475 S.W. Oak St.
Portland, OR 97223
503/246-4856

Nasscor, Inc.
P.O. Box 40569
Bellevue, WA 98015
800/331-0349 or 206/643-7500
(Maker of Amerec products)

U.S. Sauna & Steam
(formerly **Helo Sauna**)
9 Cross St.
Norwalk, CT 06851
800/243-6764 or 203/846-9192
(imported heaters from Finland, rooms and saunas built in cedar and redwood)

Vico Product Mfg. Co., Inc.
1808 Potrero Ave.
South El Monte, CA 91733
800/262-2588 or 213/686-0509 or
818/442-4420
(Ultra Sauna)

Up-Flush Basement Baths

by Richard Trethewey

F.E. MEYERS

A sewage ejector system uses a sump pump, typically installed beneath the basement floor. The sump's cover should be tightly sealed but left accessible for servicing.

Someone once simplified plumbing by saying, "Hot is on the left, cold is on the right, waste goes downhill — and if it won't, put in a pump." Such is the case if you want to install a basement bath where the drain pipe is above the basement floor level. In this case, you'll need to install a special sump pump called a "sewage ejector" to churn the wastewater and send it uphill to the main drain pipe.

This will mean a little extra work and a few thousand dollars extra expense. But it allows you to install a bathroom in virtually any basement and still get good drainage.

If you are installing less than a full bath, you might consider a couple of less labor-intensive alternatives to a buried ejector system. For example, if you need only to drain a laundry sink, a simpler and cheaper "laundry tray" pump will work. A laundry tray pump attaches directly beneath a sink or tub and is turned on as needed. There is no need for a sunken reservoir. These pumps are available through most plumbing suppliers and wholesalers and some hardware stores.

Similarly, if you want to add only a toilet to the basement, you can choose from a variety of power flushing or "up-flush" toilets. Some of these are little more than motorized marine toilets, and others are "macerators." A macerator is a small tank that allows time and/or chemicals to break down the solids before it pumps them out. Two models I've come across are the *Waterflash 2003* by Actana (French Technology Press Office, 401 N. Michigan Ave., Suite 1760, Chicago, IL 60611; 312/222-1235), which uses 0.8 gallons per flush and, according to the manufacturer, can pump discharge as high as 20 feet and as far as 165 feet horizontally (see Figure 1); and the *SaniPlus Toilet* (Sanitary for All Ltd., 550 Parkside Dr., Unit B16, Waterloo, ON N2L 5V4, Canada; 519/883-5874), which uses 1.75 gallons per flush and pumps 12 feet up and 150 feet away. Both of these products are quite new and may not be approved for local use — check with your code official.

One other option I'm aware of is an above-floor ejector system called *Qwik Jon*, made by Zoeller Co. (3649 Cane Run Rd., Louisville, KY 40216; 502/778-2731). This is probably noisier than a buried ejector system, but in most cases it is easier to install. According to the company, this unit — which attaches to a standard toilet — installs easily on the floor, can be hidden behind a wall to deaden sound, and can handle drainage from a full bathroom (Figure 2). Again, you should check your local code for compliance.

Sewage Ejector Systems

Sewage ejector systems come in a variety of shapes and sizes from various manufacturers. A typical installation consists of a drum-shaped plastic or metal reservoir, or sump, which receives discharge from the toilet, tub/shower, and lavatory. Inside the sump basin, which holds about 30 gallons of effluent, is a specially designed pump triggered by a

Figure 1. *If you're installing only a basement toilet, this up-flush model, made by the French company Actana, can do the job without a full ejector system.*

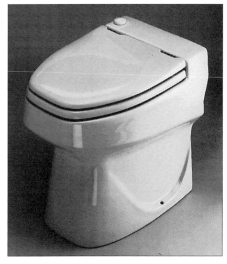

float mechanism. The unit churns the waste and periodically pumps it to the main drain pipe as needed. A whole unit is typically 18 inches around and about 30 inches deep, with a removable top cover (Figure 3).

Since the pumping unit must be slightly downhill from the bathroom (so the waste can drain to it) and be accessible for servicing, the standard procedure is to install it in the basement floor. Burying the pump in the floor means you can put your fixtures directly on the floor (instead of elevating them on platforms), and it also makes it easier to hide the low-level noise these units make.

A variety of national and regional manufacturers make ejector systems. Some common names are Zoeller, Little Giant (P.O. Box 12010, Oklahoma City, OK 73157; 405/947-2511), and F. E. Myers (1101 Myers Parkway, Ashland, OH 44805; 419/289-1144). A basic 30-gallon residential model should retail for about $400 to $600. Almost all models have a one-year warranty. I haven't found much difference between the products of these manufacturers. It may be worth paying a little extra for a good model, since it will buy a more reliable pump, and this may save a disruptive and unpleasant replacement later. (Changing the pump is not for the faint of heart.)

Design Considerations

Where can a bathroom go in the basement, where do you put the ejector?

Siting the bathroom. Upstream of the ejector, the rules for the drain piping are the same as for a standard bath connected to the main drain. That is, the drain pipes leading from fixtures to the ejector must have a pitch of $1/8$ inch to $1/4$ inch per foot of run, and, given that pitch, they can run as far horizontally as is practical. So, as far as the drain piping is concerned, you can pretty much put the bathroom wherever you wish.

Probably a more important siting consideration for the bathroom is the vent. You'll find installation easiest if you can readily connect the new bathroom's vent pipe into the existing venting system for the main plumbing system. Some plumbing codes require a future vent pipe to be left in the basement when the house is initially roughed in, which can also make things easy.

If you can't practically reach an existing venting system from the site of the new bathroom, you'll have to fish the

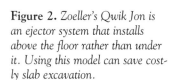

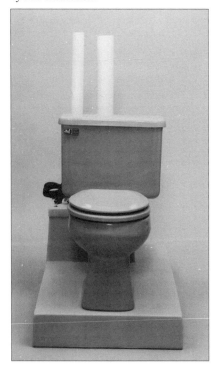

Figure 2. *Zoeller's Qwik Jon is an ejector system that installs above the floor rather than under it. Using this model can save costly slab excavation.*

vent up through the house or out through the sidewall — either of which can be challenging.

In any case, the entire system (depending on your local code) will likely need to meet the general configuration shown in Figure 4, which is from the National Association of Plumbing, Heating, and Cooling Contractors (NAPHCC) National Plumbing Standard, used by many code jurisdictions. You or your plumber should check your design with your local jurisdiction before you start.

Siting the ejector. Since the ejector may need service at some point, you'll want to put it where its hatch in the basement floor is accessible. A utility area, closet, or unfinished section of the basement near the bathroom is ideal. You don't want it beneath a finished floor unless you can gracefully leave some sort of access panel in the floor.

You should also consider noise when siting the ejector. Most units aren't very loud, but if the new room is to be a bedroom or study, the whirring and pumping noises of a nearby ejector might pose a problem. But don't let noise considerations convince you to site the ejector in an inaccessible spot — Murphy's Law always shows up on the job that takes that chance.

Installation

Once you've marked the ejector site and the path the drain lines will take, you're ready to install the ejector. Installation time will vary tremendously depending on the complexity of the job. But a standard basement bathroom with standard waste and water piping might take a two-person crew one-and-a-half to three days to rough in, with an additional half day needed to install the finish connections to the fixtures.

Excavation. You'll need a sledgehammer, a jack hammer, a chisel, and a strong back. Start by breaking the slab in a circle that is about 4 to 6 inches wider than the ejector unit. Dig a hole several inches deeper than the ejector is tall — deep enough to allow the required slope down from the bathroom to the injector inlet, plus another 3 or 4 inches for a gravel or sand base beneath.

With that done, open a trench for the horizontal drain pipes from the new bathroom group. Make the drain pipe trench deep enough to allow the $1/8$-inch to $1/4$-inch drainage slope down to the ejector inlet.

You may run into reinforcing steel (rebar) as you excavate the concrete. Cut this as necessary with a reciprocating saw or torch, but leave as much as possible intact to maintain the floor's structural integrity. Often you can slip the pipes below the rebar and hang them from it.

Setting the ejector and pipes. It's a good idea to set the ejector on a gravel or sand base and then surround it with an inch or so of sand or gravel as well. This helps to hold it firmly in place and prevent any settlement or heaving. It also eliminates the risk of puncture from jagged rocks. Put in the base first, then the ejector, and then check that the height is correct and allows the proper drainage slope from the bathroom.

With the ejector installed, but before you pack the sand and gravel around it, run the drain piping from the bathroom fixture drain pipes to the ejector. Use standard piping practices, joining all fixture drain pipes in or near the bath into a single larger drain pipe that runs to the ejector. Although you should check your local code for all these pipe sizes, the required diameters are usually 3 inches for the toilet, 2 inches for a shower or tub, and $1^1/2$ inches for the sink.

Once those pipes are hooked up, run the discharge line from the ejector to the house's main drain pipe. The discharge line is usually a 2-inch-diameter pipe (again, check your code). You can either run the discharge line straight up from the ejector site, as you see in Figure 3 or, if location dictates, run it in a trench to a spot where a vertical pipe will be less obtrusive. Don't forget to install a check valve on this line to prevent any backwards flow.

Tie this line into the main drain and vent lines. Again, check your design first with your local code official. Some jurisdictions allow you to tie the discharge line anywhere into the drain line and let venting take care of itself, while others require you to run a separate vent line to a point above the floodline of the highest fixture of the house.

Buttoning up. With the drain piping installed, connected, and double-checked by you and the inspector, it's time to replace the concrete over the trench. Fill the trench and the space around the ejector with sand and gravel. Then compact the fill and cap the trench with ready-mix concrete. Leave an open circle for the bolted cover of the ejector unit, as per the unit's instructions. Once the cover is in place, seal all openings around the ejector cover with hydraulic sealant or caulking to prevent any radon or groundwater from entering the basement.

A Word About Radon

If you're in an area that's at risk for radon, be extra careful to properly seal these new penetrations through the basement floor. In fact,

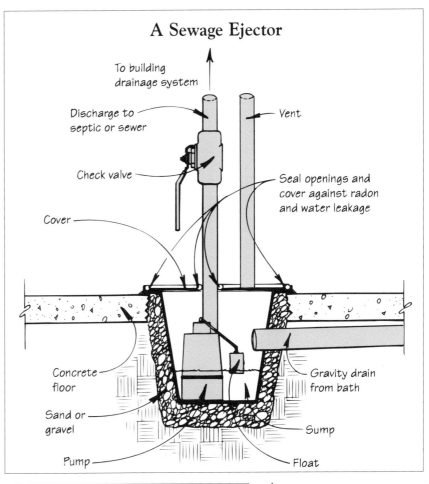

A Sewage Ejector

To building drainage system

Vent

Discharge to septic or sewer

Check valve

Cover

Seal openings and cover against radon and water leakage

Concrete floor

Sand or gravel

Pump

Gravity drain from bath

Sump

Float

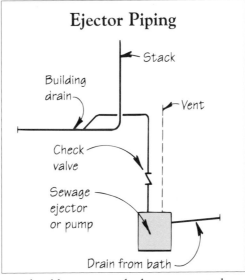

Ejector Piping

Stack

Building drain

Vent

Check valve

Sewage ejector or pump

Drain from bath

▲ **Figure 3. Typical sewage ejector.** *A surrounding bed of sand or gravel keeps the ejector unit firmly in place, while careful sealing around the cover prevents radon or moisture infiltration.*

◀ **Figure 4. Ejector piping.** *Use standard drainage piping from the bath fixtures to the ejector sump. From there, piping can go straight up or run horizontally first. Most codes require a separate vent from the pump unit.*

you should encourage the homeowner to have the home tested for radon before you start the job — this may reveal the need for a sub-slab mitigation system, and may help protect you from liability as well. Such a system will be much easier to install now, while you're tearing up the floor anyway, than later after the new finish floors are down. ■

Richard Trethewey has 19 years experience as a plumbing and heating contractor, and is currently a consultant and seminar leader in Dedham, Mass.

The Lowdown on Low-Flow Toilets

by Don Best

Despite early controversy over the performance of 1.6-gallon toilets, both gravity and pressurized models are proving themselves in the marketplace

Up until about 1980, virtually all residential toilets used gravity and five or six gallons of fresh water to rinse the bowl clean and carry the waste down the drain line. During the 1980s, however, the limitations of our nation's water resources were becoming painfully apparent, especially in the West. Municipal and state governments passed water conservation laws, bolstered by rebates and penalties. In some extreme cases, moratoriums were imposed on new construction.

Toilet manufacturers responded by offering "water-saving" models that use 3.5 gallons per flush (gpf) instead of five or six, which had been the industry standard. These quickly became the new standard.

Gravity systems. As the need grew to conserve even more water, a few American manufacturers and importers introduced "low-consumption" models — inspired by 6-liter European designs — that use just 1.6 gpf. Most models still relied on gravity, but with important changes in design. To compensate for their smaller capacity, tanks were taller and narrower to increase the head. Bowls had steeper sides to increase the gravitational pull, and the *water spots* — the surface area of the water in the bowl — were smaller (typically 4x5 inches instead of 8x9 inches).

Pressurized tank. About the time the new 1.6-gpf gravity models were being introduced, inventor Bruce Martin was pushing the development of a competing technology that used a pressurized tank (see Figure 1). Martin's patented invention features a separate plastic

tank housed inside the familiar vitreous china tank. Using ordinary supply line pressure (at least 15 psi), water enters the sealed plastic tank and compresses the air trapped inside. When the toilet is flushed, the compressed air expands, pushing the water into the bowl in a brief high-pressure surge.

When the pressurized tank system was first introduced in 1975, it was marketed as a retrofit product to convert 5.5-gpf toilets to 2.5 gpf. But not all toilets could accommodate the changeover and there were component failures — especially with the pressure regulator.

Martin fine-tuned the pressurized-tank technology, and in 1985 Mansfield used the system in its new Quantum toilet. This represented the first truly revolutionary change in residential toilets to come along in decades.

Plug-in toilet. By 1994, builders and plumbing contractors had a third low-flow technology to consider when Kohler introduced its Trocadero Power Lite, the industry's first "pumped" low-flow toilet (Figure 2). The Trocadero uses a small electric pump (0.2 horsepower) to push water through the toilet. The toilet is plugged into a regular outlet and draws about a dollar's worth of electricity a year.

Mandatory Low Flow

As recently as 1987 only a handful of manufacturers offered low-flow models. Then came the prolonged drought in California, prompting the state legislature there to make 1.6-gpf toilets mandatory in all new residential construction. One by one, other states enacted similar laws, including Massachusetts, New York, Texas, and Georgia. Toilet manufacturers had to scramble.

Federal law. To clarify the growing jumble of state and local laws, the U.S. Congress voted to pass the National Energy Policy Act, which stipulates that after January 1, 1994, all new toilets manufactured in the United States (or imported) for residential use must consume no more than 1.6 gpf.

How Well Do They Work?

Long before the National Energy Policy Act became law, the professionals who test toilets and write standards were worried that the rush to legislate the use of 1.6-gpf toilets would end up causing serious performance problems.

Drain line carry. One prime concern was that the smaller volume of water used would lead to clogged drain lines. But after extensive testing, the Stevens Institute of Technology working in tandem with the American Society of Plumbing Engineers found that 1.6-gpf toilets — whether gravity or pressurized tank type — do provide adequate drain line carry for residential use. The laboratory and field tests showed that as long as other household water fixtures and appliances drain into the same line as the toilet, clogging isn't more of a problem with low-flow toilets than with conventional fixtures.

However, the Stevens Institute recommended against using 1.6-gpf toilets in commercial projects until better performing models are developed. Although the National Energy Policy Act permits manufacturers to continue making 3.5-gpf toilets for commercial installations, some states, including California, New York, Massachusetts, and Texas, require 1.6-gpf models on commercial jobs as well. Thus, the suitability of current 1.6-gpf designs for commercial jobs is going to be proved or disproved over time in thousands of real installations.

Skid marks. Another performance concern with 1.6-gpf models is how well they evacuate the bowl and whether or not they leave "tracks," or "skid marks." In both regards, the pressurized tank models, which have a more forceful flush and a larger water spot (10x12 inches), tend to excel. Gravity models, generally speaking, are more likely to require an occasional double flush to empty the bowl and need more frequent use of a scrub brush to remove tracks.

Performance survey. In a 1992 survey, almost 9,000 Californians whose homes had been retrofitted with 1.6-gpf toilets rated the

Figure 1. *In a pressurized-tank toilet, such as this Briggs Industries' Turboflush, an inner plastic tank traps air that is then compressed by supply water under its own pressure. When the toilet is flushed, the compressed air expands, pushing the water into the bowl at high velocity.*

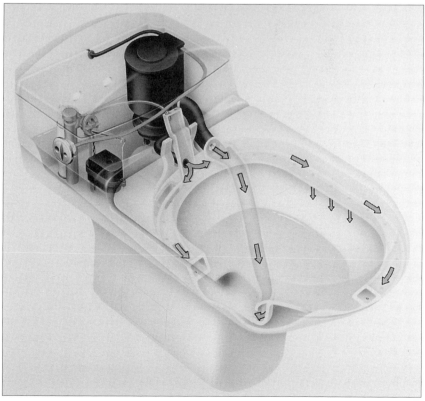

Figure 2. *Kohler's electrically operated Trocadero Power Lite uses a small pump to push water through the toilet. A dual-action push button allows the option of either a 1.6-gallon or a 1-gallon flush.*

new units on the following characteristics, listed in order of importance to users:
- Number of double flushes
- Frequency of mechanical problems
- Frequency of using a plunger to unclog
- Frequency of cleaning
- Frequency of needing a professional unclogging service

Two pressurized-tank models, the American Standard New Cadet and the Kilgore Quantum 150-1 were ranked first and second in customer satisfaction. Most gravity toilets, however, scored well too. In fact, most customers found that their new low-flows performed at least as well as their old fixtures, regardless of brand. Some did even better.

"It's fair to say that some gravity models work just as well as the pressurized tank models," says Thomas Konen, an engineer with the Stevens Institute of Technology. "The problem is, there's no way to distinguish the better gravity types at this point because the ANSI performance tests that we use are inadequate for residential toilets."

Other experts agree that ANSI's pass-fail approach — developed for earlier generations of toilets — can't adequately gauge the finer points of performance that are critical in 1.6-gpf designs.

While it can still be helpful to compare the ANSI test scores of one toilet to another (these are usually on file at state plumbing board offices), the only sure way to pick a top performer is through experience. In other words, find a manufacturer whose toilet does the job with few callbacks, and stick with it.

Costs and Savings

The wholesale price of standard gravity-type 1.6-gpf toilets, in basic white, ranges from $60 to $80. Pressurized-tank designs,

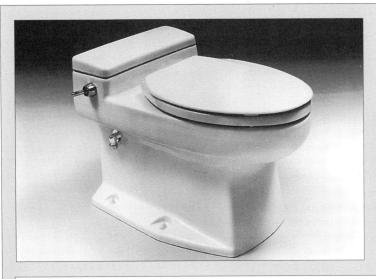

The Stingiest Flush of All

On sites where water supplies are severely limited or where the soil has poor percolation, making conventional septic system design impossible, a Microflush 0.5 gpf toilet could be the answer. The Microflush uses water to flush out the bowl, but relies on compressed air to push the wastes out of the toilet's lower chamber and down the drain line. The Microflush is manufactured by Microphor Inc. of Willits, Calif., and lists for $460 without the compressor.

— D.B.

How the Microflush Works

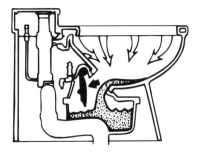

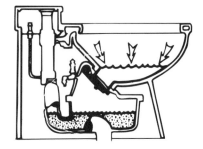

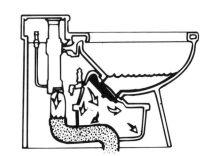

When the handle is pressed, the flapper valve opens, and the water in the bowl empties into the lower chamber. At the same time, clean water enters from around the rim, rinsing the bowl.

As clean water continues to flow, the flapper valve closes, holding the water in the bowl until the next flush.

With the flapper valve closed, compressed air forces the waste water out of the lower chamber and into the waste line.

Low-Flow Law Review

When President Bush signed the National Energy Policy Act of 1992, a new set of national standards for water conservation became law. Here are some of the key provisions that affect toilets and other plumbing fixtures:

- Starting January 1, 1994, all residential toilets manufactured in the U.S. or imported for residential use must be rated 1.6 gallons per flush (gpf) or less.
- If a component of a noncomplying toilet is broken, the customer must purchase a whole new fixture that does comply. Manufacturers will not be permitted to produce noncomplying components for sale in the United States.
- Manufacturers are permitted to make white, two-piece, 3.5-gpf toilets for commercial use until January 1, 1997. All products and containers must be marked "For Commercial Use Only."
- As of January 1, 1994, all toilets must be permanently marked to indicate their water consumption.

- Commercial 3.5-gpf toilets using pressurized tanks are exempted until January 1, 1997.
- "Blow Out" toilets used in stadiums and at other heavy-use sites are permanently exempted.
- Beginning January 1, 1994, the flow rate on showerheads and kitchen and lavatory faucets is set at 2.5 gallons per minute at 80-pounds-per-square-inch line pressure. These fixtures must be permanently marked with their actual or maximum flow rate.
- Manufacturers and distributors of plumbing products can sell their existing inventory of noncomplying products manufactured before January 1, 1994.
- All existing state laws that contain provisions that are more restrictive than those in the National Energy Policy Act of 1992 remain in effect.

—*D.B.*

which are now available from virtually every manufacturer, are priced wholesale at $140 to $180 in basic white. The new Trocadero pumped toilet is being priced in line with pressurized-tank models.

The economic arguments in favor of 1.6-gpf toilets are quite persuasive. Depending on how much a homeowner pays for water and sewage, and how many people live in the house, savings could run anywhere from $20 to $70 a year.

Low-flow toilets can also benefit homeowners who use wells and septic systems. On the supply side, the draw on the well is substantially reduced. On the drain line side, the hydraulic loading on the septic tank and leach field goes down, which extends its life. Moreover, the homeowner won't have to have the septic tank pumped out as often.

Installation

Installing 1.6-gpf toilets, whether gravity, pressurized, or pumped, doesn't present any special problems. Rough-in is still 10, 12, or 14 inches from the finished wall and a standard wax ring is used with two or three closet bolts to secure the fixture.

In the future, however, the installation of low-consumption toilets may enable builders to make money-saving changes in new construction. Experts in the plumbing field, like Dr. Larry Galowin of the National Institute of Standards and Technology, say that low-consumption toilets will make it possible for residential builders to downsize drain line

pipes from 4 inches to 3 inches in diameter, and to reduce the diameter of stack vents from 2 inches to 1 inch, or even $1/2$ inch. Also, new septic systems can be installed with smaller tanks and leach fields, a cost-cutter that's already allowed in some code jurisdictions.

"The research has already been done on downsizing drainage systems for low consumption toilets," says Galowin. "The problem is that code writers generally haven't caught up with the technology yet."

Maintenance

Both gravity and pressurized type toilets have proven themselves reliable in the field and comparable to one another in terms of maintenance. Though builders and plumbers are sometimes wary of new technology, pressurized tank toilets meet ANSI test standards that require 150,000 flushes, equivalent to 20 years of service. If problems do occur, all the moving parts are contained in a small cartridge that is easy to replace.

Perhaps the biggest drawback to pressurized-tank toilets, and the one most likely to elicit a comment from the customer, is their vigorous and relatively loud flushing action. And some types of gravity toilets, as we noted before, may draw complaints from customers who are annoyed by the occasional need for a double flush or because they have to use a scrub brush more often. ■

Don Best is a freelance writer in Surry, N.H., specializing in construction topics.

Chapter 6
CERAMIC TILE

MARGIE LITTLE, DESIGNER, COURTESY OF NKBA

Selecting & Installing Ceramic Tile

by Jay Jones

Choose the tile type and installation methods that best fit the intended use

MARK PEDERSEN

What makes a good tile job? You need the right tile, good backing, a secure bond, and a good layout. Take shortcuts on any of these, and you'll have problems with the tile installation. I've found that many problems can be traced to the customer or contractor who selected the tile because "they liked the color." But picking tile based on its color is like choosing a spouse because of hair color. You can get in a lot of trouble if you don't stop to think about the rest of the package.

Ceramic tile is made from a mixture of clay and other materials. The clay is formed and fired at high temperatures and can be glazed or unglazed. The unglazed tile, called a "bisque," has the same color on the surface as it does in the body of the tile. But with glazed tile, the beauty is only skin deep; below the glaze lies a plain-colored bisque. To choose the correct tile, you need to know about the physical properties of both the bisque and the glaze.

Choice of Tile

As you make your selection, you have three criteria to consider: water absorption, glaze hardness, and glaze wearability.

Water absorption pertains only to the bisque; it tells you whether or not the tile behaves like a sponge. Since all glazing is non-porous, any glazed tile is impermeable to water penetration from the surface. You can use any glazed tile in a shower, therefore, even if the bisque absorbs water. But water absorption of the bisque will be important if the tile goes outdoors, where freeze/thaw action can break it into pieces.

If the tile is glazed, you may need to know whether the glaze can stand up to scratches and heavy foot traffic. Glaze hardness scales and glaze wearability ratings can give you pointers here. Look on the tile packages. If nothing is listed, you can assume that the wearability and hardness are low.

Water absorption. When the tile bisque is

fired in the kiln, the clay solids and other ingredients in the mix melt, turn to liquid, and reform as a harder material. Some tile is made of clay that partially or completely turns to glass when it is fired, creating *vitreous* (or glasslike) tile. The percentage of glass in the bisque determines the tile's water absorption. Also, a more vitreous tile often makes a stronger tile.

Tile manufacturers divide tile into four groups, depending on the tile body's ability to resist moisture.

- *Impervious tile:* Less than or equal to 0.5% absorption. Mosaics and glass tile are impervious, and these are generally unglazed.
- *Vitreous tile:* More than 0.5% but less than or equal to 3% absorption. These are glazed or unglazed floor tiles.
- *Semi-vitreous tile:* More than 3% but less than or equal to 7% absorption. Quarry tile falls in this category.
- *Non-vitreous tile:* More than 7% absorption. The typical 4x4 bathroom wall tile is non-vitreous.

Glaze hardness. Manufacturers rate the tile surface from 1 to 10 based on the Mohs scale. If the surface only resists scratches from soft minerals (such as talc), the tile rates a 1. But if you can't scratch it with a diamond, it rates a 10. Most floor tile falls between 6 and 7.

Glaze wearability. The industry hasn't agreed upon a standard method to rate glazed tile's resistance to wear, but some manufacturers have borrowed a European "Roman numeral" rating system. The rating is done by visual inspection, on a scale of I to IV, with I the lowest. If you're thinking about Italian tile, keep this rating system in mind (see Figure 1).

- *Group I:* Glazed tile for light-residential traffic, baths, or bedrooms where slippers are worn.
- *Group II:* General residential use, except kitchens and entrances. Tracked-in grit or a dropped pan may damage the glaze on this tile.
- *Group III:* Glazed tile suited for anywhere in the home.
- *Group IV:* Glazed tile for medium to heavy commercial traffic, such as restaurants or lobbies.

Manufacturers generally give other clues, too, with such labels as "residential," "extra heavy duty," or "commercial."

Matching Tile and Location

To select a tile for good long-term performance, you'll need to think about where the tile will be used. You can use any kind of tile on a wall if the wall is purely decorative. But if the tile will be located in a bath, on the kitchen counter, or on the floor, you'll need to be selective.

Bathrooms. For showers and tub surrounds, you'll want an impervious (or vitreous) tile, or a glazed tile. Slip resistance isn't a factor on bathroom walls, but on floors you'll be better off with an unglazed tile, which isn't as slippery when wet (Figure 2). Many tiles, both glazed and unglazed, now add an abrasive grit to the surface to improve slip resistance. The standard non-vitreous 4x4 glazed tile can work fine for bathroom walls, but this tile cracks or chips when used on kitchen counters.

Countertops. A kitchen counter takes a lot of abuse: pans drop, knives mar the surface, and food acids (such as tomato juice) may etch

Figure 1. *Check the glaze hardness before choosing an Italian tile. On countertops, the hardness should rank in Group III or IV. This tile is set on Durock backerboard and has a hardwood edging.*

Figure 2. *Unglazed porcelain tile provides a non-slip surface on the floor in this gym shower room, while the walls take a glazed tile. Porcelain tile is a low-absorbency, vitreous tile.*

the tile. You can head off these problems with a vitreous tile or a glazed tile with a Mohs rating of 6.5 or above. I prefer the equivalent of an American Olean Crystalline, which has a good glaze because it has been fired at a higher temperature and is a harder tile. This tile comes in 4¹/4- or 6-inch squares.

Other good choices for countertops are glazed or unglazed porcelain tile or porcelain paver tile. Porcelain tile is generally high quality and durable. It is fired at a high temperature, is very hard, and has low absorption. Porcelain tile comes on sheets of 12x12-inch mesh. Porcelain pavers range from 4x4 to 12x12 inches.

The Twelve Steps of Thinset

Robert T. Young, CSI, one of the industry's leading consultants, recommends the following "Twelve Steps" for thinset tile installation. All twelve are good information for the novice and journeyman.

1 Mix thinset and grouting materials at as slow a speed as possible to prevent air entrapment (150 rpm recommended).

2 Allow thinset and grouting materials to set (slake) for 10 to 15 minutes after mixing, then remix. Consistency should be stiff enough to stick to bottom side of trowel without falling off. Do not add more liquid after material has slaked.

3 Clean surface before applying bonding material. Dampen if dry, but do not saturate.

4 Apply mortar with flat side of the trowel, pressing firmly to key into the substrate. Then select the appropriate notched trowel and comb the mortar to give a thickness of approximately ³/32 inch after the tiles have been beat in.

5 Set tiles with a sliding, twisting motion as quickly as possible to ensure that the bond coat does not "skin over" before the tiles are applied and beat in. (In hot, windy, dry weather it may be necessary to work nights or use cold water and materials to prevent "skinning over.")

6 Beat or twist tiles into fresh bonding material with a block and hammer. Pull up tiles occasionally to be sure that trowel marks are compressed to provide a minimum of 80% average coverage on interior and 95% on exterior applications.

7 Allow 48 hours after setting the tile before grouting.

8 Mix the grout at slow speed to as stiff a consistency as can be worked. Allow to set (slake) for 10 to 15 minutes and remix.

9 Dampen the surface of the tile before applying the grout.

10 Press the grout firmly into the joints; clean with a minimum amount of water.

11 Cover immediately after grouting. Wet the following day and recover in hot, dry, windy weather.

12 Do not clean with muriatic acid. If acids are required, use sulfamic acid or products recommended for the particular surface.

Owners don't always pick a product for its durability, however. If the customer leans toward the handcrafted look, encourage them to pick a handcrafted tile created for floor use rather than one that is purely decorative.

Floors. Most floor tile has higher Mohs and wearability ratings than wall tile. This is because floor tile must withstand the grit and water tracked in at entries.

If you're using tile in a kitchen or dining room, the tile must also resist scratches from chairs scooting away from the table, or from a portable dishwasher rolling across the floor. Safety is a concern as well. You don't want the family slipping on a wet floor. Unglazed tile provides better slip resistance, and some manufacturers add a surface sprinkling of grit to improve traction.

For entrances and high traffic areas, many clients like quarry tile. This isn't a good tile for countertops, but it is attractive when used in other parts of the home. Immediately after installation, the tile should be treated with a sealer to prevent spills or stains from getting into the tile.

If you prefer a glazed floor tile, choose one with a Mohs rating of 6 to 7 or more, plus some added slip resistance. Be especially careful with glazed Italian tile since many have very thin glazes. Make sure you look through the product literature to find one with an abrasion resistance of III or IV.

Tile Backing

For a shower or full tile wall, the best job is still done with mortar: a ³/4- to 1¹/4-inch bed of cement-sand mortar applied to a metal lath or mesh base. For sloped or angled surfaces, this is the way to go because you can shape the mortar to any contour (Figure 3). But if you do tile jobs only occasionally, you'll be better off with a thinset method, using a base of drywall, plywood, or cement backerboard (see "Tile Backerboards," page 149).

Floors. The main thinset methods for floors are shown in Figure 4. If the building does not have a lot of moisture in the crawlspace or basement, you can lay tile over plywood. You must have at least 1 inch of wood below the tile. Adjacent edges of the plywood sheets can't be more than ¹/32 inch above or below each other, and when you have large areas, you'll also need expansion joints. After preparing the floor, you set the tile in organic adhesive (tile mastic). Make sure the adhesive meets ANSI A136.1, an industry spec that means the adhesive is appropriate for a tile job. Use this method only for light residential jobs. The system won't stand up to wheel loads, and

Figure 3. *With a traditional thick-set mortar bed, you can level or plumb uneven framing and contour the surface to any angle. Mortar is applied over wire or mesh lath.*

SCOTT DUNCAN

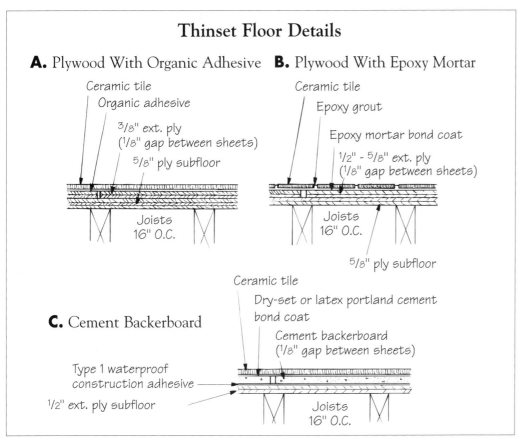

Thinset Floor Details

A. Plywood With Organic Adhesive

Ceramic tile
Organic adhesive
3/8" ext. ply
(1/8" gap between sheets)
5/8" ply subfloor
Joists
16" O.C.

B. Plywood With Epoxy Mortar

Ceramic tile
Epoxy grout
Epoxy mortar bond coat
1/2" - 5/8" ext. ply
(1/8" gap between sheets)
Joists
16" O.C.
5/8" ply subfloor

C. Cement Backerboard

Ceramic tile
Dry-set or latex portland cement bond coat
Cement backerboard
(1/8" gap between sheets)
Type 1 waterproof construction adhesive
1/2" ext. ply subfloor
Joists
16" O.C.

Figure 4. *Thin-set options:* *On light-residential floors under dry conditions, you can use mastic over plywood (A). For better quality with some water resistance, upgrade to an epoxy mortar and grout (B). For still better quality and improved water resistance, use a cement backerboard with a dry-set or latex-modified mortar (C).*

it's not recommended for wet areas.

For higher quality residential work, with some moisture resistance, use an epoxy mortar and epoxy grout over a plywood base. Make sure you fill the gaps between sheets with epoxy. Use an epoxy mortar that meets ANSI A118.3 or a modified epoxy-emulsion mortar. Epoxy mortar uses epoxy resin and hardener. Modified epoxy-emulsion mortar uses epoxy resin and hardener plus portland cement and sand. The only disadvantage to epoxy systems is that they are more expensive, and you have to clean up immediately.

For another step up in quality, you can use cement backerboard. In this system, you'll need to first put 1/2-inch exterior grade plywood on your subfloor, making sure the plywood level doesn't vary more than 1/8 inch over 10 feet. Your tile job will be only as flat as the subfloor you put it on. Line up the cement backerboard on the joists, staggering the joints, and use adhesive between it and the subfloor (Figure 5). The adhesive should be a Type 1 waterproof construction adhesive. Fasten the board with galvanized or screw-type nails, but make sure the fasteners are corrosion resistant.

To lay your tile or backerboard, use a *dry-set mortar* (a mixture of portland cement with sand and additives) or a *latex portland-cement mortar* (a mixture of portland cement, sand, and a latex additive). I always use a latex portland-cement mortar when laying impervious tile because it has a better bond strength. Fill the gaps between sheets of backerboard as you go. Some companies also recommend that you use mesh tape over the joints. This system gives you good water resistance, but it's not totally waterproof.

I use backerboard or traditional mud system beneath impervious tile and Italian tile because of special problems with these tiles. Impervious tile is so glasslike that you need the extra bond strength of a latex portland-cement

mortar (or epoxy mortar) to hold it securely. Italian tile, though often not impervious, also requires a dry-set or latex portland-cement mortar rather than an organic adhesive. This is because Italian tile is thin — about $1/4$ to $3/8$ inch thick — and if you use an organic adhesive, which can stay plastic for a longer time, you run the risk that someone will step on the tile and crack it. Also, since Italian tile has lugs that project from the back, you should use a trowel with $1/2$-inch notches to spread your mortar. This gives you good contact between the bedding mortar and the back of the tile.

Sometimes the floors on a remodeling job will be very uneven. In this case, I use $5/8$-inch exterior plywood as a backing system (4x8 sheets, or longer, depending on the length of the room). The longer sheets mean I can better span over low spots. I put dry-set or latex portland-cement mortar under the plywood to take the dips out, and I put wood screws through to the joists every 6 inches. The tile goes down with epoxy mortar or a modified epoxy-emulsion mortar. If I'm really pressed to save floor height, and water is not an issue, I sometimes use $1/2$-inch exterior plywood and lay the tile with organic adhesive.

Concrete floors. While concrete floors provide solid backing for tile, they can also present problems. If you have a crack in the concrete, it will come through the tile. Fortunately, there are new membrane products that allow you to bridge over cracks.

The surface of the concrete, ideally, should be extremely clean. Any paint spilled by painters must be removed because the tile and the bonding agent will not stick to it. To make sure the concrete is clean, I wash down the floor with a solvent. I use muriatic acid, but be careful with this stuff. It is very dangerous to work with. It can burn you and it also gives off hazardous fumes (I wear an organic vapor mask when I use it), so you must warn those around you, as well.

In addition to cleaning, the muriatic acid

Figure 5. *Cement backerboard must be laminated to the subfloor beneath it. Use an approved waterproof adhesive and apply it to fully cover the plywood substrate.*

DUROCK

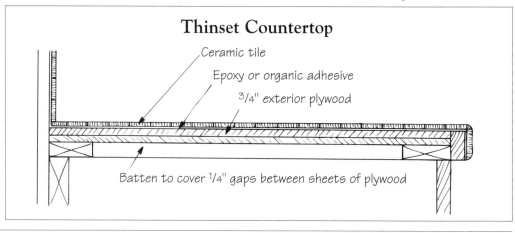

Thinset Countertop

Ceramic tile

Epoxy or organic adhesive

$3/4$" exterior plywood

Batten to cover $1/4$" gaps between sheets of plywood

Figure 6. *A $3/4$-inch plywood base with an epoxy or organic adhesive can provide a suitable base for a tile countertop.*

etches the concrete and gives it "tooth." I then use a latex portland-cement mortar to give a good bond. But on jobs that can take an extra inch of floor height, I prefer to use a 1-inch mortar bed over the concrete to ensure a totally level and appropriate surface for my tile.

Walls. Over wood or metal studs, you can use the cement backerboard system described above. The Tile Council of America approves cement backerboard as a substitute for a full thick-coat mortar ("mud") job. The installation requirements for this system are described above, with the exception that you do not have to use a plywood base. This is a system I use around bathtubs or in showers.

For walls that you know will stay dry, such as those in dining rooms or around fireplaces, you can set the tile on drywall with either organic adhesive, dry-set, or latex portland-cement mortar. Make sure you use regular drywall, not water-resistant, if you're setting the tile with dry-set mortar — or the mortar will not bond.

Countertops. Although I prefer a thick-coat mortar job for countertops, my second choice would be a cement-board underlayment, following the methods outlined for flooring (Figure 6).

You can also use a 3/4-inch exterior plywood base, but you have to measure carefully and make sure you trim out the countertop in such a way that a built-in dishwasher will still slide in. You need to leave a 1/4-inch gap between sheets of plywood to allow for natural expansion and contraction, and put a batten underneath this gap. You can use either a Type 1 organic adhesive or an epoxy mortar. With epoxy mortar, make sure you completely fill the gap between sheets. If you use an epoxy mortar, you'll get better resistance to chemicals and higher bond strength.

Layout and Installation

Tilesetters need time to plan a good layout. Rushing through this phase of the job can lead to problems. The tilesetter starts out by figuring out the center lines for walls, counters, or floors. It's best to begin setting the tile from the center as well, taking up any slack with slightly wider grout joints as you move to the corners. If you don't plan ahead, you may end up with half a tile (or less) at the inside corners. By starting in the center and planning spacing carefully, you can avoid those awkward 3/4-inch strips that break up the even look of a quality job.

Also, plan your layout so you can work in a small area at a time. Whether you're working with cement-based mortar, organic adhesive, or epoxy, you don't want the set-

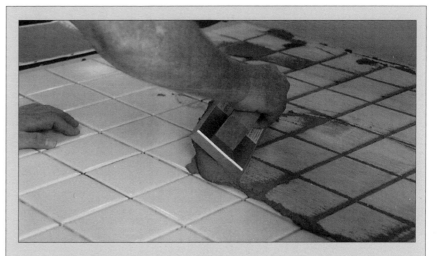

Additives for Mortar and Grout

by Joe Tarver

Setting materials are the mortars and adhesives used to bond the tile to the substrate on tile installation jobs. The modern setting materials are referred to as *thinset*. These include dry-set portland-cement mortars, furan mortars, organic adhesives, and epoxies. Generally, a thinset *adhesive* should be 1/32 inch thick after the tile has been beaten into place. Thinset *mortar* installations should be 3/32 inch thick. In both cases, two-thirds of the joint depth must be kept open for grouting.

A variety of compounds can now be added to portland-cement mortars and grouts to improve performance. The additives improve adhesion, frost resistance, color retention in grouts, flexural and impact strengths, retention of water in grout when grouting high-absorption tiles (for proper hydration), resistance to staining, and easier cleaning and maintenance due to increased density. The four main types of *latices* or emulsion additives and their characteristics are:

Polyvinyl acetate emulsions (PVAs): Excellent bond strength, good resiliency, fair color retention, high water absorption, limited water resistance. Recommended for interior use only.

Styrene butadiene rubber (SBRs): Excellent bond strength

and resiliency, fair color retention, low water absorption. Recommended for interior or exterior use.

Acrylic resin: Excellent bond strength, resiliency, and color retention; low water absorption. Recommended for interior or exterior use.

Epoxy: Two-part epoxy emulsion and hardener combined with a portland-cement sand blend. Excellent bond strength, good resiliency, improved chemical resistance, fair color retention, low water absorption. Recommended for interior or exterior use.

Furan and Furnan are also available for setting and grouting tile where resistance to chemicals and prolonged high temperatures are required.

All of these products have been developed to improve the thinset method of installing and grouting ceramic tile, pavers, thin brick, and thin marble and granite tiles.

When you go to purchase grouts and dry-set mortar, the best approach is to use products from the same manufacturer. Mixing one manufacturer's dry-set mortar with another manufacturer's latex additive could void warranties from both.

Joe Tarver is executive director of the National Tile Contractors Association in Jackson, Miss.

Figure 7. *Apply the grout with a rubber float, and work on an area no larger than 20 square feet at a time.*

ting material to skin over before you embed your tile. If you've planned the layout carefully, you can work without having to stop and think or make time-consuming cuts of fractional tile.

Grout

The two types of grouts are sanded and non-sanded. Use non-sanded grout in joints of $1/8$ inch or less, and sanded grout in joints larger than $1/8$ inch. Grout comes in many colors. With lighter colored grouts, however, you can have difficulty maintaining a consistent color as the grout dries.

This shading is especially likely if you are using tile that absorbs water (semi-vitreous or non-vitreous). The edges of absorbent tile act like a sponge and soak up moisture from the grout. If the setting mortar or organic adhesive squeezes into the tile joints, the mortar will keep the tile from absorbing moisture evenly. To avoid this, wipe out any excess dry-set (or other) mortar before you begin grouting so that the grout will dry uniformly. If you use a grout with an acrylic latex additive, you may be able to avoid the shading problem.

Be sure to follow the mix proportions outlined on the grout package. A common mistake is to add too much water to the grout. Apply the grout with a rubber float or squeegee, pushing it into the joints, and working on an area no larger than 20 square feet at a time (Figure 7). After about 10 minutes, clean the surface of the tile with a damp (not wet) sponge.

For three or four days after the installation, the tile should be washed down once a day with a damp sponge, or damp-cured by spraying with water and covering with kraft paper. If you've used a latex-additive grout, the instructions will tell you that you can skip the damp curing.

If mortar deposits remain on the tile's surface after the grout cures, you can clean off the residue from glazed-tile surfaces with a dilute solution of white vinegar and water. For unglazed tile, you can use a dilute solution of sulfamic acid; mixing proportions vary, so check with the tile store. Don't apply either of these solutions in direct sunlight, and make sure to rinse them off completely.

A good tile job takes time, and shortcuts can lead to future problems. By consulting the tilesetter before the job, the general contractor can help the work go more efficiently and successfully.

For Additional Information

For more information, contact the Tile Council of America or the National Tile Contractors Association (addresses on page 161). ∎

Jay Jones, of Baldwin Park, Calif., is a tile contractor who works throughout California.

Tile Backerboards:
Alternatives to Mud

by Jim Cavanagh

The house was barely two years old, but the tile wall in the master bath — the outside wall of the tub/shower enclosure — was simply rotting away. The base of the tile had turned black, the black had slowly crept up the seams, and no amount of scrubbing could get the clean, white luster back. The bottom of the wall felt soft, and you could push the tile in.

When the homeowner called Matt Oglesby, a professional tilesetter, he didn't even have to see the job to know what had caused the problem. Matt has been in the ceramic tile business for 42 years. This particular problem is one of his pet peeves, one which he has been pointing out to the local home builders association and the Tile Layers Union for years.

For energy reasons and to prevent damage to exterior finishes, many builders and drywall contractors now hang drywall over a polyethylene vapor barrier, effectively trapping moist air between the tile and the plastic. Drywall is not the best material to use here because the gypsum core can be damaged by water vapor or water itself. But there are several products on the market that provide low-cost, water-resistant backing for tile.

Wonder-Board, Durock, Hardibacker, and Dens-Shield are rigid, water-resistant boards that reduce flexing of the applied tile or grout. Tile contractors can use anyone with a strong back to set the underlayment, freeing the experienced tilesetter to do a careful layout.

Wonder-Board

A few years ago, Modulars, Inc., of Hamilton, Ohio, developed a fiberglass-mesh reinforced-concrete panel that is unaffected by water or water vapor. Dimensionally stable, the panels are 7/16 inch thick and come 3x4 feet, 3x5 feet, 3x5 feet 4 inches, and 3x6 feet. At just under 4 pounds per square foot, this tile base weighs about one half to one third less than a troweled mortar bed.

Wonder-Board soon became the sweetheart of the industry. The name is easy to remember, and the installation is quick and simple. To cut, you just score with a Wonder-knife, snap, and cut the glass mesh on the other side. For

U.S. GYPSUM

holes, you beat the edge with a hammer, or if you're a masochist you can cut it with a saw, using a mortar blade. It looks like a sandstorm!

Durock

Durock was created by U.S. Gypsum, and it is similar to Wonder-Board in cross section. Both use fiberglass reinforcing mesh and a cement filler. Durock weighs 12 to 15 pounds less per sheet because polystyrene beads are mixed in with the cement. Durock is also a full 1/2 inch thick and has rounded edges.

You laminate Durock to a minimum 1/2-inch-thick plywood base, using Durock Latex-Fortified Mortar or Durabond Type-1 Tile Mastic. On floors, you should line joints up with joists and stagger the joints. The cement panels are fastened to the subfloor with 1 1/2-inch galvanized roofing nails or wood screws. You have to fill the joints between panels with the adhesive or mortar used to set the tile, and you embed mesh tape in the adhesive, much like thin-coat plaster or joint compound (see Figure 1).

Durock is unaffected by water intrusion, as demonstrated by a tile salesman I know who has kept a section of Durock in a bucket of water for nearly three years. If you pull the piece out, within minutes it appears totally dry.

Figure 1. *Durock cement backerboard has polystyrene pellets in the concrete core, which reduces its weight somewhat. Panel edges have to be level, and joints must be staggered and located over joists.*

This and other cement-board products will wick a certain amount of water, but water doesn't degrade them. Because Durock and Wonder-Board are not harmed by water, you can use vapor barriers without worrying about future damage.

Hardibacker/Hardiliner

Two new kids on the block are made by James Hardie Building Products, an Australian company that has enjoyed much success "down under." One of them is called Hardibacker, and it's sold with a companion product called Hardiliner. They're similar products, the difference being that Hardiliner has beveled edges, like drywall. These edges allow you to smooth seams with tape and filler.

Hardiliner is designed for wall and ceiling applications and can be used with ceramic tile, paint, or wallpaper.

Hardibacker can be used on horizontal surfaces, including floors, and comes in 3x5- and 4x8-foot sheets (Figure 2). It weighs about half as much as the other cementitious backerboards, but then it's only half as thick, at just 1/4 inch. Hardie Building Products claims that the seemingly thin sheets hide their strength, and that when installed over 1/2-inch exterior plywood subfloors, the sheets make permanent, stable backers for tile, marble, or other slab-type surfaces.

The Hardie family of products are made up of wood fiber, sand, portland cement, selected additives, and water. These selected additives,

Bonding to Backerboard

by Harry T. Swanson

Before tiling, it is a good idea to wipe the face of the cement backerboard with a damp sponge to remove dust particles. Apply the thinset mortar with the flat side of the trowel to get a good bond. Then spread it with the proper-size notched trowel. Finally, twist each tile into place and beat it in to get a firm bond.

Some manufacturers recommend a bagged thinset cement/sand mortar mixed with water for the setting bed. We prefer a latex-modified thinset mortar. This is made by adding a latex additive — instead of water — to a one-to-one mix of portland cement and fine sand. The latex will give you four times the bond strength of the mix made with water, and longer open time on the wall to place the tile. It also provides superb resistance to wetting from any water that may reach it.

Another thinset option is mortar with epoxy or epoxy-latex additives. Although epoxy resins yield an even stronger and more chemical-resistant bond than the latex-modified mortars, they are generally too rigid to use on walls, which flex a little under live loads and with seasonal changes. The epoxy-based mortars, however, are ideal for floors and countertops, where the added strength and chemical resistance (to food wastes, for instance) will serve well.

We also recommend adding latex to the tile-grout mixture. It will make a stronger bond, complete the cure to impart maximum hardness and reduce cracking, and reduce by half the moisture absorption of the grout.

To help keep water out of the backerboard, you should place the material 1/4 inch above the surface of the tub and the shower base and caulk this space. Do not grout it. Also, do not grout the corners. They should be caulked along with the top of the walls if the tile is run

up to the ceiling. Flexible caulked joints at these locations will isolate the tile walls from each other and from the rest of the room, which may move from summer to winter in northern climates.

You need the cement board only in the wet-space areas, such as the tub surround or the interior walls of a stall shower. You can use gypsum board in the rest of the bathroom and apply ceramic tile with the latex-modified thinset mortar or with a water-resistant ceramic-tile adhesive.

There are adhesives on the market — organic mastics, for instance — that will bond to a cement backerboard, but they are resistant only to moisture and will not stand up under heavy shower usage. In addition, organic mastics will crystallize and turn brittle over time, especially near a radiator or over a heating vent. Once the material is brittle, a little flexing of the studs can pop it loose. Mastics are recommended only for light-duty residential use.

In wet areas, do the job right and use cement backerboard and latex-modified mortar. This will cost a little more than gypsum board and tile adhesive — but the owners will have a bathroom safe from the ravages of water.

Harry T. Swanson, a retired engineer, is a tile-setting consultant in Branford, Conn.

A tilesetter uses cement backerboard and thinset mortar to tile a large shower area and tub surround.

CAROLYN BATES

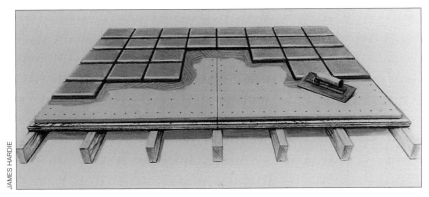

Figure 2.
Lightweight Hardibacker scores and snaps easily because it's thin — only 1/4 inch. It goes on top of 1/2-inch plywood subfloor, but is relatively new in this country.

according to a Hardie sales rep I spoke with, are secret Australian herbs and spices. Perhaps some Vegemite?

Dens-Shield

The most recent product to join the backer-board ranks is Dens-Shield, a paperless gypsum product from the Georgia-Pacific Corp. Dens-Shield was developed as a low-cost, water-resistant tile backer for wall and ceiling applications, using a gypsum core (Figure 3).

Dens-Shield covers its gypsum core with a fiberglass-matte face and a water-resistant coating. Its beauty is that it works like regular drywall, is lighter than the portland-cement backerboards, and is cheaper. It is being marketed to compete with Wonder-Board and Durock when used in shower and tub surrounds. No special tools are required, and it comes in 4x5- and 4x8-foot sheets, either 1/4, 1/2, or 5/8 inch thick.

Tile installers I have talked to think it's a good product as long as it's protected from direct contact with water. One said that the product doesn't appear to wick much, but it swelled slightly when soaked in water.

I had a sample so I decided to see for myself. I cut a 2x6-inch piece and stuck it in a cup of water for 24 hours. Then, using a magnifying glass and a ruler graduated to 64th's of an inch, I remeasured the four sides and found that the product had swollen less than 1/8 inch around its 16-inch perimeter. Perhaps this wasn't a scientific test, but it proved the product does not readily absorb water.

Competition is tight in the tile backer industry. All of the products reviewed for this article seem to do a good job when used in the correct application. It's up to the contractor to choose the best material for a given job and to make sure it's installed to the manufacturers specs. Used inappropriately, any of the products could prove to be very expensive in the long run. ■

Jim Cavanagh remodels kitchens in Kansas City, Mo.

Figure 3. *Dens-Shield is a paperless, gypsum-core backerboard with a waterproof coating. It installs like drywall and is designed as an economical backer for showers and tub surrounds.*

Sources of Supply

Durock
U.S. Gypsum
125 S. Franklin Ave.
Chicago, IL 60606
312/606-3978

Dens-Shield
Georgia Pacific
133 Peachtree St., N.E.
Atlanta, GA 30303
404/652-4000

Hardibacker
James Hardie Building Products
10901 Elm Ave.
Fontana, CA 92337
800/426-4051

Wonder-Board
Modulars, Inc.
6120 S. Gilmore Rd., Suite 201
Fairfield, OH 45014
513/868-7300

With plenty of fresh grout under the trowel, the author forces the material into the joints. The key is to apply ample force and work the trowel from several directions, holding it at 15 to 25 degrees off the tile surface.

Ceramic Tile Grouting

by Michael Byrne

A successful grout job starts with good prep work, a proper mix, and an experienced hand

There are few contractors who cannot recall a horror story about ceramic tile grout, and many homeowners have sworn off tile because the grout was so difficult to keep clean.

But it doesn't have to be that way. With the right installation and grout, tile work is durable and needs little maintenance. In new construction, the *right grout* means one with an additive — typically latex, acrylic, or epoxy. Additives enable grout to withstand the additional flexibility and movement of today's houses. Many companies now supply the additives premixed with the grout — you just add water.

A new generation of grout, referred to as "100%-solids epoxy grout," contains no cement at all — just epoxy resins and colored filler powder (see "Super Grout," page 155).

This article will explain how to get the most from any sack of grout and, I hope, dispel some misconceptions about the process of grouting.

Setting Bed

It makes little sense to skimp on the base, since a bed of tiles will never hold together a concrete slab that is cracking or a wall that is falling apart. If you're not sure of the correct specifications, get a copy of *Handbook for Ceramic Tile Installations* (available for $2.00 from the Tile Council of America, P.O. Box 326, Princeton, NJ 08542; 609/921-7050).

If the substructure is designed and built properly, the adhesive layer becomes the next weak link. Although the official specs allow some tolerance here, each tile should be bedded 100% into the adhesive, with no gaps or voids and a minimum of $3/32$ inch between the tile and the setting bed. For the purposes of this

article, let's assume that the adhesive has cured and we are ready to grout.

Prep Work

The tiles should be pre-conditioned before grouting. This includes the obvious, like removing plastic spacers and scraping excess adhesive from between the tiles (the depth of all the joints should be uniform to ensure consistent color), vacuuming the surface, and misting or sponging (see Figure 1).

But there is another condition that is frequently overlooked — temperature. Direct rays of the sun will quickly cook the moisture from fresh grout, ruining the cure. Block direct rays, even in the dead of winter, and if any areas have been overheated by the sun, you may need to let the tiles and substrate cool down.

Low temperatures can be just as harmful. Cement will not cure below freezing — so in installations where tiles butt against an outside doorway, you may have to stuff some insulation between the door and threshold to keep the chill away from the fresh grout. Room temperature must be maintained until the curing period is over (no moisture left in the grout).

If you're working with tiles or a setting bed that can absorb water, this can prematurely dry out the grout. To avoid this, wash the tiles down with a sponge and clean water. Make sure all parts of the job are moistened — top and sides of the tiles, and the exposed adhesive at the bottom of each joint. Many production crews use a garden sprayer to mist the tiles. The trick is to keep the misting or sponging uniform. Puddles or dry spots can cause the grout above to discolor or powder.

If neither the tiles nor setting bed absorb

water, misting or sponging may not be necessary. But it is still a good practice to wipe the tiles with a damp sponge just prior to dumping on the grout, and it makes cleaning a lot easier.

The Right Mix

All grout, whether it is cement based or epoxy based, needs to cure properly if it is to last. With cement grouts, the correct proportion of water to dry mix is vital for this.

Joint size will determine the kind of grout to use. With narrow joints, 1/16 inch or less, use unsanded grout since there is no room for sand. For larger joints, sand is important, primarily to reduce shrinkage and add strength. Some grout is available with custom grades of sand for joints wider than 3/8 inch. Whichever cementitious grout you use, the same results are desired: it should be smooth, dense, and have a clean appearance.

Start with a clean bucket, fresh water that is room temperature (never use hot water in cold weather), and clean mixing tools. Cleaning water should also be room temperature as should any additive you use to replace the water in the mix. Usually dry mix is poured into the bucket before liquid is added. Most grout bags have guides for determining amounts. Start by adding only about 75% of the liquid required for a proper mix.

A margin trowel makes a good mixing tool but I use a paddle mixer mounted in an electric drill and run it around 300 rpm. The paddle quickly smooths out the lumps if the blades are kept submerged. If the blades keep lifting out of the mix, or they rotate too fast, air is whipped into the mix, cutting the strength of the cured grout as much as 50%.

Add more liquid until the mix has the right consistency, which is somewhere between so wet that it pours from the bucket, and so stiff that it has no plasticity. When the lumps are gone and the consistency is right, stop the mixer and let the stuff sit and "slake" for about 10 to 15 minutes. Now is the time to check the tiles if they were misted or sponged to make sure that there is no water standing on the tiles or puddling in the joints.

The last step is to remix the grout. The short slaking period allows the liquid to completely penetrate the dry ingredients, and the remixing ensures a lump-free grout.

Packing the Grout

Don't use a steel trowel or squeegee for grouting. A steel trowel will scratch the tile and a squeegee cannot force the grout into the joint. Instead, use a Groutmaster (available

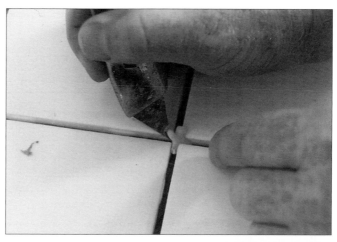

Figure 1. *Before grouting, spacers must be removed (left) or the grout around them will be weak and discolored. Use a dental pick, utility knife, or thin margin trowel. Also use the knife or margin trowel to clean out the grout joints (below).*

from American Olean and most tile suppliers) or a similar trowel designed specifically for grouting. These trowels are available in floor and wall models and have a resilient body and a sharp edge for cutting excess grout away from the tiles. The trowel allows grout to be forced into the joint under pressure while the smooth plastic edge safely removes the excess.

For floor grouting, dump enough grout onto the tiles that its weight and mass help force it into the joints (Figure 2). Hold the trowel at about a 15 to 25 degree angle and begin packing with long sweeps. Back and forth, up and down, going over each joint at least three times. It helps to hold the edge of the tool slightly askew from the joints so the edge does not drop in and force grout out of the joints.

When all the joints appear full and dense, change the angle to about 90 degrees, grasp the handle with two hands, and cut away the excess, positioning the edge of the trowel diagonally to the joints (Figure 3). Work a convenient area at a time, somewhere around 10 square feet. Make consecutive passes until each area is scraped clean. With large, smooth glazed tiles with crisp edges, you should be able to remove all but a trace of grout using the trowel. With small or irregularly shaped tiles, or those with cushioned edges, more grout will remain. The trick is to hold the face of the tool as close to 90 degrees to the surface of the tiles as possible.

At this point, you must decide whether to sponge-clean the area just filled or to continue packing joints with grout. A number of factors will speed up the set and limit how much grout you can apply before sponge cleaning. These include temperature, air conditioning, dehumidifiers, and porous tiles or setting beds.

The fresh grout needs to have "body" before it can be safely cleaned. If it is too loose, the sponge will rake out the grout from the joint. It may be possible to pack hundreds of square feet before using the sponge. On the other hand, you may have to proceed 10 square feet at a time with some installations. The trick is to never let one step get too far ahead of another. As with most crafts, experience in grouting many different types of tile is your best ally.

As the packing process continues on floor work, keep the perimeter or expansion joints free from grout and quickly backfill any voids (waiting can affect the color).

On large floor jobs, it is a routine practice for one worker to pack the joints and another to handle sponge cleaning. But for most grout work, the installer will do both.

Sponge Cleaning

Sponge cleaning has three phases. The first is to loosen and remove the excess grout on the surface of the tiles, the second is to shape the contour of the joint, and the third is to remove the water-borne particles of cement and coloring from the surface of the tiles (Figure 4).

Begin with an area about 10 square feet and go over the tiles with a circular scrubbing motion. Wring all the excess water from the sponge and scrub until the pores of the sponge begin to fill up with grout. Depending on the edge treatment of the tiles, you will have to adjust the pressure against the tile faces. Rinse the sponge in the bucket and repeat until all the solid grout remaining on the surface of the tiles has been loosened and removed.

Next begin working on the joints. They should be as uniform as possible. Pay particular attention to the edges of the tile. If they are crisp, it is easy to know where the tile stops and the grout begins. If the edge is rounded over, your eyes must be the judge. Avoid feathering the margins of the grout joint. These are weak spots that will chip off and catch dirt, making cleaning difficult and the job unsightly.

When the joints are finished, rinse the sponge and make parallel passes from left to right, using one side of the sponge per pass. Rinse after each use and repeat until all visible signs of cement or color are gone from the surface of the tiles. The trick with the sponge is to use the least amount of water possible and keep the moisture content of the sponge consistent from beginning to end. If you dribble water over colored grout you are cleaning, this can lighten the color of the cured grout and give it a mottled appearance. A ray of sunlight moving onto fresh grout will do the same thing.

These two operations, packing and cleaning, continue until the entire job is grouted. If the tiles have a smooth surface and a shiny glaze, the residual cement haze can be easily removed within ten minutes or so by rubbing with a cheesecloth or other soft cloth. Some tiles may require additional sponge cleaning.

A few kinds of tile may require special treatment before grouting can begin. An example of this would be a handmade, unglazed Mexican paver tile. The surface of these tiles is so porous that it is almost impossible to clean or even install grout unless the surface is treated with a release or a sealer. Some quarry tiles, when grouted with colored grout, need a coating of release if the body of the tiles is not to be permanently stained. On installations using large amounts of tiles like these, some manu-

Figure 2. *After allowing the grout to slake, load the trowel full with grout. The grout is too wet if it pours from the bucket, too stiff if it does not spread easily.*

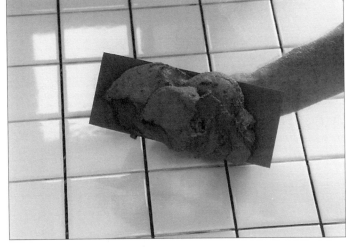

Figure 3. *After spreading about 10 square feet, scrape the tile clean with the edge of the Groutmaster trowel (shown inset). Held diagonally to the tile and tipped at 90 degrees, the resilient edge of the trowel will cut away most of the excess grout.*

Super Grout: 100%-Solids Epoxy

This type of grout gets all its strength from epoxy resins instead of cement; thus the "100% solids" in the name. The filler powder used is simply finely graded sand and a coloring agent. Accelerators are available to shorten the curing and hardening time, but if you are using this grout for the first time, it would be wise not to be in a hurry.

Epoxy grout is similar to cement-based grout in that it needs thorough and careful mixing and it needs to fill each joint completely. You must take the same precautions with temperature extremes, and you still need (more than ever) to use a grout trowel. But the method of application is completely different.

First of all, until the grout material has been placed in the joint and given a chance to set up, water will quickly and totally ruin this kind of grout! So don't do any misting or sponging of the tiles or setting bed. For the grout to stick and hold, the edges of the tiles must be bone dry, and there must be sufficient time for the adhesive layer to dry out before grouting can begin (this is important regardless of the type of grout used).

The first difference comes with mixing. Proportioning here is critical. In some products, the liquid resin and hardener do not mix in equal proportions and manufacturers usually say to mix all of both liquids. If you're using less than the entire unit, this can be tricky.

Begin with a clean mixing bucket, a clean mixing trowel, a clean grout trowel, a couple of mixing sticks, a Scotchbrite pad (included with some 100%-solids kits), buckets of fresh, room-temperature cleaning water, and a sponge. In addition, have the tiles immediately ready for grouting. The temperature must be maintained at room levels for the grout materials, the tiles, and the surrounding environment from the time mixing begins until curing ends.

The first step is to mix each liquid component in its own container and then pour each into the bucket. Keep all mixing sticks separate to avoid a premature curing reaction. Then combine the two liquids together for a minimum of three minutes and add about 75% of the supplied powder and begin mixing. Add more powder until the consistency is right. The body of this grout is different than that of cement-based grouts; the desired consistency will be something like hot peanut butter. You will not be able to get the mix "stiff" like cement grout. And because 100% solids is very sticky, you will need to adjust your movements with the grout trowel.

As soon as the grout is mixed, begin packing immediately (no slaking). The grout should pour out of the bucket slowly. Dump a pile out, hold the trowel at a low angle (15 to 25 degrees), and pack, force, coerce, and intimidate the grout into the joints. If there are any voids under the tiles, the grout will flow in until the voids are full. Keep packing until the pile of grout is used up and repack any voids or holes that show.

You will have, at room temperature, about 45 minutes to spread and clean a small unit (about 2 to 3 gallons). When you finish packing an area — about 10 square feet — hold the trowel at a 90-degree angle to the surface and 45 degrees to the direction of the joints and scrape away the excess. Don't rake the grout from the joints, but don't be too concerned about rough joints — they will smooth out in about ten minutes. Keep packing and scraping until all the grout is used up. Then, wait until the grout begins to stiffen in the joints. Test it with the tip of a margin trowel. If it has resistance and feels like it is beginning to harden, you are ready to begin cleaning. Don't wait until the grout feels hard — by then, it's too late.

The initial cleaning is done with the Scotchbrite pad and water. The pad is stiff enough to bridge from one tile to another without digging out the grout in the joint. But to clean, the pad needs water to lubricate it against the tiles and to help break the epoxy on the surface away from that in the joints. Once the epoxy particles are encapsulated within the slurry of water, they cannot reattach themselves to either the tiles or the grout in the joints.

To begin, dip the pad in the water, let some drain off, and then dribble enough water on the tiles so that the pad moves freely on the surface. Concentrate first on the surface of the tiles and add more water to the surface if necessary. Move the pad lightly with a circular scrubbing motion and when most of the excess is removed, turn your attention to the joints. Go lightly here as well, and keep the sponge from pressing into the joints and removing too much. The trick, here, is to scrub until the edges of the tiles are clean and the water begins to foam. Scrub about 10 square feet with the Scotchbrite pad, then use the sponge to remove the foam.

Remember, the pad cleans the surface and shapes the joints, and the sponge removes the excess from the surface. It is not essential that you remove 100% of the excess from the surface at this time, but it is important that you at least mix all the excess with water. You will need to change the cleaning water frequently to reduce the concentration of epoxy material on the surface of the tiles. You may have to change the Scotchbrite pad as well if the fibers begin to fill up.

If you need more than one batch of grout to finish a job, don't clean up all the grout. Keep a narrow strip between the old and new batches uncleaned so that the new stuff sticks to the old (water will prevent a bond). Also, don't mix a new batch in the old bucket because the old stuff will cause the new batch to harden prematurely.

When all the tiles have been grouted, scrape expansion or perimeter joints clean and let the grout harden overnight— don't worry about any haze on the surface.

The next day, after the grout has hardened, there will be a sticky film left on the tiles. This can easily be cleaned with a sponge and a handful of dishwashing detergent added to a bucket of lukewarm water. A word of caution here: Protect the floor with clean walking boards. At this point, you will not harm the shape of the joints by walking on the tiles, but any loose materials clinging to your shoes (or sock fibers) will stick permanently to the joints. Once this bit of cleanup is finished, the tiles are ready for traffic.

—M.B.

Figure 4. *Once the grout has "body," loosen the excess material on the surface with a clean damp sponge, using a circular scrubbing motion (top). Next, shape the joints by working the sponge back and forth with moderate pressure, being careful not to scrape too much from the joints (bottom). Clean the sponge frequently and get as much water out as possible. On additional passes, draw the sponge one clean face at a time. Remove any remaining haze with a soft cloth when the surface dries.*

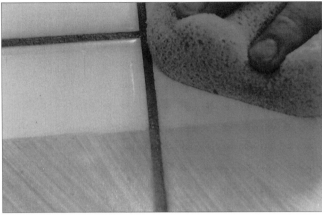

facturers can apply a thin coat of wax to the tiles before they are packed away in cartons.

With cement grouts, it is important to do all the cleaning *today*. Never wait until tomorrow; by that time the grout has become rock. So once the haze appears, get it off quickly. If it doesn't come off with a cloth, hit it with the sponge once more and the next generation of haze should come off easily. Do everything you can to avoid using acids or other harsh chemicals that can easily destroy the glaze.

If you must use an acid, make sure it is approved for use on tile, that the grout has fully cured, and that you follow the directions to the letter. Also make sure you adequately dilute the acid with several rinses of fresh water. Some municipalities have laws regulating the use of such products. And you should protect yourself with a vapor mask, glasses, gloves, and plenty of ventilation. Any wood or painted surfaces coming into contact with the acid, like baseboard molding or metal railings, should be either masked off or covered with a layer of petroleum jelly.

Finishing Touches

With the haze removed, the grout is installed but it is not finished. Now is the time to go over the entire surface and look for defects or voids, clean out expansion or perimeter joints, and clean up any grout on

surrounding surfaces. If you find any voids, pack them now before the grout dries. Also, use the tip of a margin trowel or pointer to square up the grout at inside corners or where trim tiles meet other surfaces. Painters cannot do a good job of cutting an edge if the perimeter of the tilework is rounded with grout. Once the grout has set up (usually within 30 minutes), it is easily carved away and squared up with the trowel.

The next step is to cure the grout by keeping it damp and loosely covering it with kraft paper. This will take 28 days if you use a cement-based grout with no additive. Here is another area where grout additives keep the job economical. Typical latex additives can reduce the cure time to several days. And special additives called "accelerators" will reduce the cure time to as little as four hours and require no dampening and no covering at all. Whatever product you use, read the instructions and check with the manufacturer for specifics if they are not clear.

The last step is to set up enough barriers and warnings to keep others off the tilework until the grout has hardened (again, check the manufacturer's instructions). The grout may look hard and durable after it sets up, but just a slight movement after the grout has lost its plasticity is enough to ruin the bond between the grout and the edge of the tiles. If you need to get on a freshly grouted floor, do so as soon as possible and use some 3/4-inch plywood walking boards to distribute your weight. If another trade needs to get on the floor to finish some work, tell them to come back tomorrow. If you don't protect the fresh grout, you will be responsible for any problems.

When Not To Grout

What you grout is as important as *how* you grout. Grout should never be applied to joints between tile and other materials, such as wood, porcelain, or metal. Different rates of expansion and contraction will eventually tear these joints up, and no amount of regrouting will solve the problem. For these joints, as well as expansion and cove tile joints, a resilient caulk must be used. To match colored grouts, I often use Color Caulk (723 W. Mill St., San Bernadino, CA 92410; 909/888-6225). And to ensure that the caulk can do its job, make certain that joints to be caulked are free of adhesive or grout residues. ∎

Michael Byrne is a master tilesetter, tile consultant, and contributing editor to The Journal of Light Construction.

Ceramic Tile Troubleshooting

by Michael Byrne

Even the best materials won't deliver a good job if you make these common tile mistakes

Using a 1/2-inch drill at low speed, the author mixes a batch of grout. Mixing too fast will weaken the grout.

There are few materials as durable as ceramic tile. A piece of glazed tile is, after all, a layer of glass fused to a layer of stone and should last a lifetime or more. Yet many ceramic tile installations — whether traditional mortar bed or modern thin-bed jobs — fail early in their service. And although no two installations are alike, the list of things that typically go wrong is fairly consistent, and applies even to jobs using the finest materials.

If this article tried to explain the proper way to install tile in all situations, it would be as long as an encyclopedia. Instead, it will address eight of the most common problem areas, show how these problems are caused, and offer antidotes.

Mistake One: The Wrong Tile

The easiest way to ruin a tile installation is to choose the wrong tile for the job. Unfortunately, this is where many jobs turn sour. For example, a wall tile set on a well-traveled floor will scratch (Figure 1). Or absorbent tiles in a wet location will get saturated. Although there is currently no universal system for rating tiles, some general guidelines will help.

Nearly any tile will suffice on a dry wall. For a wet wall, however, such as a tub or shower enclosure, choose a vitreous tile. Vitreous (high-fire) tiles are harder and absorb less water than non-vitreous tiles.

Vitreous tiles are generally a good choice for floors and countertops as well. But here you must check the glaze, too. A soft glaze can scratch, or even wear away completely, depending on the foot traffic.

You also need to consider appearances and the customers' expectations. For example, unglazed quarry tile is very tough and will satisfy all the sanitary and durability requirements of a meat packing plant or chemical manufacturer. But many homeowners are disappointed with the product because it shows footprints, and is prone to dusting, even with frequent waxing and cleaning.

Mexican pavers, on the other hand, a relatively soft non-glazed tile, wear well in residential settings. Although they, too, require sealers or waxes and frequent cleaning, over time the appearance of the tiles improves.

In most cases, your tile dealer can tell you whether a given tile will hold up under the intended use. If he's not certain, ask for

Figure 1. Wrong tile for the job: *The glaze along one edge of this wall tile is worn completely through — because it was mistakenly installed on a floor.*

Figure 2. *For industry specs* *on tile materials and installation, follow the recommendations of the* TCA Handbook *and ANSI Standards.*

a sample to test. Then subject the tile to the same conditions it will face when installed — scraping pots and pans, scuffing from shoes, etc. Finally, see if it cleans up to your client's satisfaction using standard cleaning techniques.

Mistake Two:
Ignoring the Specs

When a tile job fails, it seems like everyone involved has enough time and resources to redo the job properly. Wouldn't it be easier to do it right the first time? Usually, this means consulting the *TCA Hand-book of Ceramic Tile Installation* or the *American National Standard Specifications for the Installation of Ceramic Tile* (ANSI A108). Both are available from the Tile Council of America for $2.00 and $10.00, respectively (addresses at end of article).

All materials approved for use on tile-work carry an ANSI number to show that the material meets or exceeds minimum acceptable performance levels. If a product is not listed by ANSI and isn't designed for use with ceramic tile, don't use it.

The *TCA Handbook* is the industry's basic reference for setting tile (Figure 2). It shows sectional views of the most popular installation types, and tells how to properly design, construct, and prepare the substructure.

If you ignore these books and choose the wrong materials, like water-resistant drywall or blueboard for wet areas, or particleboard or lauan plywood for floors, the job is doomed, once again, before any tiles are installed.

Mistake Three:
Storing Materials Carelessly

The best tile materials won't perform their job if they are stored improperly. Take, for instance, latex or acrylic mortar additives. When properly installed and cured, they protect against freezing conditions by keeping moisture from penetrating into the mortar. In addition, they allow mortar to expand and contract as the building moves from moisture or temperature changes. But before they are mixed and cured, freezing can ruin many additives (Figure 3).

For this reason, it is important to do something very simple: Read the printed instructions very carefully. And although some installation materials can survive freezing or overheating, a good rule of thumb for all tile work is to shelter all materials from rain, overheating, and freezing. In fact, keep all materials (including the substrate) at room temperature, and provide supplemental heating or cooling if necessary.

If you have a problem with an installation material, consult the manufacturer. Don't be afraid to appear stupid. (That will happen automatically if you forge ahead with your own creative solution.)

Figure 3. *Freezing and exposure to the elements* *can undermine many tile materials — like this bag of mortar left in the weather overnight.*

Mistake Four:
Not Preparing the Substrate

Drywall compound and dust, flaking paint or floor coatings, dirt, mud, and ground-in half-eaten sandwiches are commonly found in two locations: the local landfill and the job site on which you are working. Unfortunately, all these substances are bond breakers that can prevent the best adhesives from holding on to the substrate.

Additionally, there may be substances intentionally applied that are incompatible with tile materials. Among these are floor waxes and sealers, and curing compounds used with concrete floors. Any such dirt or coating must go. And with concrete, the surface must be free of defects such as scaling and cracking (Figure 4).

In addition, each setting bed, whether concrete, cement backerboard, or mortar, must be plumb, level, square, and flat. Tiles will remain fixed to an out-of-plumb wall just as tightly as they will to one that is plumb, but the appearance will suffer. Best results are achieved by following ANSI Standards and the *TCA Handbook*.

Mistake Five:
Omitting Expansion Joints

Of the many tile failures I've inspected, few were without problems with expansion joints. Industry studies of installer callbacks report similar findings. Yet I continually find that many architects, builders, and installers do not understand this most basic detail.

Expansion joints are safety valves that protect tiles from damage due to the *normal* and *natural* movement inherent in every structure from live loads and environmental conditions. They are needed because of the laws of nature — even where there are no building codes, or on jobs done "the way my father used to."

Even where you find expansion joints, in the mall or other commercial spaces, they are often done wrong, creating cracked or broken tiles along the joints or cracks in the tiles running parallel to the joints. And the sealant used to fill the joint will usually be discolored, unsightly, or missing.

Yet, at least in theory, expansion joints are relatively simple to design, install, and maintain. They are fully described in the *TCA Handbook* (section EJ171), with their required spacing and frequency. The handbook requires them not just in large, commercial spaces, but wherever "tile work

abuts restraining surfaces such as perimeter walls." This includes residential baths, counters, and kitchens.

A good example of this is shown in Figure 5. In his haste to complete the job on time, the general contractor had the baseboard molding installed against the subfloor, and told the tilesetter to butt the tiles tight to the molding. When I was called in to inspect the tile work, the contractor was complaining that the adhesive was bad, the customer claimed the tiles were no good,

Figure 4. Bad substrates *equal failed tile: Don't even think of tiling over a crumbling slab with structural cracks $1/8$ inch or wider.*

Figure 5. *Place an expansion joint* *with a flexible sealant wherever tile meets a restraining surface, such as a partition. If not, the tile may buckle when the wood substrate shrinks.*

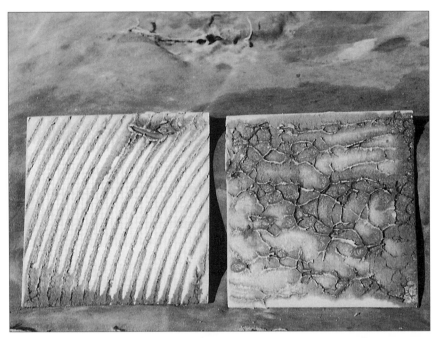

Figure 6. A *beating block* was used to properly seat the tile on the right, resulting in full coverage of adhesive. The tile on the left was simply positioned and pressed into place.

Figure 7. A *mixing paddle* for ceramic tile should have large, thick blades and run at about 300 rpm in a 1/2-inch drill. Smaller, faster blades will entrain air in the mix and weaken the grout.

and the installer swore he did the job according to contract plans and specs.

In the end, the customer was satisfied, but not before the contractor removed and replaced all the tiles, adding a new cementboard underlayment, and removing and reinstalling all the first-floor baseboard molding.

It would have been easier to follow EJ171 the first time.

Mistake Six:
Improper Tile Application

In spite of their reputation for durability, tiles are relatively fragile until they are bedded in adhesive, and surrounded by grout. If not supported properly, tiles are weak and easily broken.

For a good bond, there is only one acceptable method of application, regardless of the amount or type of adhesive or setting bed. That is to use a clean, sharp-notched trowel to spread and comb out the adhesive, followed with a beating block and hammer to seat each tile, leaving a minimum $^3/_{32}$-inch layer of adhesive between tile and setting bed.

Generally, the larger the tile, the larger the trowel notches, adjusting for specific job conditions. In addition to choosing the right trowel, you need to hold it at the correct angle. This takes dexterity and practice, but the basic method is simple: Firmly spread the adhesive with the trowel's smooth side first (the sound and feel of the trowel grating against the setting bed are good indicators of enough pressure). Next, add more adhesive to at least equal the depth of the notches on the trowel, and then use the notched side to produce the thin ridges of adhesive. Keep the notches in contact with the setting bed at all times, and, as above, use sound and feel as indicators.

After positioning the tile, it must be seated with the beating block. Unless the tile is properly bedded with 100% coverage of the adhesive, the effort is wasted (Figure 6).

The beating block does not require the same hammer blows you would use to drive a nail, but rather firm gentle taps. The idea is to seat the tile in adhesive, and level it against neighboring tiles. If the process fails to achieve full adhesive coverage, apply more adhesive with a slightly larger-notched trowel.

Mistake Seven:
Wrong Grouting Techniques

Grouting has three stages: mixing, placement, and finishing. A slipup or shortcut during any step can wreck the appearance or performance of even the most carefully installed tiles. A good grout job, on the other hand, can help to mask slight surface irregularities between tiles — although it can't improve the grip of a weak adhesive.

Grouting involves too many variables to cover in this article (see "Ceramic Tile Grouting," page 152), but let's look at the three most critical points: air entrainment, erosion by clean-up water, and finish techniques.

Air entrainment in grout. Since hand mixing infuses very little air into grout, it produces the strongest mix. But most installers use power equipment, which can potentially entrain air into the grout mix.

Since grout depends on its density to protect the tiles and resist water, care is needed when mixing.

Installers use different types of mixing devices. Small paddles are designed for use with liquids like paint, and require high speeds. This whips thousands of tiny air bubbles into the mix, perforating and weakening the cured grout, and leaving innumerable entry points for water.

For better quality grout, use a paddle with large, thick blades like the one shown in Figure 7. These typically run at about 300 rpm in a $1/2$-inch drill.

Eroding the fresh grout with cleaning water. For portland cement-based grouts, water is vital for the proper hydration of the mix. In fact, damp curing is necessary to ensure that the grout reaches its maximum strength (damp curing is not required with some latex or acrylic grouts). But the use of excess cleaning water is the enemy of grout, and can wash out the cement particles that bind the mix together.

The best way to control cleanup water is to use a specially designed grout trowel. I prefer the Groutmaster trowel (available from American Olean and most tile suppliers).

Sloppy finishes. The last step in any tile installation (other than putting sealant in the expansion joints) is the finishing of the grout after initial cleaning. If done right, this "final inspection" can make the difference between a mediocre job and one that looks polished. All that is required is a slightly dampened sponge or soft cloth and the tip of a margin trowel or utility knife.

The goal is to get each joint identical, with corners sharp and crisp, and margins squared off.

The time to begin is when all that remains on the face of the tiles is a light cement haze. Buff the tiles with the cloth or sponge, and eye each joint for consistency, packing low spots, and paring down the highs. Make certain that an equal amount of corner or edge is revealed on each tile. Also, a sharp edge on the perimeter joint makes life much easier for the painter or paper hanger to cut a crisp edge.

Mistake Eight:
No Protection During Curing

Many installers, even experienced tilesetters, think that curing doesn't start until the grout has been placed. Actually, each tile installation has at least two critical curing periods: after the adhesive has been placed, and after the grout has been placed.

If a waterproofing or crack-isolation membrane is included, there will be three. And if expansion joints are within a traffic or use area, there will be four. Here's why.

First, all adhesives, sealants, and mortars (including mortar beds, thinset mortars, and grouts) go through three phases: the plastic phase when they can be applied and generally moved about, the setting phase when they begin to harden, and the cured phase when they may accept normal traffic or use.

During the setting phase, the molecules in the material are starting to lock into place, essentially by growing bristles that intertwine. Until the material has fully cured, the bristles are fragile and can be damaged by pressure, for example, from someone's foot. Once this happens, the bristles don't grow back, and the bond is permanently damaged.

So much for amateur chemistry. The point is that movement is a problem. Even thick walking boards placed over freshly installed tiles cannot protect the setting adhesive, mortar, or grout. The only way to be sure is to eliminate traffic during the setting phase. Installers should use barricades and written notices to protect the tiles and themselves.

Tile installation is not complicated to the professional who follows the accepted standards, uses approved materials, and who realizes that the ceramic tile trade, like all others, requires ongoing study and attention to detail. ANSI Standards, and the *TCA Handbook* have taken most of the guesswork out of tile installation, but it is up to the installers to put the information to good use. ∎

Michael Byrne is a master tilesetter, tile consultant, and contributing editor to The Journal of Light Construction.

For More Information

For more information on tile materials and installation, contact:

Tile Council of America
P.O. Box 326
Princeton, NJ 08542
609/921-7050

**American National
Standards Institute (ANSI)**
11 W. 42nd St.
New York, NY 10036
212/642-4900

**National Tile Contractors
Association**
626 Lakeland East Dr.
Jackson, MS 39208
601/939-2071

**Materials and Methods
Standards Association**
P.O. Box 350
Grand Haven, MI 49417
800/678-6625

Membranes for Ceramic Tile

by Michael Byrne

To waterproof a tile job and protect it from building movement, think membranes

Ceramic tile has grown more and more popular throughout the U.S., due largely to the development of thinset systems. These alternatives to tiling over a thick mortar bed have cut down on installation costs, but have introduced new problems as well.

The new thinner, more flexible substrates, including cementitious tile backerboards, are unable to protect the tile from seasonal movement in the structure, particularly in climates with wide temperature swings like New England. In fact, even tile jobs set on thick mortar beds can have problems in modern construction due to the excessive building movement.

Also, the new substrates do not protect the underlying structure from damage when water leaks through the tiles. To guard against problems with both movement and moisture, I rely heavily on membranes to protect my work and the customer's investment.

Membranes have always been part of the tile trade. The ancient Egyptians used melted lumps of crude oil or asphalt to waterproof surfaces covered with tile. And for thousands of years, different forms of asphalt have been used successfully to back up the typical mortar-bed installation.

In our business, we rely on two basic types of membranes: the old standby of asphalt and felt paper, and the newer chlorinated polyethylene (CPE). Most major tile outlets now carry some type of membrane and each has its merits, limitations, and methods of installation. Let me explain why a membrane should be a part of your installation.

First of all, there is the problem of waterproofing. Unlike in the past, the vast majority of tiles today find their way into the bathroom, where we find water splashing over everything.

Tile itself may be waterproof and is usually not harmed by water. But the grout sur-

Two-Part Membranes

  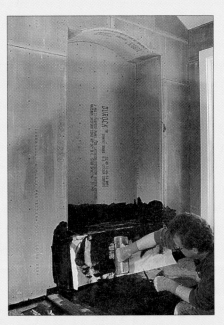

First, a thick liquid is poured on the tile backerboard and troweled into place (left), followed by a fiberglass or polyester reinforcing fabric (center). The author then laps the fabric up walls and around corners, smooths it into place with a trowel, and follows with a second coat (right). This approach works well for waterproofing complex areas like stairs leading up to a tub.

rounding the tiles can be penetrated easily if it cracks (even a hairline), or if it is installed "thin" (not packed into the joint). Then there are the inevitable cracks in corners and around tubs and other plumbing fixtures, or preformed shower pans. Once through the tiles, water is free to penetrate the substructure and start causing trouble.

Moisture-resistant drywall was one attempt to solve the water-penetration problem, but did not prove up to the task. Now, the makers of such boards tell you not to use them under tile. Mortar beds produced without effective membranes behind them don't fare any better at preventing water from reaching and damaging the wood structure underneath.

The other major area of concern is expansion and contraction of the substrate. This is usually caused by seasonal movement in the house or sometimes by water that leaks into the wood structure and causes it to swell. Tile floors thin-set over plywood underlayments are the usual victims of building movement. The problem is that tile and cementitious beds (whether they are floated mortar or manufactured tile backerboards) have a relatively small rate of expansion and contraction compared to lumber products.

Fortunately the problems of water penetration and building movement can often be solved with a single component: an *isolation membrane* installed between the tile and the substrate. Any isolation membrane will help, but like everything else in life, all membranes are not created equal. Let's begin with the simplest.

One-part membranes are not really membranes in the true sense, but rather liquid coatings that are poured, brushed, or trowelled on (see product listing at end of article). These do a fair job of waterproofing the surfaces on which they are applied, but cannot be relied on as a complete water barrier. With enough substrate movement, these materials can eventually pull apart at a joint or crack in a corner, allowing water to penetrate. Consequently, one-part membranes might be good for a floor that gets occasional spills, but not for a shower stall.

Two-part membranes are composed of ready-to-use or site-mixed liquids and a fiberglass or polyester fabric. First, the fabric is trimmed to fit the area to be treated (lapping it up walls and around corners). Then it is removed and the liquid is applied. The fabric is then applied immediately over the liquid and smoothed into place with trowels, taping knives, or other tools. Specific

CPE Membranes

After troweling a thinset adhesive onto the tile backerboard (top), the author rolls out the flexible waterproof sheeting, here Nobleseal T/S (middle). He uses a trowel to work out any bubbles and achieve a good bond to the substrate (bottom). Another layer of thinset will go on top to bond the tile.

instructions may call for additional coats of liquid to complete the installation. Although this type of membrane is not my usual choice for waterproofing or crack isolation, it may be the most practical choice when you are faced with waterproofing a complex area like a set of stairs leading into a tub or pool.

CPE membranes come in sheet form on rolls of different widths, lengths, and thicknesses. Technically, the material is a thermoplastic elastomer. We prefer this membrane for a number of reasons: the biggest one right now is that our company has been using it for over ten years with excellent results. There are two types — one is used as a water barrier on walls, floors, and countertops (Nobleseal T/S), and the other as a water container in shower pans and sunken tubs (Chloraloy 240).

Nobleseal T/S (T/S stands for thinset) has the advantage of a layer of spun polyester fiber-bonded to each side of the sheet. The fiber reinforcement helps the membrane bond to the thin-set and gives the material added strength. The membrane is bonded to the substrate (wood, concrete, drywall, metal, cement backerboard) with a compatible thinset mortar, and the tiles are then thinset to the top of the sheet. We make an effective, long-lasting waterproof connection to the plumbing fixtures with butyl caulk.

In addition to waterproofing, the layer of CPE between the two layers of polyester can absorb movement. It will "give" enough to let the substrate move underneath the tiles without disturbing them. Testing on the product has shown more than $1/4$ inch of substrate movement per 8-foot run of tile with no damage to tiles or grout. The membrane has also proven very effective in eliminating grout-line cracks when it is lapped from a countertop onto the backsplash wall. However, on large surface areas (generally bigger than 15 feet across) expansion joints in the tile work are critical.

You can use Nobleseal T/S over any substrate that's stiff enough to hold tile (follow the specs of the Tile Council of America or the American National Standards Institute). We typically use T/S on countertops and floors, and on tub-enclosure and shower walls in premium jobs.

While specifically designed for thinset use, we sometimes use T/S with floated mortar beds as well. Depending on the application, the membrane can go above or below the mortar bed. When used beneath the mortar bed, it may be loose-laid or bonded to the substrate with an appropriate thinset mortar. When used on top of the mortar bed, the CPE sheet is bonded with a latex-modified thinset mortar.

The membrane used as a water container (Chloraloy 240) is a 40-mil-thick sheet of CPE. While not having all the properties of T/S, it has been the most effective and economical alternative to hot-mopped or metallic pans. Hot-mopped pans are hazardous to deal with, can support only a limited amount of weight, and can dry out and crack. Metallic pans are expensive, difficult to fit, and are usually destroyed by electrolysis around the drain within several months. A pan made of Chloraloy can be built on-site and attached to framing with staples and to masonry with butyl caulk.

Asphalt membranes. The cold-patch asphalt gum used with roof flashing can make a reliable membrane when used with 15- or 30-pound asphalt-impregnated felt. We use this type of membrane as waterproofing behind mortar beds or cement backerboards. It functions as an isolation membrane and as waterproofing. Also, by lapping the felt over the lip of the tub or shower pan, it can form an effective watershed. And when lapped up a wall from a floor, it can keep water from leaking in and damaging subfloors.

This kind of membrane is simple to apply. Comb out a thin layer of asphalt gum with a notched trowel ($1/8$-inch notches or smaller) and cover with the felt paper, smoothing out the air pockets and giving corners nice tight creases. Then cover it with your wire mesh and mortar or with cement backerboard. For a premium job, you can then add a CPE membrane before tiling.

Membranes may seem like an extravagant expense, but over time they are cheap insurance for both your pocket and your reputation. ∎

Michael Byrne is a master tilesetter, tile consultant, and a contributing editor to The Journal of Light Construction.

Sources of Supply

H.B. Fuller Co.
315 S. Hicks Road
Palatine, IL 60067
800/323-7407
(Latex and acrylic thinset adhesives)

Laticrete Intl.
1 Laticrete Park North
Bethany, CT 06525
800/243-4788
(Two-part membranes, Laticrete 301/335, Latex and acrylic thinset adhesives)

Mapei Corp.
1350 Lively Blvd.
Elk Grove Village, IL 60007
800/992-6273
(One-part membranes, Planicrete W, Latex and acrylic thinset adhesives)

The Noble Co.
P.O. Box 350
Grand Haven MI 49417
616/842-7844
(CPE membranes, Nobleseal T/S, Chloraloy 240)

Asphalt Membranes:
Commonly available as cold-applied asphalt or plastic roof cement. Use material with the consistency of tile mastic, not the thin, paint-on variety. Also, choose the fibered type, if available, to increase crack resistance.

Glass Block and Tile in the Bathroom

by Michael Byrne

Use the right mortar and waterproof details for a durable installation

As a tilesetter, I have been working with glass blocks for years. I started out with simple "enclosed" panels (small areas of glass block surrounded by framing) and then, through experimentation, moved on to more open and freestanding designs. Thanks to special additives that greatly increase the mortar's strength, dramatic uses of glass block not possible ten years ago are becoming commonplace, especially in commercial buildings.

At present, there is not an industrywide standard for either large commercial work or residential applications. However, Pittsburgh Corning Corporation, the only manufacturer of glass block in the U.S., has conducted extensive research and provides good technical literature (see "Sources of Supply," page 170). They can also provide technical advice by telephone to help you with difficult or unusual situations.

In this article, I'll illustrate some techniques I've developed for situations that go beyond the simple enclosed panel, using a bathtub partition as an example. The material presented here is not meant to be considered a "standard." Rather, these are techniques that have served me well and assure me of a strong, durable installation.

Panel Design

On this job, the glass block panel at the end of the tub isolates the toilet area while allowing light from the window to flood the room. Rather than dim the available daylight with framing at the exposed edge of the glass block panel, which is right in front of the window, I chose to reinforce the panel with a rebar "spine" at this edge. This "spine" consists of two pieces of $1/2$-inch rebar surrounded by mortar and hidden behind a thin wrapping of tile.

Getting started. The first step on a job like this is to float the wall in back of the tub and the sill on which the blocks will sit, and cover them with tile. I include a CPE (chlorinated polyethylene) membrane to protect the framing beneath the wall and divert water back into the tub (see Figure 1).

Rebar "spine." Next, I reinforce the blocks

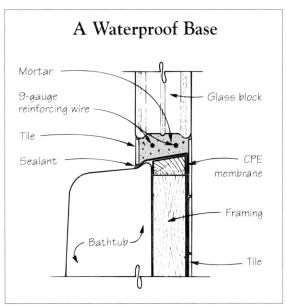

A Waterproof Base

Mortar

9-gauge reinforcing wire

Tile

Sealant

Glass block

CPE membrane

Framing

Bathtub

Tile

Figure 1. *A CPE membrane, embedded in the mortar at the base of the glass block partition, protects the framing below by diverting water into the tub.*

at the exposed edge. I begin by placing two lengths of 1/2-inch rebar from floor to ceiling, 1 inch apart and 1 inch out from the finish edge of the blocks. At the ceiling, I guide the rebar ends into holes bored into the framing, then drop the lower ends into holes bored into the floor framing. The rebars give me a place to anchor reinforcing wire at that edge.

Wiring the Grid

To secure the blocks and strengthen the panel, I wire a double grid of 9-gauge galvanized form wire for each block (Figure 2). The horizontal wires run from the wall framing, where they are anchored with metal clips and screws to the rebar. The vertical wires run from the framing at the back of the tub to the ceiling, but are not attached at either end. Where a vertical wire crosses a horizontal wire, I secure it with a snug twist of galvanized tie wire. I then connect the two grids with horizontal strips of galvanized lath 1 1/2 inches wide, which I wire into place.

At the rebar, I bend each horizontal wire into a 1 1/4-inch radius, trim it to length, and secure it to the neighboring rebar. I then cover the radius ends with bent sections of galvanized mesh, wired into place. I'll later fill this radiused end of the block panel with mortar, both to tie the edge reinforcing together and to make a base for the ceramic tile cap.

Figure 2. *A double grid of 9-gauge reinforcing wire and a mortar-encased rebar "spine" strengthen this glass block partition.*

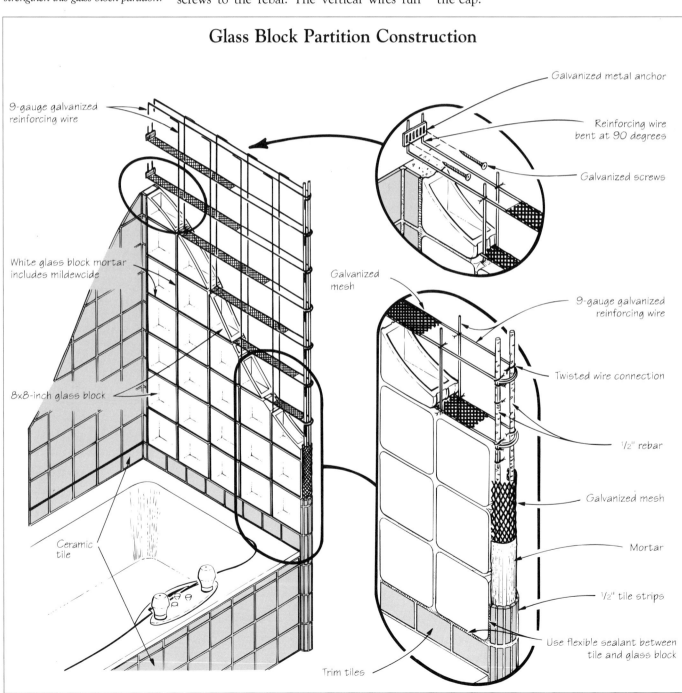

Glass Block Partition Construction

9-gauge galvanized reinforcing wire

Galvanized metal anchor

Reinforcing wire bent at 90 degrees

Galvanized screws

White glass block mortar includes mildewcide

Galvanized mesh

9-gauge galvanized reinforcing wire

8x8-inch glass block

Twisted wire connection

1/2" rebar

Galvanized mesh

Mortar

Ceramic tile

1/2" tile strips

Use flexible sealant between tile and glass block

Trim tiles

Laying the Glass Blocks

Stacking porous, square-edged masonry units, such as bricks or concrete blocks, is relatively easy compared to laying up impervious, round-edged glass blocks. For short runs and small panel areas, I feel confident enough to lay glass blocks one at a time using bricklaying techniques, but as the panel size grows, I use other methods to ensure that each block will run true.

Aligning the blocks. Because the edge on this wall must be dead plumb to match the tiles trimming it off, all the blocks must be in perfect alignment. To achieve this, I temporarily clamp the blocks to a wooden frame, pump mortar into the accessible joints, allow the mortar to set, remove the clamps, and pump mortar into the remaining joints. Here is how I do it:

First, I stack a row of blocks vertically, slipping each one into the reinforcing grid. When the entire row is stacked, I center a 1¹/₂ x 2¹/₂-inch length of straight-grained fir, as long as the stack is high, against the face of the blocks. I pass a U-shaped wire over the wood support, through a block joint, and out the other side. Holding the wire ends with vise grips, I take up the slack and give the wire a couple of twists. I then slip a 16-penny finishing nail behind the twist so that it straddles two blocks. A few more twists with the grips tightens the blocks against the wood support, which acts as a straightedge (Figure 3).

Next, I run a row of blocks horizontally, just as above, only this time, the fir straightedges are placed on the opposite side and run horizontally. Beneath this bottom run of block, I use wooden shims or wedges to start off level (Figure 4). On subsequent courses, I use short wooden shims to keep the blocks spaced right. Each twisted wire exerts a lot of force, and with all the courses attached, the fir straightedges hold the two faces of the panel in alignment. A quick check with the level, a few adjustments here and there, and the panel is ready for mortar.

Preparing the Mortar

I pump the mortar into the block joints using a heavy-duty pastry bag with a metal tip slightly smaller than the height of the joint (Figure 5). For this to work, the mortar must be able to flow through the tip, and that means absolutely zero lumps. To do this, I power up the same mixing paddle I use for mixing grout and thinset adhesive.

At this stage in the job, speed is just as important as the consistency of the

Figure 3. *The author uses straight lengths of fir — placed vertically on one side of the wall and horizontally on the other — to keep the blocks in alignment while placing the mortar. He clamps each straightedge tightly against the blocks with a U-shaped wire passed through the joint (inset) and twisted around a 16-penny nail.*

Figure 4. *The author places wooden shims (detail inset) in each joint to align the block courses as he assembles the wall.*

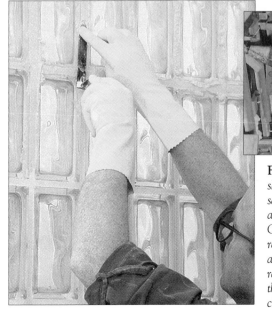

Figure 5. *With the clamping and shimming complete, the author squeezes mortar into the joints with a heavy-duty pastry bag (inset). Once the mortar has set up, he removes the straightedges, shims, and wires, and pumps in the remaining mortar. Finally, he strikes the joints with a margin trowel and cleans up any excess mortar.*

Glass Block Sources and Materials

The recent surge of interest in glass block is probably due to one thing: They let light in. With this increased interest has come new block styles — blocks with various surface textures and patterns, corner blocks, bulletproof blocks, blocks that reduce solar heat gain, and blocks that admit more or less light, depending upon job requirements. And with new kinds of glass block has come the development of new materials that speed and improve installation.

Specialty Mortars

Most mortars, even plain, old hardware store readymix, will hold a glass block wall together, but to minimize potential problems, it's best to use mixes specially tailored to glass block installation. You can mix your own, but I don't advise it.

Mortars formulated with water-activated dry polymers or latex or acrylic additives have considerably increased

Special fortified mortars have pushed the limits of what is possible with glass block. The header above the shower door is supported only by reinforced mortar and trimmed with tile (inset).

the strength of glass block panels, making preassembly of panels possible. With this method, common in commercial work, panels are assembled in jigs off site, allowed to cure, and then brought to the site and installed with the help of a crane.

In my own work, fortified mortars allow me to create strong glass block headers trimmed only with tile, like the one above the shower door in the photo.

Mortars for wet locations. The ideal mortar for glass block in wet applications contains both a polymer and a mildewcide. The polymer reduces the absorption rate of the mortar, decreasing the amount of penetration and protecting the reinforcing from rust, which can discolor the joint. The mildewcide helps when the almost inevitable breach occurs and water penetrates the mortar joint.

It is important to use clean water for mixing mortar and to keep the glass blocks packaged until they are set. Any contamination could be a food source for mildew. Once an installation is in use, advise your clients to clean it on a regular basis. Cleaning is made easier with a hand-held shower. With a rinse after each use, some routine scrubbing, and adequate ventilation, mildew should not be a problem.

White mortar. Just as important as the mortar's ingredients are aesthetic considerations. Many clients want glass block panels with white mortar joints. Unlike gray mortar joints, white joints increase the reflected light coming through a panel. Colored mortars are also available.

Installation Accessories

Accessories are available from a number of sources. For straight runs of glass block, Pittsburgh Corning is a source for reinforcing, anchors, and expansion strips, which are used at jambs and headers to accommodate movement in the framing. For curved or angled glass block panels, 9-gauge galvanized form wire can be purchased in 100-pound rolls from masonry supply yards.

There are a number of spacers to choose from. Some are crosses of plastic that ride over the raised seam formed when the two halves of a glass block are heat-welded together to form one block. While effective vertically and horizontally, spacers do allow some misalignment of faces. This problem can be addressed by installing another spacer that has a molded stop to keep the faces of the blocks in an even plane.

While there is no question that spacers can save time and energy, I am just not comfortable with the break each spacer creates within the mortar joint. Also, spacers limit you to a 1/4-inch joint. I prefer to use removable wooden shims instead.

— M. B.

mortar. For most cement-based mortars, the "life" of the mortar follows these stages:

- **Initial mixing:** combining wet and dry ingredients
- **Slaking period:** the rest stop when all the dry ingredients become wet
- **Remixing:** to break down and homogenize any remaining clumps
- **Plastic state:** the only time a mortar should be worked
- **Initial set:** when the mortar should be protected from movement
- **Hardening off:** when the mortar is hard and appears to have lost all its moisture
- **Curing:** the period until the mortar is past the 28-day mark for maximum compressive strength

The best way to ensure that the mortar will do what it is intended to do is to carefully read and follow the instructions on the bucket or bag. Also, have all the materials (block, mortar, liquid additives) and the job site at room temperature. Mortar setup will be delayed if temperatures are in the 60s, and indefinitely postponed below 60°F.

Wetter than usual mix. To get the glass block mortar through the pastry bag tip, it must be mixed slightly wetter than normal. I begin by following the recommended wet-to-dry ratio provided by the manufacturer, mix up a batch, and see if it will go through the tip. I then add only enough extra liquid to make the mix flow. With a power mixer, I could prepare the total amount needed, but I generally mix only enough to fill the bag three or four times. After the initial mixing, I let the mortar rest for about ten minutes to slake, remix with the paddle, and start filling the bag.

Placing the Mortar

To shoot the mortar, I fill the bag half full and begin twisting the open end with one hand, controlling the tip and squeezing the bag with the other. Because of the configuration of the fir straightedges, I can pump mortar into all the intersecting joints on both sides of the panel. Once this mortar has set, I remove the straightedges and wire, then pump in the remaining mortar.

Patience. After all the joint intersections have been filled, I clean the bag and tip, strike the joints with a 1/4-inch or 3/8-inch margin trowel, and go on to other work while the mortar begins to set.

If this wall were much higher than 6 feet, I would have to wait overnight before the straightedges could be safely removed. But the combination of relatively low height, warm

Simple Glass Block Panels

Interior glass block panels 25 square feet or less and surrounded by framing on four sides are the simplest to install. Using traditional mortaring techniques, you can lay up glass blocks in brick fashion. Because of the small size of the individual glass blocks, the effects of expansion and contraction are minimal. Use panel anchors where the block panel meets the framing, and embed panel reinforcing in the mortar joint every 24 inches for standard glass blocks (illustration below). Mortar the blocks in tight at side jambs, but at headers always use a fiberglass expansion strip to protect the panel from movement from above. Because of their light weight, these panels require only commonsense framing and high-quality framing materials to produce good results.

For basic information on glass block installation, contact Pittsburgh Corning. Always use informed, skilled installers. And when there is any doubt about a project, consult the architect or a structural engineer.

— M. B.

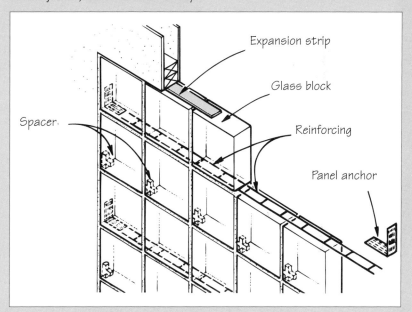

Installation of small, enclosed glass block panels is straightforward using standard accessories. Remember to use an expansion strip at the header above.

weather, and the fact that the initial pumping took place early in the day means that the fir can be stripped after about six hours, and the remaining mortar pumped in.

Removing Temporary Supports

First, I cut all the clamping wires, pull them gently through the blocks, and remove the fir strips. Then I cut away any misplaced mortar, gently clean the faces of the blocks with a damp sponge, mix fresh mortar, and fill the remaining joints. It is important to shoot the mortar in with enough force to fill all the cavities. Remember that for the mortar to achieve its maximum strength, the reinforcing matrix

Figure 6. *The author uses a site-made screed to shape the mortar for the radius end of the partition. The screed rides on the edges of the glass block.*

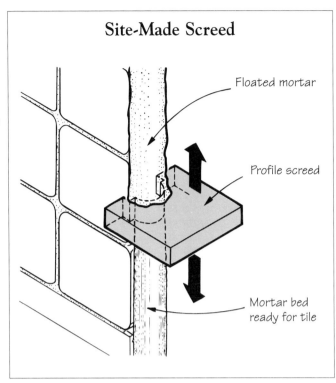

Site-Made Screed

Floated mortar

Profile screed

Mortar bed ready for tile

Screeding to shape. When the mortar has begun to firm up, I use a curved screed, made with a saber saw from 2x stock, to cut away the excess mortar (Figure 6). The screed is shaped so it rides off the edges of the glass blocks, ensuring that the mortar bed will be consistent from top to bottom. After forming the edge with the screed, I make any alterations with the tip of a margin trowel and check for flatness with a straightedge.

Tile strips. When the mortar has hardened off, I cover the semicircular edge with 1/2-inch-wide tile strips cut from a 6-inch tile using a wet saw. I round the cut edge slightly with a tile rubbing stone and then stick each strip to the curved bed with thinset mortar. After this dries, I grout the tile. You could also finish this type of radiused edge with quarter-round trim tile, but I like the dramatic and tailored look the thin tile segments give.

Block-to-tile joints. Mating glass blocks to tile need not be difficult. Whether the glass blocks are inset behind trim tiles or butted against a tile face, the joint between them should be filled with a resilient sealant, such as Color Caulk (723 W. Mill St., San Bernadino, CA 92410; 909/888-6225), instead of being packed with grout. There will be slight movement between the two materials, and the resilient sealant will provide a watertight hinge.

With the rebar locked into the upper and lower framing and encased in mortar, and the 9-gauge grid extending through the blocks, this panel will have no trouble holding up to normal use. ■

Michael Byrne is a master tilesetter, tile consultant, and a contributing editor to The Journal of Light Construction.

must be completely filled, with no voids.

To finish, strike all joints, remove excess mortar from the faces of the block, clean up with a damp sponge, and remove any cement haze with a soft cloth. The panel should be protected from bumps, shock (thermal or mechanical), and vibrations until it has hardened off — about 48 hours.

Finishing the End Cap

With the mortar hard and the panel rigid, it's time to cap the "spine" with tile. I begin by troweling mortar (the same used to set the blocks, only not as wet) through the diamond lath until the cage is filled. Then I build up a layer of mortar to form the setting bed.

Sources of Supply

Conproco
P.O. Box 16477
Hooksett, NH 03106-6477
800/258-3500
(maker of glass block mortar with dry polymer and fungicide)

Mayer Equity Inc.
38 Kinkel St.
Westbury, NY 11590
516/333-0101
(maker of Accu-Speed Connectors)

Pittsburgh Corning Corp.
800 Presque Isle Dr.
Pittsburgh, PA 15239
800/992-5769
(maker of glass blocks and supplier of reinforcing, anchors, expansion strips, and spacers)

Tec Inc.
315 South Hicks Rd.
Palatine, IL 60067
800/323-7407
(maker of white glass block mortar with dry polymer)

Chapter 7

VENTILATION

DAVID LEMKIN, CKD, DESIGNER, COURTESY OF NKBA

The hooded overhead fan (above) captures steam from both short and tall pots, even those placed on the front burner. Counter-level downdraft models (right) work well only with short pots.

Clearing the Kitchen Air

by Wanda Olson

Overhead hoods may not look as sleek as other models. But they still do the best job of ventilating combustion gases, moisture, and odors.

Rangetop cooking produces, among other things, water vapor, grease, smoke, and cooking odors. In addition, gas ranges produce nitrogen dioxide, carbon monoxide, and carbon dioxide. Left in the house, these gases pose health risks, while moisture poses the usual risk to the house itself.

For all these reasons, most new and remodeled kitchens these days have some sort of ventilation. But some of these units aren't up to the task before them, and fail to remove moisture and contaminants.

Here at the University of Minnesota, we tested the two main types of kitchen exhaust systems, overhead range hoods and downdraft fans, to see how well they capture cooking contaminants. We used steam from boiling water to simulate the exhaust gases, cooking odors, and moisture produced from typical cooking uses.

We found that the standard overhead range hood, properly installed, best meets the whole spectrum of exhaust needs that a kitchen might create. The two downdraft options, on the other hand, meet some exhaust needs very well while meeting others very poorly.

Before getting into the details of how hood and downdraft units perform, it's worth mentioning one type of "exhaust" fan that hardly performs at all: the so-called "recirculating" range hoods. These simply filter the gases, moisture, and contaminants rising from the range before blowing them back into the room. While these units trap some grease and odor in their filters, they don't remove any moisture or noxious gases from the house. They are inadequate in any kitchen. Over a gas range, they give a false sense of security while leaving potentially dangerous gases inside the house.

Hoods

The full-size overhead range hood is the only fan design that will remove all moisture and combustion gases from all conventional cooking uses. It succeeds because hot gases and moisture rising from the rangetop naturally move into the fan's most effective collection area, rather than away from it, as hap-

Typical Airflow Rates for Range Hoods

Wall-mounted range hood	150-600 cfm
Island hood	400-600 cfm
Microwave hood	200-400 cfm
Downdraft vent	300-600 cfm

How Long Is Your Elbow?

F ew exhaust fans deliver the outflows promised by the cfm rating. A recent Canadian study of kitchen exhaust fans found that their actual airflow ranged from 14% to 92% of the rated airflows; over a third of the fans produced airflows below 40% of their rated capacity. These discrepancies are typical of many installed fans.

Why the difference between rated and actual flows? Usually, the fan is not the problem — the ductwork is. Most leading fan manufacturers have their fans' flow rates certified by the Home Ventilating Institute (30 W. University Dr., Arlington Heights, IL 60004; 708/394-0150). HVI has fans independently tested to verify that the fans operate at the advertised flow rates under a standard pressure of 0.1 inch of static pressure. This is roughly equivalent to 30 feet of 3¹/₄x10-inch duct venting a 200-cfm fan. Fans perform poorly when the ductwork creates resistance much greater than this.

To avoid this problem, you must keep ductwork as short and with as few elbows as possible. You're generally safe if you use the size ductwork recommended by the fan maker and keep the ductwork's "equivalent length" to 30 feet or less — not counting the wall or roof cap. Equivalent length is the length of straight runs plus the equivalent lengths (see accompanying chart) of all elbows and transitions.

Generally, this will mean short distances from fan to cap, and no more than two elbows. For example, a run of 7-inch round ductwork with a 2-foot straight vertical section, a 90-degree elbow (10-feet equivalent length), and a 2-foot horizontal straight section running to a wall cap would have an equivalent length of 14 feet — well below the 30-foot maximum.

The 30-foot rule-of-thumb should keep you out of trouble most of the time. Some of the highest quality fans may allow more equivalent length.

When it's not possible to keep the ductwork's equivalent length under 30 feet, it's a good idea to contact the fan's manufacturer. All the major fan makers have technical staff who can help you come up with a duct configuration that will work.

— *David Dobbs*

Equivalent Lengths for Common Duct Fittings

3¹/₄x10-inch Rectangular Fittings

90-Degree Elbow

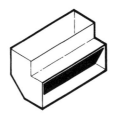

15 ft.

45-Degree Elbow

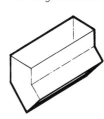

7 ft.

Wall Cap

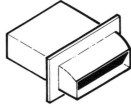

2 ft.

90-Degree Flat Elbow

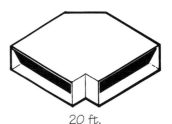

20 ft.

3¹/₄x10-inch-to-Round Transitions

Straight Transition

To 6–8 in. round = 4 ft.

90-Degree Transition

To 8-in. round = 25 ft.

Round Fittings

45-Degree Elbow

6-in. round = 6 ft.
7-in. round = 5 ft.
8-in. round = 3 ft.

90-Degree Elbow

6-in. round = 12 ft.
7-in. round = 10 ft.
8-in. round = 7 ft.

Pop-Up Downdraft Vents

by Sal Alfano

Where an overhead range hood won't do, a pop-up ventilator may answer your venting needs

Best Model DD6 pop-up downdraft vent

Often, the most practical way to vent an island or peninsula cooktop is with a downdraft vent. Downdraft vents that have intakes flush with the surface of the burners have been built into ranges and cooktops for years, but several manufacturers now make pop-up units that can be installed behind virtually any drop-in cooktop. Some are also made to fit behind drop-in ranges, and at least one manufacturer makes a line of cooking appliances with built-in pop-up ventilators.

Features differ from manufacturer to manufacturer, but the main idea is the same. A narrow intake housing, usually located at the rear of the cooktop and matching its width, sits flush with the counter when not operating. When in use, the intake housing, or "scoop," rises to a height of about 8 inches above the cooking surface. The blower, which comes on either automatically or via a separate switch, is usually a squirrel-cage fan mounted in the cabinet below the cooktop or in a remote location, such as on an exterior wall or on the roof of the building. When the ventilator is turned off, the blower shuts down and the intake housing retracts back into the counter, either immediately or after a delay of a few minutes.

Part of the appeal of pop-up ventilators is that they are out of sight when not in use, and they are inconspicuous even when operating. This is especially true for cooktops in an island or peninsula. Ceiling-mounted vent hoods in these locations are often so large that they dominate the room. And since they work best when the hood is mounted at eye-level, overhead ventilators block the line of sight of people working at the range.

Installing a Pop-Up Vent

The blower housing for most pop-up downdraft ventilators mounts in the cabinet under the cooktop. More powerful (900-cfm) blowers that mount on the wall or roof outside of the house are also available. As with any exhaust fan, it's important to limit the length of the duct run and the number of bends, both of which can have a dramatic effect on performance (see "How Long Is Your Elbow?," previous page).

When pop-up downdraft ventilators were first introduced, the housings were very large and occupied most of the cabinet below the cooktop. More recent designs are much slimmer, allowing for shelves or drawers between 12 and 17 inches deep in front of the housing, depending on the model.

Most pop-up downdraft ventilators should be installed as close to the cooktop as possible to avoid an awkward, hard-to-clean strip of countertop between the cooktop and the intake housing. This leaves little room for error. You will have to temporarily position the cooktop before you can lay out the ventilator. Then it's simply a matter of cutting a slot in the countertop, sliding the ventilator into position, and anchoring it to the wall and floor of the cabinet. ∎

Sal Alfano is editor of The Journal of Light Construction.

Sources of Supply

Best Model DD6
The Best Consortium
2323 New Hyde Park Rd.
Lake Success, NY 11042
516/328-7400 (eastern U.S.)

Purcell-Murray Inc.
113 Park Ln.
Brisbane, CA 94005
415/468-6620 (western U.S.)

Broan Eclipse
Broan Manufacturing Co.
926 W. State St.
Hartford, WI 53027
414/673-4340

Dacor Pinnacle
Dacor
950 S. Raymond Ave.
Pasadena, CA 91109
818/799-1000

Kitchenaid Retractable
Downdraft Vent
Kitchenaid
2000 M-63 North
Benton Harbor, MI 49022
800/422-1230

Thermador Cook'n'Vent
Thermador
5119 District Blvd.
Los Angeles, CA 90040
213/562-1133

pens with downdraft systems.

Overhead hoods can be either wall-mounted, hung over an island, or included as an integral part of a microwave appliance mounted over the range. Most overhead hoods have a canopy to aid in capturing contaminants. Hoods without canopies include the new pull-out "silhouette" models and microwave hoods. Our tests did not include the silhouette models.

Wall-mounted hoods. Among overhead fans, properly sized wall-mounted hoods work best, because they avoid the problems of other types, which are described below. Wall-mounted hoods should draw at least 150 to 200 cfm. The hood should be large enough to cover a large portion of the cooking surface, and should be at least 20 inches deep, rather than the 17 inches common in many models. It should be mounted 20 to 24 inches over the rangetop (Figure 1). Raising the hood above 24 inches, which is high enough even for tall cooks, reduces effectiveness.

Island hoods. Most island hoods work well because of their combination of high power and complete coverage of the cooking surface. However, because they are usually in the room's center and are installed at a higher distance above the cooking surface (27 inches is typical to preserve the line of sight across the room), room air currents can diminish their effectiveness. That is why these hoods usually have such powerful fans, up to 600 cfm.

Microwave systems. The hoods that come mounted beneath microwave ovens are similar to ordinary range hoods, with two important exceptions: They don't project as far from the wall (typically only 13 to 15 inches), and they don't have a collecting canopy, only vent openings. They do a good job of exhausting rear burners, but they miss most of the gases and vapors rising from the front burners, even if lowered as close to the cooktop as 15 inches. Because of this, their overall performance isn't that good. If cooking is limited and clients will keep the steamy stuff on the back burners, these fans can be an acceptable solution. But in most homes, you're probably better off installing the microwave elsewhere and using a conventional wall-mounted hood.

Silhouette fans. A new type of wall-mounted fan is the sleek-looking pull-out silhouette model. This has a flat horizontal shelf that pulls out for use; it stores by sliding back into a shallower cabinet. We didn't test these, but I would guess that they're more effective than hoodless microwave units, because they come out further, but not as effective as true hoods, which have canopies to aid in collecting steam and gases.

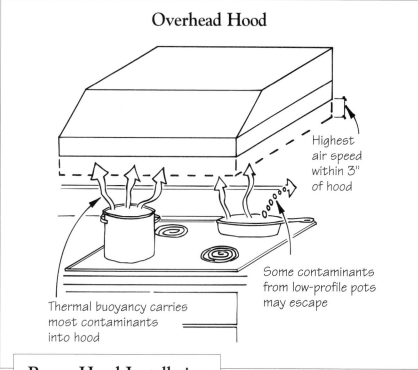

Overhead Hood

Highest air speed within 3" of hood

Some contaminants from low-profile pots may escape

Thermal buoyancy carries most contaminants into hood

Range Hood Installation

20"-24"   20" min.

Figure 1. *Overhead hoods work the best because warmed air from the cooking surface naturally rises toward the blower intake. For best results, the hood should be at least as wide as the cooking surface, be mounted no more than 24 inches above it, and project out at least 20 inches from the wall.*

Downdraft Systems

Downdraft systems come in two types:
- Counter-level downdraft units, which have vents mounted either in the center or at both sides of the rangetop; and
- Rear-mounted pop-up units, with vent scoops that typically rise 8 inches from the rear of the unit to pull exhaust back and then down (see box, facing page).

Both types are usually powered by strong fans. While neither unit performs as well as an overhead hood does for all heights of pots and all cooking loads, their relative strengths and weaknesses differ.

Counter-level units. Counter-level units typically have blowers rated at 500 cfm or higher. Whether center- or side-mounted, they successfully remove combustion gases, grease, and moisture from grills, pots, and pans shorter than 3 inches. But they capture very little rising from pans more than 3 inches high, such as spaghetti pots (Figure 2). If the household's cooking habits create considerable moisture from tall pots (do they cook a lot of pasta?), these hoods should be installed only if the kitchen is otherwise ventilated, such as by a whole-house system.

Pop-up units. Rear-mounted pop-up units, because their vents are located at roughly the height of typical tall pots (about 8 inches), perform well for pots on the rear burners. For the front burners, the capture rate for tall pots is poor, though that for pans under 3 inches is adequate with the fan on high (Figure 3).

This performance isn't ideal, but can be made to work and is often used in island and peninsula cooktops. If a client wants a downdraft unit rather than an overhead hood, ask about cooking practices. If he or she uses tall pots, your best bet is installing a rear-mounted pop-up unit capable of at least 400 cfm — and telling the client to cook the noodles and lobsters to the rear.

About High-Powered Fans

Island and downdraft models have two potential drawbacks you should watch for, both due to the high-powered fans these models use.

First, powerful fans are often loud when run at full speed. Most manufacturers list the sound level of their fans in sones. Unlike decibel ratings, sone ratings are linear: A sone rating of 4 means twice as much noise as a sone rating of 2.

The Home Ventilating Institute has set a limit of 9 sones for kitchen fans up to 500 cfm. (Refrigerators typically operate at about 1 sone.) A few range hoods operate at around 2.5 sones. Most fans, however, particularly downdraft and island hoods, range between 4 and 7 sones at full power.

Clearly, you're best off with the quieter fan, all other things being equal. Fans over 6 or 7 sones may not get used much by the client. If the fan has a variable control rather than a simple two-speed switch, the clients can find a happy medium between low and high settings that is quiet enough to use and strong enough to adequately ventilate.

Getting a quiet fan will probably mean getting a centrifugal blower, sometimes called a "squirrel-cage" fan. The alternative, the prop-like axial fans, are generally noisy even at lower airflow rates. Fortunately, most quality exhaust fans are centrifugal models, since they better overcome the resistance caused by ductwork (see "How Long Is Your Elbow?" page 173).

The other potential drawback to powerful fans is that in tight homes, they may create backdrafting. Backdrafting occurs when negative indoor pressure pulls combustion gases down natural-draft chimneys over furnaces, fireplaces, woodstoves, or water heaters. If you suspect that a backdrafting danger exists, you should test and, if necessary, provide some compensating fresh air intake before installing a powerful exhaust fan. ■

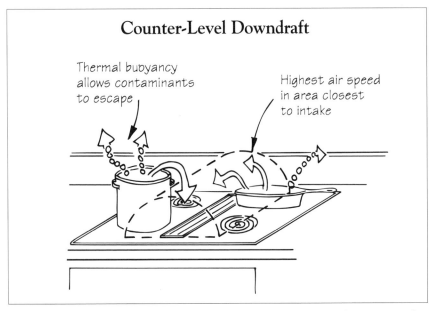

Figure 2. *Surface downdraft vents must overcome the thermal buoyancy of contaminants by pulling air down into the intake. They work best with shallow pots and pans.*

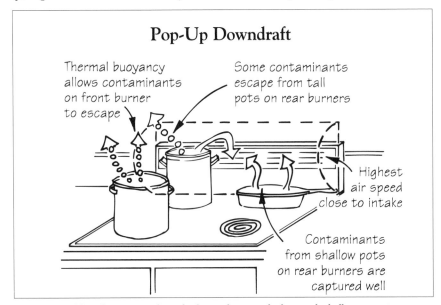

Figure 3. *Although a pop-up downdraft ventilator works best with shallow pots, it can remove some contaminants from a tall pot as long as it is on the rear burner.*

Wanda Olson is an associate professor and extension housing-technology specialist in the Department of Design, Housing, and Apparel at the University of Minnesota, in St. Paul.

Bathroom Venting That Works

by Henri de Marne

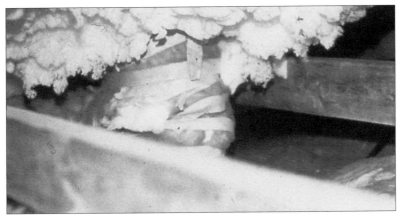

A bath exhaust that vents or leaks into the attic can cause frosty sheathing in cold climates. When the frost melts, you can get moldy wood or wet ceilings.

Bathroom ventilation in one form or another is not only desirable, it is also required by building codes. The code says that in a residential bathroom with no window that opens to the outside, you need a ducted electric fan. Although its main purpose is to provide a healthful exchange of air and to remove odors, ventilation also helps control excessive humidity.

The problem here is that a fan will remove stale air and moisture only when it is turned on, and a window will do the job only when it is opened. Both depend on the actions of the occupants.

Furthermore, even in moderate climates, bathroom fans may be responsible for stained ceilings, condensation dripping on bathroom floors, and rusting of their own metal parts. Also, cold air drafts can often be felt by wet bathers and a lot of warm air can escape to the outside through the fan.

Poor Venting Practices

Most of these problems are due to the way builders and electricians typically install the fans and ductwork. The most harmful approach, which I've seen too often, is to vent directly into the attic, either with no ductwork or a short length of duct. This commonly wets the insulation and the ceiling in the immediate discharge area, and eventually disintegrates

the ceiling finish. The situation is aggravated when the insulation is brought tight against the outlet, sometimes even covering the fan.

In the case of a small attic above sloped ceilings, or a low ranch-type roof, even with gable vents, the result generally is condensation on the sheathing and rafters — sometimes leading to delamination and decay.

Venting to the exterior is better, but can have problems, too. If the duct exhausts through the roof, it may be covered by snow for much of the winter in cold climates. And in cold weather, warm, moist air, propelled through the duct either by the fan or by natural convection, can condense inside the duct and run back inside, causing dripping, staining, and rusting.

Venting into a soffit, or through the wall just below a soffit, also creates problems. If the overhang is not vented, mildew and staining can develop on the soffit and wall. If the overhang is vented, the discharged air from the fan will be drawn into the attic where it's not wanted. The best approach, where possible, is to vent through the gable-end wall.

In many cases, although the fan is vented to the exterior, the ductwork is flawed. Bends in the ductwork are often necessary, but should be avoided as much as possible since they add a lot of resistance to airflow. Shallow turns are better

Choose a quiet fan, insulate the ductwork, and slope it downward toward the exterior

Figure 1. *In retrofits:* Run the fan up to a PVC pipe in the attic. Pitch the attic pipe downward to a wall cap in the gable end. Insulation over and around the attic duct will minimize condensation, and any that does occur should safely drain away.

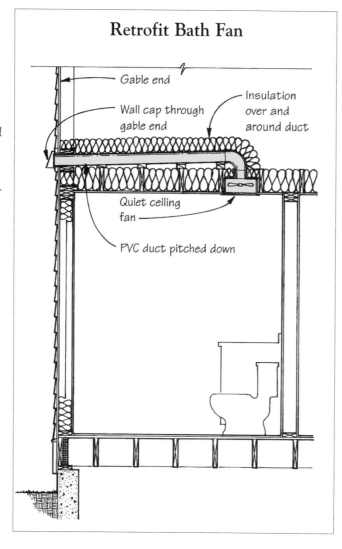

Retrofit Bath Fan

- Gable end
- Wall cap through gable end
- Insulation over and around duct
- Quiet ceiling fan
- PVC duct pitched down

Figure 2. *The preferred method:* Run the ducting down to the basement and out the band joist. The stack effect will tend to keep the damper tight, and warm air will not leak out by convection. Also, any condensation that occurs will not damage finish materials.

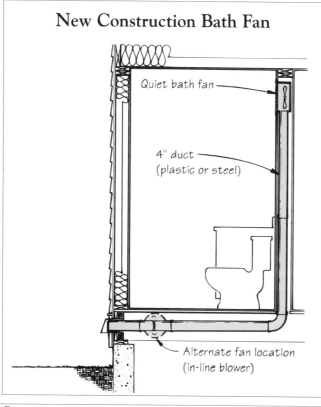

New Construction Bath Fan

- Quiet bath fan
- 4" duct (plastic or steel)
- Alternate fan location (in-line blower)

than 90-degree elbows.

On several occasions, I've found flexible duct wired up to truss webs, but left sagging between the truss and the roof vent. This creates a "trap" in the ducting that collects water, while the bends create excessive resistance to airflow.

The same is true when horizontal duct is allowed to snake over the insulation or drape over each joist on its way to the outlet. I've seen some ducts so completely folded over, or with so many bends, that no air could get through.

Simple Solutions

These problems are not hard to remedy. Primarily they require common sense and a little knowledge about moisture and ventilation.

Exterior ducting through a gable wall can be greatly improved in cold climates by insulating the ductwork to reduce condensation within the ducts. I typically do this by slicing an R-11 fiberglass batt lengthwise and laying a strip tightly on each side of the duct. Then I lay a full-width piece on top of the duct, extending over the two side pieces.

A worthwile improvement in cold climates is to connect the fan housing with flexible ducting to a rigid Schedule-10 plastic bell pipe pitched downward to the wall jack (Figure 1). This is simply done by setting the plastic pipe on progressively smaller blocks nailed to the tops of the floor joists. Any condensation that forms in the plastic pipe will flow to the outside as long as the pipe's bell ends face uphill toward the fan.

Try to install the wall jack on the south side so that any ice that forms will have a chance to melt on sunny days, and try to shield it from the winter's north winds. Use a quality wall jack with a spring-action flap. With the jack on the south, the pipe pitched downward to the outside, and insulation tightly snugged all around the duct, condensation problems and cold drafts are minimized.

This still leaves one problem, however, in very cold weather. Warm household air can leak out the vent by convection, particularly in second-floor bathrooms where the chimney effect is greatest.

But there is a way to have your cake and eat it too. It takes advantage of the fact that warm air rises and other basic principles of physics. And it solves the problems with condensation, drafts, heat loss, rusting, and dripping. I've been using the system for about ten years in new construction and whenever possible in remodeling.

Working With Physics

If we want to use the laws of physics to our own advantage instead of having them work against us, bathrooms should vent *down* instead of up.

Install the fan in the plumbing wall instead of the ceiling, thus avoiding the insulation problems the fan causes. Point the fan outlet downward and attach ducting to it firmly with clamp and duct tape (Figure 2).

Route the duct by the most direct path to the crawlspace or basement, then to the outside through the band joist. The warm, moist air is pushed down, and air that's not exhausted is stored in conditioned space instead of in a cold attic. Its heat is recaptured and little condensation occurs.

Since the vent jack is near the bottom of the house, it now is in the infiltration zone. The stack effect now has a tendency to shut the flap tighter, instead of pushing it out.

Any condensation will occur near the outside jack, and if dripping occurs, it does so in the basement or crawlspace where it is less likely to cause problems than in an insulated ceiling. (Editor's note: This bathroom venting system won both a state and federal energy award in 1985 as part of a competition sponsored by the U.S. Department of Energy.)

This venting system is easily installed in new houses or condominiums in first and second-floor bathrooms. Where two bathrooms vent to the outside, you can join them with a T-Y fitting in the basement in order to eliminate a second wall jack.

In remodeling, there are often ways to retrofit this ducting system. For example, take the case of a bathroom addition on the first floor of a house. The fan does not need to be installed near the ceiling. It can be installed lower in the wall thus permitting easier ducting down.

In the case of a second-floor bathroom, the duct may be run through a closet on the first floor, and so on. With a little ingenuity, you can usually find a way.

Your only other decisions are the choice of fan and how you will control it.

Choosing the Fan

Even though quiet fans are more expensive, you should use them — the difference in noise level is considerable and quiet fans are more likely to be used. Your supplier's catalog will typically rate the fans in sones. Look for a rating of three sones or less.

Some examples of quiet fans are Nutone's QT series (Nutone, Inc., Madison & Red Rds., Cincinnati, OH 45227; 513/527-5100); Broan's Lo-Sone fans (Broan Manufacturing

Figure 3. *This in-line fan, sold by Fantech, is powerful enough to draw against high duct resistance. It can be installed in the basement, as shown, or anywhere in the duct run. The rubber boots on either side dampen the fan noise.*

Co., 926 W. State St., Hartford, WI 53027; 800/558-1711); and the Penn Zephyr series (Penn Ventilator Co., Inc., 9995 Gantry Rd., Philadelphia, PA 19115; 215/464-8900).

In general, you should choose a fan rated at least 70 to 100 cfm for the average bathroom. The assumption is that this will deliver close to the recommended 50 cfm of ventilation after the ductwork is installed (which reduces airflow). With extra long duct runs, however, or excessive moisture loads from a hot tub, steam bath, etc., you'll need a stronger fan.

Where a stronger fan is needed, one good option is to install an in-line duct fan in the attic or basement near the end of the duct run (Figure 3). Here, fan noise will be less of a problem. High-quality in-line fans are sold by Fantech (1712 Northgate Blvd., Sarasota, FL 34234; 813/351-2947) and Kanalflakt (1712 Northgate Blvd., Sarasota, FL 34234; 813/359-3267).

Controls

Bathroom fans are frequently controlled by connecting them to the light switch. Not only is this annoying, since most of the time the fan is not needed, but it also wastes energy and can disturb sleep if the bathroom is used during the night.

A separate switch is preferable but unreliable. It may not be used when needed or it may be forgotten, causing the fan to run for hours.

By far the best fan control, in my opinion, is a 15-minute timer. When it's needed it can be turned on for whatever length of time the user chooses and then forgotten.

Compare the benefits of down-venting bathroom fans with the problems caused by standard venting, and you may decide that it's the way to go. ■

Henri deMarne is a former remodeling contractor, a building and remodeling consultant, and a syndicated columnist in Waitsfield, Vt.

Chapter 8
LIGHTING & ELECTRICAL

KATHI A. GORGES, CKD, DESIGNER; COURTESY OF NKBA. PHOTO BY DAVID LIVINGSTON

A Practical Guide to Kitchen Lighting

by Paul Turpin

The most effective lighting schemes combine both diffuse and direct lighting with plenty of switching options

Incandescent ceiling lights and undercabinet fluorescents make the work areas in this kitchen bright and functional. A ceiling fluorescent fixture and valance lights (foreground) provide even, general lighting.

Kitchens are the single most challenging rooms to light. No other room serves so many functions — from basic food preparation to evening entertaining. Often we don't know if a kitchen lighting scheme will work until the end of a project, yet all our efforts hinge on this crucial step. Good lighting will show off your work, while dismal lighting can sour the customer's appreciation of an otherwise nice kitchen.

Most of the up-front work of lighting a kitchen is knowing what lamps to spec and where to place them. In a kitchen you need three different kinds of lighting — general lighting to see your way around, task lighting at work stations, and accent lighting to show off architectural details and set a "mood."

To accomplish all of these lighting effects, I combine different types of lights. First, I look for a combination of fixtures that, used together, will give maximum illumination for general lighting and, used

separately, will give different levels of task and mood lighting.

Second, I decide on the combination of switches that will best control the fixtures. Dimmers are especially useful for controlling a fixture with several functions. For example, a bright ceiling fixture used for general lighting, or a bright floodlight used for task lighting, can become accent lighting when dimmed to a soft glow.

How Much Light?

I use a rule of thumb based on the assumption that most kitchens have about 8- to 10-foot-high ceilings, are roughly square, and are somewhere between 100 and 200 square feet.

I've found over the years that in a kitchen, you need two or more watts of incandescent light per square foot as a base figure. Because fluorescents produce about two-and-a-half times the light output (lumens) as incandescents for the same power input (watts), you'll need roughly two F40 fluorescents to equal two 100-watt incandescent bulbs. By my rule of thumb, this is enough light for a 10x10 kitchen.

The amount of light is only a starting point. Different fixtures put out different amounts of light, regardless of the bulb wattages. Also, different room configurations may require different lighting arrangements to sufficiently light the space. Depending on how much light is indirect and how big the room is, I may boost my base figure to three or even four watts per square foot. It's best to spread out the light sources, too. It is better to have two 100-watt lamps than one 200-watt lamp. The more evenly you spread the light, the more you'll diminish glare and minimize stark shadows.

General Fixture Requirements

A lighting fixture has to pass three tests before I'll use it:

First, the customer has to like the fixture's appearance. I start by showing pictures in catalogs and recommend that customers go to lighting stores and showrooms. I like to do my homework first, so I can answer any questions about the catalog specs (see "Reading a Lamp Catalog," below). Occasionally, I will model a fixture in the customer's home, and I always urge customers to look at my previous jobs to see the lighting in an actual working kitchen.

Second, a fixture has to have adequate light output. A great looking fixture with a maximum capacity of 60 watts won't work

Reading a Lamp Catalog

Lamp type:
F = fluorescent
40 = 40 watts
WW = warm white

Universal ID number

Manufacturer's description

Bulb type:
T = tubular
12 = $^{12}/8$" or $1^{1}/2$" diameter

Color temperature (CT):
The color of the light itself when it is turned on

Watts	Lamp Type	NAED Number	Description	Bulb	Base	Rated Avg. Life (Hrs.)	Approx. Initial Lumens	Nominal Length	Kelvin Color Temp.	Color Rend. Index	Stock No.	List	Each
\multicolumn{14}{c}{**PREHEAT RAPID START LAMPS**}
40	F40CW	301879	Cool White	T12	MED.BP	20000	3150	48"	4100°	67	3V478	$2.39	$1.77
40	F40WW	301994	Warm White	T12	MED.BP	20000	3200	48"	3000°	63	3V327	$3.16	$2.53
40	F40GO	396358	Gold	T12	MED.BP	20000	2400	48"	N/A	N/A	4V635	$10.98	$9.88
40	F40D	301945	Daylight	T12	MED.BP	20000	2600	48"	6500°	79	3V178	$3.63	$3.27
40	F40/C50	302034	Colortone 50	T12	MED.BP	20000	2200	48"	5000°	92	3V524	$6.14	$5.44
40	F40W	301978	White	T12	MED.BP	20000	3200	78"	3500°	58	4V568	$3.95	$3.56
\multicolumn{14}{c}{**PREHEAT RAPID START EXTENDED SERVICE LAMPS**}
40	F40T10/CW/99	250092	Cool White Ext. Serv.	T10	MED.BP	24000	3200	48"	4100°	67	4V514	$5.66	$5.09
40	F40T10/WW/99	250704	Warm White Ext. Serv.	T10	MED.BP	24000	3250	48"	3000°	53	4V515	$6.28	$5.65
\multicolumn{14}{c}{**RAPID START T-12 FLUORESCENT LAMPS**}
30	F30T12/WW/RS	313742	Warm White	T12	MED.BP	18000	2370	36"	3000°	53	2V770	$7.33	$6.50
30	F30T12/D/RS	313684	Daylight	T12	MED.BP	18000	1950	36"	6500°	79	4V088	$7.33	$6.60
30	F30T12/CW/RS	313320	Cool White	T12	MED.BP	18000	2300	36"	4100°	67	2V897	$5.30	$4.24

Base type:
Medium bi-pin

Lumens:
The approximate light output of the lamp when new. The lumens will degrade over time. Use this number as a relative guide to compare brightness between lamp models.

Color rendition index (CRI):
How true the color of an object looks in the light cast from the lamp. Look at both CT and CRI to find which lamp will give better color.

W.W. Grainger

Kitchen Lighting Case Studies

Case Study #1

This floor plan shows a partially open kitchen with a distinct separation between kitchen and dining areas, defined by the display cabinets that form one wall of the dining room. Here I include the dining room lighting as part of the kitchen lighting solution to demonstrate that lighting can be used to obscure, as well as to illuminate.

For the very small kitchen area, I used two surface-mounted fixtures, providing a combination of strong direct lighting and good reflectance from wall, cabinet, and ceiling surfaces. This combination produces strong overall light and minimizes shadows. By controlling these fixtures with dimmers, multiple light levels from these two sources can achieve almost any desired balance, including making the kitchen almost disappear when viewed from the dining area.

The dining area lighting is designed to focus attention on the table and to distract attention away from the kitchen during mealtime. The light in the display cabinets makes a "foreground" of brightness that makes it difficult to see into the darkened kitchen. The chandelier has a downlight that illuminates the tabletop plus five 60-watt candelabra bulbs. The downlight can be dimmed separately from the other bulbs for any effect from a soft glow to 350 watts of brilliance.

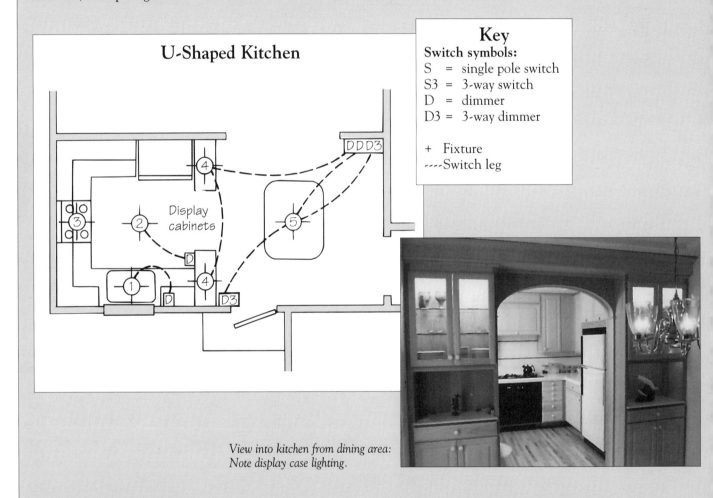

U-Shaped Kitchen

Display cabinets

Key

Switch symbols:

S = single pole switch
S3 = 3-way switch
D = dimmer
D3 = 3-way dimmer

\+ Fixture
----Switch leg

View into kitchen from dining area: Note display case lighting.

1. Sink light: Task lighting and indirect general lighting from a surface-mounted 100-watt incandescent on a Leviton 6621 slide dimmer.

2. Ceiling fixture: General lighting from a surface-mounted 200-watt 1930s fixture (salvaged from a previous job) on a Leviton 6621 slide dimmer.

3. Range hood light: Standard 40-watt incandescent bulb, which helps reduce shadows.

4. Display case lighting: Accent lighting placed inside glass-front dining room cabinets. Each side has two T-10 40-watt incandescent bulbs. Both sides are on one Leviton 6621 dimmer.

5. Suspended chandelier: Task lighting for dining table from 50-watt R-30 downlight on a Leviton 6606 touch dimmer. General lighting from five 60-watt candelabra bulbs on a Leviton 6607 three-way dimmer.

Case Study #2

This kitchen has two main areas, with a drywalled header marking the separation between cooking and dining areas. The kitchen area has a central ceiling fixture for general lighting. A recessed light above the main sink, track lights above the island cabinet, and dimmable fluorescents under the wall cabinets all perform as task or accent lighting, depending on which fixtures are operating at which level, and all add indirectly to the overall illumination. The curved island cabinet was conceived as a "stage setting" for Chinese-style stir-frying, which is one of the customers' favorite forms of entertaining. This is lit by two Capsylite/PAR 75-watt NFLs.

The dining area has dimmable fluorescents that live behind valances and wash the ceiling with indirect general lighting. Track lights are focused on the table. These consist of one Capsylite/PAR 75-watt NSP and one Capsylite/PAR 75-watt NFL. The NSP throws a bright "hot spot" on the table's centerpiece, while the broader beam of the NFL spreads just enough to illuminate all the place settings, stopping short of shining directly in anyone's eyes. This kitchen/dining area is completely open and relies on lighting to distract from work areas during mealtimes.

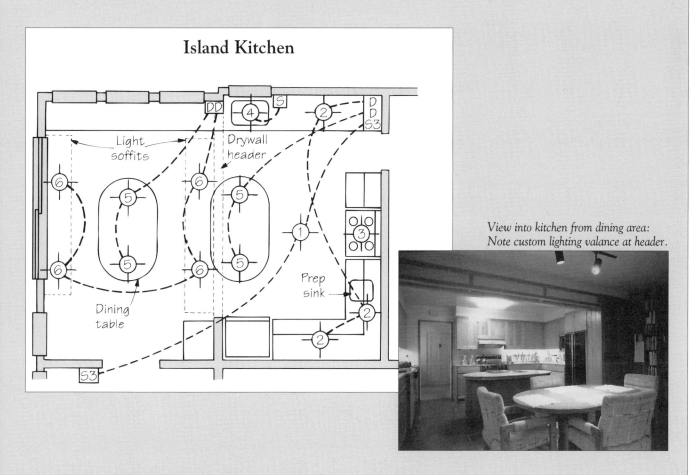

Island Kitchen

View into kitchen from dining area: Note custom lighting valance at header.

1. Kitchen ceiling fixture: General lighting from a 2'x2' white-acrylic "floating" fluorescent fixture with a 30-watt FB40/6 U-bent tube (3,000°K) on a three-way switch.

2. Undercabinet lighting: Task and accent lighting from unshielded fluorescents. Each fixture has a dimming ballast (all three ballasts are controlled by one dimmer switch) and a pair of 48" F40WW fluorescent tubes (3,000°K) protected by the cabinet valance and safety sleeves.

3. Range hood light: Standard 40-watt incandescent bulb, which helps reduce shadows.

4. Sink light: Task and accent lighting from a recessed 60-watt incandescent on a single-pole switch.

5. Track lights: Task and accent lighting at island from two 75-watt NFLs (narrow floods). Task lighting at table from one 75-watt NFL and accent lighting from one 75-watt NSP (narrow spot).

6. Dining room ceiling fixtures: Indirect general lighting from fluorescents behind custom valances built from 1"x2" oak with white acrylic diffusers. Each fixture has a dimming ballast controlled by a dimmer switch, and a pair of 48" F40WW T-12 tubes (detail shown).

Figure 1. *The author prefers a "floating"-type white-acrylic ceiling fixture (top), rather than a box-type fixture with a clear prismatic lens (bottom). The floating fixture provides both reflected light off the ceiling and soft direct light.*

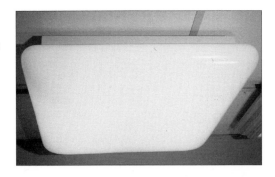

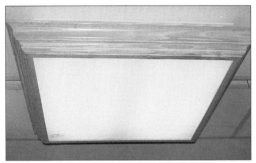

as the main light source in a large kitchen. All fixtures have a maximum wattage rating, and some are available in different versions. If you buy the 60-watt version when the situation calls for the 250-watt fixture, the customer will be unhappy with the lighting. Or worse, he may put in a higher watt bulb and create a fire risk.

Third, a fixture has to fit the specific lighting task in its given location. There are four basic locations for fixtures in a kitchen: The ceiling is for task and general lighting; the wall (above the sink, for example) is also for task and general lighting; the underside of wall cabinets and stove hoods is for task, accent, and indirect general lighting; and the top of wall cabinets is for general and accent lighting.

I select the brightest fixtures for the ceiling. Other locations can also take bright

fixtures, which serve as task lighting first and supplemental general lighting second. The most effective lighting schemes combine both diffuse and direct lighting.

A special issue here in California is that kitchen lighting is regulated by the state energy code, known as Title 24. The code says that the main light in a kitchen must put out at least 55 lumens per watt, which means it can only be fluorescent. Each municipality has its own definition of the "main" fixture. For some building inspectors, this means the one controlled by the first switch position; others call it the largest ceiling fixture.

Diffuse Vs. Direct Light

Diffuse lighting, such as light bounced off a ceiling or wall, is evenly distributed and relatively glare-free. Direct lighting provides maximum brightness, but you get shadows and have to be careful to avoid glare. By combining the two, you can soften shadows and reduce glare. Here are some guidelines for combining diffuse and direct light for each type of lighting in a kitchen.

General lighting. General lighting brightens the overall space. For this I prefer a fixture that casts some light on the ceiling and some down into the room, providing a combination of diffuse and direct light from one fixture. For this purpose, I usually use a "floating"-type fluorescent fixture that has a white-acrylic lens and sides (see Figure 1). I buy mine from Progress (Progress Lighting, P.O. Box 989, Cowpens, SC 29330; 803/463-3274), but most lighting manufacturers make similar fixtures. The most common fluorescent ceiling fixtures have wood sides with a

Figure 2. *Because of its mirror-like reflector, an Alzak fixture with an ordinary A-lamp can deliver twice the light of the more popular black-baffled fixture with an expensive R-lamp. Also, the Alzak fixture lights a much larger floor area and produces less glare.*

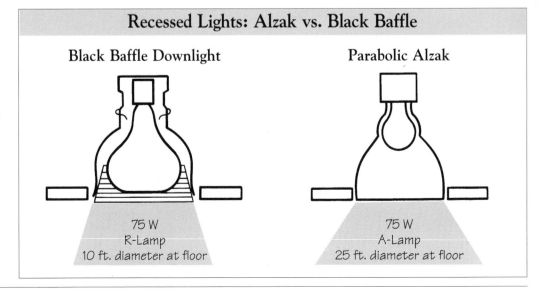

clear prismatic lens, which tend to create glare below and do not illuminate the ceiling. On incandescent lights, I also look for white-acrylic or clouded glass to avoid glare.

I avoid using recessed or track lights for general lighting in a kitchen because they tend to leave the ceiling in shadow. This reduces the amount of reflectance in the room, which is needed to reduce glare. You also get very strong contrasts (bright light and deep shadow) at the work surfaces, which make it difficult to see clearly. These problems reduce the lighting efficiency, so that you need even more watts per square foot. Surface-mounted fluorescents housed in fixtures with solid sides will also create a shadowed ceiling and should be avoided.

In cases where the client absolutely wants recessed fixtures for general lighting, I use either a Fresnel lens or a highly reflective "Alzak" fixture (Figure 2). These deliver the widest beam-spread. Space the lights 4 to 6 feet on-center for downlights, and 30 inches on-center and 30 inches away from the wall for wall-washers.

Task lighting. Once I've got the central fixture putting out reflected light, I can then add floodlights, either in track lights or recessed fixtures, for task lighting. The goal of task lighting is to provide specific work areas with adequate light. I like track lights for their flexibility. If the customers decide they want more lights or more angles, they can easily add more lampholders and even more track after the painting and finishing is done. (Here's a tip on making tracks look straight in spite of an undulating ceiling: Make a few small blocks of wood 1/2 inch thick by the width of the track, and use these to fur the track away from the ceiling 1/2 inch. The effect is attractive and the track stays straight.)

Lighting countertops with fixtures below the wall cabinets is a good way to combine very bright task lighting and, with a dimmer switch, nice mood lighting. Keep in mind that most fixtures will need a valance to hide the glare of the tube or bulb, and adding this to existing cabinets can squeeze the available space between the counter and wall cabinets (Figure 3). Also, if you use unshielded fluorescent tubes, use safety sleeves over the tubes to reduce the chance of breaking one. These sleeves are required in commercial and industrial kitchens because the innards of fluorescent tubes are toxic. In addition, fluorescent fixtures mounted on wood cabinets have to be rated for contact with combustible surfaces.

Accent lighting. Accent lighting is used to accentuate architectural details, such as spotlighting an island centerpiece. Or it can be used to achieve a dramatic effect, such as spreading a faint glow of indirect light on countertops or uplighting ceilings from behind a valance or cove (Figure 4).

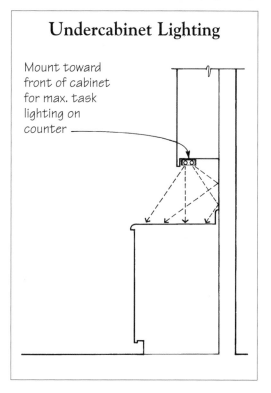

Undercabinet Lighting

Mount toward front of cabinet for max. task lighting on counter

Figure 3. *Make sure fluorescents used for undercabinet lighting are rated for contact with combustible surfaces. Also, use safety sleeves over unshielded tubes to reduce the chance of breaking one.*

Figure 4. *Coves are good for accenting high ceiling areas. They should be mounted above eye level but at least 12 inches below the ceiling. This chart shows the minimum recommended dimensions to achieve uniform brightness.*

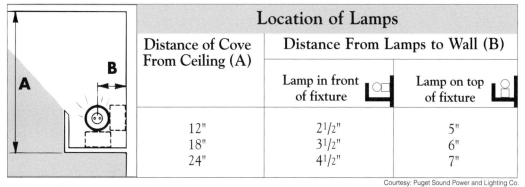

Location of Lamps		
Distance of Cove From Ceiling (A)	Distance From Lamps to Wall (B)	
	Lamp in front of fixture	Lamp on top of fixture
12"	2 1/2"	5"
18"	3 1/2"	6"
24"	4 1/2"	7"

Courtesy: Puget Sound Power and Lighting Co.

Figure 5. *The author likes Leviton Decora Slide-Dimmers for lighting control. A single fixture on a dimmer can function as general lighting at full power, or as accent lighting when dimmed.*

Figure 6. *In place of more expensive low-voltage lamps, the author often uses Capsylite/PAR halogen bulbs for task lighting. These bulbs fit standard fixtures and are known for giving off very "white," bright light with excellent color rendition.*

in dimmer switches for good looks, practicality, and energy savings (see table below).

My favorite dimmer switch is a Leviton Decora Slide-Dimmer switch (Leviton Manufacturing Co., 59-25 Little Neck Pkwy., Little Neck, NY 11362; 800/323-8920). The basic model — the 6621 Single-Pole Slide Dimmer — can be used with incandescent lights (Figure 5). You can also get fluorescent dimmers, fan speed controls, low-voltage dimmers, and three-way versions in the same product line. These are limited to a 600-watt load, which has to be reduced when ganged with other wiring devices (500 watts with one extra, 400 watts with two or more). Lightolier Controls (2413 S. Shiloh, Garland, TX 75041; 800/526-2731) makes a similar line of dimmers, including one model that can control up to 1,000 watts.

Keep in mind that standard incandescent bulbs yellow when dimmed, so you might want to choose bright white paint for walls and ceilings that are washed by dimmed light.

As a simple energy-saving feature, I like to divide the lighting load among several controls. Rather than have one dimmer or switch control 300 watts, I use three switches to control 100 watts each. This way you burn the full 300 watts only when you need maximum brightness.

Fluorescents

Most of the research on fluorescents has been done for the sake of the commercial and industrial worlds, where cost efficiency and energy savings are more critical. But residential fluorescent lighting technology continues to improve, as well. The high lumens-per-watt efficiency of fluorescents is now being complemented by a variety of color temperatures and color rendition indexes (CRI), which are more compatible with traditional residential color and lighting schemes (see "Measuring the Color of a Light").

Accent lighting can be done with conventional fixtures, but the key to successful accenting is in having flexible controls that can blend the lights from different fixtures for a variety of effects.

Controls

Most of the kitchens I remodel are central multipurpose rooms that need switches in more than one location. I am a believer

Savings Attributed to Dimming		
Incandescent Lighting	Electricity Saved	Extends Lamp Life
10% dimmed	5%	2 times
25% dimmed	10%	4 times
50% dimmed	25%	20 times
75% dimmed	50%	greater than 20 times

Courtesy: Puget Sound Power and Lighting Co.

There are still some drawbacks to fluorescents: Standard-ballast tubes flicker when powered by 60-Mghz household current. Electronic ballasts can reduce this, while also providing better energy efficiency and quieter operation. Electronic ballasts are becoming more and more common because they are cheaper to run. They are now cheaper to buy, as well, and are longer-lived (the life expectancy is now very close to the five- to ten-year life of a standard ballast). Keep in mind that most fluorescent lights can be dimmed, but you must use special dimming ballasts and dimmer switches. These end up costing about three times as much as a dimmer for an incandescent light.

Compact fluorescents have made remarkable strides in recent years. They are designed to replace incandescent bulbs and can provide outstanding energy savings. A 13-watt compact fluorescent gives out about as much light as a 75-watt incandescent, even in a recessed fixture (always use a reflector trim with a compact fluorescent in a recessed fixture). Compact fluorescents are now available with color temperatures very similar to incandescents, as well. Their CRI, however, is not quite as good. In addition, compact fluorescents blink a couple times before they come on, and the shape doesn't always fit in a conventional fixture.

Low-Voltage and Halogen Lamps

I often use low-voltage lamps in a kitchen as direct spots, and low-voltage flood lighting for task and mood lighting. Fixtures are either recessed or surface-mounted (including track-style) and are generally smaller and less obtrusive than standard-voltage fixtures.

Low-voltage fixtures and bulbs are more expensive than standard lighting and require a transformer to lower the voltage of the incoming power. But low-voltage lamps are cheaper to burn and throw off very little waste heat. With standard MR-16 lamps, they give off a crisp, bright, very "white" light with excellent color rendition.

High-voltage halogen bulbs come very close in lighting quality to low-voltage equivalents. I often use Capsylite/PARs (PAR stands for parabolic anodized reflector, which describes the bulb shape) inside cabinets with glass doors and for other task lighting in place of more expensive MR-16 low-voltage lamps (Figure 6). I typically

Measuring the Color of a Light

In a kitchen where several different kinds of lamps — incandescent, fluorescent, low-voltage, and halogen — are combined, it's important to keep track of the color temperature and the color rendition index of each light.

Color temperature is measured in degrees Kelvin (K) and indicates the color of the lamp itself when you see it turned on. Standard household incandescents have a color temperature of about 2,700°K; they look "warm" and have a red-based undertone emphasizing reds, oranges, and yellows. Halogen lamps run about 3,000°K and are noticeably whiter; these are considered "neutral." Fluorescents range from 3,000°K to 7,500°K; those on the high end, so-called "cool" wands, have a blue tone emphasizing blues and greens.

Try to keep all the lamps you use in a kitchen close in color temperature, or they'll clash. I lean toward all warm or all neutral. Cool lights don't go well with skin and wood tones.

The color rendition index (CRI) is based on an arbitrary scale of 100 and measures how true the color of an object looks in the light cast from a lamp. For the best color rendition, you want to use a light with a CRI close to 100 — the CRI of daylight. Incandescents, halogens, and low-voltage lamps generally have very high CRIs (99 to 100). But the old standard fluorescent F40-CW, which you see in supermarkets and office buildings, has a CRI around 67.

Read your lamp tables carefully: In the Philips line, one warm-white tube (F40WW) has a CRI of 53 (cost is about $3), while another (F40/SPEC30) has a CRI of 70 (cost is about $4). But the one I would use (F40/30U) has a CRI of 85 (cost is about $8). The only Philips tube with a higher CRI (92) is the Colortone 50 (F40/C50). It costs about $6, but it has a color temperature of 5,000°K, which is far too cool for my taste. Most compact fluorescents have a respectable CRI of 82.

— *P. T.*

Color Temperature Effects

Red ◄——— Neutral ———► Blue			
Warm 2,600-3,400°K	**Natural** 3,500°K	**Cool** 3,600-4,900°K	**Daylight** 5,000°K
Friendly Intimate	Friendly Inviting	Clean Efficient	Bright Alert

use Designer 16 bulbs from Sylvania (Osram/Sylvania, P.O. Box 275, Westville, IN 46074; 800/255-5042). These halogen bulbs are available in 55- and 75-watt NFL (narrow flood) and NSP (narrow spot) models. However, if fixture size or waste heat is an issue, you'll have to stick with low-voltage lamps. ■

Paul Turpin is a Los Angeles-based remodeling contractor who specializes in kitchen and bath design and remodeling.

Fixtures & Lamps for Kitchen Lighting

by Steve Topol

General or ambient lighting ensures that all areas of a room are bright and pleasant, while task lighting brings a flood of light to specific work areas. A third kind, accent lighting, is a design tool that is used to highlight walls and decor, but comes third in importance.

How much light is needed in a kitchen? This will vary considerably depending on the height of ceilings, the color of cabinets, walls, and floors, and type of fixtures. In general, higher ceilings and darker surfaces will require higher wattage.

Lighting experts suggest some ballpark figures for minimum lighting levels. For a very small kitchen — 75 square feet or less — 150 watts of incandescent light from up to three bulbs is the bare minimum. The equivalent in fluorescent bulbs is 55 to 70 watts. In kitchens of up to 120 square feet, the minimum recommendation is 200 watts from up to four incandescent bulbs, or closer to 80 watts from fluorescents. The minimum in kitchens over 120 square feet, if fixtures are carefully placed, is two watts per square foot of incandescent lighting, or 3/4 watt for fluorescent lighting.

Where most kitchen lighting goes wrong is in relying on a single source — a ceiling fixture in the middle of the room. In all but the smallest kitchens, this will create shadows at counter work areas because the person at the chopping board, sink, or cooktop comes between the light source and the activity there. A central fixture will also produce a lot of uncomfortable glare if it is bright enough to penetrate the corners of the room with light.

General Lighting

This doesn't mean you should rule out ceiling fixtures; they're an excellent source of ambient light. If a kitchen is small enough to light with a single fixture, then it should be moved away from the center of the room and mounted closer to cabinets and work areas. But in most kitchens, a central ceiling light should be combined with other fixtures, or replaced by four to six recessed lights (see Table, facing page). Although the standard R-type bulbs shown on the chart will be phased out by late 1995 (under the National Energy Act) in favor of more energy-efficient bulbs, new replacements under development will offer similar performance and draw less power.

Another approach that works well is directing light up at the ceiling. Track lighting, wall-mounted fixtures, chandeliers, and pendant lights can all provide this kind of light. These last two also help with task lighting over a kitchen table or island/peninsula.

Still another good source is indirect lighting — typically fluorescent fixtures mounted behind soffits or on top of wall cabinets. Indirect lighting offers very little glare because the light that reaches the eye is reflected. It also makes a room feel more spacious.

Task Lighting

The job of task lighting is to provide sinks, cooktops, countertop workstations, islands/peninsulas, and table tops with even light. To a large degree, the choice of fixtures depends on the location of the work area.

Undercabinet lights are easily installed over kitchen counters. These slim, compact fluorescent fixtures come in 12- to 48-inch lengths. Make sure to bring them as far forward as possible — just behind the lip of the upper cabinets — so they light the work area and not the backsplash. Another option is

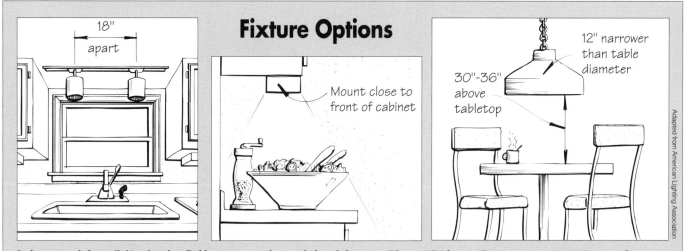

Fixture Options

18" apart

Mount close to front of cabinet

30"-36" above tabletop

12" narrower than table diameter

Sink or range lighting (left) is best handled by two recessed or track downlights using 75-watt "R" lamps. For countertops (center), use eight watts of fluorescent light under the cabinets for every foot of counter length. And keep pendant fixtures (right) over tables or breakfast bars to 120 watts with an incandescent lamp, or 32 to 40 watts with a fluorescent lamp.

a line of recessed downlights just out from the wall cabinets.

Either recessed fixtures or track lighting can be used over sinks or cooktops; these downlights should be placed 15 to 18 inches apart. Here, either 75-watt incandescent bulbs or 30-watt compact fluorescent bulbs work well. Islands and counters not under cabinets should be lit similarly. Again, recessed or track lights are ideal, although a pendant can be used.

Table Top

There are a range of choices for lighting the kitchen table. If your client chooses a pendant light, recommend a 120-watt incandescent or a 32- to 40-watt fluorescent fixture. Either should be positioned 30 to 36 inches above the table.

However, chandeliers and pendant lights aren't always the best solution because their location (which involves knowing the exact size and placement of the table to be used) has to be determined very early in the construction process, and they can detract from the clean lines of contemporary architecture.

The alternative is track lighting or recessed lights. In either case, it's important not to shine light straight down because of the hard shadows it will cast on the faces of the diners. Rather, position the lights behind and to the side of where people will be sitting. One exception is using bulbs with very tight beam spreads; a low-voltage bulb like an MR-16 or PAR-36 can be aimed directly at the table with other fixtures filling light around it.

Matching Lamps and Fixtures

The performance of any lighting fixture depends a lot on the lamp (bulb) used in it. General service "A" lamps emit light in all directions and are fine for most general lighting fixtures. But reflector lamps, or "R" lamps — which are designated either flood type (FL) or spot type (SP) — should be considered when you need to direct a beam of light. Reflector lamps put out nearly double the amount of light on a subject as an "A" lamp of the same wattage; parabolic ("PAR") lamps produce four times the light on the subject by controlling it more precisely. Low voltage bulbs — MR-16 and PAR-36 — have built-in reflectors with halogen bulbs for even finer beam control.

Choose a lamp not only by wattage — the measure of electrical consumption — but also by the amount of light it will produce, the width of the beam, and the color characteristics of the light (table above). The terms used to describe the amount of light delivered by a lamp are lumens, (measured at the lamp) and footcandles (measured at the subject being lit). Light color is measured in degrees Kelvin and the Color Rendition Index or CRI (see "Measuring the Color of Light," page 189)

The best kitchen lighting is a combination of fluorescent and incandescent bulbs. New warm-tone fluorescents have color fidelity comparable to that of incandescents, and typically use one third as much electricity as incandescents for a comparable lumen rating. ■

Steve Topol owns and operates Bay Commercial Lighting Center in San Francisco, Calif.

Lighting Coverage With Recessed Fixtures

Fixture Trim	"A" Bulb 75W	100W	150W	"R" or "PAR" Bulb 50W	75W	150W
	Sq. ft. of illuminated area			Sq. ft. of illuminated area		
Cone	25	40	50	15	30	65
Baffle	20	30	50	10	25	60
Lens	25	35	55	—	—	—
Diffuser	20	30	45	—	—	—

Note: *These coverage figures are based on providing 15 to 25 footcandles of light. Darker rooms require higher wattage, and spacing will vary with the distance from fixture to subject.*

Light Performance Chart

	Lumens per Watt	Avg. Life (hours)	Color Temp.	Typical CRI
Standard Incandescent	5-20	750-1,000	2,800° K	100
Tungsten-Halogen	15-25	2,000-4,000	3,000° K	100
Fluorescent	60-100	15,000-24,000	2,700°-5,000° K	50-90
Compact Fluorescent (5-26 Watts)	20-55	10,000	2,700°-5,000° K	80
Compact Fluorescent (27-40 Watts)	50-80	15,000-20,000	2,700°-4,100° K	80

Note: *Watts is electrical input; lumens is light output. When mixing lamp types, try to use similar color temperatures. Also consider the CRI: The closer to 100, the more colors will look accurate.*

Source: Lighting Fundamentals Handbook

Bathroom Lighting Basics

by Randall Whitehead

Place soft, diffused lights on each side of the mirror to avoid glare and shadows

Good lighting is of the utmost importance in the bathroom for close tasks like shaving and applying makeup. But more often than not, it is inadequate. The most common mistake made in bathrooms is to use a single, recessed light overhead. This creates long, dark shadows under your eyes, nose, and chin. The effect is very similar to what you got as a kid when you held a flashlight under your chin to make a scary face.

Another common mistake is to use one surface-mounted light above the mirror. This is only slightly better than a recessed fixture. At best, it illuminates the top half of the face. To function well, task lighting over the vanity needs balanced light that illuminates the face from all angles and doesn't create shadows.

Vertical Cross Illumination

The best cross lighting is provided by two vertical lights flanking the sink (see top illustration, opposite). This type of lighting originated in the theater. About 20 years ago, manufacturers started to put vanity "light bars" on the market in imitation of dressing room mirrors surrounded by bare bulbs in porcelain sockets. Soon every new house was sporting the new three-bulb brass or chrome bar. More often then not, however, only one bar was used above the mirror rather than one on each side of the mirror. These bars don't work much better than a single fixture unless they're mounted on each side of the mirror.

Vanity light bars have slimmed down from a bulky 4 inches to a more attractive 2^1/$_2$ inches. And the globe-shaped bulbs — called G-lamps — come in much smaller sizes, such as the G-14 which is only 1^3/$_4$ inches in diameter. These bright little bulbs, however, are very harsh and can create a lot of glare.

Older clients with glare sensitive eyes may prefer the traditional wide bar and oversized G-bulbs. Round G-40 bulbs, 5 inches in diameter, diffuse the light more softly and are easier to look at. But regardless of the bulb size, always use a white frosted bulb, not a clear one. A white lamp softens the illumination; clear bulbs produce too much glare to provide good task light for anyone.

The center of the light bars should be placed at eye level. Usually this is about 62 or 64 inches off the floor. And for a single sink vanity, the lights should be spaced about 30 inches apart.

I generally spec a total of between 75 to 150 watts per side. This means that each bulb in a three bulb fixture should be between 25 and 50 watts. The range depends on the brightness of the room: the more reflectance you get off the walls, vanity top, and fixtures, the less wattage you need. Regardless, I always recommend putting vanity lights on a dimmer so the homeowners can adjust the light intensity for themselves. A client may wish to apply makeup, for example, in low light that simulates a nighttime setting.

Another way to provide cross illumination is to wall-mount translucent fixtures at eye level on either side of the sink (see middle illustration, opposite). These can flank a small mirror or be floated on a full wall mirror. Most American and European lighting manufacturers make a number of fixtures that are perfect for this type of application. American Lighting, Lightolier, and Nova are a few of the bigger ones.

There are two high-end alternatives to the simple translucent wall fixture that I like because they integrate nicely with vanity coves and don't call a lot of attention to themselves. These are made by the Phoenix Day Company (1355 Donner Ave., San Francisco, CA 94127; 415/822-4414). Phoenix Day's RW 575 is a triangle-shaped fixture that mounts in a vertical corner, so it works well if the vanity is tucked into an alcove. For vanities without return walls, Phoenix Day makes the RW 550, which is recessed right into the wall to fit flush with the mirror. Both of these come in a variety of finishes with incandescent or fluorescent lamps.

Incandescent vs. Fluorescent

Incandescent light is always the best option for lighting faces. One incandescent light bulb that is especially flattering to skin tones is the Beautytone by Phillips-Westinghouse.

Fluorescents, however, are an increasingly important option to consider. Several states permit only fluorescent light sources in residential bathrooms because they are at least three times more energy-efficient than incan-

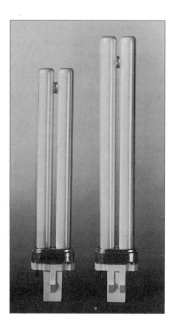

Figure 1. *Compact fluorescents such as these "PL" lamps come in a variety of color temperatures suitable for lighting skin tones.*

descent bulbs. In California, Title 24 requires that at least 50% of the ambient light in all new or remodeled bathrooms (and kitchens) must come from fluorescent fixtures.

Fortunately, many of today's fluorescent lamps are flattering to skin tones. In response to criticisms of poor color rendition, most manufacturers of fluorescents have introduced bulbs that use color-correcting phosphers. In fact, there are now over 200 different color temperatures to choose from. "Cool white" is the most common, but unfortunately the least flattering. As a rule, you should pick bulbs with a color temperature between 3,000° and 4,000° Kelvin. Above this range, skin starts looking too green; below this, it starts looking too yellow. "Deluxe warm white" is the cheapest option with a color temperature in this range.

Even the newer compact fluorescents known as "PL" lamps have the special phosphors needed to light skin well (see Figure 1). The 13-watt version not only provides excellent color rendering, but also produces enough illumination to equal a 60-watt incandescent bulb. Because the color temperatures available in the PL Lamp are close to that of an incandescent bulb, both lights can be used in one bathroom without creating disconcerting color variations.

PL lamps have two drawbacks: the constant hum and the lack of a rapid start ballast, which causes it to flicker two or three times before stabilizing. It's a good idea to let your clients know about these problems before installing PL lamps.

Unlike incandescent lamps, which become more amber when dimmed, fluorescents don't change in color temperature when dimmed, which makes them desirable for vanity lights. But if you opt for dimming a fluorescent fixture, you must specify a dimming ballast when you order the fixture. Lutron makes a solid-state ballast that is silent, but it is expensive. The old, less expensive dimming ballasts make a lot of hum at low settings. In addition, you have to install a dimming switch for fluorescents, which is also very expensive.

Lighting the Tub Area

While the task area at the vanity is the most critical to light correctly, tubs and showers also need good light. Here, ceiling fixtures with white opal diffusers that project about 2 inches below the ceiling are commonly used. These are relatively effective, but they are bright and glaring. This may be a drawback for elderly clients with sensitive eyes.

Lighting a Mirror

Vertical cross illumination (top) is the best option for lighting a vanity mirror. The light bars should use frosted bulbs and be centered at eye level, so the light will shine on the face at all angles without creating shadows. The second choice (middle) for a vanity light is two translucent fixtures mounted at eye-level. The worst choice (bottom) is a single fixture above the mirror, which creates long shadows under the eyes, nose, and chin.

Recessed Light Over Tub

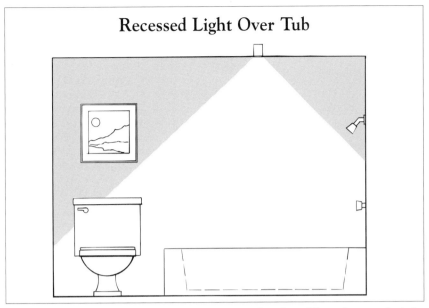

Figure 2. *A fully recessed light over the tub area reduces glare, but will leave the upper third of the room in shadow.*

Skylight With Fluorescent

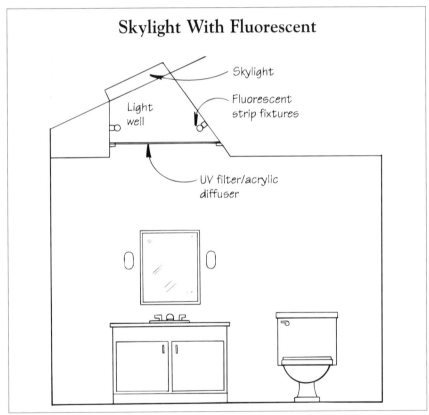

Figure 3. *Fluorescent strip lights in a skylight well will keep the skylight from looking like a black hole at night. A UV filter or acrylic diffuser is placed just above the ceiling line to keep the light from seeming like an institutional fixture.*

A fixture that is flush or recessed into the ceiling might be a better option for such older clients. Recessed fixtures reduce glare even with high-wattage bulbs. However, with a fully recessed light, the upper third of the shower or tub area will be a little dimmer (Figure 2).

Make sure that all fixtures used in wet locations are approved for this use by looking for the blue UL label. And when a light is placed in a tub or shower stall, it should always be on a ground-fault interrupter (GFI) circuit.

Lighting for Extra Elegance

Indirect lighting adds a soft, warm glow to the bath. Wall sconces or cove lighting directs light upward so it bounces off the ceiling and creates a well-diffused ambient light. Both of these can use miniature incandescent bulbs, PL lamps, or the standard-length fluorescent tubes, which not only comply with energy codes, but also provide comfortable, low-maintenance light for the entire room.

Skylights can add an elegant touch as well, and can supplement or replace electric lighting during the daytime hours. Unless you're taking advantage of a view, however, don't use clear skylights. Clear glass or Plexiglas skylights project a hard beam of light, shaped like the skylight opening, onto the floor. Bronze-colored skylights cast a dimmer version of the same shape. But a white opal acrylic skylight diffuses and softens the natural light, producing a gentle light that fills the whole room. Existing clear or bronze skylights can be fitted with a white acrylic panel at or above the ceiling line to soften the light they cast.

All skylights should have ultraviolet filters to prevent the sun from degrading or bleaching natural materials. If UV filters are not available from the skylight manufacturer, you can use UF3 ultraviolet filtering acrylic sheets made by Rohm and Haas (100 Independence Mall, Philadelphia, PA 19106; 215/592-3000). They can often be purchased from companies that manufacture fluorescent outdoor signs.

A UV filter is usually placed just inside the sash. However, if the light well is deep enough, fluorescent strip lights can be mounted between the acrylic panel and the skylight to be used at night to keep the skylight from looking like a black hole in the ceiling (Figure 3). In this case, we put the filter just above the ceiling line, leaving enough room for the lights between the filter and the skylight. If the filter is placed right at the ceiling line, it ends up looking too much like an institutional fluorescent fixture.

The most important goal to achieve in bath lighting is good task illumination. And while the overall light level should be appropriate for the size of the room, ambient and accent lighting are secondary to task lighting at the vanity. ■

Randall Whitehead is a San Francisco-based lighting consultant and owner of The Light Source.

Safe Wiring With GFCIs

by Rex Cauldwell

Ground-fault circuit interrupters can save lives in kitchens and baths — if installed correctly and tested monthly

Residential ground-fault circuit interrupters are available in two types. Use receptacle-style GFCIs where possible for convenient resetting at the point of use. GFCI circuit breakers (inset) protect an entire circuit but must be reset at the panel.

Whenever a customer asks me to defend the need for GFCIs (ground-fault circuit interrupters), I recount the old movie scene where the radio falls — or is thrown — into a water-filled bathtub, swiftly electrocuting the unfortunate bather. I then explain that if the radio had been plugged into a GFCI receptacle, the bather would still be alive. This leads us to the ultimate purpose of GFCIs — the protection of life.

Do GFCIs work? Absolutely. These devices have saved countless lives and provide much needed protection for both the tradesman and homeowner.

If you are ever unlucky enough to receive an electrical shock, but lucky enough to have a GFCI in the line, it will feel like you're being stuck with a needle, then the GFCI will trip and open the circuit, stopping the current.

How GFCIs Work

In ordinary 125-volt residential circuits using NM (non-metallic sheath) wire, the amperage leaving the panel, usually through a black wire, must equal the amperage returning to the panel through a neutral, or white, wire.

A GFCI continually monitors the amount of current going to the load and compares it to that coming back. As long as the two are equal, the electricity is doing its work properly. However, if some of the electrons are missing and the current coming back from the load is less than that going to it, the GFCI will trip the circuit. The logic of GFCI design is that if the current is not coming back via the wiring, it must be going somewhere else. Often this "somewhere else" is to earth (ground) through a person holding a tool or appliance.

Here's an example from my own experience. I was using a drill that was plugged into an extension cord that, in turn, was plugged into a GFCI receptacle in my garage. The drill was old and the shell made out of solid metal. While I was using it, one of the wires inside the drill shorted to the metal case, which made it electrically hot. Since electricity can cause muscles to contract, my hand tightened around the metal handle so that I could not release it. The current was now leaving the service panel, traveling through the black wire of the house wiring to the GFCI, then through the extension cord into the drill. From the drill, the current was

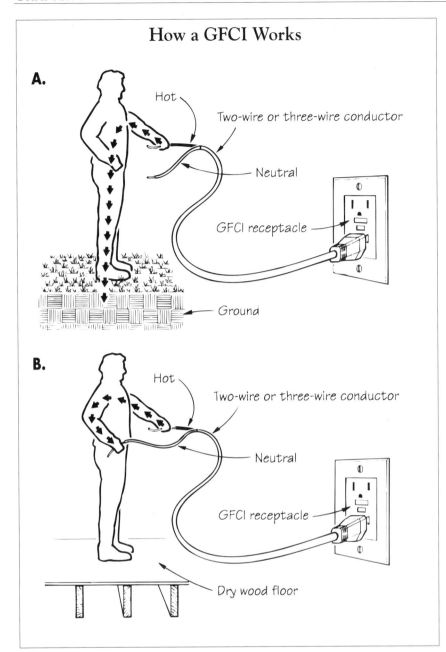

How a GFCI Works

A.

Hot

Two-wire or three-wire conductor

Neutral

GFCI receptacle

Ground

B.

Hot

Two-wire or three-wire conductor

Neutral

GFCI receptacle

Dry wood floor

Figure 1. *A GFCI trips when it senses a current imbalance, protecting you from shock if you accidentally contact a hot conductor while you are grounded (A). If you come between a black and white conductor and are not grounded, however, a GFCI may not protect you (B), since there will be no current imbalance.*

an amp), also a UL standard. Theoretically, the average person can tolerate four to six milliamps of current for $1/30$ of a second before his or her heart goes into fibrillation. (Fibrillation means that the heart goes out of sync; the result can be death.) With GFCI protection, you may still get a shock, but its duration will be limited to $1/30$ of a second.

Why doesn't the circuit breaker trip? Most circuit breakers controlling general purpose receptacles will not trip until at least 15 or 20 amps of current flow has been exceeded. This amount of current is normally fatal. In order to protect against fatal shocks, you need a device on line, like the GFCI, that will trip before the circuit breaker can trip.

Common sense. Just because you are plugged into a GFCI doesn't mean that you can cast all common sense to the wind. You can still die if your body — your heart in particular — is placed between the incoming black wire and the outgoing white wire. In this case, your body is in series with the electrical current, just like a light bulb. As long as your body isn't grounded, you are no different to the GFCI than a normal working load (see Figure 1). If you get caught in this situation, the GFCI will not trip because there is no current leakage to ground to create an imbalance...and you could be killed.

GFCI Types

For residences, GFCIs come in two types. One type looks like a receptacle. It has a test button on it and sometimes a light. The second type looks like a 15- or 20-amp circuit breaker with a test button on it. In both designs, the purpose of the test button is, when pressed, to place a current imbalance on the circuit. The GFCI should then trip if it is working properly.

Circuit breaker GFCIs. Use a GFCI circuit breaker only if all receptacles on the circuit require ground-fault protection. It fits into the service panel like a standard breaker but wires a little differently. Circuit breaker GFCIs have two main disadvantages: They cost more than receptacle GFCIs and are somewhat inconvenient. Because they're located in the service panel, the homeowner has to walk to the panel each time the GFCI trips the circuit.

Receptacle GFCIs are fed from the service panel through a standard circuit breaker. The GFCI receptacle is then placed at the point of use so that when it trips, the homeowner can immediately reset it without leaving the room.

flowing through me to ground. This was a classic ground fault: The electrical short within the drill caused the current to pass through me to ground, rather than flowing back to the service panel via the white wire. The GFCI detected this imbalance and opened the circuit immediately, saving my life. My only discomfort was the pin prick feeling.

Split-second response. The time it takes for a GFCI to open a circuit will vary from manufacturer to manufacturer, but it should be no more than $1/30$ of a second to comply with UL standards. The actual amount of current imbalance that the GFCI must detect before it trips is four to six milliamps (thousandths of

I recommend using GFCI receptacles wherever possible inside the house, both for cost and convenience. However, the cost can escalate far above the cost of a circuit-breaker GFCI if you install them at several locations on a single circuit.

To power outdoor receptacles, however, I definitely recommend using a GFCI circuit breaker. Experience has shown that GFCI receptacles can have a short life span when located outside, even in watertight boxes. The boxes and lids may be watertight but they are not vapor tight. The water vapor seems to shorten the life of the electronics within.

Incorrect Wiring of GFCIs

A GFCI receptacle may be wired incorrectly by a homeowner or novice electrician. GFCI receptacles have a "line," or input, side and a "load," or output, side. The line side must be connected to the wiring that originates at the service panel. The load side must be connected to any downstream receptacles that are to be protected (Figure 2).

Often a receptacle GFCI is wired incorrectly by pigtailing the downstream receptacles off the line side. These receptacles are now in parallel with the GFCI and are not ground-fault protected. Only those receptacles feeding out of the load side will be protected.

Remember to label any downstream receptacles as ground-fault protected. Use the stickers supplied with the receptacle expressly for this purpose. Inspectors often overlook this, but be sure to do it anyway. Without the label, the homeowner has no way of knowing that a particular outlet is protected.

It is also possible to wire a circuit-breaker GFCI incorrectly. However, the incorrect hookup would be immediately apparent if the "test" button doesn't trip the device. Under test, this type of device typically places an eight milliamp ground-fault on the circuit.

Testing

Always test GFCIs (using the test button located on the GFCI) immediately after installation. If you are at a site where you will be using a preexisting GFCI to power your tools, always test it first to verify that the ground-fault protection is still working. It's possible to obtain 125 volts from a GFCI receptacle without its ground-fault protection working. Manufacturers normally recommend monthly testing of GFCIs.

Plug-in tester. Do not test a GFCI by shorting across the hot-to-neutral slots in the receptacle. This will not test the GFCI and may cause damage. Three-prong plug-in

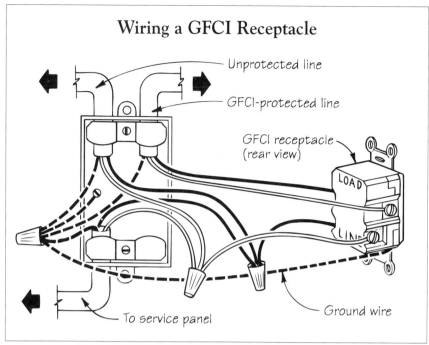

Wiring a GFCI Receptacle

Unprotected line
GFCI-protected line
GFCI receptacle (rear view)
LOAD
LINE
To service panel
Ground wire

Figure 2. *To give ground-fault protection to downstream receptacles, you must wire them off the load side of the GFCI.*

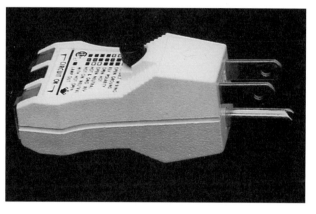

Figure 3. *This plug-in tester can test a GFCI receptacle and any downstream receptacles it protects, but only in a grounded circuit.*

testers with a push button are specifically designed for the testing of GFCIs and are commonly available at most electrical supply houses. This type of tester typically places a .0068-amp current imbalance on the line to trip the GFCI. All electricians, contractors, and inspectors should carry and use these little testers (Figure 3).

You can also use a plug-in tester to test a GFCI that has several receptacles on its load side. First test the actual GFCI receptacle or GFCI circuit breaker. Then test the most distant receptacle working off its load side. The GFCI should trip when you push the button on the tester.

Testing GFCIs in an ungrounded circuit. Plug-in testers create an actual fault to the ground wire in a three-wire circuit, causing the GFCI to trip if it is working properly. However, this can lead to uncertain test results for a GFCI installed in an ungrounded (two-wire) circuit. The GFCI may actually

Figure 4. *GFCI-protected extension cords are recommended by OSHA for power tool use in outdoor or damp locations (right). Another option is a portable plug-in GFCI (below).*

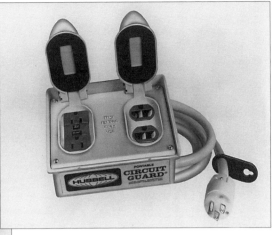

work fine, but it will not respond to the tester since there is no ground wire to short to.

However, for UL-approved receptacle GFCIs, the test button on the device itself will still yield an accurate test. This is because the built-in test device works by taking some of the current from the black wire on the load side of the GFCI and shunting it back to the white wire on the line side to unbalance the circuit. This is, in effect, a ground-fault simulation rather than a true ground fault, but the imbalance effect is the same.

Code Requirements

The National Electric Code (NEC) defines where and how GFCIs should be used. Here are some of the more common regulations affecting residences. (Unless otherwise stated, "receptacle" refers to a 125-volt, single-phase, 15-amp or 20-amp standard residential receptacle.)

Kitchens. All countertop receptacles within a 6-foot straight-line distance from the kitchen sink must have GFCI protection. Since, according to code, two separate circuits must feed the countertop receptacles, I normally wire my kitchens with one GFCI circuit to the left of the sink and one GFCI circuit to the right (assuming the sink is in the center of the countertop). This normally separates the load evenly and, if I come back ten years later to troubleshoot a problem, I know exactly how the circuits are wired. I use GFCI receptacles, as opposed to circuit breaker GFCIs, since the former can be reset at the point-of-use in the kitchen. Countertop receptacles beyond the 6-foot limit, as well as other general use kitchen, dining, and pantry receptacles, can be wired into the line, or unprotected, side of the GFCI.

Bathrooms. All receptacles installed in bathrooms must have GFCI protection. I always use receptacle GFCIs for reset convenience.

Garages. Every receptacle in a garage must have GFCI protection unless it is not readily accessible, such as a receptacle located on the ceiling for a garage door opener, or one serving a plug-in appliance occupying dedicated space, such as a freezer. Any 230-volt outlet is exempt, as is the laundry circuit.

Outdoors. All receptacles installed outdoors that are readily accessible and within 6 feet 6 inches of grade level must have ground-fault protection.

Unfinished basements and crawlspaces at or below grade level. All receptacles installed in these locations must have ground-fault protection, except for:
• A single (not duplex or triplex) receptacle supplied by a dedicated branch circuit for a plug-in appliance such as a freezer or refrigerator
• A laundry circuit
• A single receptacle supplying a permanently installed sump pump

Job-site protection. In most areas of the country, builders are required to use a GFCI-protected temporary panel. This type of panel normally protects single-phase, 125-volt, 15-amp and 20-amp receptacle outlets. If you use a generator of five kilowatts or less, you may be exempt. (See Section 305(6)(a) of the NEC for more information.) Extension cords with built-in GFCI protection are also available for job-site use and are recommended by OSHA (Figure 4).

Where Not To Use GFCIs

Even though it isn't against code, room lights should not be placed on a GFCI unless there is a specific need for doing so. The reason is simple: If the GFCI trips, you don't want to be left in the dark trying to find your way out of the room — especially in the bathroom, where the floor might be wet and slippery, with many objects to bump against or trip over.

Avoid this by wiring only the receptacles in the room, if you want them protected, off the load side of the GFCI, but put the lights on the line side.

Also, unless there is a specific reason, don't use a GFCI for equipment and appliances that cannot go without power for an extended time, such as a freezer or sump pump, since GFCIs are sensitive and are subject to nuisance tripping. ■

Rex Cauldwell is a master electrician and plumber, and owner of Little Mountain Electric Company in Copper Hill, Va.

Chapter 9
PLUMBING & MECHANICAL

CAROLYN BATES

Roughing-In for Kitchens & Baths

by Jim Hart

A successful rough-in starts with a good lead carpenter, detailed plans, and appliance spec sheets on site

Having the right or wrong rough-in dimensions on a bathroom or kitchen remodel can make or break a job. Chipping out tile, hacking out drywall, butchering a cabinet, or yanking on Romex are sometimes the only ways to correct poorly located rough-ins.

Unfortunately, a bad rough-in usually remains undiscovered until near the end of the job, when the painter is finished and the tile-setter has collected his check. That's when the plumber finds out that the shower wall mortar was floated too thick and it's impossible to get the fixture knobs on. A tightly planned, two-week bathroom remodel can suddenly expand to a three- or four-week job — not good news to you, or to a client who has been living with one less bathroom.

Key Characters

There are several key elements that contribute to a successful kitchen or bath rough-in.

Lead carpenter. Invariably, a general contractor will take on full responsibility, but won't always have time to meet with the subs on the job. So information ends up getting passed through one or more workers. The result can be a disaster. To avoid problems, the contractor should assign one worker who has a well-rounded knowledge of all aspects of construction to the task of overseeing the layout and making sure subcontractors accurately place the rough-ins. As my company's lead carpenter, this responsibility falls to me. Spreading this responsibility over more than one person multiplies the potential for errors, and adds a lot of unnecessary communication.

Good plans. A detailed set of plans is essential to locating dimensions. If good plans don't exist, I draw them myself. If a drawing differs from the site dimensions by more than $1/2$ inch, I get out a notebook and redraw the plan accurately, or make note of it on the plans. I've seen a fraction-of-an-inch error in a plan cause a door casing need to be scribed around a countertop or a switch plate to be cut down to fit next to a cabinet. This is not a pretty sight.

Spec sheets on site. Whenever possible, have the appliances and fixtures on site. At a minimum, have the manufacturers' specification sheets available for all appliances that must be built in. It's helpful with whirlpool baths, sinks, mixing valves, cooktops, and range hoods to have the fixture itself on site before rough-in begins.

Good client communication. Some rough-in locations are fixed according to the appliance or fixture requirements — those of a range, for example. No need for client input there. But the height of a shower head is usually of interest to the user. Asking your clients' opinions will make them happier with the job, even if you end up telling them how high you think the shower head should go, or how high everyone else plumbs their shower heads.

I've discovered that clients often have high expectations for under-sink storage. Unfortunately, under a three-basin sink with P-trap, garbage disposal, and instant water heater, the homeowners are lucky if they can get even a small wastebasket on the cabinet door. Make sure clients understand that the more appliances they have, the less storage space there will be.

Good subcontractor communication. I try to get all the subs together for one meeting before the job starts. It's helpful to have a contractor who does both heating and plumbing, since it isn't uncommon to have a DWV line conflict with a vent duct. Having the electrician there at the same time is helpful, just in case one of those ducts interferes with a recessed can light. Though hashing through these details with so many subcontractors at the same time is difficult, it's the best way to troubleshoot problems and come up with economical solutions.

Don't be shy about making things crystal clear to a sub. Post-it notes, ink markers, and spray paint are all helpful in directing subs.

Make a checklist. Once the demolition is done, the lead carpenter must visualize what the finished room is going to look like, even when the walls are nothing but open studs. To make this easier, I make a checklist of key rough-in dimensions. Making the checklist is a helpful way to consider each appliance location before it's too late. Referring to the list during the course of the job ensures that I won't have to call subs back to move things around.

Bathroom Rough-In

Here is a list of typical bath rough-ins, and some important considerations for each one.

Bathtub with shower. I don't attempt to precisely locate a 2-inch drain until after the bathtub is installed. But I do need a rough idea of the drain location when framing the floor. I usually cut a 12x12-inch cutout in the subfloor to give the plumber room to install the P-trap and the drain overflow, and this cutout must fall between joists. Because tubs are usually 32 inches wide, I often have to deviate from a standard joist layout if the joists run parallel to the tub.

For shower controls, I frame a standard 16-inch stud bay, centered on the width of the tub (Figure 1). I also install a piece of 3/4-inch plywood between the studs in this bay as a base for the faucet body. Plywood won't crack as easily as a 2x block with the many screws used to fasten the faucet body.

As I mentioned earlier, I leave the decision of where to locate the faucet body and shower head to the client. Before soldering in the faucet body, put all the escutcheons and handles on, and make sure the handles don't hit each other. I've discovered that the more expensive shower fixtures tend to be larger and require more space than economy models.

Deciding the depth at which to place the faucet body (and the plywood block) is largely determined by the thickness of the faucet body itself and the thickness of the wall surface. Most drain bodies give you at least 3/4 inch to

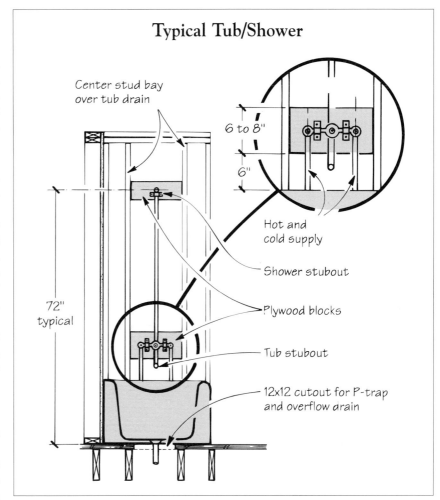

Typical Tub/Shower

Center stud bay over tub drain

6 to 8"

6"

72" typical

Hot and cold supply

Shower stubout

Plywood blocks

Tub stubout

12x12 cutout for P-trap and overflow drain

Figure 1. *Though most plumbers place the shower head and controls at standard heights, the author always consults with clients on this since many have individual height preferences.*

play with in relation to the faucet. Many manufacturers have faucet extensions available, too, but don't depend on it. Grohe's (241 Covington Dr., Bloomingdale, IL 60108; 708/582-7711) newer faucets, which I install frequently, have an incredibly large range — close to 3 inches — that allows me to place the faucet just about anywhere within a wall, and not have problems getting the finishes on.

Sink. For a pedestal sink, the 1 1/2-inch drain must be centered exactly. For a vanity cabinet rough-in, jogging the P-trap over 2 to 4 inches to one side of center is desirable (Figure 2).

To quickly and accurately space the hot and cold supply lines the required 8 inches apart, I use copper straps with 1/2- and 3/4-inch holes at regular intervals. The copper pipes are then soldered to the strap for support.

Toilet. Most toilets have standard rough-in dimensions. Nearly all require the flange to be centered a minimum of 12 inches from the finished wall surface. With a typical drywall interior, I center the flange 13 inches from the framing, giving me 1/2 inch for drywall and 1/2 inch additional clearance. One plumber told me this additional clearance is essential for accommodating the inconsistencies in porcelain castings. If there is to be tile with a mortar

Vanity Rough-In

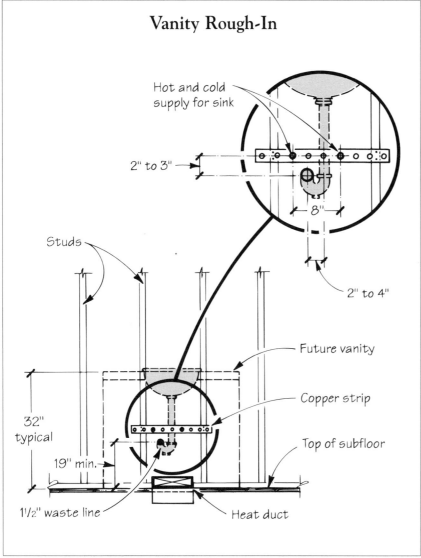

Figure 2. *Place the vanity sink drain 2 to 4 inches off center to allow room for the trap. Use copper strap to secure the hot and cold supply lines.*

bed on the wall around the toilet, another ³/4 inch is needed (Figure 3).

Code here requires a minimum of 15 inches of space on either side of the toilet, and 24 inches in front. I've found that additional space is helpful on at least one side for a wastebasket and toilet paper holder. I used to put the toilet paper holder on the back wall if the toilet rough-in had minimum side clearance, until an occupational therapist alerted me to the risk of back injury that occurs when twisting 180 degrees to reach for the toilet paper.

With a linoleum floor, I usually rest the toilet flange directly on the subfloor. If the floor has tile on a mortar bed, I build up the flange ¹/2 to ³/4 inch with a plywood ring so that the flange isn't recessed too far below the finished floor. Otherwise you need two wax rings, which creates a risky seal. However, installing the flange too low is better than placing it too high.

If the cold water supply comes through the wall, it must be below the tank and above the baseboard, but not so close that the escutcheon is hanging half on the baseboard and half on the wall. I aim for the pipe to be 6 inches to the left of the toilet's center, and at least 5 inches above the subfloor. When it comes through the floor, place it 6 inches from the toilet's center and 2 inches from the wall.

Fans. I've rarely moved a ceiling joist to make room for a bath fan, unless it's a light/fan combination and the homeowner wants to center it in the room. I usually rough-in the bath fan near the bathtub/shower, but not inside. Make sure you position the fan with the louvers facing away from the bathroom entry, so that people can't see into the mechanical

Built-Up Flange

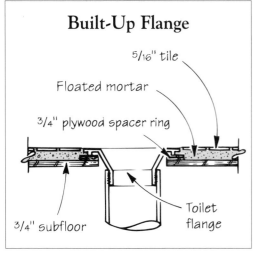

Figure 3. *Remember to allow room for the escutcheon plate when bringing the toilet supply line through the wall (right). For a tile floor, the author installs a ¹/2- to ³/4-inch-thick plywood spacer ring to ensure that the flange isn't recessed too far below the finished floor (above).*

Toilet Clearances

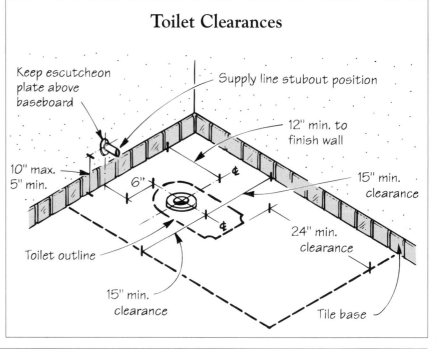

part of the fan when they come in the door.

Vanity lights. Symmetry is critical with vanity lights. In order to rough-in the electrical box, you often need to know the mirror or medicine chest height. I've often reframed a wall and even moved plumbing to make room for a recessed medicine chest. Strip vanity lights are nice because they usually allow you to rough-in the electrical box anywhere along the length of the fixture, as long as the height is accurate.

Outlets. Homeowners usually want outlets along the longest stretch of cabinet. Through-the-backsplash outlets require careful consideration of cabinet, substrate, tile, and backsplash dimensions. Set the outlet boxes far enough out to accommodate the thickness of the backsplash.

Outlet boxes need to be at least 3/4 inch above the backsplash so the plate doesn't hit the backsplash. If the wall above the vanity is tiled, I try to vertically center the outlet in a tile course. I usually don't worry about the horizontal placement of the outlet in relation to the tiles unless it's a high-end job. Then I'll either center outlets and switches in both dimensions of the tile or center them at the corner of four tiles. But this means you have to know the exact countertop placement, the tile dimensions, and the grout line width when the boxes are placed. If these aren't available (and they rarely are at the framing stage), I may let a wire run wild and cut in my boxes just before setting the tile.

Heating ducts. Whenever possible, I try to rough-in the heat through the kick of the vanity cabinet. Most homeowners don't like the look of a register on the wall or floor of a kitchen or bath. Standard 3x10 duct works best in a kick space, but getting a custom sheet-metal boot to make the right angle is often difficult. In my area, it is permissible to seal the kick cavity with caulk to make a wood plenum. Then I cut a simple 2 1/2x14-inch rectangle out of the cabinet base for the register.

Kitchen Rough-In

Kitchens require fewer plumbing rough-ins than bathrooms, but have more appliance rough-ins. When laying out the rough-ins, the cabinets are the main consideration. With the subfloor swept clean, I mark out the location of the upper and lower cabinets. It's a good idea to use an optical level to locate the high and low points on the floor, to see how that will affect the height of the countertop. In general, the countertop will be the cabinet height plus counter thickness. Snapping a line or nailing a 2x4 at the top of the backsplash and the bot-

tom of the lower cabinets is helpful for locating the rough-ins, especially the electrical outlets, on a framed wall.

Kitchen sink and dishwasher. A kitchen sink drain comes through the wall lower than a vanity drain to make room for the garbage disposal — even though the kitchen sink is nearly always higher (Figure 4). In a standard 36-inch-high base cabinet, roughing in the 2-inch drainpipe 12 to 15 inches above the subfloor works well.

In most cases the dishwasher will drain into the garbage disposal if there is one. The hot water supply to the dishwasher can be tapped off the sink hot water supply, but good plumbers will provide another supply near the dishwasher. This will keep the sink's hot water pressure from falling when the dishwasher is running.

Ranges and cooktops. Freestanding or slide-in ranges require accurately placed gas and electrical rough-ins. Most ranges have a back panel that allows space for the gas valve and electrical outlet. If not placed accurately, the

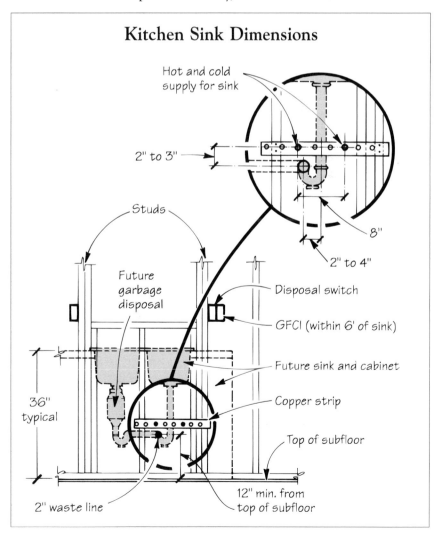

Figure 4. *For a double-basin sink with disposal unit, place the waste pipe 2 to 4 inches off center from the sink drain that doesn't feed into the disposal.*

Locating Range Hood Ductwork

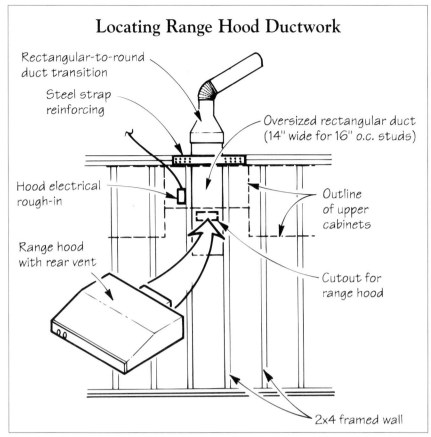

Rectangular-to-round
duct transition

Steel strap
reinforcing

Hood electrical
rough-in

Range hood
with rear vent

Oversized rectangular duct
(14" wide for 16" o.c. studs)

Outline
of upper
cabinets

Cutout for
range hood

2x4 framed wall

Figure 5. One way to locate the duct for a range hood is to frame a full stud bay in the center of the hood location, then install an oversized duct before drywall goes up. After the cabinets are installed, cut through both drywall and sheet metal to connect the range hood duct.

I have found two solutions: One, I find the hood location to the best of my ability, using cabinet drawings. Then I make sure the duct rough-in falls in a stud bay with enough latitude to move either way a couple of inches. When the duct is installed, I ask the heating contractor not to fasten it in this bay, and to extend it a couple of inches above the plate line in the attic before turning a corner. This allows me to shift the boot a few inches vertically and horizontally after the drywall and cabinets are in place.

The second solution, suggested to me recently by a plumbing/heating sub, is to have the duct built oversized, then drywall over the entire duct. When it's time to position the hood, cut through the drywall and sheet metal at the correct location (Figure 5).

Either solution is better than removing a cabinet and tearing into a wall only to move a duct an inch or two. If you are wrestling with a 50-pound microwave/hood combination over an expensive countertop, you want the connection to be as painless as possible.

Downdraft cooktops are the toughest. Most subcontractors won't attempt to rough in the ductwork for these monsters without having them on site. Often, the duct must run through the back of the cabinet, underneath the subfloor, and through the exterior wall. If the downdraft cooktop isn't on site, a lead carpenter can spend hours trying to communicate to the cabinetmaker and subcontractors the best way to install it, and still end up modifying a cabinet to make it fit.

Lights. Architects often draw recessed lights centered between upper cabinet doors and above the front lip of the counter. This often means that ceiling joists have to be moved or headed off. Sometimes the top of the can light comes too close to a rafter, which is a more serious problem. In this case I've usually been able to convince the client to deviate slightly from the plans.

Outlets. Above-counter outlets are handled in a manner similar to that for bath vanity outlets. The refrigerator, microwave oven, trash compactor, and garbage disposal all need outlets. The garbage disposal also needs a switch. Most clients prefer it to be placed to the right of the sink.

Sometimes I photograph the open walls before drywalling, just in case an outlet gets accidentally covered. This saves me from trying to find the "lump" in the wall. ■

Jim Hart is a lead carpenter in Mountain View, California, and a contributing editor to The Journal of Light Construction.

electrical cord or gas line can keep you from pushing the range all the way back to the wall.

With a drop-in range, keep in mind that the cabinet space below is usable unless the range has a downdraft vent. Keep the outlet or gas rough-in just a few inches below the bottom of the countertop.

Hoods. In my opinion, ducted hoods are the most difficult appliances to rough in. There are two basic ways to duct a range hood: through the cabinet or into the wall.

A through-the-cabinet vent is the easiest to install. At worst, a ceiling joist will have to be moved to make way for the rectangular duct. Most clients still want to use what little space is left in this cabinet. It's worth finding out if you can get a piece of 1/4-inch plywood and the correct stain from the cabinetmaker so the duct can be hidden. Then there's usually room for a spice rack.

For an into-the-wall duct, which is preferable to many homeowners because of the storage that's saved above the hood, the rectangular sheet-metal boot needs to be precisely roughed in before drywall and cabinets are installed. If you're 1/4 inch off, it might be impossible to get an adequate seal between the hood and the duct.

Drain, Waste & Vent Systems

by Lanny Watts

It pays to understand drains, vents, and traps — and to stay friends with your plumber

It usually begins something like this: You call a plumber onto a job to confirm the specs and discuss faucet styles and fixture colors. Then your plumber says, "Of course, this will need a vent running up through that wall to the roof." Your eyes go wide. You've already given a price to the customer and now you have to cover additional plumbing, carpentry, and finish work out of your pocket.

The purpose of this article is to help you avoid such surprises. First I'll explain how drains, traps, and vents are laid out by a plumber. Then I'll discuss some common venting problems and their solutions.

Basic DWV

Vents and traps are the least understood elements of a house's DWV (drain/waste/vent) system, but to explain how they work, it's useful to examine what they serve: namely, drains.

Drains. Drains carry waterborne waste from the various fixtures (sinks, toilets, floor drains, etc.) to the sewer or septic system outside the building.

Horizontal drains should have a 2% slope, equivalent to 1/4-inch drop per foot of length. This allows the contents to develop a velocity (approximately 2 feet per second) which is not so slow that things bog down and not so fast that the water flows ahead of solid and semi-solid wastes.

For sizing a drain, fixtures are rated in *drainage fixture units* (dfu). One dfu equals one cubic foot of water per minute. The specified dfu of a fixture determines the trap size and the individual drain that leads from it. A combined drain from several fixtures is sized based on the total dfu, using a

Typical Drainage Fixture Unit (DFU) Values

Fixture	DFU	Min. Drain Size
Bathtub	2	1 1/2"
Dishwasher	2	1 1/2"
Kitchen Sink	2	1 1/2"
Lavatory	1	1 1/4"
Shower	2	1 1/2"
Toilet	4	3"

Horizontal Drain Sizes

Total DFU	Min. Drain Size
3	1 1/2"
6	2"
12	2 1/2"
20	3"
160	4"

Note: Numbers may vary somewhat depending on local codes.

Save The Seals

Sewer gases may be unpleasant to smell, poisonous, explosive, or a combination of these. Traps prevent these gases from coming out of the drain pipes into the living space. Each plumbing fixture (toilet, shower, sink, etc.) in a building has to have some variation of a simple water seal trap.

Types of Traps

The standard trap is called a P-trap. Turned on its side, a P-trap resembles the letter P (see illustration). When wastewater leaves the sink, it goes down the vertical leg, around the U, and then most of it flows out the horizontal drain. A small portion of the water will be left behind in the trap and is known as the *water seal* or *trap seal*. The spillway where the water overflows from the U into the horizontal drain is called the *weir*. The top side of the lowest section of the U is called the *top of the dip*. The water located between the top of the dip and the weir forms the effective trap seal. Sewer gases forming and collecting in the drainage system will not normally pass through this barrier of water. The water in the inlet half of a trap, however, is not an effective seal because gases can bubble upward through it.

There are three common variations of the P-trap. A toilet has what is called an integral trap. The trap is actually a part of the toilet. The water we see in the bowl is matched by a trap seal of equal depth on the far side of the dip.

In some situations, where it would be hard to reach a P-trap to clean it, or where greater protection for the trap is required, a drum trap is used. A drum trap is typically the size and shape of a coffee can, and either the top or the bottom of the trap has a large threaded cover for cleaning. The depth of the water seal in a drum trap (about 4 inches) is greater than in a P-trap (about 2 inches), but drum traps are not accepted by every code.

The third common exception to the P-trap is called an S-trap. Instead of the outlet drain heading off horizontally, the trap bends and discharges vertically. S-traps are not accepted in any modern plumbing codes because they can fail easily.

When Traps Fail

Traps fail to function as gas traps when they lose their water seal. There are eight common ways this can happen: siphonage, oscillation, momentum, back pressure, evaporation, capillary attraction, aspiration, and mechanical failure. (In trade school, apprentice plumbers learn the word SOMBECA to remember every way except mechanical failure, which is presumably the most obvious.) Some of these problems can be reduced or eliminated through proper plumbing design. Others require that the trap be periodically inspected and maintained.

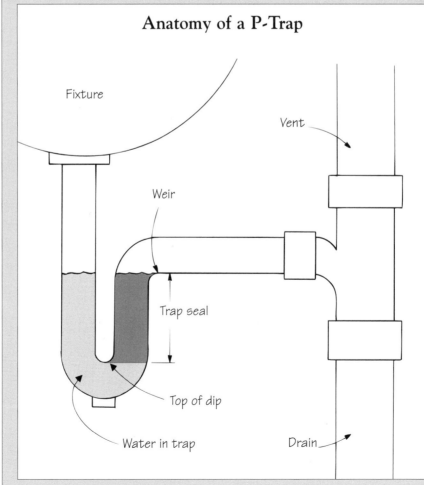

Anatomy of a P-Trap

Fixture

Vent

Weir

Trap seal

Top of dip

Water in trap

Drain

When waste water leaves the sink or other fixture, most of it flows out the horizontal drain. A small portion of the water is left behind in the trap, creating a seal to block gases.

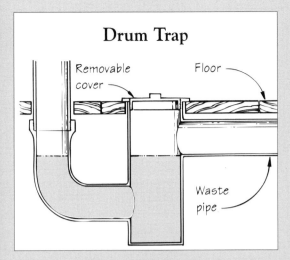

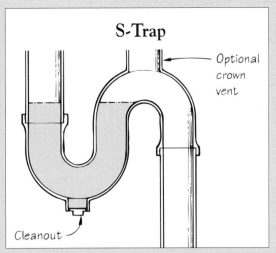

A drum trap (left) has a deeper water seal than a P-trap, but is not accepted by some codes. It may require a hole in the floor for the cleanout. Old-style S-traps (right) are not accepted by any modern code because they fail easily, even with the addition of a crown vent.

Siphonage. Anyone who has had to borrow a little gasoline from a friend's car is familiar with the effect of a siphon. When a siphon hose is filled, it will draw liquid from a high place to a lower place until the upper end of the hose is exposed to air. Water can siphon out of a trap if there is no air in the intervening pipe.

An S-trap will siphon at least some of its seal every time a large amount of water is drained. Siphonage is prevented by draining the water away from a trap horizontally, and by installing a vent pipe in the top of this horizontal drain.

A toilet trap also discharges downward and tends to siphon its contents. This, however, serves the function of a toilet well since it is required to carry away solid waste. The trap seal of a toilet is replenished by shunting a portion of the water that refills the tank into the bowl.

Oscillation. Oscillation is caused by pressure variations in the plumbing vents, especially those that penetrate the roof. On a gusty day, the air pressure in the drainage and vent system will fluctuate rapidly. This will cause the water in the traps to slosh back and forth. Every time the water sloshes, a little bit is lost over the weir. If enough water sloshes away, the seal is lost. Traps are designed to be deep enough to prevent this.

Momentum. The surface tension of water holds it together, so water tends to form into blobs, or slugs. If a slug has enough momentum, it can overcome gravity and travel up out of a trap. Placing the trap close to the fixture drain stops the slug from gaining enough momentum to overcome gravity.

Back pressure. When a fixture such as a toilet discharges a large volume of water, the resulting slug pushes air in front of it and sucks air behind it. Without proper venting, the air in front of the slug will push the water of other traps back into their respective fixtures. The trap seal will be temporarily lost and sewer gas will belch into the room.

Evaporation. In a seldom used trap, such as in a flood drain, the seal can simply evaporate away. The usual way of preventing this is to provide a regular source of water for the trap, either by periodically discharging water onto the floor surrounding the drain or by bleeding a small amount of water from a water supply line directly into the trap. This latter method is called a trap primer. If it is used, make sure your plumber takes precautions to prevent contaminated water from siphoning back into the supply system.

Capillary attraction. Capillary attraction is a form of absorption which can occur when a mass of hair or a piece of string is caught in a trap and extends down the drain. The strands will soak up water until saturated. Water can then drip off the lower end of the strands as a siphon. Smoothly constructed traps, sufficient volume of discharge water, and periodic maintenance are required to prevent this problem.

Aspiration. After a slug of water has passed a drainage branch that leads to another fixture, it will pull a vacuum on that line. Unless the trap is protected by a vent, the vacuum will suck the water seal from the trap.

Mechanical failure. If there is a crack in the trap, a broken gasket, or a crossed thread on a cleanout plug, the seal water will simply drip out.

So, the next time you go fishing in a trap for some matted hair, an earring, a chopstick, or perhaps a contact lens, think about all the horrid sewer gas it's been keeping out of the house... and of all the problems that were overcome to accomplish this.

— *L.W.*

table like the one on page 205. The table takes into account the low probability that all the fixtures will discharge at the same time.

Vertical drains should be plumb to allow the water and waste to fall as a unit (called a slug). On a horizontal run that drops to vertical, the turn can be abrupt. But a vertical drop that turns to horizontal, or a turn on a horizontal run, should have room to make a wide sweep and should have a

cleanout, if practical.

If the drainpipe is plastic, it should be supported every 4 feet. Also, nail guards should be installed to protect plastic drains if they are near the surface of studs or joists.

Traps. As materials decompose in a drainage and sewer system, gases and odors are produced. The trap at each fixture holds a pocket of water, which is a highly effective seal for keeping the gases and odors out of the living space. As long as water remains in the trap and there is no undue pressure from the sewer gas, the occupants of the building are protected. (For a discussion of trap maintenance, see "Save the Seals," previous page).

Vents. The vent system is a continuation of the drainage system and penetrates the roof in one or more places. Its purpose is to maintain neutral pressure within the system by relieving positive pressure caused by the creation of sewer gases, and both positive and negative pressures caused by discharges traveling through the system. This keeps water draining smoothly and quietly, and keeps traps functioning properly.

Unlike drains, vents don't need to be sloped to maintain a smooth flow of waste. Horizontal runs simply need to be routed without any low spots where condensation could collect — one percent pitch is plenty. High points, which cause parts of the vent to drain in different directions, are not a problem.

Each fixture in a plumbing system must have a trap, and each trap must be protected by a vent. As a general rule, vents need to be at least half the diameter of the trap and drain they serve, but never less than $1^1/4$ inches in diameter. Vents, like drains and supply lines, can be combined in a manifold. In this case, the pipe is sized to meet the combined dfu requirements.

A vent should rise vertically from the drain it serves until it is at least 6 inches above the highest flood rim (the top of a lavatory, for instance) of the fixture group it serves. Plumbed this way (see Figure 1), if a drain becomes plugged, the contents will overflow into the room before filling a horizontal vent. This eliminates the risks of leaving waste material behind to clog the vent, or of allowing the vent stack to act as a part-time drain.

Vents should extend only one foot above the roof and, in cold climates, they should be increased to at least 3 or 4 inches in

Basic Drain/Waste/Vent System

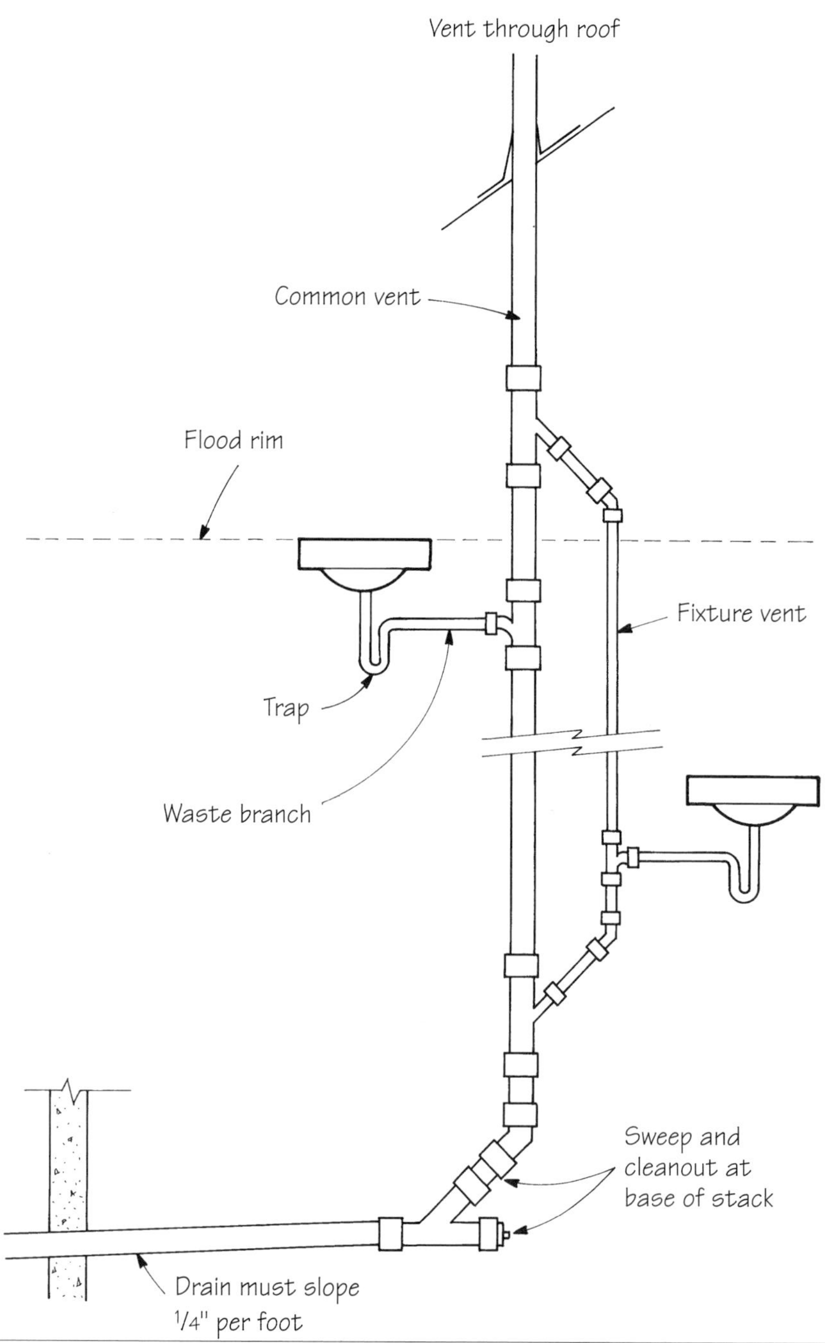

Figure 1. *In a household DWV system, each fixture has a trap and vent. The vents must connect at least 6 inches above the flood rim of the highest fixture.*

Wet Vent

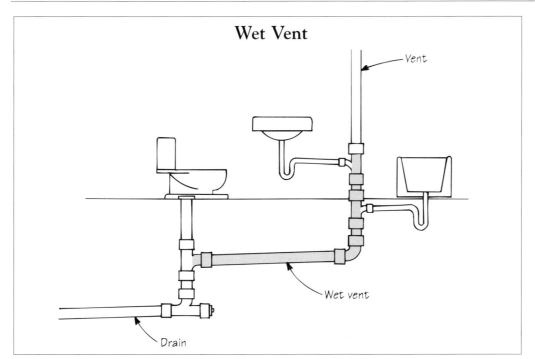

Figure 2. *A wet vent (shaded portion of illustration) also serves as a drain for lesser fixtures, and is usually one pipe size larger than normal. Here the sink and tub drain serves as a wet vent for the toilet.*

diameter before going through the roof. This will eliminate frozen condensation in the pipe from closing the vent.

Vent terminations should be 8 feet above or 10 feet away from windows, roof decks, or ventilation inlets.

Wet vent. A wet vent is a vent pipe that also serves as a drain for a lesser fixture or fixtures (Figure 2). It is usually sized one pipe size larger than normal. Because the vent is washed by the upper fixture, the vent can safely come off the drain horizontally. For health reasons a food preparation sink cannot wet vent a toilet.

Venting Problems

Sometimes just moving the location of a kitchen sink can cause venting problems. Some common problem layouts are:

• a sink on an outside wall with a window above it;
• a sink in a room with a low shed roof;
• a sink on a solid wall (log or concrete);
• an island sink in the middle of a room; or
• a sink over an unheated crawlspace.

Similar problems occur with other fixtures such as tubs and toilets. Generally the venting solutions are the same, but the drains, traps, and vents must be sized according to the dfu of each fixture.

Window sinks and low shed roofs. The drain and vent for a sink placed on an outside wall can be safely tucked just behind the drywall on the outside wall. All the insulation should be behind the piping, to keep condensation from freezing in the

Bow Vent

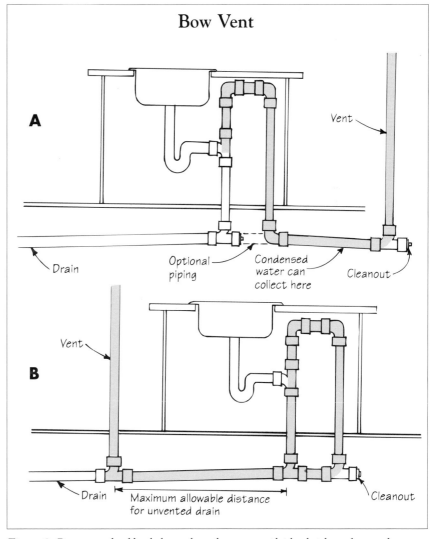

Figure 3. *Bow vents should only be used as a last resort with island sinks or fixtures that are not near a usable wall. The vent makes a U-turn just below the countertop and drops to the level of the drain. From there, it either runs horizontally until it can rise like a normal vent (A), or connects back into the drain (B), which is vented as soon as possible.*

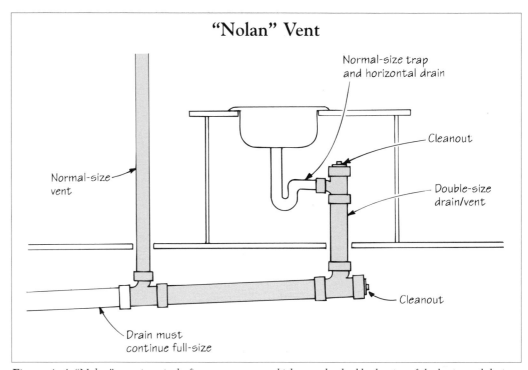

Figure 4. *A "Nolan" vent is a single-fixture wet vent, which must be double the size of the horizontal drain. This setup costs more in materials, but is more reliable than a bow vent for island sinks.*

pipe. If the sink is in front of a window, the vent should rise to just below the rough opening and then bend around and up. Once at ceiling height, the vent should come across the ceiling into the main part of the house to minimize its exposure along an outside wall. This is true for a shed roof also. Doing this keeps the vent from penetrating along the edge of the roof. Unless absolutely necessary, the vent should also be reconnected with the main vent system and brought out through an upper roof to reduce the number of penetrations.

Island sinks and solid walls. A sink that is placed on a solid wall, or away from walls (island sink), needs either a *bow vent* or what I call a *"Nolan" vent*, named after the inspector who introduced it to me.

With a bow vent, the vent starts upward as a normal vent does, but then hangs a U-turn just below the countertop and drops down to run parallel with the drain (Figure 3).

Once the vent is at the level of the horizontal drain it can do one of two things: (1) The vent can continue horizontally to the nearest available wall that will allow it to rise like a normal vent; or (2) the vent can connect back into the drain with a second vent is taken off at a location where it can rise normally.

The second layout would allow the vent to function as a drain should the actual drain become plugged in its vertical drop. Both setups require a cleanout since, in either case, a bow vent is below the flood rim allowing the vent to become fouled before a stopped sink overflows. For this reason, every bow vent must be preapproved by a plumbing inspector for a specific application. I try to avoid bow vents altogether.

A slightly bulkier, but mechanically simpler, solution is what I call a "Nolan" vent (Figure 4). This is basically a double-sized, single-fixture wet vent. From the $1^1/_2$-inch trap outlet, the drain runs horizontally to the corner of the sink base cabinet and discharges into a $3 \times 1^1/_2$-inch tee. The top of the tee is capped with a cleanout and the 3-inch drain drops to below the floor. The drain remains oversized for its entire run, and a regular $1^1/_2$-inch vent is taken off at the first opportunity. This setup involves increased materials cost — especially if there is a long run to a full-sized stack — but it won't fail.

For fixtures over an unheated space. An unheated crawlspace creates a problem for the water supply more than for the drain. If the drain is pitched properly and protected from cold drafts and from small or continuous discharge, such as a drippy faucet, it will do fine. ■

Lanny Watts has been a master plumber in Chittenden County, Vt., for 18 years. He currently teaches plumbing theory to third year apprentices.

Plumbing Pointers for Remodelers

by Dodge Woodson

For accurate estimates, learn how to identify plumbing pitfalls on your pre-bid walkthrough

Relocating and adding to plumbing systems can be very expensive on a remodeling job. Since plumbing codes are stringent and complicated, it's always best to call in a professional plumber before giving a final estimate. Still, there are many red flags you can learn to recognize on an initial visit to a site. Sizing up the system can help you and your client plan well and avoid surprises.

For any plumbing system you should ask four basic questions:

- Has the existing plumbing caused hidden damage that you will be responsible for once the job is started?
- Will your plumber be able to work with the existing plumbing, or will it be impractical to connect the new to the old?
- Will the existing system handle the increased demands of your remodeling work?
- Are there existing code violations your plumber will have to correct in performing the desired work?

All of these questions must be answered before you can compile accurate cost projections.

Hidden Damage

Water is a powerful force; it can carve rock, erode the earth, and destroy your remodeling budget. If you fail to disclaim unseen damage or don't notice evidence pointing to a problem, you could lose serious money.

In bathrooms, look for places where water may be getting behind and underneath fixtures. Check to see that the trim plates around faucets, drains, and overflow outlets are well-sealed with plumber's putty. Look at the caulking around tubs and showers; if it's dried and cracking, you may have rotted lumber in the walls or floors. Check around the base of the toilet. Water damage can be caused by faulty wax seals or condensation dripping off the tank — particularly where cold well water is used.

In the kitchen, inspect every area you can gain access to. Whenever possible, go below all the plumbing fixtures and inspect the structure supporting them. This will often reveal subflooring stained by water.

Remove the access panel of the dishwasher if there is one and look under the appliance. Refrigerators with ice makers can leak and rot the floor underneath. Look also for any water heaters, washing machines, and well and water conditioning equipment that might be installed in the living areas of the house.

Assessing Existing Supply Lines

One of the main things to look out for, especially with an older home, is the type of

Water will penetrate the wall at the faucet handles (above) whenever the shower is used. The holes should have been covered with trim plates sealed with plumber's putty. The curling and torn linoleum around the toilet (left) indicates water damage to the underlayment, probably from a faulty toilet seal.

water supply lines.

Galvanized. Galvanized water pipes are commonly found in older homes. Get rid of them; if you don't, you're asking for trouble. Galvanized pipe will gradually close up with rust and mineral deposits until, ultimately, pressure is reduced to a trickle.

Worn threads on galvanized fittings are a frequent cause of leaks. When working around old galvanized fittings, any significant jarring or vibration can cause the fittings to let go at any moment. If this happens to a riser hidden in a wall, it will cause a lot of trouble and expense to fix.

When tying into old galvanized pipe, you may want to protect yourself in the contract. If the client doesn't want to replace the galvanized piping and you have to tie into it, your plumber may have to remove several sections

Galvanized pipe should be replaced when found in older homes. The threads rust, causing leaks, and can eventually break off altogether if the pipe is jarred.

Rust, grease, and hair completely clogged this galvanized drain pipe. The author attempted to unclog the pipe with a snake, but succeeded only in punching a hole through the blockage.

to find solid pipe to make a good connection. This will increase your costs unless your contract has a clause disclaiming responsibility for the condition of existing piping.

CPVC. Another type to watch out for is CPVC plastic water pipe. It's fragile and hard to work with. Also, do-it-yourself types like CPVC because it does not require soldering skills. They can cut it with a hacksaw and glue it together. If I see CPVC in a house my crew has to work on, I automatically increase the expected labor to allow for potential problems.

Polybutylene. This pipe is gray and very pliable, but unlike CPVC, "polybute" is very rugged. Remodeling plumbers like polybute because it can be snaked through walls without any concealed joints. In freezing temperatures, it will expand to reduce the risk of splitting. When polybute was first introduced, there were problems with faulty connections, so you need to watch out for these.

PVC. If you find PVC supply pipe, you'd better talk with your plumber. Most codes limit the use of PVC water distribution pipe to cold water. The code generally requires your cold water piping to be of the same material as the hot water pipe, and since PVC cannot be used for hot water, it's not suitable for residential use.

Copper. If you find copper supply line you're probably in good shape. It's easy to repair, add on to, and install.

Main shut-off. Locate and test the main water shut-off valve to see if it works properly. If water leaks past the valve, the plumber will have trouble soldering copper connections (the water turns to steam and causes voids in the solder joint). With CPVC pipe, water will prevent the glue from setting up properly. With polybutylene connections, a small amount of water will have no adverse effects on the connection.

Accessibility. Keep in mind that the plumber not only has to be able to see the plumbing, he will need room to work with it. In general, if you can easily put your hand around the water pipes, the plumber will be able to do his job. But if the pipes are tight against the subfloor, or notched into the top of floor joists, you may have to remove the floor to make a connection.

Placement of lines. In cold climates, pipes in attics, crawlspaces, and outside walls may freeze and burst if not insulated properly. In some cases, pipes in an outside wall may have been saved from freezing only because there was *no* insulation in the wall. In a house where you encounter distribution lines in an outside wall, make sure that you don't isolate the pipe by insulating on the wrong side — the insulation must not be between the pipe and the heated space.

Assessing Existing Drainage

Residential drains are typically installed with a grade of 1/4 inch per foot, and you'll have to maintain this pitch with any new lines. Make sure that any new drain pipe will not be lower than the existing pipe when it reaches the point of connection — an installed, sewage-ejector system can cost in excess of $1,000.

The plumber will need 18 to 24 inches of straight pipe to work with to cut a new fitting into the existing drain line. Also, make sure he has the room to install any new pipe and traps that may be necessary.

Cast-iron drain lines. Most of the main drain lines in older homes are cast iron, usually 3 to 4 inches in diameter. As long as these pipes are properly graded, they will give years of good service. Cast iron is generally easy to tie into, using a rubber coupling with stainless-steel hose clamps.

However, because cast iron can rust, the interior of the pipe becomes rough and can catch hair, grease, and other objects. Cast iron can also rust through from the inside. Rust stains on the outside of the pipe are reason for some concern.

Galvanized and lead drain lines. Galvanized and lead drain pipe are the ones to watch out for. Galvanized pipe is a metallic color, with heavy fittings at the connections. It was used as recently as 20 years ago for sink, shower, and tub connections (it's still code-approved for drainage). Over the years, it becomes restricted with rust and accumulated buildup of hair and grease.

As with galvanized supply lines, galvanized drains are prone to leaking because of rusted threads. This can cause water damage as well as health hazards, since sewer gas can escape. If the connections show a buildup of rust or a white efflorescence around the threads, the pipe will probably leak in the near future. Or the threads may simply break off when worked with. It's best to replace galvanized drain pipe.

In very old homes, you might find lead pipe and traps. These will be a dull gray color and very soft. The drains will rarely be straight and properly graded. When lead is bent, it creases and cracks and will leak. If the pipe runs through a spongy area of the floor, the effects of walking across the floor can take its toll on the soft material. When you see lead plumbing, plan to replace it.

Copper. You may find copper in the drain/ waste/vent (DWV) system. Copper drains usually work very well and cause few problems, remaining smooth and blockage-free. Except for rare circumstances, there will be no reason to replace a copper DWV system.

Plastic. Schedule 40 plastic pipe — either PVC or ABS — is now the most commonly used DWV material. Your plumber should have no problems tying into a correctly installed plastic DWV system.

Fixtures

It is not unusual to find odd-sized bathtubs and sinks. Trying to find a modern unit with comparable measurements may be impossible. If you have to alter the opening for a bathtub, it is best to know it before you submit your proposal.

When choosing a location for tubs or showers, provide an access wall for the faucet in case it ever needs to be replaced. Also, if you are replacing a bathtub with a shower, you'll need to increase the size of the drain. Bathtubs, even those with showers, require a 1 1/2-inch trap and drain. Shower stalls, though, require a 2-inch trap and drain. This conversion may require removing the bathroom floor, or the ceiling below the floor.

If the customer wants to replace a lavatory or vanity with a pedestal sink, you'll have to relocate the plumbing; pedestal sinks require special spacing on the waste and water lines.

Assessing the Demand: Water Distribution

Undersized water pipe is a common problem. It was not unusual in the past for plumbers to install 1/2-inch pipe throughout a house. Unfortunately, this is not in keeping with current codes and creates problems. In a house with all 1/2-inch pipe, if someone is taking a shower when another fixture is turned on, they get drenched with cold or hot water. Adding another bathroom can make the water pressure even worse.

If you are unable to see what size the water pipe is, run a test. Turn the water on at full volume in the tub and notice the pressure. With the tub running, have someone turn on the kitchen sink. Then flush the toilet near the tub. Watch the pressure at the tub. If the house has more than one bathroom, try the test with both tubs running at full capacity. You may find some extreme differences between an upstairs and downstairs bath.

Sizing distribution lines. You should never have more than two fixtures being fed by a single 1/2-inch pipe. There should be at least a 3/4-inch line up until the point of the last two

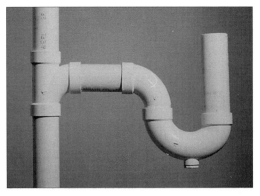

The chrome S-trap, above, does not meet code because it is unvented. A fixture drain should have a vented P-trap (right).

fixtures. With a 3/4-inch water service, most houses will have adequate pressure and be in code compliance.

Assessing the Demand: Drainage

The size of a house's building drain will be determined by the number of fixtures it handles. Most codes will not allow more than two toilets or bathrooms grouped on a 3-inch drain. A 4-inch drain can handle all ordinary residential demands.

Slow drains. When your work involves tying into the existing DWV system, you may become responsible for slow or clogged drains. Kitchen remodeling, for instance, may include the addition of a garbage disposer. When this device is installed, the existing kitchen drain may no longer be adequate.

To test a kitchen drain, fill the sink to the flood rim with water. If it is double-bowl, fill both sides. Release all the water at the same time. Repeat this procedure two or three times. Occasionally, if there is a clog down the line, a single bowl of water may appear to drain fine, even with the clog. By draining several bowls of water quickly, though, you'll discover the problem.

Check any fixtures your work may involve. Flush the toilet, fill and drain the tub, and test the lavatory. Follow this rule: If it has a drain, test it.

The absence of a vent can cause a drain to operate slowly. If you have a fixture that drains, but does so without force, it may need a vent. In any case, note existing drain problems and have the customer acknowledge the condition before you begin work.

Code Violations

Beware of existing code violations. If you alter existing plumbing, you may be required to correct all code deficiencies. Remodeling can expose all types of plumbing code violations.

Undersized distribution pipe. Undersized water distribution pipe is a common code problem. If the whole house is piped in 1/2-inch pipe, the plumber may connect to it, in most cases, without changing the existing pipe. However, if there is larger pipe available in an accessible location, the plumber will be required to make his connections to the larger pipe. This can mean running pipe for a much longer distance than you planned.

Unvented fixtures. Unvented fixtures are a frequent problem with older homes (most states require every fixture drain to be vented). If the drain goes straight down through the floor, the fixture is not properly vented and your plumber will have to install a vent for the new fixture being installed. Under remodeling conditions, you may be able to use a mechanical vent, a small plastic device that screws into a female fitting installed in the fixture drain line. Check with the local code official to see if mechanical vents are allowed.

Illegal traps. If the drain comes straight up through the floor, to an "S" trap, you have a code violation. But if the drain comes out of the wall, into a "P" trap, you should be okay. Drum traps are prohibited in most states.

Illegal drains. Sink drains dumping into a sump-pump pit are in violation of code. If this condition exists, your plumber will have to tie the drain into the sanitary drainage system. This could result in additional costs of several hundred dollars.

Space requirements. If you are doing an extensive bathroom remodel, you may have to expand the size of the bathroom to meet modern code requirements. For example, the center of the toilet drain must have 15 inches of clear space on each side and 18 inches of clear space in front.

Septic capacity. Another issue to consider, if you are adding space to a home, is whether the existing septic system will be adequate. Adding bedrooms may necessitate enlarging the septic system, which can cost several thousand dollars, depending on the soil type and the local code requirements. Locate and inspect the septic system. If you find the leach field to be soggy and saturated with liquid, the system may be defective. Strong odor in the air is another warning of a failed system.

Conclusion

Even if the plumbing you anticipate seems trivial, give the entire system a full inspection. A checklist is helpful. After a general walk-through, go back over the specific plumbing you plan to deal with. With the expense of plumbing work, this phase of your estimate deserves your concentrated attention. ■

Dodge Woodson is a master plumber and general contractor in Topsham, Maine.

Antiscald Protection for Showers

by Rex Cauldwell

Although the solution is simple and readily available, scalding in the tub or shower is still a severe problem throughout the U.S. — especially for the very young and the elderly. It's easy for a two-year-old standing in the bathtub to reach up and turn the water on to full hot — possibly to get blasted with dangerously hot water. Elderly bathers may also be at risk because their reaction time is slower and their sensitivity to heat may be greater than normal. Or they may panic and turn the wrong handle or turn it in the wrong direction. Either way, serious injury can result.

Scalding can also occur if the cold water pressure drops suddenly while someone is showering. This typically happens in houses with undersized or otherwise poorly designed water supply lines. Someone flushes the toilet while another person is showering, and the person in the shower is hit by an untempered spray of hot water. The problem is exacerbated by low-flow shower heads: There is already such a small volume of cold water being delivered that any further decrease has even greater effect.

Water Heater Settings

There are several ways of attacking the scalding problem. The simplest first step is to reduce the temperature setting on the water heater. In most cases, the temperature setting can be lowered without greatly affecting the hot water supply. In the past, water heaters were commonly set at higher temperatures to produce the hot water needed for dishwashers. Today, however, the trend is toward dishwashers that heat their own water. Clothes washers and bathroom vanities need only warm water, so with the possible exception of soaking dishes, extremely hot water isn't really required.

Still, I often find water heaters adjusted as high as 160°F! Water at this temperature will give a second-degree burn in a second or less. Even a medium setting of 130°F can cause first- and second- degree burns in 30 seconds, — even faster on the sensitive, thinner skin of small children. *I recommend setting the water heater no higher than 120°F.*

Water heater manufacturers have responded to the problem and are now presetting the electric thermostats at 120°F. Gas water heaters, which are sent from the factory in the "off" position, now have explicit instructions ex-plaining the risks of temperature settings higher than 120°F.

Even with these measures, however, it is still possible for a gas water heater to deliver scalding water, because of a phenomenon called the *stacking effect*: After a series of short draws from the water heater, the water at the top of the tank can become much hotter than the setting on the thermostat, which is located near the bottom of a gas water heater. Manufacturers are required to keep the temperature at the top to within 30°F of the thermostat setting, but with a 120°F setting this would still permit 150°F water to exit the tank at the top — plenty hot to cause scalding.

Pressure-Balancing Valves

Lowering the water heater temperature is a good first step in scald prevention, but this alone cannot guarantee protection. In many cases, customers will still choose to have the water heater at a higher setting — either because the tank is not large enough to supply all the hot water they want, or because they are accustomed to having very hot water in the kitchen.

The best way to protect your clients against scalding in the shower is to install a pressure-balancing shower control. If installed correctly, these valves have a physical stop, set by the installer, that limits the maximum mixed-water temperature to 120°F. They also keep the water temperature within 3°F plus or minus of where the user sets it, regardless of pressure fluctua-

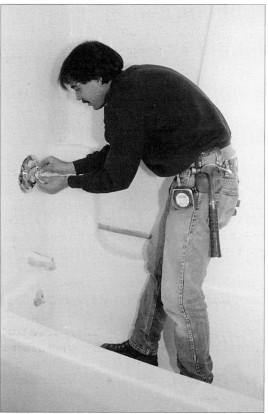

CAROLYN BATES

Pressure-balancing valves give reliable and affordable protection against scalding in the shower

How Pressure-Balancing Valves Work

Piston Type

Equal Pressure: Under normal water pressure, equal volumes of hot and cold water pass through the pressure-balancing cartridge.

Balanced Pressure: With a drop in cold water pressure, the balancing spool is pushed over by the greater hot water pressure, instantly reducing the volume of hot water coming through the cartridge.

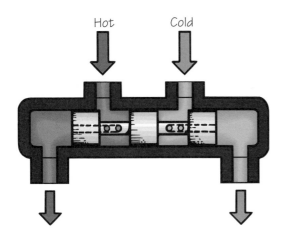

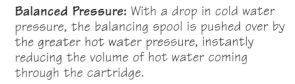

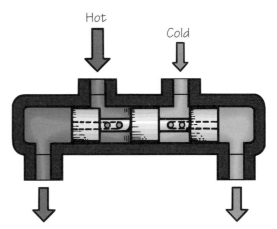

Diaphragm Type

Equal Pressure: Under normal water pressure, the rubber diaphragm remains in the center of the cartridge, allowing equal volumes of hot and cold water to pass through.

Balanced Pressure: With a drop in cold water pressure, the diaphragm is forced over by the greater hot water pressure, simultaneously reducing the volume of hot water.

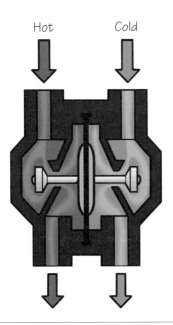

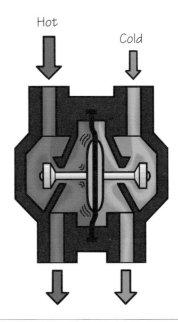

Pressure-balancing valves come in two main types. With piston, or spool, mechanisms (top), increased water pressure on one side pushes the piston over, simultaneously closing the inlet on that side and balancing the pressure of the mixed water. With diaphragm types (bottom), a flexible rubber diaphragm responds to pressure fluctuations, closing the inlet on the side with greater pressure.

tions in the house (see Figure 1).

There are two types of pressure-balancing valves: those that use a piston, or spool, mechanism and those that use a flexible rubber diaphragm (see box, facing page).

Sliding piston type. The pressure-balancing valve I am most familiar with is the Moentrol, manufactured by Moen, which uses a stainless-steel piston mechanism to regulate the incoming water. When you are showering under normal water pressure, both cold and hot water flow equally through the spool, and up to the shower head. When someone turns on the cold water elsewhere in the house and the pressure on the cold water side drops, the piston instantaneously moves to reduce the flow of incoming hot water, preventing scalding. The hot water flow matches the reduced cold water volume, so the mixed-water temperature remains the same. Likewise, if a sudden pressure drop occurs in the hot water supply, the pressure-balancing piston moves instantly to decrease the flow of cold water into the valve body.

Diaphragm types. The second type of pressure-balancing mechanism uses a rubber diaphragm to respond to pressure differences. One example is the Danfoss pressure-balancing cartridge, which is used in valves made by Briggs, Central Brass, Gerber, Grohe, and other manufacturers. Another is the Kohler Rite-Temp pressure-balancing unit.

As the rubber diaphragm moves in response to pressure differences, it restricts the flow of the side with the greater pressure, working in a manner similar to the piston-type mechanism.

Thermostatic Valves

The vast majority of residential antiscald valves are pressure-balancing units of one of the types described above. Another category of antiscald valve is the thermostatic control valve. These come in two types — those that respond only to temperature changes, and so-called combination valves, which have both a thermostatic device and a pressure-balancing mechanism.

Thermostatic valves are widely used in Europe but are not common in the U.S. They typically cost two to four times what a pressure-balancing valve costs, so they are installed mainly in high-end jobs.

I have not had wide experience with thermostatic valves. Most of my customers are more comfortable with the cost of a pressure-balancing valve. However, I have installed one model — a combination type — in my own home. Yet with this valve, expensive as

it was, I cannot adjust the water temperature while I'm showering unless I turn the faucet off first and then turn it back on at the new temperature. This particular model has a bimetallic thermostatic element. The technology has improved, and most makers are now using wax thermostatic cartridges, which are reportedly more reliable. If a client insists on having a thermostatically controlled valve, look for one with a wax element.

CAROLYN BATES

Figure 1. *A plumber sets the adjustable stop that limits the mixed-water temperature of this Moentrol pressure-balancing valve to 120°F.*

Shopping for Pressure-Balancing Valves

There are many pressure-balancing valves on the market. I generally use the Moentrol because it's reasonably priced and reliable. Plus, I've been installing them for years and have never had a callback.

Currently, only single-handle pressure-balancing valves are available. They come in two types. With one type — those like the Moentrol — the handle pulls out to adjust the volume and rotates to adjust temperature (Figure 2). With the other type, called a cycling valve, you rotate a lever to adjust the temperature but there is no volume adjustment — the valve operates only at full volume. Manufacturers claim that with the advent of low-flow shower heads, volume adjustment is less important, since most people will prefer to shower at full volume anyway. But I happen to prefer the units like the Moentrol because you can preset the temperature before you turn on the water.

Retrofit jobs. Although pressure-balancing valves must be plumbed for single-handle operation, some manufacturers make a cover plate that allows you to convert double- or triple-handle controls to single-handle operation — without having to retile over the holes left by the previous valves. Sometimes, the cutout for the plate is even large enough to allow room for the new connections — even when there is no rear access panel. However, most of the time you need rear access.

You get what you pay for. Never buy a bottom-of-the-line unit. Because the new codes (see "Antiscald Code Update," next page) are boosting the sale of pressure-balancing valves, many manufacturers have introduced less-

MOENTROL

MOEN POSI-TEMP

Figure 2. *All pressure-balancing valves currently have single-handle controls. With one type, the handle rotates to adjust temperature and pulls out to adjust the volume (top). Cycling-type valves (bottom), have no volume control; the lever turns the water on at full volume and rotates to adjust the mixed-water temperature.*

expensive, do-it-yourself models. I suggest sticking with the older proven designs — your plumbing sub will undoubtedly have a recommendation.

Installation Tips

These tips apply to all valve installations, though careful installation is even more important with pressure-balancing controls.

Read and follow instructions. This goes without saying. Even so, most instructions leave a lot to be desired — which is where your plumber's experience comes in.

Buy a unit with IPS (iron pipe size) connections. These valves have threads on the inside of the faucet body, as opposed to copper sweat connections. With sweated connections, it's possible that the heat from the torch can ruin heat-sensitive parts in the delicate pressure-balancing mechanism or the valve cartridge itself. Using IPS bodies solves that problem. However, if you must use copper sweat connections, either disassemble the entire faucet so that the heat cannot warp or destroy the plastic cartridge parts, or use a heat sink (a wet rag wrapped around the faucet) to absorb the heat once it enters the main body. Either way, do not use any more heat than is necessary to sweat the joint.

Thoroughly wash out new plumbing pipes before installing the valve. Sediment is the bane of pressure-balancing valves. New water lines must be totally purged of sawdust, dirt, sand, wood and rock chips, solder globs, and pieces of teflon tape before connecting the fixture. Renovation jobs pose even more problems. With old galvanized water lines, bits of rust will invariably break loose during installation. A bit of debris lodged in the wrong place will prevent the balancing assembly from working.

Turn the water on and have it "fountain up" to get rid of as much loose sediment as possible. When you work on old water lines, treat the pipes gently to keep pieces of rust from breaking off inside.

When water pressure is released into the fixture, have the fixture valve on full, both hot and cold, with the shower head removed. Do not turn the fixture handle to the off position until enough water has been run through the fixture to purge the lines of any foreign material. If the handle is turned off when a sharp object, like a rock shard, comes through, the fixture could be ruined. If the client's water supply is notorious for incoming sediment, install an in-line filter.

Do not pressurize one side only. Slowly release both hot and cold water pressure to the fixture at the same time. I've had pressure-balancing valves jam when they were hit with 50 to 80 pounds of water pressure on one side only. When this happens, pressurizing the other side by itself usually unjams the piston. If not, you have to remove the pressure-balancing spool, open it up, and free up the piston.

Set the temperature limit stop carefully. By code, the installer must limit the maximum hot water temperature to 120°F. I have used a meat thermometer to check this, but typically I use my hand and adjust the hot water just below where it starts to feel really uncomfortable on my skin. If the installer sets the limit stop too high, scalding can still occur. ∎

Rex Cauldwell is a master plumber and electrician, and owner of Little Mountain Plumbing Co. in Copper Hill, Va.

Antiscald Code Update

In a drive to prevent scalding injuries, many state and local plumbing codes now require antiscald valves in residential showers. That's because all four of the national plumbing codes — the *National Standard Plumbing Code* (1993), the *National Plumbing Code* (1993), the *Standard Plumbing Code* (1994), and the *Uniform Plumbing Code* (1994) — have adopted the rule. The codes call for all showers, including bath/shower combinations, to be equipped with pressure-balancing or thermostatic controls that comply with ASSE standard 1016 (American Society of Sanitary Engineers, Bay Village, Ohio). The valve must be installed according to the manufacturer's instructions and adjusted to deliver a maximum mixed-water temperature of 120°F.

What does compliance with ASSE 1016 mean? Among other things, that the valve can maintain a set water temperature within 3°F plus or minus when either the hot or cold water pressure drops by 50%. Also, if the cold water fails altogether, the valve must be able to reduce the hot water to a trickle within 5 seconds while not allowing the temperature to exceed 120°F.

Manufacturers must have their products tested by independent laboratories for compliance with these and other standards.

There are a couple of exceptions in the codes: Instead of a pressure-balancing or thermostatic control in the shower, the *National Standard Plumbing Code* allows the supply piping serving the shower to be designed to slow the water velocity down to 4 gpm, making it unlikely that pressure imbalances would occur. But because this requires using larger pipe, it would probably cost more than simply installing a pressure-balancing shower control. Likewise, under the *National Plumbing Code*, you can use a master thermostatic mixing valve in the supply lines, set at 120°F, instead of an antiscald control in the shower.

Check with your plumbing inspector for local regulations on pressure-balancing valves. As in all code matters, it's up to the local jurisdiction to decide which rules to adopt and how to enforce them. For example, some inspectors may require upgrading to pressure-balancing controls for any remodels that affect the bathroom; others may require the valves in new installations only.

Some Cautions on Fancy Faucets

by Lynn Comeskey

CAROLYN BATES

They look great in the showroom, but upscale faucets can be a real challenge to the installer. It's often best to "dry-fit" the parts at the supply house.

One of the Twelve Commandments of Remodeling is "Thou shalt not start the job until all materials are in hand." This commandment was written with "decorative" faucets in mind. These new faucets, many of them imported from Europe, are popular with designers and clients and now are used on half of my jobs.

It's tempting to start a job with just the valve body in hand and worry about the trim later, but don't. In fact, as cautious as it may sound, you or your plumber may want to "dry-fit" all of the parts of the faucet when you pick it up. This way you can make sure that you have everything you need. It also allows you to ask questions of your supplier if part of the assembly isn't clear.

If it's not possible to see the fitting ahead of time, you might offer to install it on a time-and-materials basis. But even then, make sure you or your plumber ends up with the printed instructions. A few years ago, we neglected both of these pearls of wisdom when installing a Danish tub/shower mixer. After many more hours than any of us care to remember, our plumber finally figured out how it was supposed to be installed.

Putting the Pieces Together

Beware of tub/shower or lavatory mixers that are assembled from several pieces, because how these pieces are put together can make all the difference. For instance, we have received mixers with the hot and cold valves operating in the same direction. Obviously we were given a unit made with two rights or two lefts.

Another assembly problem to watch for is valve stems that don't align in mixers that are silver-soldered together. Unlike threaded or corrugated connections to the valves that are easy to line up, the silver-soldered versions are impossible to budge. We recently had to get three Broadway mixers off our distributor's shelves before finding one we could use.

Some Italian mixer valves don't have these assembly problems — they come unassembled, and you get to put them together. Our local imported faucet expert won't even stock these. And while you would assume that any plumbing fitting offered for sale in this country would either have U.S. threads or come with adaptors, this is not always the case. The only answer is to be thorough. At the $55 to $65 an hour

Polished brass finishes can rapidly tarnish unless they are sealed with a durable finish such as a polymer resin.

we pay plumbers in this area, it's important they have everything they need to complete the installation on the first trip.

Plumbing the Depth

Another disturbing fact about many European faucets is that they are intended for finished surfaces with little depth. This can be a real problem for tiled shower/tub walls. While trying to install the Danish mixer I mentioned earlier, we discovered after much head-scratching that it was made for a 3/8-inch-thick wall. We were trying to install it in tile over a mortar float that exceeded an inch in thickness. With some good luck, we were able to locate an extra lavatory faucet escutcheon and refashion it at a local machine shop. Thank goodness! We never would have been able to duplicate the distinctive yellow-enamel finish.

Remember that tile needs some latitude because the thickness of the mortar bed can vary considerably depending on how plumb and square the framing is. Our plumber is used to having over an inch of flexibility with domestic mixer valve bodies because they are deep and have lots of thread. By contrast, we have encountered some imported mixers with approximately 1/4 inch of thread. This means the valve body has to be installed very accurately to make the trim work later.

But this problem isn't unique to tub/shower installations. Although plastic laminate and solid surfacing materials like Corian aren't usually a problem, tiled lavatories and kitchen countertops can be. Grohe, Dornbracht, and Broadway do offer valve stem extensions, and another manu-

facturer, Phylrich, will custom-make stems to the length you need.

A Solid Finish

Another popular item is the reproduction, white-ceramic cross or lever handles. However, they don't make them like they used to. The handles seem to break with ease — so I always test them ahead of time.

The truth is that some of the decorative faucets in the higher price brackets, which the homeowner naturally equates with the highest quality, just aren't made very well. In this vein, talk to your supplier about brand names you don't have experience with; they know what comes back and what doesn't.

One expectation that the homeowner carries after many years of owning chrome-finished fixtures is that even an aging faucet will continue to sport that flawless, showroom gleam. This is fine for chrome, but not for polished brass and other more exotic finishes that are experiencing a wave of popularity. One manufacturer purposely doesn't apply a protective finish so the faucet trim tarnishes right away. That's okay if the homeowner is aware of it; but that's usually not the case.

Most manufacturers spray their fixtures with a lacquer finish to protect the raw metal or plating. Lacquer finishes have a nice warm sheen, but won't take a lot of abuse and allow rapid tarnishing once this coating is scratched. We've tried to have tarnished pieces repolished and lacquered locally, but the finish doesn't last long. To put off the inevitable tarnishing, look for brands with a polymer resin finish; they are much more durable. Artistic Brass, for example, offers a five-year guarantee on its finish.

Despite this litany of cautions, I'm not trying to discourage anyone from using decorative faucets. Most are good-looking and functional, and they continue to rise in popularity. But they do require extra diligence and attention from you, and a new set of expectations from your client. ■

Lynn Comeskey, of Palo Alto, Calif., is a remodeling contractor who specializes in kitchens and baths.

Taking the Worry Out of Drinking Water

by Don Best

To guarantee clean water for your clients, choose the right equipment and make sure it's serviced regularly

A subcontractor installs a water-softening system to treat all incoming water.

Whether it's an outbreak of dangerous protozoa in a municipal water system, news of a private well contaminated with nitrates, or fresh warnings about the dangers of lead in our drinking water, rarely a day goes by without a worrisome new headline about water quality.

Polls show that seven out of ten Americans are concerned about the quality of the water they drink, and that millions of homeowners have already resorted to bottled water or installed some type of water filtration equipment in their home.

If you're a builder or plumbing contractor, it's important to the health of your clients — *and* your business — to understand the water quality issues that affect your area. Armed with the facts, you can answer your customers' questions and make confident recommendations. If some type of water treatment is called for, you're in a good position to either install and service the equipment yourself or to work through a subcontractor.

How's the Water?

About 85% of all homes in the U.S. are serviced by municipal water systems, which are governed by both the Safe Water Drinking Act, a federal law administered by the U.S. Environmental Protection Agency (EPA), and state health laws.

Enforcement of these laws, however, is far from perfect. In a highly publicized case last summer, 370,000 people in Milwaukee became ill with flulike symptoms from drinking public water contaminated with a parasite. While this incident was unique in the number of people affected, smaller outbreaks of illness from contaminated drinking water occur every year, according to Dr. Thomas Navin, epidemiologist at the Centers for Disease Control in Atlanta. The problem, says Navin, is that "with increasing population pressure, there is increased risk in raw water [sources] that must be addressed by municipal systems."

In a controversial report called "Think Before You Drink," released in September 1993, the Natural Resources Defense Council (NRDC), an environmental group based in Washington, D.C., charged that many contaminants "are not adequately controlled under EPA rules because of inadequate … standards and weak or nonexistent enforcement." Particularly at risk are

Choosing the Right Filter

| Problem/Pollutant | Reverse Osmosis | Distillation | Filtration | | | Activated Alumina | Water Softening (Cation Exchange) |
			Carbon	Mechanical			
Aluminum	✔	✔				
Arsenic	✔	✔			✔	
Asbestos	✔			✔		
Barium	✔	✔				✔
Cadmium	✔	✔				✔
Chloride	✔	✔				
Chlorine	✔		✔			
Chromium	✔	✔				
Color	✔		✔	✔		
Copper	✔	✔				✔
Endrin			✔			
Fluoride	✔	✔			✔	
Giardia Cysts	✔	✔		✔		
Hardness	✔	✔				✔
Iron (Fe^2)	✔	✔		✔		✔
Iron (Fe^3)	✔	✔				
Lead	✔	✔	✔		✔	
Lindane			✔			
Manganese	✔	✔				✔
Mercury	✔	✔				
Methoxychlor			✔			
Nitrate	✔	✔				
Particulates	✔	✔		✔		
Pesticides, Herbicides, PCBs			✔			
Radium	✔	✔				✔
Radon			✔			
Selenium	✔	✔			✔	
Silver	✔	✔				
Sulfate	✔	✔				
Tannic Acids		✔	✔			
Taste & Odor			✔			
Total Dissolved Solids	✔	✔				
Total Trihalomethanes			✔			
Toxaphene			✔			
Turbidity	✔	✔	✔	✔		
VOCs			✔			
Zinc	✔	✔				
2,4-D			✔			
2,4,5-TP Silvex			✔			

Note: *Adapted from NSF International. Performance for a given unit may vary from the chart. For example, not all carbon units are effective for lead reduction. Always ask for proof of performance according to NSF standards.*

Major Contaminants Found in Drinking Water

Contaminant	Type	Main sources	Health effects	Main risk group
Health Hazards: The following contaminants are widely found in water; their threats to health are well established.				
Lead	Inorganic chemical; heavy metal	Soft or acidic water in lead pipes, copper pipes connected by lead solder, or brass faucets	Developmental and learning disabilities, low birth weight	Children, fetuses
Radon	Radioactive gas	Groundwater	Lung cancer	Anyone
Nitrate	Inorganic chemical	Wells in agricultural areas	Methemoglobinemia, a blood disorder	Infants under 6 mo.
The following contaminants are found in water less often than those listed above, or the seriousness of the hazard from low levels of contamination is unclear.				
Pesticides	Organic chemicals	Runoff and seepage in agricultural areas	In high doses, liver, kidney, or nervous-system damage; possibly cancer	Anyone
Trichloroethylene	Organic chemical	Industrial effluents or hazardous-waste sites	In high doses, nervous-system damage; possibly cancer	Anyone
Trihalomethanes	Organic chemicals	Chlorination of surface water	Possibly cancer	Anyone
Bacteria, viruses, *Giardia*	Microorganisms	Insufficiently disinfected or filtered water	Intestinal and other diseases	Anyone
Taste Killers: The following contaminants, in sufficient quantity, may degrade the taste, odor, or appearance of water but are not known to be hazardous to health.				
Ferrous iron, manganese	Minerals	Groundwater	—	—
Hardness minerals (calcium, magnesium)	Minerals	Many water sources, especially groundwater	—	—
Chlorine	Water-treatment chemical	Excessive residue of chlorination	—	—

the elderly, infants, and people with weakened immune systems, says the report.

While EPA officials feel the NRDC report exaggerates the health risks and maintain that most tap water in the U.S. is safe, EPA's deputy director of drinking water standards, Stephen Clark, admits that a number of the smaller, poorer water districts cannot afford to meet current standards for monitoring.

Given this uncertainty, more municipal water customers are turning to in-home water treatment as a safeguard against possible *health* risks (see table, above). Most purchasers of in-home systems, however, want their water treated primarily for *aesthetic* concerns, such as taste, smell, hardness, or color.

For example, many people dislike the taste given to water by chlorine, a disinfectant widely used in municipal water systems. As shown in the chart (facing page) "Choosing the Right Filter," a carbon filter can effectively remove chlorine from the water and address some color and odor problems as well.

Another frequent source of complaints is "hard" water, which leaves scaly deposits on toilets and tubs, makes it difficult to rinse the soap out of clothes, and can give drink-

Combined Water Softening & Reverse Osmosis System

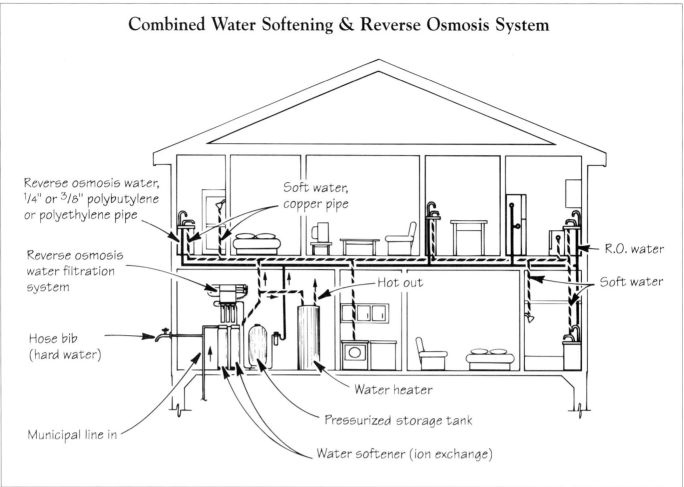

Reverse osmosis water, ¼" or ⅜" polybutylene or polyethylene pipe

Soft water, copper pipe

Reverse osmosis water filtration system

R.O. water

Soft water

Hot out

Hose bib (hard water)

Water heater

Pressurized storage tank

Municipal line in

Water softener (ion exchange)

Figure 1. *This high-end, point-of-entry system has both water softener and filtering equipment clustered near the water main. Filtered water is routed through separate plastic piping to dedicated drinking-water taps throughout the house, and to a connector for the refrigerator's ice maker.*

ing water a cloudy appearance. A water softener can remove most of the dissolved calcium and magnesium that cause these problems.

Some water quality problems are evident to the eye, nose, or tongue, but many others are not. To find out what the water quality issues are in your area, start by asking the local water utility for an analytical breakdown. Since the quality of the water leaving the treatment plant is constantly monitored, it is easy for them to provide a printout for you. If there's no one at the water utility willing to help you interpret the information, get some help from your local or state health officials. You can also get some answers by calling the EPA's drinking water hotline at 800/426-4791.

Even if the water leaving the treatment plant is clean, contaminants can get into municipal drinking water *after* it leaves the plant, from either the utility's distribution pipes or household plumbing. Lead, which can cause serious neurological problems, especially in children, is the most common example. This dangerous contaminant, which is tasteless, colorless, and odorless in the water, leaches out of lead pipes, sol-

dered joints, and brass faucets, creating a potential health hazard to some 40 million Americans, according to EPA estimates.

Since lead pipes and lead-based solder were banned nationwide in 1986, newer homes don't present a risk. But if you work on older houses, especially those built between 1910 and 1940, when the use of lead service pipes was common, it would be smart to have the homeowner test his water through a reputable lab.

If you work in an area with private wells, your local and state health officials can give you an overview of the groundwater quality. Using historical test records, they should be able to alert you to potential well water problems, including high levels of radon, arsenic, nitrates, pesticides, and other contaminants.

Local well drilling contractors are another good source of expertise on groundwater quality. In recent years, many of them have begun to sell and service water softening and filtration equipment as a natural extension of their drilling business.

Of course, neither historical nor anecdotal information can take the place of a site-specific water well test, which will precisely identify any substances that need to be removed to meet your customer's goals. All private wells should be periodically tested by a certified testing laboratory that's recommended by your state health department.

Should You Subcontract?

Once you've done your homework, you'll know whether or not there's a genuine need for in-home water treatment in your area. If there is, you must decide whether you want to become a dealer yourself or to work with an established dealer who will install and service the equipment on a subcontract basis.

Most home builders choose the latter course, since there's usually not enough volume and profit in the work to justify the relatively large investment of time and effort it takes to become a dealer. (Plumbers, k&b remodelers, and well drillers, on the other hand, may find it worthwhile to start their own dealership.)

Since there are a lot of hucksters loose in the field — as well as some questionable equipment — it pays to choose a sub with care. Look for an established business with a good reputation, permanent location, and a stable relationship with one or more reputable manufacturers. It is also worth checking with the Better Business Bureau and Federal Trade Commission for a clean record.

The water filtration equipment should be certified by the NSF International or a reliable lab that tests to NSF standards. NSF is an independent, nonprofit group that tests products to see if they remove the specific contaminants that their manufacturers claim.

Some water contractors take the time to become Certified Water Specialists, which means they've completed at least a basic training course with the Water Quality Association (WQA). About 500 dealers nationwide have gone on to become level-five specialists, having completed advanced course work with the WQA.

Service and Maintenance

Since all water treatment equipment requires ongoing maintenance to remain effective (e.g., periodically replacing the activated charcoal in a carbon filter or the membrane in a reverse-osmosis system), you must be able to count on your subcontractor to reliably service the system for years to come.

"One of the first things I looked for was a company that had the horsepower to stand behind their equipment and deliver good service," says custom builder Mark Falcone, president of Falcone Builders in Laguna Beach, Calif. "I didn't want any callbacks or problems down the road to end up on *my* desk."

Falcone says that he doesn't make a profit on the $4,000 water softening and reverse-osmosis systems that his subcontractor, Water Factory Systems, of Irvine, Calif., installs.

"The water treatment system goes into my homes just like the refrigerator and the other appliances," he explains. "I have them put in as a service to my clients, without any markup."

But most builders mark up the systems. For example, Maracay Homes, which develops subdivisions in the Phoenix area, adds $1,850 to $1,950 to the price of a new home for including a built-in water softener, reverse-osmosis filtration system, and related piping. Maracay pays its subcontractor, All About Water-Eco Water, in Gilbert, Ariz., about $1,000 for the equipment and installation.

"Builders can make a nice margin on these systems with little or no effort," says Joyce Crissman, co-owner of All About Water-Eco Water. "While the home is being framed, our crew goes in and plumbs in the softener loop and the polybutylene lines for the filtered drinking water. Once the home is finished, we install the equipment. After the new owner moves in, we do all the service and maintenance. All the builder has to do is offer the option to potential buyers."

Point-of-Entry Systems

The upscale systems that Falcone Builders and Maracay Homes use are called "point-of-entry" water treatment systems. The equipment is typically clustered in a basement, garage, or utility room near the point where the water line enters the house.

With the exception of the outside hose bibs, all household water — hot and cold — is typically routed through the softener. Using water line pressure, some of the softened water is diverted through the reverse-osmosis unit into a storage tank. As demand calls, the filtered drinking water is distributed through separate piping to various service points throughout the house (Figure 1).

For customers concerned about the salt content of softened water (for example,

Water Treatment Technologies

The four main types of in-home water treatment devices are described below. Capabilities vary from model to model, so look for proof of performance. There are also special filters available for specific problems, such as lead, that may solve the problem at less expense.

Reverse Osmosis

With RO systems, line pressure forces molecules of pure water through a thin semipermeable membrane. The purified water is slowly collected in a one- to three-gallon storage tank while dissolved contaminants, unable to pass through the membrane, are drained away. Most undersink units take from two to three hours to process one gallon of water.

Reverse osmosis can remove 90% to 99% of the impurities in water, including lead and other toxic metals, arsenic, nitrates, and organic contaminants. It is not effective against high levels of minerals. Most models come with a sediment or carbon prefilter and/or a carbon postfilter. Depending on the model, RO units waste three to five gallons of water for every gallon used. The membranes need to be replaced every one to two years. Installed retail prices for point-of-use models run from $450 to $1,500. Replacement membranes cost $150 to $300.

Distillation

Water is electrically heated inside a vessel to make steam, which is then condensed in a coil to produce distilled water. This removes most dissolved solids, including salts and heavy metals such as lead, but is not effective against volatile organic compounds. Some models work with line pressure alone; others have a built-in pump.

This is a slower process than RO, requiring up to two hours to produce one quart of distilled water. The process requires about three kilowatt hours (kwh) of electricity to make one gallon of distilled water, making operating costs high where electric rates are high. Distillation units also release appreciable amounts of heat into the room, a plus in winter, a negative in summer. Some units are prone to scaling on the inside surfaces, so frequent cleaning may be required. Installed retail prices for distillation units range from about $250 to $1,000.

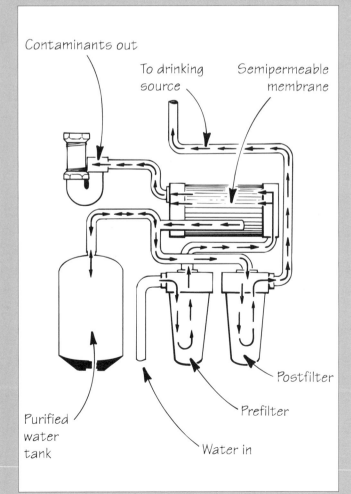

Contaminants out

To drinking source

Semipermeable membrane

Purified water tank

Prefilter

Postfilter

Water in

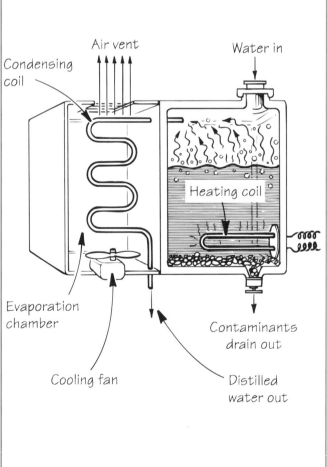

Air vent

Water in

Condensing coil

Heating coil

Evaporation chamber

Cooling fan

Contaminants drain out

Distilled water out

Water Softeners

Line pressure pushes hard water through a canister filled with a synthetic resin. Through a process called ion exchange, the hard calcium and magnesium ions dissolved in the water are exchanged for soft sodium ions affixed to the resin. (Because the sodium-based process leaves the water relatively salty, water softened with sodium may not be suitable for people on low-sodium diets. Potassium-based softeners are an alternative.)

When the resin is saturated with calcium and magnesium, the system automatically regenerates itself by flushing the resin with salt water from a companion tank filled with brine. Most models require electrical hookup to power the regeneration cycle and use either a timer or a flow monitor to regulate the process. Softeners typically treat about 2,000 gallons between regeneration cycles, depending on the size of the unit and the hardness of the water. The brine tank must be periodically reloaded with salt. Installed retail prices range from about $750 to $2,200.

Activated Carbon

With this system, line pressure forces water through one or more canisters packed with activated carbon granules, which trap and hold contaminants. Carbon filters are best at removing bad odors and tastes, chlorine, organic chemicals, and pesticides. Many are also effective against lead. Carbon filters work most effectively when equipped with a prefilter to remove sediment, which can clog the carbon prematurely.

High-volume models typically deliver one-third gallon to three gallons per minute — suitable for families with high water usage. These use large canisters about 10 inches high by 3 inches in diameter and will last approximately six months or process about 1,000 gallons of water before the carbon needs to be replaced. If filters are not replaced when needed, they can actually breed bacteria.

Small faucet-mounted filters are effective only against odors and tastes and need frequent filter changes. Installed retail prices for under-the-sink and countertop models range from $50 to $450. Replacement filter elements for high-volume filters range in cost from $15 to $75.

— D.B.

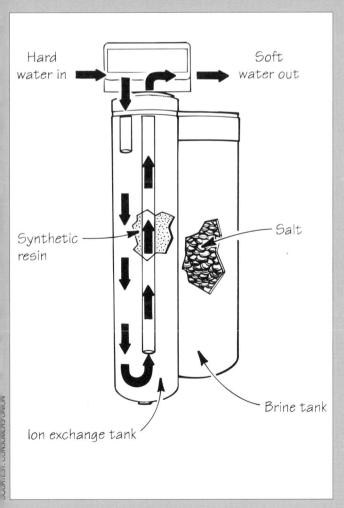

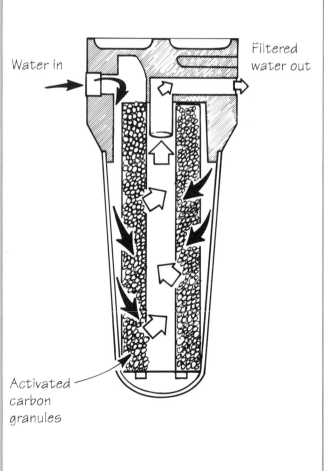

Figure 2. *Point-of-use filtration is more common and less costly than central systems. This undersink reverse osmosis system from Culligan can deliver 1/2 gallon per hour and costs from $500 to $800 installed.*

those on low-sodium diets), you may want to bypass the water softener for their drinking water loop. The harder the water, the saltier it will be after softening, so this is mainly a concern with very hard water. However, hard water will more quickly scale up filter and distillation equipment or wear out the membranes on reverse-osmosis units. Another option for those on low-salt diets is to use a potassium-based softener rather than one using sodium.

The piping used to deliver the filtered drinking water is usually 1/4-inch or 3/8-inch polybutylene or polyethylene tubing. Not only is plastic tubing less expensive than copper, it also holds up better in contact with filtered water, which is very aggressive.

Point-of-Use Systems

A more common and less expensive option is to install some type of "point-of-use" filtration (Figure 2). This approach places the water-treatment unit under the sink or on the countertop close to where the water is going to be used for drinking or cooking. (Water softeners are *always* placed at the point of entry, in order to treat all household water, since it would be impractical to put a softener on each plumbing fixture.)

The installed retail price for a point-of-use filtration unit varies dramatically from under $100 to over $1,000, depending on the technology used and the unit's capacity and features (see "Water Treatment Technologies," previous page.)

Bear in mind that the lifetime operation and maintenance costs on these filtration systems can be several times their original purchase price, especially when the cost of wasted water (reverse osmosis) and electricity (distillation) is factored in. ■

Don Best is a freelance writer in Surry, N.H., specializing in construction topics.

For More Information

To find out whether a specific brand of water filtration equipment performs as the manufacturer claims, contact:

NSF International
(formerly National Sanitation Foundation)
3475 Plymouth Rd., P.O. Box 130140, Ann Arbor, MI 48113
313/769-8010

For information on drinking-water quality standards, contact:
U.S. Environmental Protection Agency
Office of Drinking Water (WH5500)
401 M. St., SW, Washington, DC 20460
800/426-4791

For a list of Certified Water Specialists in your area, contact:
Water Quality Association
4151 Naperville Rd., Lisle, IL 60532
708/505-0160

Instant Heat & Hot Water

by Paul Turpin

Whether or not you're looking forward to the day when you build electronic houses that anticipate your clients' every whim, there are several uncomplicated devices — thermostats and sensors — that can be used today to make a house "smarter." Wiring these controls into standard 110-volt circuits offers greater comfort, convenience, and even energy savings in rooms such as the bath, which are used only intermittently.

Heating Controls

Built-in electric space heaters are often used in bathrooms — even those with central heat — to raise the temperature of the room quickly during a shower or bath. The heater I use most often for this is Dayton's Low Silhouette Kickspace Electric Heater from the Grainger catalogue (800/473-3473); it fits nicely in either a cabinet kick space or a soffit. These heaters offer an optional built-in thermostat, but I can provide more flexibility with slightly different controls.

When this electric heater is the only source of heat in the bathroom, I use two 24-volt thermostats. The first maintains the room at normal temperature. White-Rodgers makes a moderately priced, fully programmable, low-voltage thermostat (#1F60-22) that is carried by most electrical supply houses and hvac suppliers.

The second thermostat is an inexpensive one (White-Rodgers #IC20-2) that remains set at the high temperature needed during baths and showers. This thermostat can be wired so that it's activated by a spring-wound timer. It allows customers to "twist and forget" when they want the bathroom extra warm for awhile, so they don't have to reset or reprogram a thermostat. Figure 1 shows how to wire these devices so the high-temperature thermostat overrides the maintenance thermostat when activated.

In order to make use of these low-voltage thermostats, you have to use an electric heat relay. I use a White-Rodgers #24AO1G-3 to control noninductive heating loads up to 6,000

watts. At the panel, I use a GFCI breaker as a safety measure in case of flooding.

A note on selecting heaters: I always use the highest BtuH (Btus per hour) output available, so that the room will warm up quickly when necessary. For example, the Dayton heater has a range from 500 to 2,000 watts. I typically use the 2,000-watt configuration on a 15-amp, 240-volt, GFCI-protected circuit. This gives me a very respectable 6,824 BtuH output (multiply watts by 3.412 to get BtuH).

Hot Water Recirculating System

Anyone who's ever laid out plumbing knows to keep hot water runs as short as possible. The closer that fixtures are to the water heater, the better, since this saves both energy and water.

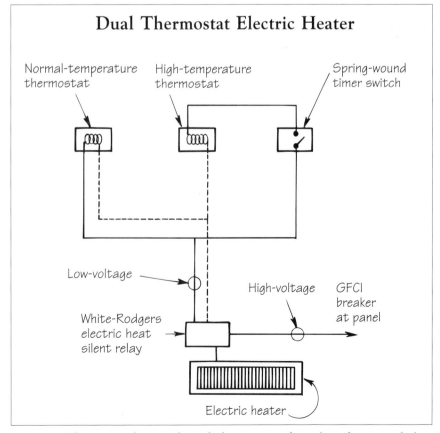

Figure 1. *This wiring schematic shows the basic wiring scheme for a short-term, high-output baseboard heater that can be controlled by the homeowner with a spring-wound timer switch at bath or shower time.*

Hot Water Recirculating System

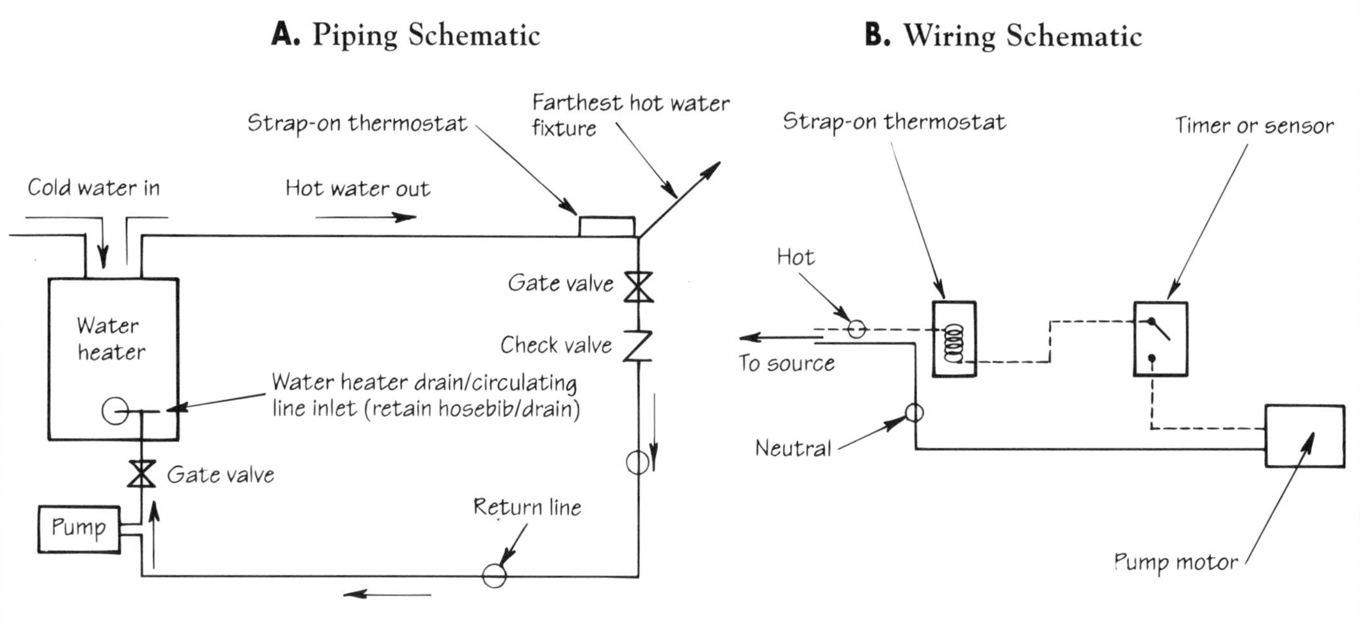

A. Piping Schematic

B. Wiring Schematic

Figure 2. *The plumbing diagram (A) shows how to set up a recirculating loop with a small pump so that fixtures a long distance from the water heater deliver hot water on demand.*

The wiring diagram (B) demonstrates how an inexpensive, strap-on thermostat and a timer or motion sensor can be used to efficiently control the system.

Unfortunately, this isn't always possible. Sometimes, added bathrooms are far from the rest of the house, or the water heater needs to be moved to make room for other alterations.

If you're facing a situation where there is a long lag time in hot water delivery, a recirculating system can solve the problem. This system requires running a return line back to the water heater from the most distant hot water fixture, and installing a small, stainless-steel pump to feed the recirculated water back into the water heater through the drain outlet near the bottom of the tank (see Figure 1).

You have to pay attention to the overall hot water distribution layout. All fixtures should be on the loop since a separate branch line to only one fixture would "starve" other fixtures. The recirculating loop should, of course, be insulated as heavily as possible to reduce heat loss during cycling.

To connect the pump (I use a Grundfos #UP 15-42SF), you have to remove the hosebib/drain cock on the water heater and put in a tee. The pump outflow attaches to one side of the tee, and the drain cock goes back in the other.

The next step is to control the flow. Not only does it waste a lot of energy, but it shortens the life of the pump when it runs continuously. And the point of the system is to improve hot water delivery to the fixture on demand.

The way to do this is to have two switching devices wired in series (Figure 2). The first is a strap-on thermostat control (I use a White-Rodgers #1127-2) that you fasten onto the hot water pipe at the farthest point of the loop. This thermostat functions as a low-limit control; it should switch the pump on when the pipe temperature falls below the limit set on the thermostat.

The second switching device responds to anticipated demand, and is wired to the thermostat in series so that both of them need to be "on" in order for the pump to run. There are two basic kinds of switches that can be used here: timers and sensors.

A programmable timer is set to the periods of the day — early morning, dinner hour, late evening — when the demand for hot water is most likely. Motion or infrared sensors (two sources I know of are BRK Electronics, 708/851-7330, and Hubbell Industries, 203/333-1181) can be used to activate the system by installing them in the bathroom or in the hallway leading to it.

The sensor has the advantage of actually responding to the movements of the homeowner, rather than just predicting them. When residents are moving around the area, the hot water's available; when they're not around, the system remains inactive.

Sensor switches can also replace normal light switches. These are useful in utility rooms, large walk-in closets, garages, and other rooms without outside light sources. ■

Paul Turpin is a Los Angeles-based remodeling contractor who specializes in kitchen and bath design and remodeling.

Chapter 10

ACCESSIBILITY

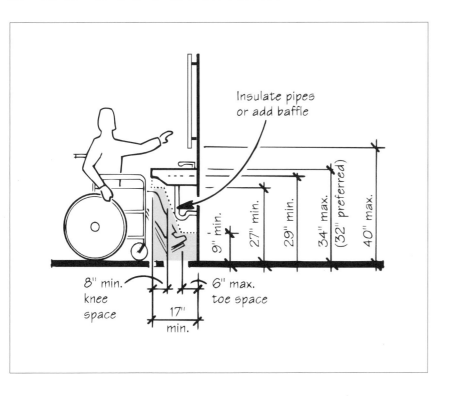

Insulate pipes or add baffle

9" min.
27" min.
29" min.
34" max. (32" preferred)
40" max.

8" min. knee space
6" max. toe space
17" min.

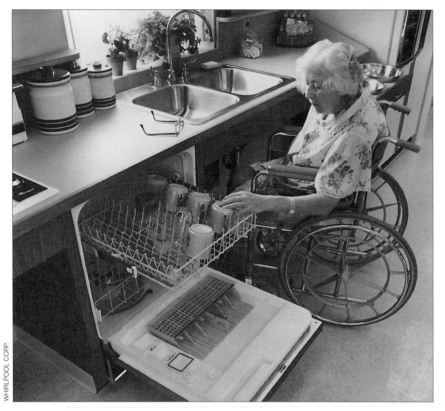

WHIRLPOOL CORP.

Remodeling for Accessibility

by Kenneth Hoffman

In an accessible kitchen, an opening below the sink allows space for a wheelchair.

Accessible design doesn't have to be expensive or look institutional. Knowing your client's specific needs is the key.

I work on Cape Cod in Massachusetts. The Cape is a magnet for the newly retired and so has a significant percentage of older residents. As they strive to live independently in their own homes, I am asked more and more often to make modifications that allow for individual personal difficulties. I did not consciously seek this type of business, and at first I was unprepared, even reluctant. But eventually I found I had filled a niche and I built up my business with regular customers. This article is meant to share information gleaned by trial and error to assist you if you ever find yourself working with similar clients.

Planning the Project

I have discovered that many older folks have two major concerns: that the end result should not look "institutional" and that modifications should not cost too much. Since my policy is to include close family members in planning the project, I have observed that they share similar concerns. They generally request that alterations enhance the value and marketability of the property, or that the modifications are easily reversible when the loved one moves into nursing care or passes on. These are sensitive issues, but I have found it helps to discuss them early in the process —

it makes for a satisfied customer long after the job is done.

Identify the problem. During the family conference, it is important to get the client to describe his or her physical limitations. Is it a relatively short-term condition that will improve? Will it remain the same for the rest of the client's life? Will it worsen? Are additional problems likely or foreseeable? This information should be factored into the design at the planning stage. Often, a short-term plan will meet the client's current needs only, but a long-term, multi-stage plan can accommodate new problems should they arise.

Candid discussions and an evaluation of specific physical limitations are essential to a successful project and a satisfied customer. If you work in private homes, as I do, you may not be bound by accessibility codes. You can focus on helping your customers overcome personal barriers so they can enjoy as much independence as possible.

Observe your client. I believe the best thing you can do is to listen to and closely observe your client. One of the tricks I use when the problem involves arm or hand mobility is to seat the person comfortably at a table, spread out an old newspaper, and have him or her hold a marker and trace motions that are comfortable to make. A

Accessibility Resources

Rather than fumble around as I did when first confronted with accessibility issues, you should first read some of the guides available that deal with public access for the handicapped. Your state building code is an excellent starting point. Another is *ANSI A117.1: Providing Accessibility and Usability for Physically Handicapped People*, and the *Uniform Federal Accessibility Standard* (see list at right).

Other readily available sources include rehabilitation hospitals or local Council on Aging staff, who can provide valuable insight. You might also look in the Yellow Pages under "Hospital Equipment and Supplies."

In researching this article, I came across what seems to be a treasure chest of information. Funded by the U.S. Department of Education, ABLEDATA has a file of over 17,000 individual products from over 2,000 companies. You can call or write, but try to be specific about the type of product you are seeking and your end goal. They will forward up to 20 entries at no charge; from 21 to 100 entries, the charge is $5.

If you are building or designing for accessibility on a regular basis, you may want to buy one of the comprehensive sourcebooks listed here. *The Remodeling and Building for Accessibility Sourcebook*, by the Housing Resource Center, brings together information on design, codes and standards, financing, products, and sources into one large three-ring binder. The Barrier-Free Design Center's *Sourcebook* is intended for use by architects and designers. It provides a clearly organized and well-illustrated approach to accessible design, beginning with site considerations and exterior entrances, and moving room-by-room through the house. A case study provides a useful introduction, and a chapter on developing a client profile includes a very thorough nine-page checklist.

—K.H.

ABLEDATA
National Rehabilitation Information Center
8455 Colesville Rd., Suite 935
Silver Spring, MD 20910
800/346-2742
First 20 entries, no charge; 21 to 100 entries, $5

The Accessible Bathroom
Design Coalition Inc.
2088 Atwood Ave.
Madison, WI 53704
608/246-8846
$12 (plus $2 shipping/handling)

Adaptable Housing
Dept. of Housing and Urban Development
HUD User
P.O. Box 6091
Rockville, MD 20850
800/245-2691
$4 (includes shipping)

ANSI A117.1: Providing Accessibility and Usability for Physically Handicapped People, 1992 ed.
American National Standards Institute
11 West 42nd St., 13th Floor
New York, NY 10036
212/642-4900
$30 (plus $5 shipping/handling)

Designs for Independent Living
Tools for Independent Living
Whirlpool Consumer Assistance Center
2303 Pipestone Rd.
Benton Harbor, MI 49022
800/253-1301
No charge

Directory of Accessible Building Products
National Assoc. of
Home Builders Research Center
400 Pince Georges Blvd.
Upper Marlboro, MD 20772
800/638-8556
$3 shipping charge

The Sourcebook
The Barrier-Free Design Center
Access Place Canada, Collete Park
444 Yonge St., Toronto, ON M5B 2H4, Canada
416/977-5010
$45 (plus $7 shipping/handling)

Figure 1. *For clients who have trouble grasping, the HandiLever by Extend Inc. is an inexpensive way to convert a doorknob to a lever-action handle. It comes in a variety of finishes in sizes to fit standard doorknobs.*

Swing-Clear Hinges

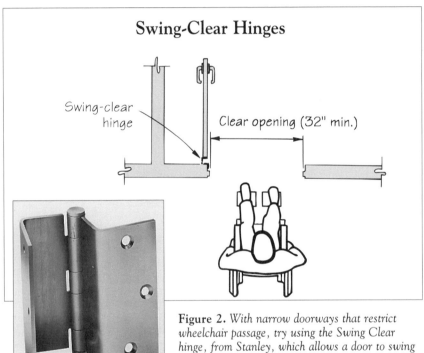

Swing-clear hinge

Clear opening (32" min.)

Figure 2. *With narrow doorways that restrict wheelchair passage, try using the Swing Clear hinge, from Stanley, which allows a door to swing beyond the door jamb. This effectively widens the opening by the thickness of the door.*

forget to suggest corner protectors and plates on door jambs to protect them from damage.

Doorways

Use of doors may require only a simple hardware change, from a standard-twist doorknob to a lever-action handle (for those with arthritic hands, who have difficulty grasping). An inexpensive way to make this modification is to use a HandiLever (Extend Inc., P.O. Box 864, Moorhead, MN 56560; 218/236-9686), which attaches to an existing doorknob (see Figure 1). One common problem is that doors are too narrow — not only entry doors, but doors within the house, too. For most wheelchairs a 32-inch door is the minimum you can use; in most cases a 36-inch door is preferable.

Stanley Hardware (480 Myrtle St., New Britain, CT 06053; 800/622-4393) makes some special offset hinges, called "Swing Clear" hinges, which allow the existing door to swing completely free of the opening to 95 degrees (Figure 2). By installing these hinges, you will gain about an additional 1 1/2 inches in the doorway with a minimum of labor and cost. Unfortunately, if you need more space than that, the only solution is to rip out the old door framing and reframe for a new, larger door.

Thresholds

Thresholds seem innocent enough at a glance, but for those with impaired mobility they can be toe grabbers, and for people in wheelchairs they can seem like hills to climb. I try to remove thresholds whenever possible. If for some reason I can't remove a threshold, I devise a wedge that tapers to the floor on both sides of the threshold. On a recent job, I lifted the carpeting, glued down squared wood shingles, and then put the carpeting back in place.

Any change in floor surface elevation that cannot be eliminated (such as a sunken living room or dining room) needs to be marked with a visual cue, such as balusters or a railing.

Grab Bars

Probably the most helpful and cost-effective product for elderly customers is a securely attached, appropriately placed grab bar (Figure 3). Properly chosen and installed, grab bars enhance the value of a home and help prevent the most common household accident by people of all ages — falling. I often encourage people living independently to even put them in long hallways, just for reassurance.

tape measure can then easily convert this exercise into working measurements.

Closed fist test. Another trick to use is the "closed fist" test. Simply stated, if a device is meant to be opened, can you do it with a closed fist? The answer should be "yes." Make a list of everything in the house that has to be opened. Cabinet doors, drawers, and pull boards all fall into this category.

Knobs can be replaced with loop hardware. Twist-action knobs should be replaced with lever-action hardware. One simple kitchen cabinet modification I have made many times is to replace friction catches with magnetic catches. This simple, inexpensive modification makes a big difference in the lives of some people. Closing can be made easier by adding push plates or kick plates to cabinet doors. For homes that are being modified for wheelchair use, do not

Yet grab bars are often a source of strong customer objection. The first objection is usually that they look institutional. Use some persuasion and try to educate your clients otherwise. Tubular Specialties Manufacturing Inc. (13011 So. Spring St., Los Angeles, CA 90061; 800/421-2961) has an attractive catalog that I bring along to back me up. It has a wonderful assortment of grab bars for every need, in different styles and colors.

The next objection is usually something like: "I don't need a grab bar. I've been using the such and such for years and it works fine." Where there's no grab bar present, people use towel bars, toothbrush holders, mirrors, doorknobs, soap dishes, bureau drawers — any number of items not intended for such use.

A word of caution on installing grab bars: Make sure you have them well anchored. Do not be charmed, coerced, or bullied into shortcutting. They must be fastened into solid blocking or studs (Figure 4, page 237). No mollies, sleeves, or even toggle bolts. The minimum test, according to ANSI A117.1, is that they should be able to support 250 pounds in shear or pull-out. You could find yourself with major liability if a grab bar fails from customer use.

Most of the guidelines for railings apply to grab bars. They should be 1¼ to 1½ inches in diameter, with a profile the hand can easily grasp (no sharp edges), and they should be no further than 1½ inches away from the wall. Aside from the obvious, the dangerous thing about using a towel bar as a grab bar is that the arm can slip between the bar and the wall and twist or break under the weight of the body.

The biggest difficulty I have encountered with grab bars is proper installation in older bathtub/shower areas. Sometimes it is impossible to find anything to secure them to. In such cases, I refuse to do second-rate work. I encourage the customer to either remove the wall surfaces so that proper blocking can be installed or invest in a new tub or shower unit that has built-in safety and accessibility features.

Accessible Kitchens

After access difficulties have been remedied, I think you will find that the kitchen poses the most obstacles for independent living. Most existing kitchens have problems that could have been solved at the drawing board, if only we were starting from scratch.

But with some understanding of your client's difficulties and a little imagination, there are modifications you can make that are not budget busters but still allow you to make a profit. Keep in mind that changes should either enhance the home's value or be easily reversible when no longer needed.

Most modifications in the kitchen are for wheelchair access or to accommodate reaching and bending difficulties. For example, the standard 36-inch-high counter may be too high. I have solved this with the least expense in two ways. The

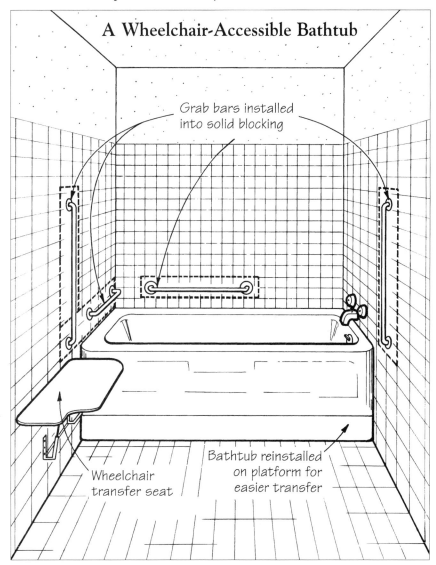

A Wheelchair-Accessible Bathtub

Grab bars installed into solid blocking

Wheelchair transfer seat

Bathtub reinstalled on platform for easier transfer

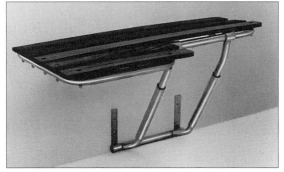

Figure 3. *Grab bars are one of the easiest and most economical ways to make a home safer. A wheelchair transfer seat (left), such as this one from Tubular Specialties, can be added near the bathtub to assist your client in moving from wheelchair to tub and back. When not in use, the seat can fold against the wall.*

Elderly K&B Design Tips

by Carol E. Klein

A shallow sink, set at 32 to 34 inches, with drain in the rear and open underneath, allows easy access for wheelchair users.

Consider the physical changes people experience with aging. Provide for changes in mobility, reach, hand grip, strength, vision, and hearing. In your design, eliminate unnecessary movement; build in easy-to-reach cabinets, lever handles on doors, non-glare lighting, flexible shower hoses, grab surfaces, and sliding or casement windows.

In all designs, be aware that you are not necessarily preparing for a single individual. The occupants of the home might be a family with only one person who has a limitation.

Kitchens

An efficient kitchen layout is a basic triangle composed of work centers for food preparation/dishwashing, cooking, and storage. In the kitchen, people spend most of their time at the sink. So the most important element in your triangle would be the sink. Locate it in the pivotal corner so that the resident can turn easily to other work areas. If the countertops are unbroken, residents can slide, rather than carry, heavy items across the countertop to the other work centers, such as the stove.

What follows are desirable features and some layout suggestions for senior adult kitchens and baths.

• Your layout should place the sink and the stove on the same wall, so residents don't have to carry heavy items across the room.
• For people in wheelchairs, countertops should be about 32 inches high, with at least 29 inches of free space

below, and with the finish floor continuing under the counter. If possible, make counter heights adjustable between 30 and 36 inches.
• Make cabinets, drawers, and shelf storage handy: not too high. Also, residents should not have to bend too far to reach the low shelves. Shallow shelves are good for storage and retrieval; pull-out drawers are best.
• Drawer interiors should be light colored. Door pulls and handles for wall cabinets should be mounted close to the bottom of cabinet doors, base-cabinet handles close to the top.
• Include a counter-mounted cooktop and a separate wall-mounted oven. (Avoid under-counter ovens.) A side-opening oven is preferable to the usual pull-down style.
• Electric stoves with front controls are best. A smooth cooktop, without raised burners is preferable. Also look for a unit with staggered burners, which are safer.
• Light switches, disposal controls, and electrical outlets should be placed on the back walls above the countertop.
• Place the drain at the rear of the sink to create under-counter clearance.
• Faucets should have lever or push handles. A spray hose is useful for filling pans on the stove.
• A vertical side-by-side refrigerator/freezer is best, with a minimum of 18 inches of counter space adjacent to it.
• Provide at least 30 inches of counter space for food preparation.
• A front-loading dishwasher is best.

Put it within 12 inches of the sink.
• Consider light, glare, and color together. Provide twice the normal level of illumination. In general, walls, ceiling, and floor should be light colored; furnishings should be of medium-shade colors.

Bathrooms

Bathrooms need to provide for the full gamut of physical abilities of residents, including the most challenged and the most able. Make bathrooms large enough to accommodate wheelchair users, and provide reinforced walls that can support grab surfaces. Focus your design decisions on maintaining independence for residents.

• Wheelchair space should be a minimum 5-foot-diameter circle.
• The bathroom door should open outward, so if a person falls near the door, it can still be opened.
• Put a vertical bar at the head or foot of the tub. Be sure that any protrusion from the wall — like a soap dish or toilet paper dispenser that might be grabbed by a panicked resident — is secure enough to hold 250 pounds.
• Ideally, the tub and shower should be separate units. Provide space at the side or end of the tub for a transfer seat, and provide a flexible spray hose.
• Provide adjustable-height storage. ■

Carol E. Klein is technical communications director at Advanced Living Systems. Adapted with permission from Commercial Renovation.

first is to remove a base cabinet, carefully cut out that section of countertop, and lower it so it's suspended between the two remaining side cabinets.

Another method, when there is a blank cabinet end or peninsula, is to hinge a new surface at the correct height off the vertical cabinet end, using card-table hinges. This new counter can be raised for use, then folded down for floor space as needed. Also, depending upon the existing cabinet design, pull-out boards can sometimes be added to provide work surfaces at the desired height.

Most wheelchairs require a 29-inch minimum clearance under counter surfaces, but this is another case of paying attention to your client's specific needs. You can gain access to the sink by removing the base cabinet and rehanging the sink at the proper height, but it is always necessary to pad the exposed plumbing. Sometimes the drain can be relocated further to the rear. False panels or fabric skirts can be added to conceal the plumbing and still allow for access.

Again, some of the simplest things can go overlooked. On my initial customer call, I often take the time (no charge) to remove the food from the refrigerator and adjust the shelving to meet the customer's "reach" needs. Changing the kitchen sink faucet to a long-lever, single-action type is another easy change that can make all the difference in the day-to-day life of an older independent adult.

To make cabinets more accessible, you can remove upper cabinets from the wall and rehang them 4, 5, or 6 inches lower. Lazy susans can be added for access to base cabinets, and large drawers can be fit into unreachable lower cabinets, using existing cabinet doors as the new drawer fronts. Shallow, pantrylike shelving can be added in appropriate places to assist people with reaching difficulties.

Sometimes changing the direction of the refrigerator door swing will allow it to open 180 degrees. That may not sound helpful to you, but if you were in a wheelchair you would now be able to pull up sideways to reach even the deepest shelf with greater ease. If it's not possible to rehinge the door in the refrigerator's present location, it may be useful to the customer to swap around some cabinets and relocate it.

In terms of customer relations, the kitchen has the potential for the greatest number of difficulties. You are invading a very personal space, one that is used at least three times a day and has an almost ritual routine associated with its use. Based on my

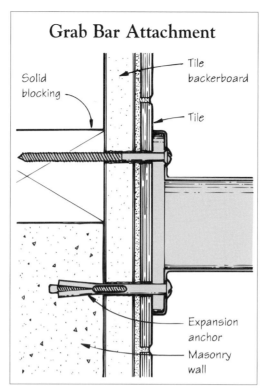

Grab Bar Attachment

Solid blocking — Tile backerboard — Tile — Expansion anchor — Masonry wall

Figure 4. *Make sure you fasten grab bars securely. They need to support 250 pounds in pullout or shear.*

experience, it is worth taking the time to learn that routine and plan ahead with the customer so as not to disturb them while the work is in progress.

I try to break the job into manageable chunks that can be started and completed in the same day. And always, clean up the job daily: use drop cloths, sweep, dust, and vacuum. Older adults are sometimes the least tolerant of disruptions to their personal schedules, but most appreciative of your caring and consideration.

Barrier-Free Baths

Another area of the home that often requires modification, but can cause customer relations difficulty, is the bathroom. Now you are not only in the personal space, but in the private space. Careful planning and discussion should take place ahead of time. All the rules for the kitchen apply here. Like the kitchen, the bath may need to be gutted and completely remodeled. But again, there are some useful minor modifications that I have made many times.

Lowering the bathroom mirror is required if there is a wheelchair. That means either rehanging the mirror or tilting the top forward and slightly downward to allow for full viewing for grooming.

Showerheads can be replaced with flexible hose. But if a wheelchair customer lives alone, the best suggestion is to build an entirely new bathroom with either a no-lip shower unit so it can be directly wheeled

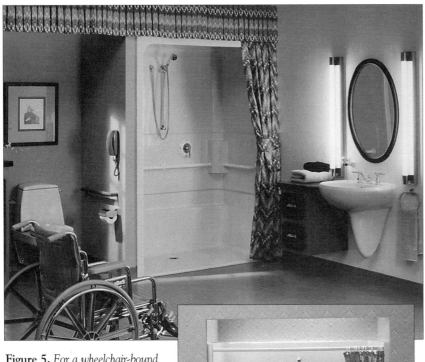

ously discussed, and space for transferring to the bath/shower or to the toilet. On older open-at-one-end bathtubs, a tiled platform can be built at the same height as the open end. The person can then transfer from the chair to the platform bench seat, swing the legs up and into the tub, and, using grab bars, slide forward and down into a seated position. In some cases a wheelchair transfer seat may serve the same purpose.

Unfortunately, not all customers' needs can be met in the space available in some bathrooms. In those cases it becomes necessary to move walls and "steal" space from an adjoining room — costly, but sometimes necessary. If possible, I try to expand into a closet and then construct a new closet elsewhere in that room, but sometimes a large part of a room has to be sacrificed to accomplish the goal. This is a case where goal-setting during the family conference can ease the way into the project.

Business Rewards

Accessibility is more in demand as people live longer and remain independent longer. For successful projects, I cannot emphasize enough the importance of the initial interview, family conference, and overall development of a multistage concept with clear budgetary guidelines and expectations. Listening and planning are your best tools in this trade.

At this point, you may be having some thoughts about maintaining "the bottom line." There's no need to be concerned. We maintain the same profit margin on adaptations for accessibility as for the more traditional jobs. We charge for consultation/planning services after the initial no-charge visit to see if the customer is comfortable with what we have to offer. A consultation charge shows that your expertise has a value; it also helps get the discussion down to specifics very quickly. Through this session, you will get a sense of a customer's expectations and just how much lifestyle disruption can be tolerated at one time.

We began working with accessibility issues with some apprehension and not much knowledge. Over the years, however, helping folks remove or work around architectural barriers has become the most personally rewarding aspect of our work. Helping older adults to remain alone in their homes, preserve their dignity, and maintain their personal lifestyles has added an entirely new component to our "bottom line." ■

Kenneth Hoffman is a remodeler in So. Yarmouth, Mass.

Figure 5. *For a wheelchair-bound client, installing a no-lip shower unit like this one from Kohler (above), may be the best option for safe bathing. For people who can walk, but can't climb over the side of a tub, the BathEase unit with a side door (right) may be suitable. Wall-hung sinks and toilets are also a big help.*

into (Figure 5), or a molded unit with a bench seat that the client can get to and from without assistance. There are devices that can be used in a standard tub to lift a client in and out, but I usually suggest a new accessible unit if the budget can afford it.

Toileting is another problem area that can be made easier with the proper grab bars. If a new toilet is to be part of the remodeling work, I usually recommend a wall-hung unit. Not only can it be mounted at a convenient height, but it also simplifies the ordinary chore of cleaning the bathroom floor — it can be easily mopped under from a standing position. Bathroom sinks can also be wall-mounted at a desirable height and are obstruction-free underneath.

Bathrooms often have limited floor space. This can be a problem for the wheelchair-bound older adult trying to live independently. Wheelchairs require turning space, as previ-

A Custom-Built Accessible Shower

by Don Jackson

If you do a lot of remodeling work, sooner or later you'll be asked to rework a shower to make it more accessible for someone who uses a wheelchair. If you shop around for one of the prefab accessible units, you'll notice two things: One is, they don't come cheap, especially the nicer acrylic ones. And second, these units take up space you may not have in the bathroom, not without knocking down walls and stealing from an adjoining room. The problem with a small bathroom is that a wheelchair needs a comfortable turning radius — usually 5 feet is specified — and the sidewalls of a shower unit get in the way unless it can be recessed.

Architect Larry Lundy of Madison, Wis., uses a different solution — a custom ceramic tile roll-in shower without walls. Lundy works for the Design Coalition, a nonprofit community design center specializing in accessible design. According to Lundy, space constraints are almost always a problem with accessible remodels. This means you usually have to move walls to make room for a prefab shower stall. Also, many of the so-called "accessible" shower units require a short, steep ramp to get into — a barrier for someone in a wheelchair.

So Lundy prefers to use a mortar-based tile shower pan set flush with the rest of the bathroom floor. A hospital-style shower curtain, the kind that hangs from tracks mounted on the ceiling, keeps the water in while still allowing an attendant, if there is one, to assist without getting drenched. A well-designed roll-in can actually turn an inaccessible bathroom into one that is much easier for someone in a wheelchair to use. Without a curb and with the shower curtain drawn back, the whole floor becomes available for maneuvering (see illustration at right).

Installation Tips

Lundy designs his roll-in showers with details developed with tile contractor Scott Duncan of Classic Enterprises in Saratoga, Calif. The construction details (see illustration, next page) are an adaptation of a standard curbed shower pan.

Essential ingredients of the installation are the plastic shower pan membrane and a two-piece clamping-type drain. It is critical to slope the mortar bed under the membrane $1/4$ inch per foot to ensure that any water that soaks through the tile runs out to the weep holes in the drain. Otherwise, bacteria will grow under the tile and create odors that will be impossible to get rid of.

Lundy recommends installing a membrane under the entire bathroom floor if the budget will allow. If not, it should at least extend a couple of feet beyond the shower area to catch drips and splashes. The membrane should run up the wall at least 8 inches around the shower area; use 2x10 blocking between the studs. You'll need to notch the bottom of the studs about $1/4$ inch so that the membrane doesn't push the cement backerboard out at the bottom.

When modifying the floor framing, make sure the floor has no more than L/360 deflection, as for any tile floor. As you reduce the depth of the floor joists to make room for the recessed shower pan, you'll probably have to double several joists to stiffen the floor.

The mortar and tile work should be done by a tradesperson skilled in the use of shower pan membranes. Specify cement backerboard substrate, not moisture-resistant drywall, for the shower walls. At the inside corner joint where the two tile walls meet, use silicone sealant instead of grout. The walls may deflect slightly over time, and the flexible sealant will absorb the movement without allowing water to penetrate behind the membrane.

Make sure when the mortar bed is floated so that the slope toward the drain is limited to the immediate shower area.

Small Accessible Bathroom

Hospital-type curtain track

Use sealant at corners

5' min.

Extend membrane 18" to 24" beyond sloping shower area

Slope starts here

For a small bathroom, a custom roll-in shower may be the best solution for accessible bathing. With the shower curtain pulled back, the entire floor area becomes available for maneuvering the wheelchair, while the walls of a prefab shower stall would get in the way.

Recessed Mortar-Bed Shower with Membrane

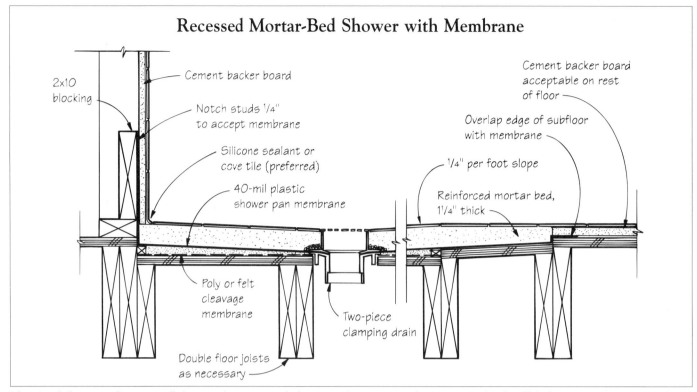

2x10 blocking

Cement backer board

Notch studs 1/4" to accept membrane

Silicone sealant or cove tile (preferred)

40-mil plastic shower pan membrane

Poly or felt cleavage membrane

Two-piece clamping drain

Double floor joists as necessary

Cement backer board acceptable on rest of floor

Overlap edge of subfloor with membrane

1/4" per foot slope

Reinforced mortar bed, 1 1/4" thick

The 40-mil plastic membrane, installed over a sloping mortar bed, ensures that any water that penetrates the tile will find its way to the two-piece drain assembly. Note the transition from the shower area to the main bathroom floor (at right in the drawing), where the subfloor steps up to finish floor level.

Otherwise, the wheelchair user may be forced to use the brake to keep from rolling when using the other fixtures.

Curtains and Other Accessories

You're not going to find a hospital-style shower curtain at the local building supply. Try the Yellow Pages under "Hospital Equipment & Supplies." Kirsch (309 N. Prospect St., Sturgis, MI 49091; 800/528-1407) makes a track (part #9046) that you can site-bend to a 12-inch radius using a bending tool the company makes. A 16-inch drop chain with hooks allows the use of a standard-height shower curtain. Expect to pay $50 to $75 for the track and chain. The rig is easy to install — the track surface-mounts on the ceiling and finishes with end caps. Mount the track so that the curtain hangs about an inch inside where the floor begins to slope.

Hand-held shower heads. These are available from many manufacturers. Where the budget can afford it, Lundy likes models by Kohler (Kohler Co., 444 Highland Dr., Kohler, WI 53044; 414/457-4441). On occasion, he also uses a less expensive model from Alsons Corporation (525 E. Edna Place, Covina, CA 91723; 818/966-1668) that has a flow control right on the handle — a preference of some customers.

Grab bars. Horizontal grab bars in the shower area are usually necessary for wheelchair use. They help for maneuvering the wheelchair, and many people need them for support when they lean to reach the controls or soap dish. Grab bars are a good idea for anyone, standing or sitting, who uses the shower — even textured tiles get slippery.

Place grab bars 33 to 36 inches from the floor. Don't forget to add solid blocking during the early stages of the work. Also provide grab bars beside the toilet and in the area where the person makes the transfer into the bathing wheelchair.

Lundy advises using caution when buying grab bars. Many of the ones he's seen in local hospital supply stores stick out as much as 3 inches from the wall. These are very dangerous because a standing person can slip and get his arm wedged behind the bar. Look for bars that have only a 1 1/2-inch space to the wall. They should be from 1 1/4 to 1 1/2 inches in diameter. A good source for grab bars is Tubular Specialties (13011 S. Spring St., Los Angeles, CA 90061; 800/421-2961).

Other items. A single-lever pressure-balancing control valve is a good idea in any shower, but it's a must in an accessible shower. A person in a wheelchair cannot quickly maneuver out from under a sudden stream of scalding water.

Don't forget to place a soap dish at a workable height — usually 30 to 36 inches from the floor. (The best way to get dimensions for most items in an accessible bath is to get out the measuring tape and have the client show you what's comfortable — it will vary from client to client.) As with any shower, install a good ventilation fan. And make sure that all electrical outlets are GFCI-protected.

Cost Considerations

Compared with the cost of simply installing a prefab accessible shower unit (no demo work), building the custom ceramic roll-in shower will cost more — perhaps twice as much. However, where space is at a premium, Lundy says the tile shower is definitely cost-competitive with moving walls to make room for a prefab. From a serviceability standpoint, the tile shower is easier to use because it requires no ramp; it's also more resistant to scrapes and bumps from the wheelchair. ∎

Don Jackson is managing editor of The Journal of Light Construction.

Accessibility on a Shoe String

by Sam Clark

With creative design, ordinary building products can make any home more accessible

Accessibility is becoming an important part of more and more building projects. Disability ultimately affects every family and most individuals; we are all eventually subject to illness, accident, and aging. In an important sense, accessibility is for everybody.

As a designer and builder, I have included accessibility in everything I've designed in the last few years. When it isn't practical to make a place accessible at the time of construction, I try to make it easy to adapt later.

People often expect accessibility to be expensive, difficult to build, and institutional looking. And indeed this is often the case when buildings are poorly adapted after the fact. But when it's emphasized from the start, accessibility can be simple and affordable without calling attention to itself. As a bonus, the features that make buildings usable for people with disabilities make life and work easier for all.

Defining Accessibility

Though we identify accessibility with wheelchairs, it's really broader and simpler: Accessibility means detailing buildings so that all potential inhabitants, their visitors, and their families can get about without impediment and do ordinary tasks and activities conveniently, whatever their age or physical condition. People experience a wide range of impairments or challenges that influence mobility, strength, hearing, vision, and cognition. When we keep these varieties of experience in mind as we

design, many of the features of accessible design become obvious.

Accessible design comes down to careful site planning and layout, and thoughtful selection and use of ordinary building products. There will be some extra costs, but most accessibility comes from using ordinary things in an educated way.

This article summarizes some key features needed for accessibility, using examples from a recent Habitat for Humanity house built in Barre, Vt. The house was designed by David Scheckman of Iron Bridge Woodworkers and Builders, in Plainfield, Vt. I worked on the accessible features of the plan.

Circulation: Doors and Halls

The pathways in an accessible house must be spacious. To begin with, a hall or other pathway should be at least 3 feet wide for convenient wheelchair travel along a straight line. A doorway requires a minimum clear opening of 32 inches. This refers not to the nominal door size but to the available space between the door stops or any other projections into the opening. The best solution is to use 3-foot doors everywhere, although a 2-foot-10-inch door can also work.

Circulation becomes more complex when turns and transitions are considered. Though whole book chapters are devoted to this subject, there are a few key points.

First, a right-angle turn is difficult to make from a 3-foot hallway into a 32-inch-wide door opening. To provide more maneuvering

Wheelchair-Accessible Floor Plan

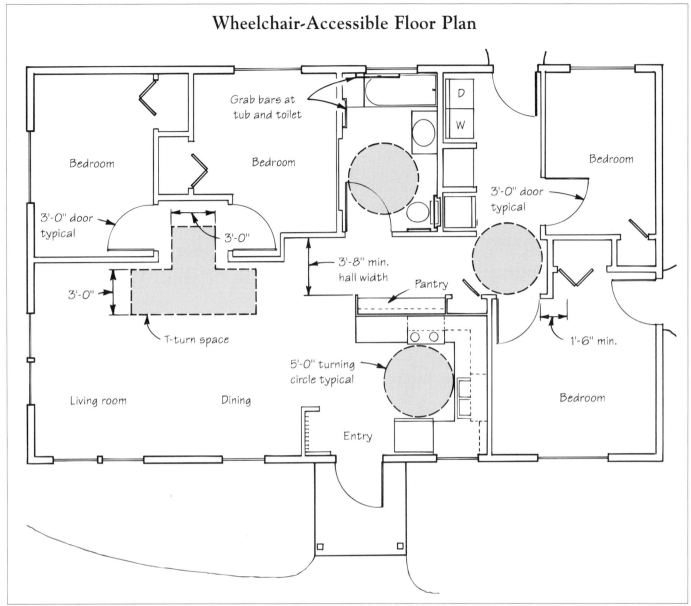

Grab bars at
tub and toilet

Bedroom

Bedroom

Bedroom

3'-0" door
typical

3'-0" door
typical

3'-0"

3'-0"

T-turn space

3'-8" min.
hall width

Pantry

1'-6" min.

5'-0" turning
circle typical

Bedroom

Living room

Dining

Entry

Figure 1. *The pathways in an accessible house must be spacious. The halls in this accessible floor plan are all at least 3½ feet wide and the doorways 3 feet wide for convenient wheelchair travel. In addition, a wheelchair user needs a 5-foot-diameter "turning circle" to reverse direction and at least 18 inches free on the swing side of doors. In the kitchen, a wheelchair needs a minimum floor space of 30x48 inches to approach an appliance, closet, or phone.*

room, make halls with doorways along them at least 3 feet 6 inches wide.

To reverse direction, a wheelchair user needs either a 5-foot-diameter "turning circle," or a 3-foot-wide space to pull into to make a "T turn." Turning areas will occur naturally on the plan, but it's important to make sure they are provided where people will need them most.

To open a door inward (from the swing side), a person using a wheelchair or walker usually takes a position next to the door, pulls the door open, pivots, and then goes through. This is impossible unless there is a space of at least 18 inches (preferably 24 inches) beside the door on the handle side. This is the feature most often omitted when spaces are adapted.

A wheelchair needs a minimum floor space of 30x48 inches to approach an appliance, closet, or phone.

These necessary clear spaces are shown on the floor plan in Figure 1. Usually they can be provided by repositioning partitions, adjusting door locations, reversing door swings, or other small adjustments. In the Habitat design, the hallways were widened somewhat at the expense of the bedrooms. The designer also eliminated as much of the hallway as possible by creating a relatively open plan. Putting the laundry and other services along hallways also conserved space.

Door details are important. Lever handles are much easier to turn and pull than knobs. I can't think of any reason to use regular knobs.

Door sills or thresholds should stick up no more than ½ inch if beveled, and ¼ inch if square-edged. For interior doors, it's easiest to do without thresholds. Few standard exterior door sill profiles meet the standard when installed in the usual way, on the subfloor. Some — such as traditional oak thresholds — can be made to work by setting them down onto the framing. Some companies, such as Weather Shield, sell a low-profile aluminum threshold that can be installed with either wood or steel doors. Most sliding doors and center-hinged exterior French doors will not work at all unless the screen door is eliminated, although Andersen has developed a mini-ramp accessory that offers a partial solution.

Extra costs for doors are less than expected. Three-foot-wide doors are only $2 to $8 more than 32-inch models. The lever handles that make it easy for anyone to open a door now cost about $4 more than knobsets.

Windows

A casement, or crank window, is the easiest to operate, particularly over a counter. For high-end brands, casement prices are within a few dollars of double-hung prices. Other companies charge about 15% more for their casements. For tall casements, companies such as Andersen and Marvin sell an accessory that connects the two window locks so they can be operated from a single, low position. These cost about $45 each. In general, window costs will be determined as much by design and choice of manufacturer as by accessibility requirements. Better quality, more costly windows of any type will operate more easily than cheaper versions.

To reduce costs, the Habitat house used double-hung windows and sliders, perhaps less than ideal, but more economical. In the kitchen, we provided one casement above the counters where a double-hung is extremely awkward to operate. In the master bedroom, we provided an extra door. A door is a better egress for mobility-impaired people than a window, because it eliminates the need to climb out in an emergency.

Bathroom

The bathroom is perhaps the trickiest part of an accessible design. Also, the needs of specific users drastically influence the design, particularly for bathing. For example, a person with a strong left arm needs a different layout than a right-handed person. It's best to design a bathroom for a particular user whenever possible.

The Habitat design, though nonstandard, illustrates some typical accessible features (Figure 2). The bathroom door itself is always a problem because of its extra width.

If it opens in, it can obstruct wheelchair movement in the bathroom. An outward opener can crowd the hall. A pocket door or sliding door can be hard to keep working smoothly, and can also be somewhat awkward to operate. We chose the inward opener, since the bathroom was rather long, and recessed the toilet 2 inches to provide additional clearance between the door and the toilet.

The toilet is in the corner centered 18 inches from the wall. This allows for grab bars behind and beside it if needed. The space beside it makes room for a wheelchair. This basic configuration allows for a variety of "transfers" from and to a wheelchair. We used a standard toilet, not one of the "accessible" models, which can be too tall for some people. Raised seats can be purchased to increase the effective seat height if needed.

The tub has a transfer seat at its foot. The shower control, which has a temperature limit and a lever handle, is mounted where it can be reached from the transfer seat. Ideally, there would be maneuvering

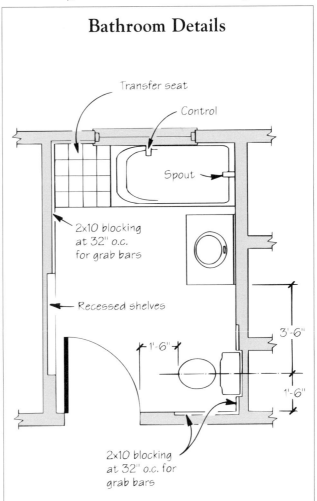

Bathroom Details

Transfer seat
Control
Spout
2x10 blocking at 32" o.c. for grab bars
Recessed shelves
1'-6"
3'-6"
1'-6"
2x10 blocking at 32" o.c. for grab bars

Figure 2. *In this bathroom plan, a standard toilet is recessed 2 inches to allow 18 inches of clear space for a wheelchair user to open the door from inside. The toilet is placed in the corner with ample open space on one side for "transfers" from and to a wheelchair, and the tub has a transfer seat at the foot. Two-by-ten blocking was provided wherever grab bars might be useful.*

space at the other end of the tub, also. Two-by-ten blocking was provided wherever we thought grab bars might be useful. I saved a sketch showing blocking locations for future reference.

The vanity must provide knee room below and be adjustable in height without major replumbing. To create the knee space, the sink is shallower than usual — no more than 3 inches deep at the front and sloping to no more than 7 inches at the rear. Some standard models fit the bill nicely, and some companies are coming out with affordable models. We chose to use a drop-in, but some wall-hung units will also work. To maximize knee room, the drain swings back to the wall, and the trap is mounted on the wall.

The sink counter is mounted on plywood brackets, which can be moved up or down from 29 to 34 inches. The pipes are covered to prevent burns from hot water. The water supplies use flexible tubing to make changing the height easier.

The mirror goes right down to the counter splash to make it visible to seated users. The faucet is a lever model. Recessed shelves replace the medicine cabinet.

These adjustments add perhaps 10 or 12 square feet of space not found in a typical small bathroom. In a small home, this space

could cost about $600. Of course, in a big house, that space might be there anyway.

The grab bars, blocking, and the transfer seat might add $400 to the cost of the bath. None of the other detailing adds cost directly, but there is extra design work needed, including working closely with the family who owns the house. More labor is also needed during installation; good support from all trades really helps.

Kitchen

Even when disability is not an issue, people differ in the counter heights they like. A variety of work heights is essential. One of these choices should allow for working seated — if only at a nearby kitchen table. We addressed this by providing an adjustable-height sink counter.

There are a number of simple ways to make the sink height adjustable. I chose to leave a knee space under the sink, and ordered a short cabinet to put under the sink counter to the left of the sink (Figure 3). This short cabinet is also removable in case a wider counter for working seated is desired.

The counter sits on wooden cleats screwed to the cabinets at either end. The 5/4x4-inch wood apron under the counter makes it strong enough to span this distance. The

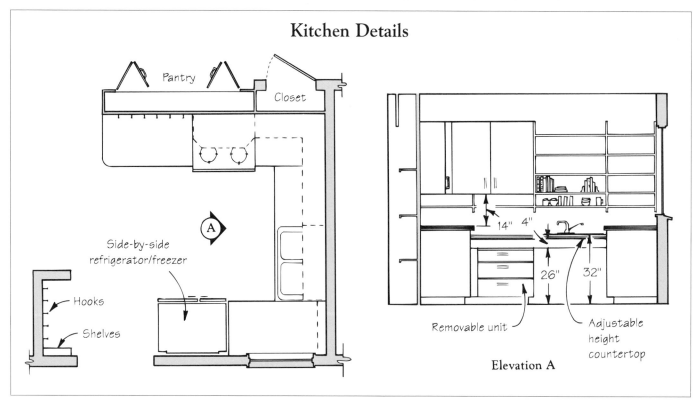

Figure 3. *In kitchens, a variety of work heights is essential. A site-built adjustable-height sink counter, installed with wooden cleats over a short cabinet, can be repositioned to raise and lower the countertop. The cabinets have lots of drawers, which hold more than shelves and allow the contents to be easily found and retrieved. Overhead cabinets are positioned only 12 to 14 inches above counter height.*

counter can be raised or lowered by repositioning the cleats.

The sink should be shallow (6$^1/_2$ inches maximum), and the drain should be at the back to maximize knee space. The former feature is essential, the latter highly desirable. I mention this because shallow sinks are easy to find. The cheapest, off-brand models sold at home centers are often shallow. But the rear drain sink is a special model at a much higher cost. Therefore, we chose the standard model.

The cabinets have lots of drawers, which hold more than shelves and allow the contents to be easily found and retrieved. Drawers are essential for anyone who has trouble bending, reaching, or seeing. Overhead cabinets should be positioned only 12 to 14 inches up from the standard counter height. This is more easily reached by shorter people, and essential for wheelchair users.

We chose D-shaped handles for the cabinets; they're easier to grab than round pulls.

The greater number of drawers increases kitchen costs $200 or $300, though I would argue that the drawers would improve a kitchen designed for any users. Beyond that, the accessible kitchen need be no more costly than a conventional design.

Electrical

The most important electrical changes cost nothing. Switches should be lowered to 42 or 44 inches on-center, where they are convenient for everyone, and outlets raised. As standard practice, I locate outlets 24 inches from the floor. It is also helpful to add outlets and switches where the standard locations might be awkward for some users. The service panel should be on the ground floor where anyone can get to it, and should be positioned somewhat lower on the wall. In the kitchen, outlets should be located as conveniently as possible.

Selecting Appliances

When selecting appliances, pay attention to controls — the knobs, pulls, and switches that regulate appliances or equipment, and the dials, screens, notches, or markings that indicate what setting the equipment is on.

First of all, good controls are easy for anyone to reach. For a stove, hood, or refrigerator, they should be near the front. They should be easy to grab and turn, even for people with little hand strength. A good test is to operate the handles with a closed fist. If this is possible, they are probably okay.

Good controls are also easy for anyone to understand. Many modern appliances use electronics to do lots of things, but are difficult to make sense of. They may have to be programmed, and the appearance of the controls themselves offer few clues to their uses. Switches may be tiny and hard to distinguish from each other and from their background. Such devices will be useless to many people. The feedback system, which lets the user know what's going on with a device, should also be clear. Numbers should be large, stops or clicks on a knob easy to feel, signal lights or displays large and bright. It's excellent if a device has more than one way to signal the user, to accommodate people who take in such information in different ways. A timer that gives an audible tone plus a visual cue is better than one that gives one cue only.

These requirements don't always mean higher costs. Cheaper equipment, being simpler, may in some cases have excellent controls. This is largely an issue of product selection and careful shopping. In the case of the Habitat project, in addition to lever faucets, we had to purchase a stove and a hood. We shopped with the family to find the best affordable units.

The big problems with refrigerators is that the freezer is usually hard to reach from a wheelchair. Side-by-side or bottom-freezer models are best, though they do tend to be $200 to $300 more expensive and are very wide. A less expensive alternative is to find a conventional fridge with a freezer that begins lower than 4 feet. You could also provide a 36-inch-wide opening so a side-by-side unit could be added later.

In Brief

I also recommend plan reviews, particularly on your first projects. It's easy to get the basic concepts of accessibility right, yet make small errors that leave the house less successful and less in conformance with codes or good practice. Local advocacy agencies, state officials, or designers in this specialty can review your plans.

Finally, if you are building for a specific disabled client, that person and his or her family should be heavily involved in the details. They know best what will work. ■

Sam Clark is a builder and designer who works with UserNeeds Design, accessibility specialists in Plainfield, Vt.

Accessible K&B Design Guidelines

Compiled by *JLC Staff*

The dimensional guidelines on the next four pages are adapted from the federal Americans With Disabilities Act (ADA) and the standard ANSI A117.1 from the American National Standards Institute. Other recommendations and "preferred" dimensions shown reflect the opinions of accessibility specialists. While the ADA and ANSI guidelines were developed for use in public and commercial facilities, they provide a good basis for accessible residential design as well.

WHEELCHAIR ACCESS

Adult Wheelchair Dimensions

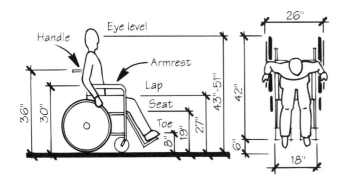

Minimum Wheelchair Clear Floor Space

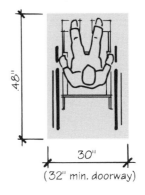

Forward Reach Limits

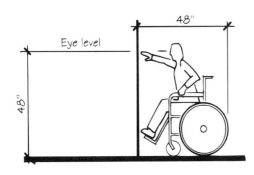

Side Reach Limits

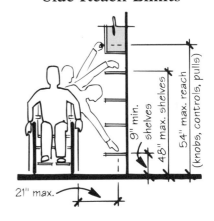

Forward Reach Limits Over Obstruction

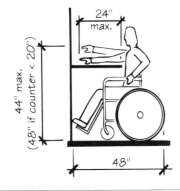

Side Reach Limits Over Obstruction

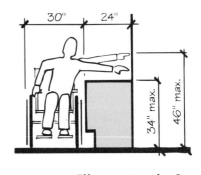

Illustrations by Joseph Petrarca

KITCHEN PLANNING

Work Surfaces
(recommended near sink and stove)

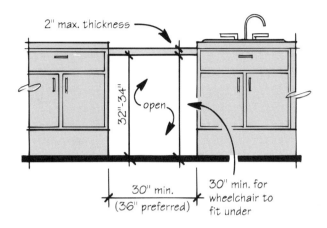

2" max. thickness

open

32"-34"

30" min.
(36" preferred)

30" min. for wheelchair to fit under

Base and Wall Cabinets

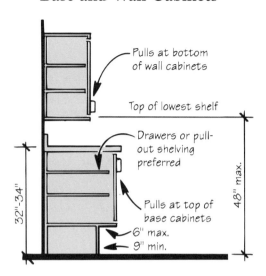

Pulls at bottom of wall cabinets

Top of lowest shelf

Drawers or pull-out shelving preferred

Pulls at top of base cabinets

32"-34"

48" max.

6" max.
9" min.

Clear Floor Space: Cabinet to Wall

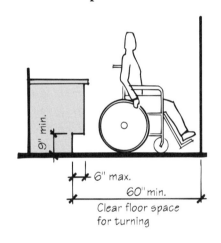

9" min.

6" max.
60" min.
Clear floor space for turning

Clear Floor Space: Cabinet to Cabinet

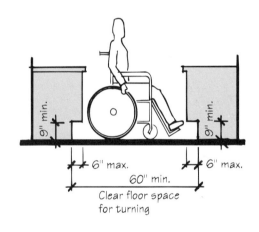

9" min.

9" min.

6" max.
60" min.
6" max.
Clear floor space for turning

Kitchen Sink Clearances

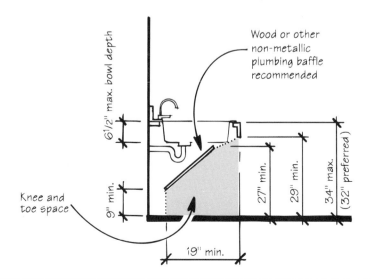

6½" max. bowl depth

Wood or other non-metallic plumbing baffle recommended

Knee and toe space

9" min.

27" min.

29" min.

34" max. (32" preferred)

19" min.

BATHROOM PLANNING

Lavatory Clearances

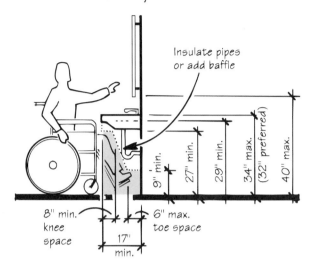

Insulate pipes or add baffle

9" min.
27" min.
29" min.
34" max. (32" preferred)
40" max.

8" min. knee space

6" max. toe space

17" min.

Clear Floor Space at Lavs

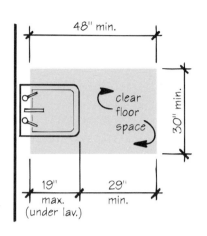

48" min.

30" min.

clear floor space

19" max. (under lav.)

29" min.

Clear Floor Space at Toilets

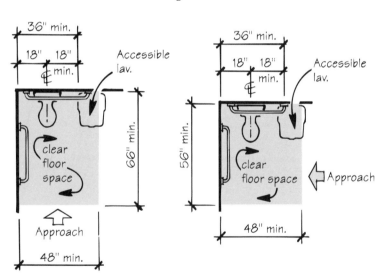

36" min.

18" 18"
min.

Accessible lav.

66" min.

clear floor space

Approach

48" min.

36" min.

18" 18"
min.

Accessible lav.

56" min.

clear floor space

Approach

48" min.

Grab Bar Dimensions

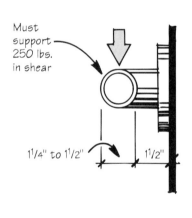

Must support 250 lbs. in shear

1¼" to 1½"

1½"

Grab Bars at Toilets

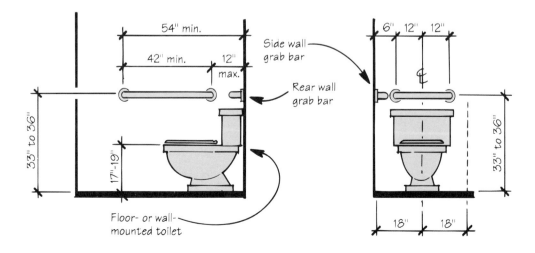

54" min.

42" min.

12" max.

Side wall grab bar

Rear wall grab bar

33" to 36"

17"-19"

Floor- or wall-mounted toilet

6" 12" 12"

33" to 36"

18" 18"

BATHROOM PLANNING

Clear Floor Space at Tubs

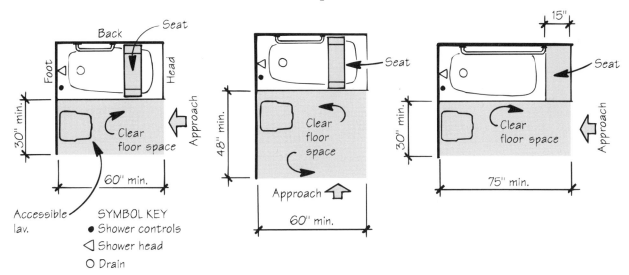

SYMBOL KEY
● Shower controls
◁ Shower head
○ Drain

With seat in tub

With seat at head of tub

Grab Bars at Tubs (Seat in Tub)

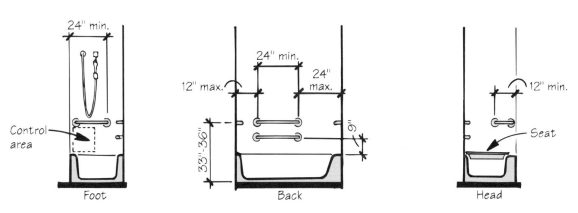

Grab Bars at Tubs (Seat at Head of Tub)

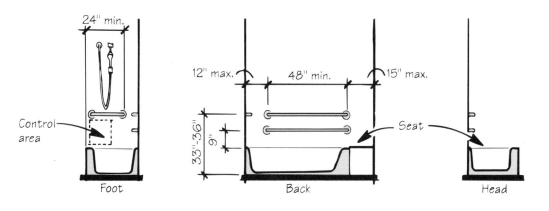

Index